TRADITION AND INCARNATION

Foundations of Christian Theology

WILLIAM L. PORTIER

Paulist Press ▪ New York/Mahwah, N.J.

ACKNOWLEDGMENTS
The Publisher gratefully acknowledges the use of the following: Scripture Text taken from The New American Bible, NABOT Copyright 1970, NABWRNT Copyright 1986, NABWRP Copyright 1991 by the Confraternity of Christian Doctrine, Inc. Washington, D.C. All rights reserved; Quotations from the three-volume English Dominican translation of Thomas Aquinas, *Summa Theologica,* copyright © 1947, Benziger Publishing Company, Mission Hills, California; quotations from *Decrees of the Ecumenical Councils,* edited by Norman P. Tanner, S.J., published in 1990 by Georgetown University Press, copyright © Sheed & Ward Ltd, London, England; quotations from *Bhagavadgita* in *Hindu Scriptures,* edited by R.C. Zaehner, original copyright © 1966 by J.N. Dent; copyright © David Campbell Publishers, London, England.

Library of Congress Cataloging-in-Publication Data

Portier, William L.
    Tradition and Incarnation : Foundations of Christian theology/
William L. Portier.
      p.   cm.
    Includes bibliographical references.
    ISBN 0-8091-3467-5
      1. Theology, Doctrinal—Introductions.   2. Revelation.
    3. Tradition (Theology) 4. Incarnation.   5. Jesus Christ—Person
    and offices.   6. Catholic Church—Doctrines.   I. Title.
    BT65.P67   1994   93-42702
    230′.2—dc20   CIP

Published by Paulist Press
997 Macarthur Boulevard
Mahwah, New Jersey 07430

Printed and bound in the
United States of America

Contents

CONTENTS

TO

My Mother
Ethel D. Portier

and

My Father
William Portier, Jr.
(1918–1984)

. . . [O]n my heart
Deeply hath sunk the lesson thou hast given,
And shall not soon depart.
—WILLIAM CULLEN BRYANT (1815)

Acknowledgments

The project of writing this book began in the fall of 1987. At the time I thought I could complete it with relative dispatch. But I soon found out that one of the first things one learns in writing an introductory text is how much one doesn't know. Having already acknowledged in the text the authors from whose ideas I have drawn, I have now the happy task of thanking the other people who helped me learn about the things I didn't know or who have helped me in any way in writing this book.

This book is based on the introductory theology course which I teach in Mount Saint Mary's nationally recognized core curriculum. The first people I want to thank, therefore, are my students. From interacting with them, I've learned to reach for a substantive theological idiom open to intelligent Christians who are neither professional clergy nor theologians. Though I'm tempted to say that these students are too numerous to mention by name, there are a few whom I wish to thank personally: Michelle Blackmon, Anne Bloom, Joanne Cahoon, Kay Carter, Stephanie Caulfield, John Cominsky, Tim Dore, Mary Gallant, Jen Hagan, John Lee Holmes, Joe Kilner, Monica Marselli, Adam Miller, John Muse, Dave Owens, Helen Richards, Sally Rodgers, Vanessa Silva, Patrick Smith, Becky Sparks, Keith Snider, Lisa Tarker, Linda Winkler.

For the past five years in their classes, my colleagues in the Mount theology department have used this book in its various draft forms. Patsy McDonald and Bill Collinge provided pages of detailed written comments and suggestions. For their critical comments and suggestions as well as for their fellowship, I am grateful to Patsy and Bill and also to Jim Forker, *eminence grise* of the department, Bill Buckley, Paul Russell, and the late Vince Molloy.

Thank you too to all of my friends at the Mount. From our community I have learned much about God. Among many others, thank you especially to Sue Goliber—"A faithful friend is a sure shelter; whoever finds one has a rare treasure" (Sir 6:14)—to Jim Forker, Patsy McDonald, Ken and Myrna Eshleman, Rita and Alan Carroll, Linda Winkler, John Drummond, and to the most excellent and visionary academic administrator I can ever hope to know, Tom Flynn.

For financial assistance I am grateful to Mount Saint Mary's College and to the National Endowment for the Humanities. Mount President's Pride Summer Grants (1987–89) supported my work. As part of their support for the core curriculum, NEH funded the philosophy and theology faculty development seminar during the summer of 1988. It contributed significantly to the development of the course upon which this book is based.

Thank you to Patsy McDonald and John Cominsky who carefully proofread and commented upon the entire manuscript. Thank you to Rosilee Litz who regularly turns my scrawled-over pages of type into laser jet art works, and whose tolerance for my personal idiosyncrasies and primitive technology is greatly appreciated.

Thank you to Larry Boadt at Paulist Press for his patient encouragement of this work over the past six years, and for providing me, as a student of Isaac Hecker, with the singular pleasure of having this book published by the present successor to Hecker's own publishing ventures.

Significant portions of this book were written and revised in a little yellow house near Currituck Sound in Point Harbor Beach, Harbinger, North Carolina. For the gift of this house and for a raft of other precious gifts, I am grateful to my wife, Dr. Bonnie Portier, whose idea of this house as a sanctuary from life's chaos typifies her unique and salvific blend of loving care and practical acumen. I am also grateful to my mother, Ethel Portier, for helping us to buy this house, and to my mother- and father-in-law, Jane and Al Krempel, for their North Carolina hospitality during my visits south to work on the book.

To our children—Phil, Thea, and Laura—whose company I treasure and of whom I am so proud: I hope you will read this book some day and recognize in it something of what I have learned from you about life and about God.

Finally, as always, thank you to my mother and father, Ethel Portier and William Portier, from whom, among other things, I first learned to pray and to talk about God. Because it has greatly to do with handing on what has been received, I dedicate this book to you.

The way of God, who disposes all things with gentleness, is to instill religion into our minds with reasoned arguments and into our hearts with grace.

—Pascal, *Pensées,* 83

Introduction

Each Sunday throughout the United States, Christians go to church. They go to churches with denominational names such as Elias Lutheran Church, Incarnation United Church of Christ, St. Joseph Catholic Church—to pick three from Emmitsburg, Maryland. The Bible plays a key role in the worship of each of these churches. Christians of every denomination study it in their Sunday schools, celebrate its message in songs and hymns, proclaim it in their assemblies, and preach about it in their sermons and homilies.

Some Christian churches have strong formal traditions of public worship (liturgy). The order or organization of their Sunday worship, e.g. the relative places of Bible, sermon, and song in it, is based on ancient liturgical texts found in books with names such as the *Lutheran Book of Worship*, or the Episcopalian *Book of Common Prayer*, or *The Rites of the Catholic Church*. In addition to proclaiming the scriptures and preaching on them, such worship also often includes a public profession of faith, based on a creed from the fourth and fifth centuries, and a more frequent carrying out of the Lord's command at the last supper to "do this in memory of me" (Lk 22:19; 1 Cor 11:24–25). The creed and the sacramental re-presentation of the last supper are a regular part of Catholic worship (the mass) on at least a weekly basis. The eucharistic (thanksgiving) prayer, through which the sacramental re-presentation takes place, tells again each week the story of salvation culminating in Jesus' death and resurrection.

Readers who have any familiarity with the subject matter of this book will most likely have derived a good part of it from participation with their families in some form of Christian worship. They will have heard the biblical word proclaimed and/or taken part in the sacramental re-presentation of the story of Jesus.

1

Treatments of the Bible, the Nicaean Creed, and the story of Jesus, therefore, form the heart of this book and reflect my conviction that Christian theology is deeply related to Christian worship. As you pray, so you believe.

In addition to its rootedness in the experience of Christian worship, this book also grows from my experience of teaching theology to undergraduates. Since 1979, when I began teaching the first course in theology in the Mount Core Curriculum, I have felt the need for a single basic text addressed to college students. To meet this need, I present Christian theology as part of the conversation among the humanities and sciences. Christian theology is here understood as a humanities discipline in which the Bible, supplemented with the creed and other traditional sources, is the primary text. Christian theology uses historical, philosophical, and literary approaches to answer questions about the revelation Christians believe God to have communicated in Jesus Christ, and that, through a long tradition of text and commentary, they have handed on. As a humanities discipline, Christian theology is primarily about reading and understanding texts.

The critical appropriation of texts is always contextual. Critical inquirers ask questions out of an inherited historical and linguistic context. Another word for such a context is *tradition*. My philosophical commitment to a contextual understanding of human thinking and living accounts for the way in which this book is put together.

The book's fourteen chapters (one for each week of a typical semester) are divided into two parts under the respective headings of *Tradition* and *Incarnation*. Extending a contextual understanding of human thinking and living to the religious sphere, *tradition* emphasizes the belief that God comes to us not simply as separate individuals, but as living members of a people with a heritage. Presumed throughout Part I is a sense of the church as an historical and linguistic community of faith which spans all particular times and places, and unites the living and the dead in Christ.

Chapters I-IV can be read as a unit moving from the general to the specific. They move from a very broad inquiry about the human condition (Chapters I and II) to one that is more sharply focused on religious inquiry in general (Chapter III) and finally on specifically Christian inquiry.

Chapter I introduces the "Great Questions" we ask about the meaning of life. It also draws attention to the fact that our posing of these questions takes place within our particular histories. Chapter II distinguishes philosophical inquiry and discourse about God from theological inquiry and discourse about God. The key religious question about God is not about God's existence but about whether we can trust God.

In Chapter III, the enlightenment or age of reason (1650–1800), mentioned briefly in Chapter II, appears substantively for the first time. It is a central and inevitable part of the historical context in which contemporary Americans and other westerners conduct religious inquiry. Chapter III uses the modern concept of religion, offers an alternative to the narrowness of modern understandings of religious experience, and argues that experience of God is in principle open to everyone.

Chapter IV deals with revelation as a theological concept and as an alternative to the deliberate ambiguity of the modern term *religious experience*. Chapter IV emphasizes Christianity's Christ-centered understanding of God's self-communication and the resulting distinctiveness of Christian experience of God.

Chapters V and VI can be read as a second unit. They focus on the Bible as the privileged witness to God's self-communication in Christ, and on the church as the living historical and theological tradition of which the biblical witness is a constitutive part. These chapters deal with the contents and historical origins of the Bible as a text (Chapter V) and the theological issue of how to read the Bible as a religious book or inspired scripture at the traditional, historical-literary, and canonical levels of interpretation (Chapter VI).

With the fundamental theological idea of revelation in place, along with the Bible (understood in terms of tradition) as an authoritative witness to it, Chapter VII brings Part I to a close by taking up the issue of theology's definition. Chapter VII contrasts pre-enlightenment understandings of theology as prayerful-liturgical and scientific with post-enlightenment understandings of theology as context-based and *praxis*-oriented.

Since Christianity and its understanding of revelation are Christ-centered, Part II focuses on the figure of Jesus Christ as the heart of Christian theology. The leading idea of Part II is *incarnation*. This term refers to the ancient and common Christian belief that in Jesus Christ God became a human being. This belief has its origin in the experience of early Christian worship. Chapter VIII, therefore, uses the Nicaean-Constantinopolitan Creed to study the doctrine of the incarnation and the trinitarian understanding of God that follows from it.

Chapters IX and X form a unit. Chapter IX looks at modern challenges to the classical Christology of the creed. These challenges raise the question of the "historical Jesus." Twentieth century Christians responded by applying historical-critical method to interpretation of the New Testament. Chapter X surveys fundamentalism, skeptical historical criticism, and moderate historical criticism as alternative responses to modern challenges.

Chapters XI and XII use a moderate form of gospel criticism to sketch an historical-theological portrait of Jesus. This portrait is intended both to respond to the modern critique of classical Christology and to present Jesus in a way that is faithful to the tradition as well as religiously compelling. This historical-theological portrait presents Jesus in the context of first century Palestinian Judaism as God's Son-Servant-Wisdom.

Chapter XIII uses the approach to religious experience from Chapter III to address, in the person of David Hume, the enlightenment's radical critique of Christianity's claim to a special revelation from God. Hume's Newtonian understanding of the world as nature is contrasted with a biblical understanding of the world as creation. Miracles are treated as manifestations of or signs from God rather than as God's interventions in or violations of nature's mechanical laws.

With Chapter XIII as a base, Chapter XIV presents Jesus' resurrection, in the context of Jewish eschatological hope in the resurrection of the dead, as the manifestation of or sign from God to which Christianity is the response in faith. A brief conclusion argues that the Jesus of this historical-theological portrait can indeed be recognized as truly God.

A word about the perspective from which this book is written. If it is true that inquirers always ask questions out of a tradition, then their inquiries will always be perspectival, i.e. located somewhere. Further, if understanding is indeed contextual, then the absolutely objective, neutral observer is not only illusory but represents a fundamental misunderstanding about inquiry. When they ask questions, questioners stand somewhere.

My location as a white, middle-class, North American male is reflected, though not uncritically, I hope, in my focus on the enlightenment and separation of church and state, as well as in the choices I have made in constructing an historical-theological portrait of Jesus. As a professor of theology I also stand in the Catholic theological tradition. This location is evident, for example, in my choice of *tradition* and *incarnation* as the leading ideas of this book. It is most obviously evident in my treatment of the Bible as a privileged moment in the process of tradition, in my understanding of the church, and in various other options too numerous to mention. This doesn't render what I have written useless or less valuable because it is not disinterested. It simply locates what I have written. Being situated, writing from a perspective, is part of being finite. To become aware of this is to become critical.

In making a critical appropriation of my perspective, I have done my best to keep faith not only with the Catholic tradition, but also with my sense of the demands of historical evidence, and with the ecumenical imperative of contemporary Christianity. In terms of historical integrity, this means that what I say from my perspective as an inquirer who stands in the Catholic tradition, even if arguable, must be in keeping with serious and plausible interpretations of historical evidence.

Though I am situated within the Catholic tradition, the ecumenical imperative means that this cannot be a narrowly Catholic book. Christianity does not exist in abstract form but only in its various historical forms. Likewise there are no generic Christian theologians, only situated ones. And so I have written in the only way I as a finite inquirer could write, i.e. as a Catholic. In view of the present division among Christian churches, however, I have written as a Catholic in a way that is intended to recognize respectfully and be open to dialogue with other Christians. Finally, I have tried to write about Christianity in a way that would be understandable and open to, as well as respectful of, those who are not Christians, but who read in good faith from other perspectives.

Having described theology as a humanities discipline concerned with the interpretation of texts, I need to say something about the primary texts used in this book. The version of the Bible used throughout, unless otherwise indicated, is the *New American Bible* (with Revised New Testament, 1989). I have chosen it, first, because of its connection to Catholic liturgical life in the United States. It is the translation American Catholics hear at mass. The second reason for choosing it is the availability of the *Catholic Study Bible* (Oxford University Press, 1990) with its excellent notes and commentary.

Though I refer to it throughout as the Nicaean Creed, the creed used in the text (especially in Chapter VIII) is again the version that is used in Catholic liturgy in the United States. It is more properly called the Nicaean-Constantinopolitan Creed. It comes to us from the documents of the Council of Chalcedon (A.D. 451). Because it is a liturgical text, I have retained its present non-inclusive translation.

Mention of the Council of Chalcedon recalls the frequent use in this book (especially in Chapters IV and VIII) of texts from church councils. Except for the creed, I have taken these from the *Decrees of the Ecumenical Councils*, edited by Norman P. Tanner, S.J., 2 volumes (London & Washington, D.C.: Sheed & Ward and Georgetown University Press, 1990). This edition was chosen, first, for its comprehensiveness. It gathers in one place the documents of all the councils recognized by Roman Catholicism as ecumenical, i.e. as councils representing the whole church. Second, the translations in Tanner's edition use inclusive language. For alternative translations of the documents of Vatican II, students are urged to consult the editions by Walter A. Abbott, S.J. or Austin Flannery.

PART ONE
TRADITION

For I handed on to you as of first importance what I also received.

(1 Cor 15:3)

This recognition that all understanding inevitably involves some prejudice [inherited prejudgments] gives the hermeneutical problem its real thrust. . . . And there is one prejudice of the enlightenment that is essential to it: the fundamental prejudice of the enlightenment is the prejudice against prejudice itself, which deprives tradition of its power (239–40).

Long before we understand ourselves through the process of self-examination, we understand ourselves in a self-evident way in the family, society and state in which we live. The focus of subjectivity is a distorting mirror. The self-awareness of the individual is only a flickering in the closed circuits of historical life. That is why the prejudices of the individual, far more than his judgments, constitute the historical reality of his being . . . (245).

Hans-Georg Gadamer, *Truth and Method* (1960)

Tradition is the expression through the centuries—at every moment living, and at the same time taking body—of the Holy Spirit who animates the totality of the faithful.

Johann Adam Möhler, *Unity in the Church* (1825)

This tradition which comes from the apostles progresses in the church under the assistance of the holy Spirit. There is growth

7

in understanding of what is handed on, both the words and the realities they signify. This comes about through contemplation and study by believers, who "ponder these things in their hearts" (see Lk 2,19 and 51); through the intimate understanding of spiritual things which they experience; and through the preaching of whose who, on succeeding to the office of bishop, receive the sure charisma of truth. Thus, as the centuries advance, the church constantly holds its course towards the fullness of God's truth, until the day when the words of God reach their fulfillment in the church.

Vatican II, *Dogmatic Constitution on Divine Revelation* (1965)

Chapter I

The Great Questions

THE RELIGIOUS DIMENSION

Our world is full of religions. Most cultures exhibit what we can intelligently recognize as religious behavior. Putting aside until Chapter III the task of defining the term *religion*, we can note that wherever we find human beings we usually find a god or gods, religious behavior, and religious faith. Critics of religion both ancient and modern have dismissed it as a mere human creation, a fire around which people who can't bear to imagine a cold and indifferent universe huddle. Religious people believe that the gods are quite real and have manifested themselves. Critics cannot deny that the religions of the world, along with their share of charlatans and hypocrites, have also inspired many selfless and truly holy people whom we can't help but admire. In spite of recurring prophecies that humanity will soon outgrow them, religious faith and practice remain.

Whether we agree with religious people or their critics or simply don't know, the near-universal appeal, the persistence, and the transforming power of religions are intriguing. What is there about human beings that opens them to religions and their claims about things unseen? Where do religious experience and religious language fit into human experience in general? This chapter will address these questions by trying to lay open what we might call the depth-dimension of human experience, that innermost part of us, best represented by some combination of the traditional symbols of heart and head. It is at this level that we can best hear the words of the philosophers, poets, and gods. We will begin by distinguishing between ordinary and extraordinary human experience.

ORDINARY HUMAN EXPERIENCE

What is meant here by "ordinary" human experience takes place at the level of what is often called common sense. It is routine. We don't have to think about it. Getting out of bed, taking a shower, brushing your teeth, putting on your shoes, starting your car, driving to school or work are all the kinds of stuff of which the ordinary is made. For our purposes, its distinguishing feature is that we don't have to think about it. The ordinary, day-to-day routine doesn't usually give rise to reflection. We tend to take it for granted.

But to describe ordinary experience as routine is far from dismissing it. Without the basic structure it provides, we might all go mad. What would happen, for example, if you had to figure out the inner workings of the internal combustion engine every time you wanted to start your car? The routine is comfortable. It lets us know what to expect.

Each culture puts at human disposal a set of ready-to-hand things from which we put together our pre-reflective routine. What is common sense for one culture, e.g. cars and planes and how to use them, may be quite extraordinary for another. What you regard as routine or ordinary will be related to your culture.

EXTRAORDINARY HUMAN EXPERIENCE

At certain points in every life, the routine of ordinary experience is broken or interrupted in a dramatic way. By contrast with the routine, we can call these disruptions "extraordinary." The terms *ordinary* and *extraordinary* are correlative or defined in relation to one another. To have one you need the other. We recognize and name the extraordinary by its contrast with what we know as ordinary. This gives us the relatively routine or ordinary and the relatively extraordinary or special. One of the distinguishing features of extraordinary experiences is that they can lead people to think more deeply or at a different level than they usually do when they are performing day-to-day tasks. Extraordinary experiences are quite common in the sense that they happen to everyone at different times. They are only extraordinary in relation to the routine of the person who has them. Four examples will be used to clarify extraordinary experience and its effects: birth, death, love, and evil. Birth and death establish the boundaries of a given routine. Love and evil shape its highs and lows.

FOUR EXAMPLES

1. *Birth*. Although some psychologists speak of the "trauma of birth" and its effects on us, our own births are not an issue here. I am referring rather to births that occur in one's own family or in other families that are close to us. Although millions of people are born each day and, in that sense, birth is quite common, it usually only happens in the lives of individual sets of parents, for example, a relatively few times in their lives. In that sense, birth is statistically and personally extraordinary. Some women have described childbirth as an experience of often but not always unspeakable physical pain to be followed by exhilarating joy. Babies represent for us a renewal and reaffirmation of life. They remind us of new beginnings and human possibilities. While we have all seen diagrams of the hit-or-miss process that unites sperm and egg and know quite well how the baby comes into being, we still speak innocently of the "miracle of birth." To hold a newborn baby that is your own flesh and blood, and to realize that this little human being didn't exist before and now it does, and that you and everybody else got here this way, is to know this wonder. The wonder will not last as birth gives way to the demanding routine of infant care and child rearing. But it returns with our occasional reflective binges about what the future might hold for this new being and about the possibly prodigious consequences of how we treat it. These are not the thoughts of which routines are made, and were we to sustain them indefinitely, they would probably drive us crazy.

For a pregnant woman who is alone and abandoned, for parents who, for whatever reasons, do not want the routine to be intruded upon by new life and all its attendant complications, the wonder turns to dread. The two responses are closely related. In both cases, the awesome magnitude of new being invades our lives. It can be greeted as a gracious gift or resisted as an intolerable imposition. Often we greet new life with complex combinations of the two responses.

2. **Death**. As with birth, we are not concerned here with our own deaths, but with those of people close to us: parents, children, relatives, and friends. Death puts a final end to the routine and to life as we know it. In the process, it raises the deepest and most disturbing questions about the possible meaning or absurdity of human life. Is this it? Why are we even born if it is only to come to this? Do we just return to the chemical elements out of which we are composed? Anyone who has held a dead child, watched a loved one die slowly and painfully, touched the cold, dead face of one's mother's or father's corpse, knows the awful pull of these questions. This is part of the power of Michelangelo's *Pietà*.

The end of the routine makes us wonder why there is any routine at all. It throws into question the very nature of what we are dealing with in human life. Death enables us to see life whole, and so we use the term *life*, as in "Life is sad, life is a bust," or "Life, I love you, all is groovy." What about this "life" we talk about? Is life such that it has it in for us, as it seems when the lives of our fellows are taken away and we are left to face our own mortality? Is life gracious, as it seems when it bestows the gift and promise of new life? Or is life simply cold and indifferent? Do we even have any justification for speaking this way? Such questions become more poignant when death involves the innocent, a young child, or an obviously good person who has suffered more than we would wish on even the worst of us. Can we expect anything better out of life? Why do we even want to or think we have a right to? The old retort that no one ever said life had to be fair cannot take away the sadness or the anger or the longing. We seem to want more than life has to offer. Is this a clue that points to the nature of reality or simply a warning that we need more "realistic" expectations?

Although death raises in dramatic form the question about the ultimate meaning of our lives, we can and do find short of ultimate meanings. If someone were to ask you, for example, why you are here, you could answer at various levels with reference to livelihood, career goals, and personal preferences. These are all short of ultimate meanings. The ultimate meaning is what is true "in the last analysis," the last meaning, the meaning of all the little meanings, the last "why" that would answer at the most radical level the question about the reason you are here. Perhaps there is no such answer, no ultimate meaning. Death brings us to the point of facing up to this possibility. Life gives us death but it doesn't tell us what death means. This leaves us in an ambiguous situation. Life might not mean anything in particular beyond the finite meanings we give it in terms of our various cultures. The question about ultimate meaning might just be a silly one.

3. *Love*. Love and evil are used here to stand for what happens in us when we experience the human capacity for selfless behavior and the human capacity for cruelty and inhumanity. In the case of love, we are speaking of the effects that unselfish behavior, done for the sake of someone else, might have on the person who receives it. Romantic love is certainly not excluded from such an understanding of love. But love as selfless behavior is much broader than romantic love, and some forms of romantic love can be quite selfish. Although I am committed to the proposition that unselfish behavior is preferable to cruelty, the point here is not primarily an ethical one. It is rather to explore the kinds of questions that our experience of love and evil raise about the human condition. This is pre-ethical.

Experiencing love in the sense meant here often brings one up short. It comes to us as a gift, unowed and often unexpected. While we might try to manipulate the feelings and behaviors of others more often than we'd like to admit, we cannot coerce or control love freely given. The record of human history, as well as the experience of most people, testifies to the extraordinary human capacity for heroic self-sacrifice. Among the examples we could include are courageous soldiers who give their lives for their comrades, daring rescuers who risk their own lives to save others, women and men who devote their lives to care of the poor, the sick, the elderly, and the dying, and mothers and fathers who carry out the daily nurture of their children. Often we have a hard time believing that others could really love us unselfishly, just for us. We tend to wonder at their gifts, suspecting that we don't deserve them, or fearing that they'll be taken away.

We tend to be in awe of genuine human goodness when we

encounter it in such phenomena as faithfulness to promises that we might have broken. Another's love is a potential judgment on our own frequently selfish behavior. Often it makes us feel unworthy, challenging our own patterns of behavior, making us wonder if what we consider good in others is really the way we ought to behave. Again the emphasis here is not on ethics, especially if that is understood in its most primitive form as the imposition of external standards. The emphasis is rather on the deep pre-ethical questions about the human condition raised by the experience of love.

4. *Evil*. This section is not about what modern theologians and philosophers sometimes call the problem of evil or theodicy. (see Chapter II). Nor is evil being used as a primarily ethical category. Rather, the emphasis is on the deep questions about the human condition raised by our own experiences of cruelty, inhumanity, and seemingly undeserved suffering. We can experience this kind of evil ourselves or witness as others suffer it. In discussing the problem of evil, theologians and philosophers sometimes distinguish between the kind of evil that others do to us, like cruelty or inhumanity, and that which befalls or overtakes us by accident, such as cancer or other diseases. Because diseases such as cancer are often caused by the refusal of human agents to take public health into account when they make business decisions, this distinction cannot be too rigidly applied. But it works in a general enough way that we can limit our present concerns to the kind of evil that is done to us by others. Evil is being used in a common-sense way that precedes ethical reflection. This use presumes our natural revulsion at the cruelty and inhumanity human beings inflict on one another.

The cruel taunts with which children torment one another provide a frightening indication that the human capacity for inhumanity runs as deep as our capacity for heroism. Who among us has not been the clumsy one, the fat one, the handicapped one, the one that was too smart, the one whose clothes were wrong or whose parents were strange? Who among us doesn't know someone who is just downright mean? Who has been spared the sting of human cruelty? On a grander and more ghastly scale, we have the ovens of Dachau, the "colored" water fountains, lunch counters, and schools, and their nagging but subtle residues in American society. What would you have felt if you were a Jew being experimented upon or incinerated simply for being a Jew, a black man being lynched in the segregated south simply for being black? These are the taunts of children raised to the most gruesome powers. Anger, rage, determination, resignation, or despair cannot take away the radical sense that such things should not be allowed to happen to us. Religious people ask where their God has gone. We feel we have the right not only to complain but to lament and protest such treatment to whatever powers there are. At some deep level such behavior strikes at our very sense of humanity. Like life itself, the human begins to emerge against the background of the recognizably inhuman. What is human anyway? What are human beings that they seem to have such divided capacities?

The most disturbing moment in our reflections on our responses to human cruelty comes when we begin to realize that we are brothers and sisters to the grand inquisitors and the Hitlers of our world. Our hearts can twist themselves into the kinds of knots that lead to the point where we can write off whole groups of people as less than what we are. We have all invoked our own particular versions of the final solution.

We are weak composites of conflicting motives and impulses. We fail to live up to the very ideals we have set for ourselves. We break faith with the ones we love. This is not to deny that sometimes we can be heroically faithful. Sometimes we do come through. It is precisely this ambiguity that raises the deepest questions about us. What kind of beings are we? How ought we to act? Should our behavior lead to profound regret at our weakness or only to cynicism about all forms of oughts, whether they come from within or without us?

SUMMARY CHARACTERISTICS
OF EXTRAORDINARY EXPERIENCES

The four examples used here to illustrate extraordinary experiences are by no means exhaustive. In his book *Faith and Doctrine*, Gregory Baum, a Canadian theologian, adds more descriptions of what he calls "depth-experiences," both secular and religious.

Among his examples of secular depth-experiences he includes friendship, conscience, truth, human solidarity, and compassionate protest. These and many other examples could be developed along the lines indicated here to formulate the kinds of questions about the human condition that open up its depth dimension. We can summarize the preceding experiences in the following way:

First, extraordinary experiences are strikingly different from the routine or the ordinary against which they appear. They tend to break the patterns of our experience in dramatic ways. To locate them in the geography of experience, we often use spatial metaphors. Thus we speak of the "depths" of human experience or its "borders" or "limits" or "peaks."

Second, in themselves extraordinary experiences are ambiguous. Death, for example, does not also tell us what death should mean, how we should interpret it, or answer the questions that it raises. Death is therefore ambiguous, admitting of more than one possible interpretation.

Third, we tend to remember extraordinary experiences, and they can exert powerful influences on the direction of our lives. The stronger or more striking they are, the more power they have to affect us.

Fourth, because of their unusual character, extraordinary experiences often lead us to think seriously about the meaning and direction of our lives. This kind of thinking or reflection takes place at a different level, usually we call it "deeper," than the kind of thinking we do in the everyday world of common sense. Extraordinary experiences often give rise to questions that are very difficult to answer with our usual problem solving methods.

THE QUESTION OF ULTIMATE MEANING

From the discussion of extraordinary experiences and the questions they raise, we can conclude that, at its "depths," or whatever metaphor we choose, the human condition can be described as mysterious. Because we are talking about the extraordinary, the term *mystery* is not being used in the ordinary sense it has when we refer to "mystery stories." In this latter sense, mysteries can be solved conclusively on the basis of evidence. The

French philosopher Gabriel Marcel (1889–1973) distinguishes between a *problem* and a *mystery*. For Marcel, problems have solu-
tions and mysteries do not. As mysterious, human life can only be
lived. The ordinary questions of the workaday world have definite
answers. We can look them up in the prose of memoranda and
instruction manuals. Because the deep or great questions about
the human condition involve us personally, we can only answer
them with personal decisions. At this level of mystery, the poem,
the song, or the story is more appropriate than the memorandum,
the manual, or the encyclopedia.

We find that at its deepest levels, human experience cannot
account for itself in a purely theoretical way. It raises questions
that cannot be answered unless we acknowledge our personal
involvement in them. We can say that human experience carries
within itself this possibility for reflection, because certain experiences lead us to question the meaning of all experience. This last
is what is meant by the question of ultimate meaning. It asks
about the final meaning of all the short-of-ultimate meanings in
our lives. Why are we here? What becomes of us in the end?
What is our final purpose? What is a human being and how ought
we to behave toward one another? These are the great questions,
the deep questions about the human condition.

"Numberless are the world's wonders," said the Greek play-
wright Sophocles, "but none more wonderful than man" (*Antig-
one,* Scene I). It is important to emphasize that the wonder about
the human condition expressed by the great questions has not
been imposed on experience from outside by out-of-touch scholars and professors. Though we would each give voice to them in
our own way, we have all felt the great questions. They are given
with experience, rising up from out of its depths.

To return to the question with which this chapter began, we
can say that religion fits into experience and appeals to us at the
same deep level where we encounter life as mystery and the various questions that reveal it as mysterious. All serious literature
operates at the same level, exploring and rendering the great
questions into the literary forms of poetry and narrative. To treat
religious matters as routine, disposable commodities in the everyday world is to trivialize them and turn religion into a banal form
of magic or a sick game that the gods force us to play. Serious

religious faith and practice can only make sense to someone who has felt the deep and mysterious ambiguity of the human condition and felt the urgency of the question to which it gives rise. At the level of mystery, life requires of us a certain openness represented by the pilgrim attitude of the wayfarer. Marcel calls us *Homo viator*, human being on the way.

If human experience is open-ended and mysterious, then it can admit of, but does not require, religious interpretations. We can exclude religious interpretations, if we choose to, but we cannot demonstrate that the evidence of experience requires this of us. None of the examples discussed above is, strictly speaking, religious. As we shall see below, however, religious people often so experience them. At this point, we can only conclude that the ultimately mysterious quality of human existence, opened by the great questions, leaves life open to a religious interpretation.

THE POSITIVE ROLE OF TRADITION IN QUESTIONING

Why are we here? What becomes of us in the end? What is our final purpose? What is a human being and how ought we to behave toward one another? These are some of the great questions. As one begins to reflect on them, two approaches present themselves. The following pair of images captures the contrast between them.

First image: Picture yourself at your desk in your room. You are alone. It's evening. In the lamplight you can see the paper in front of you as you write. The paper is blank, and you are free to fill it with your own thoughts. It is as if you were the only person in the world.

Second image: Picture yourself in church on Sunday or on a city sidewalk for a Fourth of July parade. You are surrounded by other people, but also by the inherited words and symbols of your religion or nation. You share these words and symbols with the other people in church or on the sidewalks. Sometimes you speak the words together as in the creed or the pledge of allegiance to the flag. Your imaginations respond similarly, though not identically, to common symbols such as the cross and the flag.

The first is an image of a solitary individual questioner. This unfettered self, unconscious of prior connections to family and history, feels completely free to ask the great questions and sufficiently mobile and unbound to follow wherever the questions lead. This image has a certain heroic or larger-than-life aspect. In the stories of our culture, the heroic, solitary searcher holds a noble place.

The second image is that of an individual in context, situated in a particular place and time and in a particular network of relations to people in family, community, nation, and church. This image reminds the questioner to pay attention to the settings in which the great questions might arise. The inheritance of shared language, culture, and religion shapes such settings and supplies terms in which we can ask and answer questions about the human condition.

Each reader is both a solitary and a contextual questioner. Academic life tends to emphasize the disengaged posture of the first image. It teaches us to "trust lonely reason primarily" (Rodriguez, 46). But experience should teach us that we don't encounter the human condition raw. Though our questions about human life are deeply personal, historical contexts shape their forms and tones. Our thoughts and questions about death, for example, don't occur in a vacuum. They must be posed in some particular language or other.

In this chapter on the great questions, readers have been addressed as if they were simply solitary, disconnected questioners. Emphasis on the individual inquirer is useful at the outset. Its abstract approach minimizes the historical differences among readers and thus appeals to the widest audience. Subsequent chapters, however, will challenge readers increasingly to take account of the fact that questioning is not only private and personal, but also profoundly social or contextual.

Another word for context is *tradition*. I want to use it to refer to the sea of historical connections (linguistic, national, and religious) in which individuals swim. A tradition is an historical context or network of linguistic, personal, and cultural relationships. Within such networks, individuals learn how to be individuals. They learn the categories in terms of which they talk and act and work and find meaning in their lives. Traditions are not monolithic or uniform or one-sided. Rather, they are like ongoing conversations. The points of view and the shades of emphasis in the conversation are often functions of money and power. Thus traditions embody not only conversation but also bitter argument and political struggle. The key aspect of tradition, however, is that it provides the framework and the terms in which conversations or political struggle can be conducted and sometimes moved forward. As a result of such movement, power relationships are often changed.

An excellent example of a tradition is American law. It is itself a particular development in the Anglo-Saxon legal tradition. The body of precedent doesn't provide ready-made answers to each new legal question. Rather it provides the framework and the terms in which answers emerge from a process of dialogue that is designed to test competing claims to truth in a conflictual setting.

If you are an American, the legal tradition of the United States is part of your cultural context or inheritance. You carry it around inside of you even if you never think of it. It shapes your ideas of what is fair and what you have a right to expect in public dealings with people, especially people you don't know. To realize how much your own legal tradition has shaped your sense of what is fair, you need only compare it with an alien legal tradition.

The fact that you could make such a comparison illustrates that traditions are not absolutely closed and isolated from one another, but open to dialogue. The example of American law also illustrates that traditions are open to political change. When the leaders of the civil rights movement in the United States wanted to end segregation, they made an internal critique of the laws that made it possible. They criticized segregation as unjust in the legal terms provided by the American tradition. They appealed to the American legal tradition and to its sense of what is fair. They struggled and they won, and power relationships changed.

Tradition so understood is both limiting and enabling or freeing. Tradition literally means "what has been handed on." The term is intended to emphasize the historical or inherited character of context. Each of us carries around within ourselves—even when we are alone at our desks—an inherited language, an inherited family from an inherited people in an inherited cultural setting. To try to think seriously without adverting to our manifold inheritance is naive in the extreme. If we should decide that our inheritance is too limiting and needs to be overcome to some degree, we will find that the best resources available for overcoming it are, paradoxically, those we have inherited. Though appeals to tradition are often used to suffocate growth and repress questions, we must acknowledge that the very terms we use to question and challenge inherited authorities have been themselves inherited from a living tradition. Tradition or inheritance is alive and constantly being refashioned by individuals who inhabit it and contribute to its ongoing conversation.

Catholicism has been called the longest-lived intellectual tradition in the west. One of the goals of this book is to convey to the reader a sense of how the Catholic intellectual tradition works. I have emphasized context, historical setting, inheritance, and tradition—intending them as virtually synonymous—because one cannot understand what it means to think and question as a Catholic without a positive feel for tradition as simultaneously enabling and limiting. What we inherit not only limits what we can do—the usual emphasis of our culture—but it also enables us to do what we can do. Tradition is not simply inert and suffocating. It is also

Pope John Paul II on the dynamic nature of traditions:

From this open search for truth, which is renewed in every generation, the culture of a nation derives its character. Indeed, the heritage of values which has been received and handed down is always challenged by the young. To challenge does not necessarily mean to destroy or reject *a priori*, but above all to put these values to the test in one's own life, and through this existential verification to make them more real, relevant and personal, distinguishing the valid elements in the tradition from false and erroneous ones, or from obsolete forms which can be usefully replaced by others more suited to the times.

Centesimus Annus, 1991, Paragraph 50

alive and enabling. It harbors its own resources for self-criticism and growth.

Questions for Review and Discussion

1. Discuss the difference between complex, everyday questions, such as how to repair a transmission or program a computer, and ultimate, or deep, questions.

2. What is ambiguous about our experience of birth and death?

3. Why is the discussion of love and evil called "pre-ethical"?

4. Based on your experience, how would you pose the question of ultimate meaning?

5. Are music and literature "just entertainment," or can they also open us up to the depth-dimension of human life?

6. Argue for or against the claim that human life is ultimately open-ended and mysterious.

7. This chapter has claimed that human life has a depth-dimension, and further that religion becomes meaningful to us at this level. Do you agree or disagree with these claims? Explain.

8. From what has been said in this chapter, how would you define the term *tradition*?

9. What is the role of tradition in asking the great questions?

10. How can you be an individual and make your own free choices, if you always carry around inside you so many connections to the past?

For Writing and Reflection

1. Write a descriptive essay about an extraordinary experience you have had. Show how it opened up the depth-dimension by raising ultimate questions or causing deep reflection.

2. Write a descriptive essay about an extraordinary experience you have encountered in a film, novel, play, poetry, or song, or

about the reflections such works of art might have occasioned in you.

3. Write an autobiographical essay in which you discuss both the limiting and the enabling aspects of the tradition(s) you inherited.

For Further Reading

The kinds of reflections that appear in this chapter are often simplifications of lines of thought found in the writings of the continental philosophers known as "phenomenologists" or, more popularly, "existentialists." Gabriel Marcel's *The Mystery of Being*, 2 vols. (Chicago: Henry Regnery Co., 1960), originally delivered as a series of lectures in 1949 and 1950, offers useful access to this kind of thinking.

The approach to tradition taken in this chapter is indebted to the German philosopher Hans-Georg Gadamer (1900-). His book *Truth and Method* (New York: Seabury Press, 1975; original edition 1960), pp. 235–344, especially 245–58, provides an account of how tradition is a component in all of our understanding.

In his autobiography *Hunger of Memory* (New York: Bantam Books, 1983), Richard Rodriguez offers a moving narrative approach to the interaction between an individual and tradition, the *private* and the *public*, as he terms them.

Chapter II

Philosophy

PHILOSOPHY AND THEOLOGY

In the previous chapter, we examined some extraordinary experiences and saw how the great questions can arise from them. Religious people believe that God speaks to us at this same deep level where the great questions arise. But before we can examine religious questions, especially the question of God, we must take a detour into philosophy. Philosophers also speak about the great questions. When they do, they often speak of God. In order to appreciate what is distinctive about a religious approach to the great questions and to God, we must have a clear sense of how philosophy and theology are related and how they are different.

In this chapter, we will explore the relationship between philosophy and theology, asking how they are related and how they are different. This will involve two tasks. First, we will examine some philosophical approaches to the great questions and to God. Second, we will consider how philosophy's approach to God differs from a theological approach rooted in the biblical tradition.

These two tasks involve two separate arguments addressed to two different audiences. To those who take skeptical or relativist approaches to the great questions, this chapter argues for the legitimacy of philosophical inquiry. To those religious people who tend either to distrust or to overemphasize philosophy, this chapter will argue for both the autonomy and the limitation (from a biblical perspective) of philosophical approaches to God.

SKEPTICISM AND RELATIVISM IN THE
FACE OF THE GREAT QUESTIONS

Faced with the ambiguity of the human condition, one can adopt various postures toward the ultimate questions raised by experience. Some decide that these questions are so complex and confusing that we can never answer them. Dallying with them is therefore a waste of time. We simply cannot know about such things as the ultimate meaning of life. People who feel this way have been called "skeptics." They are extremely suspicious of human claims to know the truth in general, and the truth about ultimate questions in particular. What is often called "healthy skepticism" is necessary for the life of the mind and for any advances in science and other forms of human learning. George Santayana (1863–1952), a Spanish-American philosopher, called skepticism the "chastity of the intellect." If we are too open or credulous, we become gullible and easily deceived by appearances. An attitude of radical skepticism, however, can become a disease of the soul that closes us to the riches of human experience. Santayana thought that, after preserving it like chastity "coolly and proudly" through youth, skepticism could eventually be "safely exchanged for fidelity and happiness" (*Skepticism and Animal Faith*, 1923, p. 69).

In addition to the skeptics, others have been overwhelmed to discover the vast diversity of human cultures in history. It's disconcerting to find that what you consider "normal" or "human" is really only the common sense of your culture. The multiplicity of cultures, religions, forms of government, and so on makes us extremely conscious of the relativity of our own. The discovery of the richness of cultural diversity has led many people to conclude that our answers to the ultimate questions—and even the fact that we ask ultimate questions—are merely functions of our history and culture. There will be as many answers as there are cultures where people ask such questions. What we take to be the truth about the human condition is relative to our history and culture.

Comparative study demonstrates cultural diversity, and we would be foolish and provincial to ignore the evidence for the cultural relativity of many of our beliefs and preferences that we take to be universal. A healthy sense of this relativity helps to engender tolerance, another necessity for the life of the mind and for politics in a modern state. As with skepticism, however, absolute relativism can paralyze the spirit, especially when it is faced with the ethical demands raised by those who suffer inhuman treatment at the hands of others. Philosophy offers an alternative to skepticism and relativism in the face of the great questions.

THE APPEAL TO REASON AND THE DECISION
TO PURSUE THE GREAT QUESTIONS

In western culture, the classic symbol of the philosophical alternative to radical skepticism and relativism is the bald and crooked figure of Socrates, the "gadfly" of Athenian society in the fifth century B.C. His own relentlessly critical spirit had taken in healthy doses of both skepticism and relativism. But his reliance on the trustworthiness of critical human reason always stopped him short of their radical and absolute forms. So far as we can reconstruct his thought from the literary dialogues of his student Plato, Socrates worked out his philosophical position in dialogue with a group of itinerant teachers of the day known as "sophists." The sophists, at least as Plato portrays them in his Socratic dialogues, tended to be radical skeptics and cultural relativists. Widely traveled, the sophists well knew the diversity of human customs. They came to recognize contemporary Greek culture as a human convention rather than as some natural state of affairs. In their work as traveling teachers, they probably acquired the image that we find in Plato, who seems to portray them as not much better than deceivers, serving argument and expedience rather than truth.

Philosophy appeared in ancient Greece at a time when many people had lost faith in their traditional religious answers to questions about human destiny. Philosophy offered a rational alternative to doubt and confusion in the face of the great questions. While Socrates himself was something of a skeptic and a cultural relativist, he thought there was something deeper, something that enabled and even required the sophists to be skeptical. This was reason. Even to demonstrate its limits, the sophists had to use it.

He thought that they tended to trivialize their own powers of questioning and thinking by in the end denying them. By contrast Socrates, again as we have him from Plato, tried to develop a different attitude toward life and the ultimate questions it raises about what we are and how we should behave. We have come to call this habit of mind which Socrates tried to communicate to his students *philosophy*, or the love of wisdom. According to Plato, in his *Theaetetus* (155 d), philosophy begins with a sense of wonder. It was this sense of wonder before the mystery of reality and the human condition that Socrates tried to cultivate in his students.

Plato and his student Aristotle developed Socrates' way of arguing with the sophists into a method known as "dialectic." In this form of argument, one begins with the conclusion of one's opponent, a conclusion one believes to be false. The point is to show that if one accepts this position, one must also accept other positions that one admits to be false or self-contradictory. In attempting to disarm the radical skeptic, for example, the practitioner of dialectic might point to the inner contradiction of the claim that it is true that we cannot know the truth. The claim that all truth claims are culturally or historically relative, except of course the present one, meets a similar fate in the dialectical process.

Aristotle moves similarly against those who claim that philosophy, the attitude of open wonder before the ultimate questions, is a useless waste of time. The direction he takes is well-encapsulated in the saying attributed to Socrates, "The unexamined life is not worth living." In his *Protrepticus*, Aristotle writes: "If you are obliged, to philosophize, then you must do so, and even if you are not obliged, you will still have to philosophize." In examining this position we begin to get a sense of why we just can't throw up our hands in the face of the great questions. If we try to avoid them, or so Aristotle thought and the western tradition in the main agrees, we diminish the quality of our lives as human or thinking beings.

WHY ASK THE GREAT QUESTIONS?

Although Aristotle doesn't do it in exactly this way, we can unfold the "not to philosophize is to philosophize" position in four basic steps.

1. Seriously asking the great questions places the questioner at risk. The great questions are personal and therefore don't have impersonal or theoretical answers. Answering the great questions requires not only reasoning but also personal decision.

2. The personal or at-risk nature of the great questions should not disturb us. We deal with these kinds of engaged questions throughout our lives, e.g. marriage and career decisions.

3. Even if we never reflect on the great questions, we live our answers to them. Our accumulated decisions imply our statements about what life means.

4. The Socratic or philosophical option is that it is better (more rational, more liberating) to reflect on our answers to the great questions than to live them unawares. Philosophical reflection is one of the primary means of recognizing the tradition we have inherited and learning to overcome its limitations.

Step One

First, we must admit that the question about ultimate meaning can't be given a certain theoretical answer. What is the final purpose or meaning of human life? A certain answer at the theoretical level would require pre-defined terms. But we are asking here about the ultimate terms. In terms of what could they be defined? We can achieve certain answers in mathematics and sometimes in science only under carefully controlled conditions. Given base ten, two plus two must be four. Given standard conditions, when what we call hydrogen combines with what we call oxygen in a ratio of two to one, what we call water will result. The terms here are all humanly pre-defined in keeping with what appear to be the demands of reality. Certitude, either theoretical, as in some forms of mathematics and geometry, or virtual, as in science, derives from demonstration based on given definitions. In mathematics and science, we can presume the world and human beings. Ultimate questions ask about the final meaning of the world and human beings.

Human life does not come equipped with anything like an instruction manual. The terms in which to discuss the ultimate meaning of human life are not given. What is at issue is the very task of constructing the terms of the discussion out of reflection on human experience in dialogue with those who have gone before us. The task of reflection is further complicated by the fact that we do not approach ultimate questions with anything like the disinterested objectivity we have been taught to associate with mathematics and science. We have a strong personal stake in ultimate questions. They involve not only our attitude toward death but also our whole approach to how we ought to live now. Ultimate questions, therefore, are not theoretical questions in any abstract, easily dismissed sense. They are radically practical. Or, as some twentieth century thinkers would have it, they are "existential" questions. Existential questions are self-involving. They include the questioner in the question. We should not, therefore, expect to resolve them at the level of theory understood in some detached and disinterested way. If ultimate questions place the questioner into question, then they can only be resolved by a process that includes personal decision as well as reasoning.

Step Two

The second step is to realize that the lack of scientific or mathematical answers to ultimate questions is no reason to abandon them. We face these self-involving kinds of questions all the time in matters such as marriage and vocational choices. We would not dream of abandoning all prospects for marriage or career simply because we could not achieve mathematical certitude in choosing among the alternatives. While it is true that we could discuss the relative merits of the married and unmarried states or of various vocational choices in the abstract, questions about marriage or career become self-involving when they face us as concrete options. How do I know that I should marry this person, this one now? How do I know for sure that I should be an accountant rather than a teacher or a musician? One can never know in the same way we know that, given base ten, two plus two must be four. Self-involving questions require personal decisions, but responsible personal decisions are not arbitrary or whimsical. We have reasons for and reasons against, and we can list and examine them. But reasons alone will not settle the issue. In the end we must decide to commit ourselves to this person or this course of action rather than that. However difficult or unfair this might appear, people do it all the time. Ultimate questions place us in a similar position.

Step Three

Third, we have been given a life, and life, so to speak, forces the issue. We must do something with ourselves. We must make existential choices that involve how we will dispose of the limited resources of time and energy we have been dealt. Even if we never think explicitly about ultimate questions, we will live our answers to them. The accumulation of our choices tends to point in one direction or another, making our statement about what is of final importance in human life.

In the tradition that comes down to us from Plato and Aristotle, as opposed to the tradition of the sophists, it is taken for granted that thinking about your answer is better than living it unawares. Since you must live and choose and will answer the question in any case, it's better that the answer be considered. The unexamined life is not worth living. Who is right, Plato and Aristotle or the sophists? This is one of those self-involving questions.

Step Four

But if we choose the way of Plato rather than that of the sophists, what do the philosophical attitude and the kind of reflection it engenders accomplish? This leads to the fourth step. Philosophical reflection accomplishes a number of humanly useful purposes. First, through reasoning processes similar to Aristotle's dialectic, philosophical thinking helps us to find what can't be true because it involves self-contradiction or leads to conclusions we know to be false on other grounds. Second, philosophical reflection applies the acids of skepticism and cultural relativism to our common-sense assumptions about life and human purpose. It helps us to clarify our assumptions. Third, it forces us to explain or give the reasons for what we take to be the case on the ultimate questions. We learn the crucial political skill of arguing intelligently about matters that do not admit of scientific or mathematical proof, but are essential to human life. Fourth, from all of this, we learn to construct a critical, guiding vision about human life and its purpose. This vision, revised and augmented as future experiences require, will serve us well when we have to make important human choices. The point of philosophy is that, since in any case we will assume such a vision as it comes to us from our culture, it is better or more humanly enriching to have a reasoned or examined vision than one we might call uncritical or taken for granted.

GOD AS A PHILOSOPHICAL QUESTION

Since both philosophers and theologians speak about God, it is necessary to clarify the difference between philosophical and religious approaches to the God-question. For most philosophers in the western tradition, the question of God has been implicit in the ultimate questions about the world and human life. In reasoning about God, they have attempted to ground on a transcendent principle the intelligibility of the cosmos, the seeming order that makes science possible, and the dignity and purpose of human life. This last or ultimate reality transcends or goes beyond analysis in terms of the physical or social worlds. It is reducible neither to the world nor to humans. In philosophy, therefore, God is in a sense the conclusion of an argument. God is the one reality thought to be required to explain and give meaning and purpose to everything else. If one wants to make a political appeal for natural rights, as Thomas Jefferson did in the Declaration of Independence, the most convenient way to ground it is by an appeal to God or the Creator. If there is no God, then everything comes up for grabs.

The serious atheist, as opposed to the cocktail party variety, must resolutely face up to the threat of being engulfed in absolute meaninglessness. By the same token, if theistic philosophers wish to be honest in dealing with the God-question, they must take seriously all the signs of meaninglessness in human experience.

These include all the evidences against order presented by the cosmos and especially by seemingly needless human suffering. Since the enlightenment (1650–1800), the question of God and the question of evil have been closely linked in what is called *theodicy*. This term, first used by the German philosopher G.W. Leibniz in 1710, refers to modern attempts to justify belief in God in the face of the so-called "problem of evil."

Philosophical Approaches to God from the Cosmos

By definition there can be no other categories in terms of which to define ultimate reality. In attempting to clarify its meaning, however, philosophers have compared ultimate or transcendent reality to various worldly realities. We shall look briefly at four examples of cosmological, or "from the world," approaches to God, those of Aristotle (384–322 B.C.), Thomas Aquinas (ca. 1225–1274), William Paley (1743–1805), and Alfred North Whitehead (1861–1947).

For Aristotle, who described philosophy as an "ascent to the divine," the ultimate reality was necessary in order to explain motion. In Book XII of his *Metaphysics*, he speaks of "something which moves without being moved, a being purely actual," that "can in no way be otherwise than it is." This is the "first mover," a "necessary being," a "first principle."

St. Thomas Aquinas, a Christian theologian, followed Aristotle in referring to the "first mover." In his famous "five ways," which appear in Question 2, Article 3 of his *Summa Theologica*, Aquinas adds four more terms for the ultimate reality which "all men speak of as God." They are:

"a first efficient cause";

"some being having of itself its own necessity, and not receiving it from another, but rather causing in others their necessity";

"something which is to all beings the cause of their being, goodness, and every other perfection";

"some intelligent being by whom all natural things are directed to their end."

The rise of the "new science" during the modern period brought a new variation on the cosmological approach. The "argument from design" or the "teleological" argument reasoned to God from the design of objects in the universe such as the human eye. This approach is well illustrated in William Paley's *Natural Theology* (1802), which argues for a designer of nature.

In the twentieth century "panentheism" of Alfred North Whitehead, God's actuality, but not God's necessity, comes to be identified with the world. Related as intimately to God as body is to soul in Aristotle, the world is seen in this "process" perspective as "God's body" in a very real sense. As Whitehead puts it in *Process and Reality*, we experience God as "the lure for feeling, the eternal urge of desire." He is the "great companion, the fellow-sufferer who understands" (522, 532).

Philosophical Approaches to God from the Human Person

While Aristotle and Aquinas approached God in terms of the world and spoke of God as what was needed to account for the world as we know it, others have approached God in more specifically human or subjective terms. This approach via the human subject is well illustrated in St. Augustine's (354–430) analysis of the restless heart. Augustine summarizes his approach in this well-known passage from Book I of *The Confessions*: "[Y]ou have made us for yourself, and our heart is restless until it rests in you." Adopting a more intellectualist, subjective approach, St. Anselm of Canterbury (1033–1109) addressed God as "something than which nothing greater can be thought." Anselm argued that it was self-contradictory to deny such a being existed; therefore, God necessarily exists. Relying on Whitehead's philosophical foundations, Charles Hartshorne has spent a lifetime reinterpreting and refining Anselm's argument. God emerges as the one necessary and "the not conceivably surpassable being." Anselm's approach has come to be known as "the ontological argument," while that of Aristotle and Aquinas is usually referred to as the "cosmological argument."

ANALOGY

The history of philosophy offers a whole catalogue of every-day terms that have been used to speak of God: mover, cause, being, designer, good, companion, and so on. All of them go back to our routine experience of the cosmos and human subjectivity. In an attempt to get at what ultimately conditions or makes possible this experience, philosophers have stretched these terms to their limits.

In the philosophical tradition that comes down from St. Thomas, and that has dominated Catholic thought since the nineteenth century, this way of speaking about God is called "analogy," and it is possible because reality exhibits what Thomists call the analogy of being. As in the common-sense understanding of the term, analogy involves comparison. God is compared to something cosmic or human, e.g. a being or a designer. But the comparison is thought to involve two important qualifications or reservations. To make the proper qualifications about our affirmations of God, we must take both the "way of negation" and the "way of eminence."

The Way of Negation

On the way of negation, we must realize that, if God is God, if God is ultimate or infinite, then God cannot simply be one cause or being or companion among many others. This would make God finite or limited, a Zeus or a Wotan, a magnified version of what we are. To treat the reality of God with the proper reverence, it is necessary to grasp and appreciate the radical elusiveness of the very notion of a monotheistic Godhead. With the possible exception of absolute nothingness—to which God is likened in some religious traditions—I cannot think of a more difficult notion, impossible to imagine except in obvious anthropomorphism, nearly as difficult to conceive in reflective thought.

According to the way of negation, then, we must admit that God is not the kind of a being or a cause or a designer that we would expect to find in the world. The literal or univocal meaning of whatever we affirm of God must, therefore, be simultaneously denied. Although we are not speaking directly of it here, we must

SOME PHILOSOPHICAL APPROACHES TO GOD	
FROM THE WORLD	**FROM THE HUMAN PERSON**
Aristotle first mover or necessary being	*Augustine* the rest for the restless heart
Thomas Aquinas first cause or some being having of it itself its own necessity	*Anselm* something than which nothing greater can be thought
William Paley designer	
Alfred North Whitehead great companion and fellow sufferer who understands	*Charles Hartshorne* the one necessary and not conceivably surpassable being

also admit that biblical language about God is subject to the same logical limitations as philosophical language about God. The way of negation denies that God is literally my father. Even the term *infinite*, used so often with reference to God, is simply a seemingly positive way of denying human and cosmic limitations to God.

The Way of Eminence

According to the doctrine of analogy, then, in what sense can we say that God is a cause, a being, or a companion? In taking the way of eminence, we say that God is whatever God is to a supereminent or superlative degree. We find trivial examples of supereminence in such advertising slogans as "better than best" or "whiter than white." Contemporary advertising speaks of products the way religious people speak of God.

The basis for the way of eminence lies in our experience of what medieval thinkers called the *analogy of being*. The world

presents us with seemingly graded degrees of reality, life, freedom, and perfection. Rocks and trees and human beings (min-
eral, vegetable, and animal) are different yet comparable. We can
compare and contrast. This experience of the analogous character
of reality leads to the positing of an ultimate degree, as in St.
Thomas' "five ways." On the vector provided by our experience
of the analogy of being, i.e. the seemingly graded degrees of
reality, life, freedom, and perfection, we launch our affirmations
of God off into limitlessness or supereminence. We do not have a
clear concept of the goal, but our experience of the world and of
human beings gives force and direction to our affirmations about
God.

A good example of the limitations of analogical language
about God is the issue of which gender we should use to refer to
God. Although our human sexuality serves as a created image of
God's own creativity (Gn 1:27), God's creative capacities must,
by the way of negation, transcend the finitude of human sexual
differentiation. Strictly speaking, by the way of negation, God is
neither male nor female. But in reading the same text from Genesis by the way of eminence, we can conclude that comparisons
from both male and female experience can in principle serve as
the basis for our analogical language about God. It is as male and
female that human beings are the image of God. From a Christian
perspective, because Jesus addressed the God of Israel with the
intimate form of Father ("Abba" in Aramaic) and taught his
disciples to dare the same, Christians will continue to pray the
Lord's Prayer and address God as Father. But Jesus' use of
"Abba" did not prevent him from using both male and female
imagery in his teaching about God, e.g. Luke 15:4–10. Nor
should it prevent his latter-day disciples from using female imagery in their analogical language about God.

Critics of analogy have argued that, in trying to stretch human language to divine proportions, philosophers have abused
and broken it, drifting off into meaninglessness and incoherence.
Thomists have argued among themselves about how our concepts
of God manage to do minimal justice to the reality of God. Philosophers from the contemporary schools of Anglo-American language philosophy have analyzed the kinds of meanings to be given
to our affirmations about God. The initial skepticism of this tradi-

tion has gradually given way to more sympathetic responses to religious language. In the United States, those who deal with such questions are usually called philosophers of religion.

A BIBLICAL PERSPECTIVE ON THE GOD OF THE PHILOSOPHERS

Philosophers who speak of God profess to reason from their study of the world and human beings to what they say about the divine. They make statements about God independently of any appeal to divine revelation. For some Christian theologians, such claims to know God apart from God's revelation border on blasphemy. Since God is so completely different from us, we cannot know God without a self-manifestation or revelation. We do not look for God. God looks for us.

This approach, however, has not been that of the Catholic tradition. It has insisted by contrast that if God wishes to make a revelation to us, created human limitations require that God use a means suited to human reception. If we are to recognize God when God appears, we must be able to have some idea of God, however impoverished. The Catholic tradition, therefore, has affirmed that we can know God by reason and has kept philosophy and theology closely related. In addition to forming in theologians the basic habits of mind needed to deal with ultimate questions, philosophy has traditionally helped theology to clarify the terms it uses in speaking about God and revelation.

Catholics often claim, following St. Thomas, that philosophy proceeds according to the light of human reason, while theology proceeds according to the light of faith. This seems a clear enough explanation of the difference between philosophy and theology. But Christians, Jews, or Muslims who believe in God on religious grounds might have a hard time separating their believing from their reasonings, distinguishing reason's light from that of faith. Given our historical human condition, the reasoning of those who have faith is not always as "pure" as the apparent clarity of this distinction would suggest. More must be said.

On the one hand, philosophical attempts to speak of God in cosmic or human terms are quite consistent with biblical insistence that the created world and the human heart bear the recognizable traces of the one who made them. The heavens are said to proclaim God's handiwork, while God's law is said to be inscribed on our hearts (Ps 19; Rom 2:14–15; 1:20). On the other hand, such attempts remain impoverished and insufficient when compared with God's revelation in the history of Israel and in Jesus Christ.

The example of Blaise Pascal (1623–1662) will help to illustrate the difference between philosophical and theological approaches to God. Pascal is the author of an often quoted contrast between the "God of Abraham, God of Isaac, God of Jacob" and the "God of philosophers and scholars." Pascal is an especially appropriate example because, in addition to being a profoundly religious spirit, he was a mathematician and scientist of world-class stature. His contributions are in areas as diverse as probability theory and hydraulics. The computer language that bears his name honors his pioneering work on a calculating machine that helped prepare the way for the computer. Because Pascal's genius encompassed both science and religion, his contrast between the living God and the God of philosophers and scholars deserves our attention.

After his death in 1662, a "Memorial" was found sewn into his clothes. Dated November 23, 1654, it served to remind him of a soul-searing experience he had had that night. In the "Memorial," Pascal addresses the God he had encountered.

Pascal's Memorial

The year of grace 1654.

Monday, 23 November, feast of Saint Clement, Pope and Martyr, and of others in the Martyrology. Eve of St. Chrysogonus, Martyr and others. From about half past ten in the evening until half past midnight.

Fire
'God of Abraham, God of Isaac, God of Jacob,'
(Ex 3.6) not of philosophers and scholars.

Certainty, certainty, heartfelt, joy, peace,
God of Jesus Christ.
God of Jesus Christ.
My God and your God. (Jn 20.17)
'Thy God shall be my God.' (Ruth 1.16)
The world forgotten, and everything except God.
He can only be found by the ways taught in the Gospels.
Greatness of the human soul.
'O righteous Father, the world had not known thee, but I have
    known thee.' (Jn 17.25)
Joy, joy, joy, tears of joy.
I have cut myself off from him.
They have forsaken me, the fountain of living waters. (Jer 2.13)
'My God wilt thou forsake me?' (cf. Mt 27.46)
Let me not be cut off from him forever!
'And this is eternal life, that they might know thee, the only true
    God, and Jesus Christ whom thou hast sent.' (Jn 17.3)

Jesus Christ.

Jesus Christ.

Pensées, 913 (Penguin Edition)

    The frequent scriptural allusions bespeak Pascal's habitual, prayerful dwelling with the Bible. His deep concern in the "Memorial" is not for the question of God's bare existence, but for the question of God's disposition toward him. The last prayerful question shows that the issue is framed in terms of fidelity and trust. "My God wilt thou forsake me?" This is an allusion to Jesus' prayer to the Father from the cross in the words of Psalm 22 (Mt 27:46). It places the issue of trust at the center of religious life as it is lived within the biblical tradition. Repeated references to certainty, peace, and joy indicate that on this night Pascal had been given to know this trust in an especially deep way. The final prayer indicates his awareness that such trust is a grace in Christ. Several times in the "Memorial" Pascal uses Jesus' words to the Father as his own.

    Pascal's "Memorial" bears powerful witness to the key religious or theological question about God. It is not "Is there a God?" or "Does God exist?" More than 90 percent of Americans already say they would answer those two questions in the affirmative. The key religious question is rather the one Pascal asks or prays in the "Memorial." "Can I trust God?" Is God the "My God and your God" of the "Memorial"? "My God wilt thou forsake me?"

The passion in the "Memorial" is clearly for God for God's own sake, "the world forgotten, and everything except God." It would be interesting to compare the "Memorial" to Descartes' argument for God in his *Meditations*. Rightly or wrongly Pascal feared that philosophers and scholars who spoke of God— perhaps he had his contemporary Descartes in mind—had more of a passion for intelligibility, clarity, and distinctness than for God.

In a biblical perspective, as the "Memorial" illustrates, God is not merely the "last cause" or the "one necessary being," but also and primarily the "one we can trust." God's history with Israel, and especially the life of Jesus, teaches that God remains the "one we can trust" even in the face of the apparent meaninglessness of suffering and death. Biblical faith does not simply ask people to believe that there is a God whose existence explains why things are intelligible. Rather it asks people to believe that God can be trusted even when things look meaningless.

In the Old Testament, God presents two aspects: Job's Lord "out of the storm" (Job 38:1) and Elijah's "tiny whispering sound" (1 Kgs 19:12). In the next chapter, we shall look more carefully at both these texts. The Lord "out of the storm" is terrifyingly other than we.

> For my thoughts are not your thoughts,
>   nor are your ways my ways, says the LORD.
> As high as the heavens are above the earth,
>   so high are my ways above your ways
> and my thoughts above your thoughts (Is 55:8–9).

Before the Lord "out of the storm," Job is reduced to the status of a speechless worm (Job 42:1–6). Scripture asks us to believe that God the unutterable, whose name we dare not say, whose image we dare not fashion, has drawn near and is found in Elijah's "tiny whispering sound"—the "still small voice" of the King James Version. This tension between the sense of who God really is (the awesome, unutterable one) and the sense that God is near as the one we can trust gives the Old Testament its epic character.

The stories of the great biblical heroes of faith illustrate that the task of trusting God involves personal struggle. Abraham, Jacob, and Moses all struggled with God and his call. Jacob is said to have wrestled with God (Gn 32:23–32; Hos 12:5) while Abraham and Moses simply argued with God. Sometimes people think that if we could just encounter God as Abraham, Jacob, and Moses did, the life of faith would be so much easier. A second look, however, would show that arguing with God, resisting the call, and struggling in faith are at the heart of the biblical story.

CONCLUSION

If God is anything like what both the philosophers and the scriptures testify, there can only be one such reality. But the God who is the conclusion of the philosopher's argument for cosmic or moral order is not sufficient to sustain the religious life of a Christian or a Jew. So while we must say that, if there is a God, philosophers and theologians can only be talking about the same one, we must add with Pascal that the God of the philosophers is only a pale shadow of the God of Abraham, the "Awesome One of Isaac" (Gn 31:42,53).

On the other hand, the context of Pascal's famous contrast between the God of Abraham and the God of the philosophers helps us see that Pascal's dictum is better used to communicate the richness of biblical faith and worship than to diminish philosophy. Believers should keep in mind that the God of philosophers and scholars comes in handy when someone asks, or when you ask yourself, what the term *God* could possibly mean. But the God of the philosophers is not nearly enough. St. Thomas put it well in his *Summa Contra Gentiles*:

> If the only way [open] to us for the knowledge of God were solely that of reason, the human race would remain in the blackest shadows of ignorance. For then the knowledge of God, which especially renders men perfect and good, would come to be possessed by only a few, and these few would

require a great deal of time in order to reach it (Book I, Cap IV, Pegis edition, 67-68).

Questions for Review and Discussion

1. What are skepticism and relativism? Contrast Socrates and the skeptics on the great questions.

2. Summarize the chapter's four-part argument for why it is better to pursue the great questions than to ignore them. Do you agree with this argument? How would you change it?

3. In general, what is the difference between philosophy and theology? How do philosophical approaches to God differ from theological approaches?

4. Describe the two paths philosophers have used to approach the question of God.

5. Of the various philosophical attempts to speak about God, which do you find most compelling or interesting? Which do you find least successful?

6. Apply the "way of negation" and the "way of eminence" to the question of God's gender.

7. Does philosophy have any positive role to play in our understanding of God?

8. Using the example of Pascal and his "Memorial," explain from a biblical perspective the limitations of philosophical approaches to God.

For Writing and Reflection

1. Pick one of the philosophical approaches to God and develop it in an essay. Or write an essay criticizing philosophical approaches to God.

2. The New Testament books Romans (4:17–25) and Hebrews (11:8–19) present Abraham as a model of faith and trust in God. Read the story of Abraham and Sarah in Genesis 12–25. Compare it with what Romans and Hebrews say about Abraham. Write an essay in which you discuss Abraham's trust in

God and any examples you find of Abraham questioning or arguing with God. What does the story of Abraham and Sarah tell you about what God is like?

3. Go to the library and find either Descartes' *Meditations* or Aristotle's *Metaphysics*. Descartes' third meditation argues from his own imperfection and incompleteness to the existence of a perfect being or God. Aristotle's *Metaphysics*, XII, 7, argues from motion to a first mover, "a primary being, eternal and unmovable and separate from sensible things." Pick one of these texts and write an essay that compares and contrasts it with Pascal's "Memorial." For example, why are the respective authors interested in God? How do the tones of the two texts contrast? From your reading of these two texts (the "Memorial" and either Descartes or Aristotle), how would you contrast philosophical and religious approaches to God? Don't be vague. Use references to and examples from the texts to support whatever you say.

For Further Reading

Anton-Hermann Chroust, *Aristotle: Protrepticus, A Reconstruction* (Notre Dame, Ind.: University of Notre Dame Press, 1964), pp. 48–49.

Frederick Ferré, *Basic Modern Philosophy of Religion* (New York: Charles Scribner's Sons, 1967). Surveys the various philosophical positions on God. It is written from the point of view of analytic philosophy of religion.

James C. Livingston, *Modern Christian Thought from the Enlightenment to Vatican II* (New York: Macmillan Publishing Co., 1971). A history of religious thought approach, clearly written, with extensive citations from primary sources.

Blaise Pascal, *Pensées*, trans. by A.J. Krailsheimer (Harmondsworth, Middlesex, England: Penguin Books, 1983).

Thomas V. Morris, *Making Sense of It All, Pascal and the Meaning of Life* (Grand Rapids, Mich.: Eerdmans, 1992). A very readable set of reflections on Pascal's religious thought.

Hans Urs Von Balthasar, *The Glory of the Lord, A Theological Aesthetics*, Vol. III (Edinburgh: T. & T. Clark, 1986; original edition 1962). In this volume of "Studies in Theological Style: Lay Styles," Von Balthasar devotes a long section (pp. 172–238) to Pascal. He numbers him among "the supreme figures of theological aesthetics" (172).

David Hume, *The Dialogues Concerning Natural Religion* (1779). Presents the skeptical case against the various arguments for God.

Germain Grisez, *Beyond the New Theism* (Notre Dame/London: University of Notre Dame Press, 1975). Presents a developed philosophy of religion and a reinterpretation of analogy in dialogue with its critics.

Elizabeth A. Johnson, *She Who Is, The Mystery of God in Feminist Theological Discourse* (New York: Crossroad, 1992). Presents an argument for the use of both male and female imagery in our analogical language about God.

Alfred North Whitehead, *Process and Reality, An Essay in Cosmology* (New York: Harper Torchbooks, 1960). The book was first published in 1929.

Charles Hartshorne, *A Natural Theology for Our Time* (La Salle, Ill.: The Open Court Publishing Company, 1967), p. 17.

John F. Haught, *The Cosmic Adventure, Science, Religion and the Quest for Purpose* (New York/Ramsey: Paulist Press, 1984).

Ian Barbour, *Religion in an Age of Science* (San Francisco: Harper & Row, 1990).

Terrence W. Tilley, *The Evils of Theodicy* (Washington, DC: Georgetown University Press, 1991).

Carl Sagan, *Contact* (1985) and John Updike, *Roger's Version* (1986). These two novels explore the tension between the spirit of scientific rationality and that aspect of religious faith that seems to distrust science.

Terms To Identify

relativism

skepticism

analogy

way of negation

way of eminence

sophist

dialectic

panentheism

theodicy

Chapter III

Religion

WHAT IS RELIGION?

If this were a book on the philosophy of God or natural theology, we would at this point examine the various arguments for and against God. But since we are on our way to a study of Christian theology, we must for now leave aside the philosopher's path to God and enter that explicitly religious dimension of human experience of which theology is a part. Like philosophy, the religions too concern themselves with the depth dimension of human experience. In the words of the Second Vatican Council's *Declaration on the Church's Relationship to Non-Christian Religions*:

> Women and men expect from the different religions an answer to the obscure riddles of the human condition which today also, as in the past, profoundly disturb their hearts. What is a human being? What is the meaning and purpose of our life? What is good and what is sin? What origin and purpose do sufferings have? What is the way to attaining true happiness? What are death, judgement, and retribution after death? Lastly, what is that final unutterable mystery which takes in our lives and from which we take our origin and towards which we tend? (Paragraph 1)

In studying religion, the first problem one faces is the need to decide what will be included in the study. This is the problem of definition. To what does the term *religion* refer? This problem appears in a concrete way in our society when the courts have to decide what forms of behavior should be protected under the laws that are intended to recognize and guarantee religious freedom or prevent the establishment of religion.

VATICAN II

The Second Vatican Council (1962–1965), convoked by Pope John XXIII, assembled the Catholic bishops of the world in an ecumenical council (an assembly representing the whole church). Vatican II was the twenty-first ecumenical council, as they are reckoned by the Catholic Church, and the first since 1870. In addition to the college of bishops in union with the pope (bishop of Rome), Eastern Orthodox, Anglican, and Protestant representatives also attended the council as official observers. Pope John asked the council to address the spiritual needs of the contemporary world by engaging it in dialogue. The council produced sixteen documents: four constitutions (solemn doctrinal statements in which the church rearticulated its own self-understanding in a contemporary setting), nine decrees, and three declarations. The latter have a more practical significance and address such modern conditions as religious pluralism and religious liberty. Among the council's most important documents are: the Dogmatic Constitutions on the Church and Divine Revelation, the Pastoral Constitution on the Church in the World of Today, the Constitution on the Sacred Liturgy, the Decrees on Ecumenism and on Eastern Catholic Churches, and the Declarations on Religious Freedom and the Church's Relationship to Non-Christian Religions. Along with the founding of the World Council of Churches in 1949, Vatican II is one of the most important religious events of the twentieth century.

"RELIGION" IN THE AMERICAN CONTEXT

The brief reference above to American law indicates that the question "What is religion?" is always asked in a specific context. The American environment has unique conditions that influence the way Americans tend to answer this question.

Two forces have in the main shaped American cultural ideals.

The first is the dissenting English Protestant Christians who settled what is now the east coast of the United States. The second is the European enlightenment or age of reason, a period that dates roughly from 1650 to 1800. The first is represented in our cultural and historical symbols by the New England Puritans, the second by Thomas Jefferson. Under the force of various circumstances, these two cultural streams flowed together to form one of the most distinctive features of American public life. We call it "separation of church and state." It is enshrined in the First Amendment to the U.S. Constitution. It would be fair to say that for the first half of the republic's history, the dissenting Protestant heritage shaped our understanding of church-state separation. More recently the enlightenment side has predominated. Doubtless this is because the more inclusive enlightenment symbols, e.g. reason, law, and the individual, are better suited to a more diverse population. The ascendancy of the enlightenment side of our heritage in public life has had a tremendous effect on how Americans view "religion."

Though it is often treated as a fundamentally intellectual movement associated with the rise of modern science, the enlightenment was primarily a movement for the political emancipation of individuals from various forms of traditional authority, the established Christian churches of Europe being chief among them. Freedom of scientific inquiry is one important instance of such emancipation. The chief enlightenment ideal is individual political liberty and the freedoms of speech, assembly, and religion that it implies. Enlightenment commitment to individual political liberty is based on a nearly absolute faith in the competence and autonomy of individual reason. In this text, I will refer to this complex of enlightenment ideals and beliefs by the shorthand term *modernity*.

In contemporary American culture, as it is shaped by law, media, and political discourse, modernity has a strong influence on how we perceive "religion." In a sense, the very idea that there is a universal phenomenon known as religion is a creation of the enlightenment. In fact, there are only particular religions and they are not accustomed to presenting themselves as one among the many religions we can choose from. The very category of *religion*, as moderns use it, does violence to what it describes.

The religions have most often understood themselves as both *concrete* (God is the God of Abraham) and *true* (there is only one God). There are almost as many such claims as there are religions. They appear mutually exclusive and bound to conflict. Such competing claims, when pushed, lead to religious wars, persecutions, and other forms of intolerance. By replacing the concrete religions with *religion* as an abstract and universal category, modernity sought to avoid or submerge conflict and secure political freedom. In so doing, however, it changed our approach to the religions.

By adverting to how religions worked prior to the enlightenment, we can grasp the extent of modernity's impact on our understanding and use of the term *religion*. Before the enlightenment in the west, the idea of a people or nation implied shared gods and shared public prayer and ritual. Consider the examples of the ancient Roman empire, the Holy Roman Empire of medieval Christendom, the Islamic empire, and even the modern confessional nation states that emerged in Europe after the reformation and the Peace of Westphalia in 1648. They all had what in enlightenment terms we would call "established religions" or "churches." A look at how religions work in contemporary cultures that are in tension with modernity shows a similar situation. From an historical point of view, Islamic republics are not unusual—we are. Today's Americans are among the first people in history not to consider their religions as primarily shared and public. We generally call this disconnection of the gods from the public life of the people "separation of church and state" and we consider it a very important political good. Under modern conditions, religions have become voluntary associations.

The point here is not to argue against the voluntary character of religion in modern society, but to emphasize how modernity has changed the religions and our understanding of them. By rendering them voluntary, modernity has thereby rendered problematic the essential public and communal dimensions of traditional religions. Religion has become: a) privatized or interiorized, b) separated from shared daily life, and c) focused on personal "belief."

a) *Privatization*—Under modern conditions, religious faith and life tend to become private and interior as opposed to public and communal. In order to prevent legal establishment and the religious intolerance and persecution that went along with it, the gods had to be banished from public life and confined to the individual soul. When modern people want to find God, the first place they are inclined to look is within themselves.

b) *Separation from Shared Daily Life*—Once the religious sphere is located primarily in the soul, the rest of life becomes secularized or separate from religious influences. We no longer expect to find God in ordinary daily life, the activities we share as members of American culture—business, politics, law, sports, entertainment. In a world-historical perspective, what we take for granted is a most unusual development.

Because of the Christian side of its founding heritage, the United States, throughout most of its history, has managed to avoid the full impact of these changes. Instead of having one established church, the United States had many voluntary churches, denominations, as they came to be called. In spite of the multiplicity of denominations, the United States had a shared religious culture. All the churches—Catholicism and Judaism were conspicuous exceptions—were descended from the reformation. Public structures such as law, schools, and language supported their communal life. By the first decades of the twentieth century, however, public life had become sufficiently secularized to complete the privatization of American religion.

c) *Focus on Personal "Belief"*—One common effect of privatization or interiorization is that religious faith and life come to be equated with "belief." When we talk about religion, we often speak of our "beliefs." We often divide the world into "believers" and "non-believers," the latter a more civil term than "unbelievers." In an academic setting, belief takes on an intellectual cast. To study religion is to study different beliefs. To be a Catholic, for example, is to share certain esoteric beliefs with other Catholics. Catholics "believe in" the pope. Protestants don't. Catholics, Lutherans, and Episcopalians are all just like their other fellow Americans except they have different beliefs. The scriptural and traditional idea of having one's entire life (heart and soul and strength) transformed in God goes by the way.

In more popular religious settings, "belief" takes on a more devotional than intellectual cast. This preserves some of the sense that God appeals to the entire person and not just to the part that "believes." But belief as religious devotion still remains relatively separate from the rest of life. In the table of contents of the standard news magazine, "religion" is only one among many more important headings. It comes pretty close to the end of the issue and is comparatively brief and often sensational. Most of us would be surprised if it were otherwise.

Modernity has created a situation in which most people do not expect to encounter God in their daily affairs. God is not expected to appear in our shared public life. If we are interested in God, we pray privately or go to church. From a religious perspective, modernity presents a challenge of the highest order. Religious faith and life are not likely to survive unless they can be publicly shared in worship and service and community life. Our culture no longer provides public structures for such shared activity. Where traditional religions have remained vital under modern conditions, people have *voluntarily* built such structures. The profoundly counter-cultural nature of this effort comes to light when such people try to pass their faith on to their children.

DEFINING RELIGION

As a curiosity in the modern world, traditional religions have become an object of study. This gives rise to the problem of definition. When religion is no longer taken for granted as part of daily life, we arrive at the problem of defining it. A brief survey would reveal that scholars have devised various approaches to the problem of definition.

As examples we can consider the efforts of two philosophers who have influenced the academic study of religion in the United States, William James (1842–1910) and Alfred North Whitehead. Both James and Whitehead are strikingly and refreshingly original in their approaches to religion. But their common aversion for the public or institutional dimensions of the religions lends to their language about religion a naively individualistic ring. Its public dimension is relegated to the category of the merely external.

In the second of his prestigious Gifford Lectures at Edinburgh in 1901, James tackles the problem of definition. He begins

by noting that the term *religion* "cannot stand for any single principle or essence, but is rather a collective name" (James, 39). He
then goes on to distinguish between "institutional" and "personal" religion. The former is a merely "external art, the art of
winning the favor of the gods" (James, 41). For religion so understood James has little use. He declares personal religion to be
more fundamental and defines it as

> the feelings, acts, and experiences of individual men in their
> solitude, so far as they apprehend themselves to stand in rela-
> tion to whatever they may consider the divine (James, 42).

James' comments on human relations to the divine are extra-
ordinarily insightful, but they remain limited by his characteristi-
cally modern focus on "individual men in their solitude."

Speaking a quarter-century later in 1926, Whitehead echoes
James' dichotomy between the internal and the external. He recognizes the dimensions of "ritual, emotion, belief and rationaliza-
tion" as giving religion "external expression in human history"
(Whitehead, 18). But again for Whitehead, the primary religious
category is "solitariness." Barely paraphrasing James, he defines
religion as "what the individual does with his own solitariness"
(Whitehead, 16). Like James he is eloquent on the development
of the individual's relationship to God. But like James, Whitehead remains profoundly innocent of the social dimensions of
interior life.

> Thus religion is solitariness; and if you are never solitary, you
> are never religious. Collective enthusiasms, revivals, institu-
> tions, churches, rituals, bibles, codes of behavior, are the trap-
> pings of religion, its passing form (Whitehead, 16).

In their emphasis on the solitary individual, these two definitions are almost quaintly modern. Their radical separation of the
external and the internal blinds them to the enabling role of tradition or inheritance, and to a full appreciation of the public and
communal dimensions of religious life. Any primarily sacramental
or incarnational approach to the relationship between the so-
called external and internal is excluded at the outset.

If students were to approach the study of religions with such definitions, the behavior of serious Jews, Christians, and Muslims, for example, would be incomprehensible except in condescending terms. The Passover meal, the eucharist, the pilgrimage to Mecca would be consigned to the merely external. Readers must be aware that such modern understandings of religion as James' and Whitehead's are historical exceptions. Traditional religions are usually not anything like what James, Whitehead, and other modern people assume religion is supposed to be.

In his book *The World's Religions*, Ninian Smart offers a richer but more tentative and heuristic approach to the problem of definition. Recognizing *religion* as a modern category, and one that religions don't usually use to understand themselves, he finds it more profitable to study particular religions rather than to search for the essence of something called *religion*. As an aid to such comparative study, Smart proposes a sevenfold schema of dimensions. It provides some initial basis for comparison and contrast among religions.

One category that cuts across Smart's dimensions, and appears as well in many of the classical religious traditions, is that of worship. *Worship* is a difficult word for the modern, secular mind to understand. While we might speak analogically of people worshiping money or the state, the primary sense of the term *worship* implies what in the previous chapter has been called the transcendent. The transcendent is a reality that is not reducible to us or to the world, but that is made manifest through them. The presence

---

SMART'S SEVEN DIMENSIONS

1. practical-ritual
2. experiential-emotional
3. narrative-mythic
4. doctrinal-philosophical
5. ethical-legal
6. social-institutional
7. material

of transcendence, which we perceive as worthy of our worship, is arguably one of the most significant, distinguishing features of the religious dimension of human existence. If worship (awe-filled appeal to a transcendent) is allowed a key role in a working definition of religion, then we would think of Judaism, Islam, and even some forms of Buddhism as religions. Humanism and Marxism, for example, could only be called religions by analogy. Not only would such an approach be more respectful of the self-understandings of humanists and Marxists, it would also mean that key religious ideas, e.g. God, are best understood in terms of worship.

Throughout human history, people in disparate places and cultures have claimed special kinds of extraordinary experiences, in which transcendent reality erupts into their routine and makes itself known as "holy" or worthy of worship. Such claims are recognizable as religious by their appeal to the transcendent. In the following sections, we will examine two classic examples of religious experience claims from the history of religions. The first one is taken from the Hindu holy book known as the *Bhagavadgita*. The second is taken from the religious tradition of Judaism and appears in the biblical book of Exodus. The divinities in these examples are not abstract and removed from the world. They are identifiable precisely by their historical connections to family and people.

ARJUNA'S ENCOUNTER WITH VISHNU/KRISHNA

The name of the Hindu religion, like that of India itself, is related to the name of the Indus River which separates contemporary India and Pakistan. The Indus Valley saw the emergence of an ancient urban civilization going back to the third millennium B.C. Religious elements from this civilization, especially its emphasis on yogic meditation techniques, combined with elements from the religion of the "Aryan" warriors, who invaded the Indian continent ca. 1500 B.C., to form the tradition out of which contemporary Hinduism has developed.

A remarkable diversity and all-inclusiveness (one might even call it "catholicity") distinguishes Hinduism as a religious tradition. In its highly developed incarnational/sacramental sense, just about anything is a potential means for manifesting the transcendent. One senses here a certain kinship with the analogical imagination of Catholicism.

One of Hinduism's most fascinating aspects is the role played by polytheism, the belief in many gods, in symbolizing the infinite fullness and mystery of ultimate reality. While there is a sense of the inevitable oneness of the ultimate or absolute, the depths of its infinity are mirrored by an endless multiplication of divinities drawn from local traditions. These lesser gods embody the various attributes of divinity and function in a way that is very similar to that of Mary and the saints in Catholicism's "communion of saints." Those contemporary Jews and Christians, who have learned to think of monotheism and polytheism as opposites, will have a difficult time appreciating the positive role of polytheism in Hindu religious practice and belief.

Without using the term *polytheism*, the Second Vatican Council's *Declaration on the Church's Relationship to Non-Christian Religions* has recognized this positive role, noting that

> In Hinduism the divine mystery is explored and propounded with an inexhaustible wealth of myths and penetrating philosophical investigation, and liberation is sought from the distresses of our state either through various forms of ascetical life or deep meditation or taking refuge in God with loving confidence. (Paragraph 2)

In the text from the *Bhagavadgita*, or "Song of the Lord," we encounter more of the devotional than the meditative or ascetical side of Hinduism.

The *Bhagavadgita* is only one of the many scriptures or sacred writings of the long Hindu tradition. Others include the earlier *Vedas* and the *Upanishads*. The latter evidences more of the "searching philosophical inquiry" and "ascetical practices" or "deep meditation" referred to by Vatican II. The *Bhagavadgita* represents the height of the devotional, or *bhakti*, strain of Hinduism. It is a small part of the great Sanskrit epic, said to be the longest poem in the world, the *Mahabharata*. The *Mahabharata* tells the story of a great war. In the *Bhagavadgita* we find a Hindu

knight of the warrior caste named Arjuna on the plains of
Kurukshetra with his chariot driver. It is the eve of the great battle
that may have taken place sometime between 850 and 650 B.C.
Thoughts of the upcoming battle fill Arjuna with distress. The
threat of death is compounded by the fact that the opposing army
includes many of his own relatives. He does not want to fight.

> Those for whose sake we covet
> Kingdom, delights and things of pleasure,
> Here stand they, arrayed for battle,
> Surrendering both wealth and life.
>
> They are our venerable teachers, fathers, sons,
> They too our grandsires, uncles,
> Fathers-in-law, grandsons,
> Brothers-in-law, kinsmen all;
>
> These would I nowise slay
> Though they slay [me], my friend,
> Not for dominion over the three [wide] worlds,
> How much less for [this paltry] earth.
>
> (I, 33–35)

Arjuna and his chariot driver spend the night in deep conversation. Unknown to Arjuna, the charioteer is really the Lord Krishna
in disguise. Krishna is one of the avatars, or incarnations, of the
Hindu god Vishnu. Along with Shiva, Vishnu is one of the two
chief deities in the devotional strain of Hinduism. The climax of the
Bhagavadgita occurs in Chapter XI when Krishna reveals himself
to Arjuna in his multi-faceted heavenly form. Smart describes this
passage as expressing "a shattering religious experience, which is
here clothed in the mythology of the cult of Vishnu. . . ."

Upon learning Krishna's true identity, Arjuna makes the following request:

> Even as Thou hast described [thy] Self to be,
> So must it be, O Lord Most High;
> [But] fain would I see the [bodily] form
> Of Thee as Lord, All Highest Person.
>
> (XI, 3)

Highlighting the central role of *darsan* (seeing) in Hindu practice,
the ensuing theophany or manifestation of God is rendered in
imagery that is primarily visual. The repetition of "I really want to
see you" in George Harrison's 1970 popular song, "My Sweet
Lord," in reality a devotional hymn to Vishnu, exemplifies the
same religious motif.

> So saying Hari,
> The great Lord of Yogic power,
>
> Revealed to the son of Pritha
> His all-highest sovereign form,—
>
> [A form] with many a mouth and eye
> And countless marvelous aspects;
> Many [indeed] were its divine adornments,
> Many the celestial weapons raised on high.
>
> Garlands and robes celestial He wore,
> Fragrance divine was his anointing:
> [Behold] this God whose every [mark] spells wonder,
>   The Infinite, facing every way!
>
> If in [bright] heaven together should arise
> The shining brilliance of a thousand suns,
>   Then would that [perhaps] resemble
> The brilliance of that God so great of Self.
>
> Then did the son of Pandu see
> The whole [wide] universe in One converged,
> There is the body of the God of gods,
> Yet divided out in multiplicity.
>
> Then filled with amazement Arjuna,
> His hair on end, hands joined in reverent greeting,
> Bowing his head before the God,
>   [These words] spake out:
> . . .   (XI, 9–14)
>
> Gazing upon thy mighty form
> With its myriad mouths, eyes, arms, thighs, feet,

Bellies, and sharp, gruesome tusks,
The worlds [all] shudder [in affright], —
    how much more I!

Ablaze with many coloured [flames] Thou touch'st the sky,
Thy mouths wide open, gaping, thine eyes distended, blazing;
I see Thee, and my inmost self is shaken:
I cannot bear it, I find no peace, O Vishnu!

                                        (XI, 23–24)

More terrifying visions follow and, apologizing for any undue familiarity he may have been guilty of before he knew Krishna's true identity, Arjuna pleads with his Lord to return to the way he was before:

Things never seen before I've seen, and
    ecstatic is my joy;
Yet fear and trembling possess my mind
Show me, then, God that [same human] form [I knew],
Have mercy, Lord of Gods, Home of the universe!

                                        (XI, 45)

Krishna's subsequent instruction to Arjuna expresses the heart of Hindu devotionalism:

The Blessed Lord said:
Right hard to see is this my form
    Which thou has seen:
This is the form the gods themselves
    Forever crave to see.

Not by the Vedas or grim ascetic practice,
Not by the giving of alms or sacrifice
Can I be seen in such a form
    As thou didst see Me.

But by worship of love (bhakti) addressed to Me alone
Can I be known and seen
In such a form and as I really am:
[So can my lovers] enter into Me.

Do works for Me, make Me thy highest goal,
Be loyal in love (*bhakta*) to Me,
Cast off [all other] attachments,
Have no hatred for any being at all:
For all who do thus shall come to Me.

(XI, 52–55)

MOSES' ENCOUNTER WITH YHWH (I AM) IN THE BURNING BUSH

Moses can be regarded as the founder of Judaism. His experience with the burning bush precedes both the exodus from Egypt and the experience at Mount Sinai. Together with them it forms the basis of the Jewish religious tradition. The biblical book of Exodus, as well as the books containing the Mosaic law, Leviticus, Numbers, and Deuteronomy, provides our only information about Moses. There are no accounts in Egyptian history that correspond to the Exodus account, and some of what we do know of the period of the nineteenth dynasty in Egypt is difficult to harmonize with Exodus. Since we are dealing with the thirteenth century B.C. and evidence is scanty, these discrepancies need not imply a critical decision against the belief that the Hebrews fled Egypt approximately 1,300 years before the birth of Christ and migrated to Canaan under the leadership of Moses. Moses is indeed an Egyptian name, and the traditions that ascribe the origins of Jewish cult and law to him are ancient and strong.

From the final chapters of the book of Genesis, we learn how the Hebrews, the descendants of Abraham, came to be in Egypt. This is the story of Joseph, the favorite son of his father Israel, thrown into a well by his jealous brothers and carried off to Egypt by Midianite merchants. As Genesis ends, a famine reunites Joseph and his brothers in Egypt. With the beginning of Exodus, Joseph has died and a new Egyptian pharaoh has begun to persecute the Hebrews. Newborn males are to be cast into the Nile. According to the well-known account in Exodus 2, Moses' mother puts him in a basket and sends his sister to hide him in the reeds along the Nile. Pharaoh's daughter finds him there and raises the Hebrew child as a member of the Egyptian royal household. The young Moses is deeply moved by the plight of his fellow Hebrews.

One day when he sees an Egyptian strike a Hebrew laborer, he gets into a fight with the Egyptian and kills him. Fearing for his own life, Moses flees to the land of Midian, probably in the Sinai peninsula, and marries a local woman. As Exodus 3 begins, we find Moses in Midian tending his father-in-law's sheep.

> Meanwhile Moses was tending the flock of his father-in-law Jethro, the priest of Midian. Leading the flock across the desert, he came to Horeb, the mountain of God. There an angel of the LORD appeared to him in fire flaming out of a bush. As he looked on, he was surprised to see that the bush, though on fire, was not consumed. So Moses decided, "I must go over to look at this remarkable sight, and see why the bush is not burned."
>
> When the LORD saw him coming over to look at it more closely, God called out to him from the bush, "Moses! Moses!" He answered, "Here I am." God said, "Come no nearer! Remove the sandals from your feet, for the place where you stand is holy ground. I am the God of your father," he continued, "the God of Abraham, the God of Isaac, the God of Jacob." Moses hid his face, for he was afraid to look at God. But the LORD said, "I have witnessed the affliction of my people in Egypt and have heard their cry of complaint against their slave drivers, so I know well what they are suffering. Therefore I have come down to rescue them from the hands of the Egyptians and lead them out of that land into a good and spacious land, a land flowing with milk and honey, the country of the Canaanites, Hittites, Amorites, Perizzites, Hivites and Jebusites. So indeed the cry of the Israelites has reached me, and I have truly noted that the Egyptians are oppressing them. Come, now! I will send you to Pharaoh to lead my people, the Israelites, out of Egypt."
>
> But Moses said to God, "Who am I that I should go to Pharaoh and lead the Israelites out of Egypt?" He answered, "I will be with you; and this shall be your proof that it is I who have sent you: when you bring my people out of Egypt, you will worship God on this very mountain." "But," said Moses to God, "when I go to the Israelites and say to them, 'The God of your fathers has sent me to you,' if they ask me, 'What is his name?' what am I to tell them?" God replied, "I am who am." Then he added, "This is what you shall tell the Israelites: I AM sent me to you."

God spoke further to Moses, "Thus shall you say to the Israelites: The LORD, the God of your fathers, the God of Abraham, the God of Isaac, the God of Jacob, has sent me to you.

"This is my name forever; this is my title for all generations.

"Go and assemble the elders of the Israelites, and tell them: The LORD, the God of your fathers, the God of Abraham, Isaac and Jacob, has appeared to me and said: I am concerned about you and about the way you are being treated in Egypt; so I have decided to lead you up out of the misery of Egypt into the land of the Canaanites, Hittites, Amorites, Perizzites, Hivites and Jebusites, a land flowing with milk and honey."

SOME GENERAL CHARACTERISTICS OF RELIGIOUS EXPERIENCE

Bhagavadgita 11 and Exodus 3 provide two classic examples of religious experience claims. Because of their antiquity, longevity, and foundational role in their respective traditions, we can take them as in some sense typical or representative. The approach taken in the following discussion of them derives from what students of comparative religion call the "phenomenology of religion." As a general method in philosophy, phenomenology "brackets," or sets aside, questions about the extra-mental existence of whatever is being studied. Phenomenologists focus their efforts on finely nuanced descriptions of what appears to consciousness.

Phenomenology literally means the study of what appears. Since religious questions cannot be solved by strict demonstration, but are nevertheless important, the method of phenomenology is particularly well suited to the study of religious experience. One of the fruits of its use in religious studies has been the emergence of a sense of the remarkable structural similarities among religious experiences from disparate times, places, and religious traditions. The best-known practitioner of this method is the Roumanian-

born historian of religions Mircea Eliade (1907-1986), who taught
for many years at the University of Chicago.

In Chapter I, we used the correlative terms *ordinary* and
extraordinary to open up the depth-dimension of human experience. Similarly, Eliade uses the correlative terms *sacred* and *profane* to elucidate the religious dimension of human experience.
He develops these categories at an introductory level in *The Sacred and the Profane* (1957). It is important to keep in mind that
these terms are not to be equated with *good* and *bad*. The profane
is simply the ordinary background against which the sacred appears. It has absolutely nothing to do with "profanity" in our
sense of the term. In Eliade's cosmos, every aspect of the profane
offers a potential medium for the manifestation of the sacred.
This capacity of the visible world to body forth the invisible, along
with Eliade's easiness with cosmic symbolism, gives his approach
a striking affinity with the incarnational/sacramental ethos of Roman Catholicism. Doubtless this affinity has something to do with
Eliade's own religious background in the Roumanian Orthodox
Church. When we analyze religious experience in Eliade's categories of sacred and profane, we can identify five characteristics or
structural elements.

1. *The Ordinary Person in Ordinary Space and Time* – In our
two examples, Arjuna and Moses are ordinary figures in the sense
that no supernatural claims are made for their origins or natures.
Although they have both achieved heroic stature in their respective traditions, there is no question that they are human beings in
the ordinary sense. They are likewise engaged in the routine tasks
proper to them, Arjuna as a warrior, Moses as a shepherd. Obviously, Arjuna's situation on the eve of a battle puts him in a more
extraordinary situation than Moses and heightens his sensitivity to
the depth-dimension.

Reconstructing the inner lives of such shadowy figures from
the past as Arjuna and Moses is risky business. Nevertheless, we
might hazard some observations from a psychological point of
view. Both Arjuna and Moses have arrived at what might be
termed crisis points. Both texts indicate that they are experiencing certain tensions in their hearts and minds. At the end of the
first chapter of the *Bhagavadgita*, Arjuna slumps down in his
chariot and "let slip his bow and arrows, his mind distraught with

grief" (I.47). The kinship Moses feels with the people of his birth leads him to murder one from the people who raised him. Fearing that he will murder them as he had murdered the Egyptian, the Hebrews too reject him (Ex 2:13–14). Both Arjuna and Moses exhibit characteristics of what William James called the "divided self" or the "sick" or "twice-born" soul. This state of tension or dividedness keeps both Moses and Arjuna open to the depth-dimension and in a state of readiness for a possible sign from the gods of their ancestors.

2. *The Sacred Appears* – The *sacred* is the name Eliade gives to what religious people think they have experienced. In phenomenological terms, the sacred is the object of religious consciousness. Although it could refer to a personal God, it is a broader term, intended for use across the entire range of the history of religions. A nearly identical concept is developed in Rudolf Otto's (1869–1937) *The Idea of the Holy*, first published in German (*Das Heilige*) in 1923. Otto wanted to use the category of the holy to reach beyond the rational and ethical dimensions of our language about God, to touch upon the distinctively religious, i.e. that which elicits the distinguishing religious response of worship.

The texts we are examining both describe the dramatic eruption of the sacred or the holy into the lives of Arjuna and Moses. Both Krishna/Vishnu and Yahweh are experienced as coming unbidden and on their own initiatives. Though the ground seems to have been prepared, neither Arjuna nor Moses is portrayed as expecting to encounter his respective Lord. The same could be said of St. Paul on the Damascus road (Acts 9) or the other New Testament figures, such as Mary Magdalene or Peter, who are given to see the risen Lord Jesus.

The holy never appears "directly," but through a non-sacred or profane medium. As long as the term is not used in a reductionist sense, we could say that the holy is *symbolically* mediated. The chariot driver and the bush are the mediums in our texts. "There the angel of the LORD appeared to him in the flame of a burning bush" (Ex 3:2). The sacred is recognizable as such precisely through the distortion of the medium by which its presence is disclosed or made manifest. This is not an ordinary bush. It burns but is not consumed. This is what initially catches Moses' attention and draws him near. Hundreds of years later, Blaise

Pascal will begin his "Memorial" commemorating his own encounter with the God of Abraham, with an allusion to the same "fire" of Exodus 3.

In a similar manner to the bush, the chariot driver is distorted before Arjuna's eyes into the kaleidoscopic vision of Vishnu. The visual imagery of the *Bhagavadgita* contrasts with Exodus' emphasis on the conversation between Moses and the Lord. This contrast reflects the general biblical stress on hearing and the corresponding Hindu stress on seeing.

In neither text is there any question of Arjuna or Moses confusing the holy with the medium through which it is made manifest. Moses does not identify the bush with Yahweh, nor does Arjuna think that the charioteer is Vishnu. The sacred is not reducible to the worldly or visible medium through which it appears. This is another way of saying that people, even so-called "primitive" ones, do not worship rocks and trees. From a religious point of view, the great advantage of the phenomenological approach to religion is that it lets the sacred be itself without reducing it to something else, i.e. without reductionism.

Among others, Sigmund Freud (1856–1939) at the individual, and Karl Marx (1818–1883) and Emile Durkheim (1858–1917) at the level of society, each practiced some form of reductionism. They took for granted that religious people have gotten it wrong and that what they think they experience must really be something else. We find a good example of reductionism in Freud's opinion that "what is sacred was originally nothing but the perpetuated will of the primeval father" (*Moses and Monotheism*, 156).

As irreducible in its manifestation, the sacred is also self-defining. It gives itself in experience precisely as the "totally other." Its initial definition is to be other than or not the profane. Both Yahweh and Vishnu identify themselves. It is very important to Moses that he learn the name of Abraham's God. The tetragram YHWH (transliterated from Hebrew as "Yahweh") is really no name at all. Like the Mosaic prohibition against graven images of the Lord, its primary intent is in saving the divine transcendence: "I am who am" (Ex 3:14). Although the issue of the divine name does not assume the importance that it has in Exodus 3, Vishnu identifies himself similarly. "Time am I, wreaker of the world's destruction . . ." (XI, 32). Arjuna addresses his Lord as "[Thou] the first Creator, God's Lord, the world's [abiding] home, unending. Thou art the Imperishable, Being, Not-Being and what surpasses both . . ." (XI, 37). "Thou, of this universe the last prop and resting place" (XI, 18).

3. *The Sacred Evokes Worship*—In both texts, the manifestation of the sacred elicits a twofold response consisting of a powerful attraction and a simultaneous fearfulness. Moses is drawn to the bush, but he is also fearful: "Moses covered his face, for he was afraid to gaze on God" (Ex 3:6). After begging the Lord to reveal his true form to his sight, Arjuna cannot bear what he has seen: "I see Thee and my inmost self is shaken: I cannot bear it, I find no peace, O Vishnu!" (XI, 24).

The fundamental religious attitude, as typified by Arjuna and Moses, is one of awe and reverence. This is the attitude of worship. God doesn't have to command it, it comes naturally. To the holy or the "numinous," that which inspires worship, Rudolf Otto has given the Latin name *mysterium tremendum et fascinans*, the awful and fascinating mystery. Jews and Christians might accept Otto's phrase as an apt designation for the God of Abraham and Jesus.

4. *The Sacred Involves a Calling*—The sacred never gives itself as an ordinary object in experience. It is not simply there among the other objects. One does not know the sacred in the manner of everyday information. Life does not go on as usual. Encounter with the sacred is a transforming experience that profoundly alters one's perception of things and calls one to act in a new way. Religious experience often involves a calling or a mission, a vocation. We find this with Arjuna and Moses, as well as with figures such as Paul from the other great conversion stories in the religious traditions. Arjuna must fight on the plains of Kurukshetra. Moses is called to lead his people out of Egypt.

Neither one finds these missions personally appealing. Moses is less than reassured by Yahweh's initial promise that, when all of this is over, the people will worship God on Mount Horeb (Ex 3:12). Like the prophets who will come after him, Moses resists the Lord and his call. He protests five separate times (Ex 3:11; 3:13; 4:1; 4:10; 4:13). Arjuna spends the entire first ten chapters of the *Bhagavadgita* arguing unawares with his Lord over the traditional Hindu view of death. Neither Arjuna nor Moses is portrayed as having surrendered his freedom or human faculties. In the end, the tension is resolved. They relent and freely acquiesce to their respective Lords.

5. *The Return to the Ordinary*—"But they will never believe me or listen to me; they will say, 'The LORD did not appear to you' " (Ex 4:1). Even in the midst of his awe-inspiring experience, Moses never stops thinking like a human being. He works to fit this experience in with the rest of his life experience. For prophets like Moses, the most difficult moment occurs when they come down from the mountain and return to the people.

RELIGIOUS EXPERIENCE

As the examples of Arjuna and Moses illustrate, phenomenology serves, in a modern context, as a particularly apt means for studying religions. By its refusal to reduce religious faith and life to something other than they claim to be (see above), phenomenology directs our attention to what is specific to the experiences we call "religious," namely, manifestations of the sacred and worshipful responses to them.

In his classic study, *The Varieties of Religious Experience* (1902), William James popularized the term *religious experience*. Because of its currency, and in spite of its limitations, we shall continue to use it. James focused in his work on "that element or quality in them [religious experiences] which we can meet nowhere else." In defending his own choice of examples, he argued that the specific quality he sought "will be of course most prominent and easy to notice in those religious experiences which are most one-sided, exaggerated and intense" (James, 52). In choosing the classic examples of Arjuna and Moses, I have followed James' example. Such dramatic examples, however, run the risk of giving readers the false impression that religious experiences only happen to shadowy heroic figures who lived long ago. This would reinforce the modern tendency to separate religious life from the rest of life.

This tendency seems to be a built-in hazard of the phenomenological approach. This is not surprising when we consider that the method arose under modern conditions. The very term *religious experience* suggests that there is a special kind of experience distinct from political, economic, or athletic experience. It happens only rarely and to very unusual people. Phenomenology of religion's crucial distinction between the sacred and the profane seems to reflect the modern dichotomy between the religious and the secular, which we find embodied in certain contemporary interpretations of separation of church and state.

Such an approach to religious experience, with its emphasis on the *difference* between the sacred and the profane or God and creation, we can call *dialectical*. In the Old Testament, the call of the prophet Isaiah (Is 6) provides a dramatic example of the dialectical approach. Rudolf Otto uses Isaiah 6 extensively in *The Idea of the Holy*. God's final speech to Job from "out of the storm" (Job 38–41) provides another example. In the New Testament, St. Paul, with his dramatic conversion on the Damascus road (Acts 9) and his emphasis on being created anew in Christ, fits this dialectical pattern well. In Christianity's long history, figures such as St. Augustine, Martin Luther, Blaise Pascal, and Søren Kierkegaard provide further illustrations.

But if James is correct, such dramatic examples are simply exaggerated instances of a phenomenon that appears most often in more ordinary people in less one-sided and intense forms. In addition to its insistence on the difference between the sacred and the profane, phenomenology of religion also emphasizes that the sacred only appears in and through the profane. Anyone or anything is a potential medium for the sacred. Recall the examples of the charioteer and the bush. This latter emphasis means that phenomenology of religion is open on its own terms to an approach that emphasizes not the difference but the *continuity* between the sacred and the profane, between God and creation. Borrowing a term from the previous chapter, we can call this approach *analogical*.

Analogical and dialectical approaches to religious experience differ in their presentations of God and of the people who experience God. The rest of this chapter will be devoted to developing the analogical approach by contrasting it with the dialectical approach. The purpose of this contrast is to emphasize that religious experience can happen to anyone.

THE DIALECTICAL APPROACH
TO RELIGIOUS EXPERIENCE

a) *God in the Dialectical Approach* – The dialectical moment of the phenomenology of religion emphasizes that the sacred appears precisely in its *differentiation* from the profane. As is the case with the God who addresses Job from "out of the storm," the emphasis here is on the wholly Other character of the object of religious experience. In a modern context, however, such emphasis on God's otherness tends to promote the common view of God as separate from the world. God becomes a separate being who competes with other beings for our attention. Time spent with God is time spent away from work and family. Loving God with our whole heart and soul and strength becomes a cruel and impossible command. Only those with no family or no work could even dare attempt it.

If God is totally Other, we ought not to expect to find God in the affairs of daily life. To find God, we would have to go to a separate place, either our own interior or perhaps a church. From within such a perspective on God, pastors can chide their people for not being able to give God "even one hour a week." The possibility of paying attention to God and loving God in and through creation remains dim.

b) *Religious People in the Dialectical Approach* – If religious experiences are always as dramatic as St. Paul's on the Damascus road, then they are relatively rare and only happen to the "great souls" among us. In *The Varieties of Religious Experience*, James spoke of "twice-born souls," people such as Paul, Augustine, Luther, and Pascal, whose inner divisions could be healed only by momentous experiences of conversion. For the great saints and mystics of the modern period, such conversion experiences are most often interior. The great saints and mystics do not appear to be like the rest of us. Though we go to church, it might not occur to us to describe that as "religious experience."

THE ANALOGICAL APPROACH
TO RELIGIOUS EXPERIENCE

a) *God in the Analogical Approach*—The story of Elijah in the first book of Kings provides an Old Testament example of the analogical approach to God. After his well-known face-off with the prophets of Baal in 1 Kings 18, Elijah slit all of their throats. This enraged Jezebel, the Sidonian wife of King Ahab of Israel and the one under whose influence Ahab had promoted the worship of Baal. With the forces of Jezebel in pursuit, Elijah fled to the desert and finally took shelter in a cave on Mount Horeb, the same holy mountain where God had appeared to Moses. The disheartened prophet was instructed that only upon leaving the shelter of the cave would he meet the Lord.

> A strong and heavy wind was rending the mountains and crushing rocks before the LORD—but the LORD was not in the wind. After the wind there was an earthquake—but the LORD was not in the earthquake. After the earthquake there was fire—but the LORD was not in the fire. After the fire there was a tiny whispering sound. When he heard this, Elijah hid his face in his cloak and went and stood at the entrance of the cave. A voice said to him, "Elijah, why are you here?" (1 Kgs 19:11–13).

In this story, Elijah did not find God in the great wind, nor in the earthquake, nor in the fire. Storms, earthquakes, and fires are the kinds of places where the dialectical approach might lead us to expect to find God. Rather Elijah recognizes God in "a tiny whispering sound" (1 Kgs 19:12). According to the analogical approach, we should expect to find God in the kinds of everyday occurrences suggested by some of the varied English translations for what came after the fire in 1 Kings 19:12: "a faint murmuring sound" (Revised English Bible), "a sound of a gentle breeze" (Jerusalem Bible), "a still small voice" (King James Version).

The God of the analogical approach to religious experience speaks not only "out of the storm," but also in "a still small voice." God is the kind of God we experience in and through other realities of creation. We are actually experiencing God all the time. As St. Paul insisted in his speech before the Athenians, though we might seek and grope for God, God "is not far from any one of us" (Acts 17:27). "For 'In him we live and move and have our being' . . ." (Acts 17:28). This is a consoling thought that is in keeping with the analogical moment of the phenomenology of religion. The sacred appears in and through the profane but is not identified with it. The analogical approach takes very seriously the religious truism that God is everywhere.

In the writings of the medieval English visionary and mystic Julian of Norwich (1342–1413?), we find a highly developed sense of God's presence in the "tiny whispering sounds" of creation. In the following passage from *Showings*, probably the first book written in English by a woman, God's abiding presence to creation is manifested to Julian through the mediation of a tiny hazelnut. Julian's analogical text provides an instructive contrast with Pascal's dialectical one from the previous chapter.

> And (our Lord) showed me something small, no bigger than a hazelnut, lying in the palm of my hand, and I perceived that it was as round as any ball. I looked at it and thought: What can this be? And I was given this general answer: It is everything that is made. I was amazed that it could last, for I thought that it was so little that it could suddenly fall into nothing. And I was answered in my understanding: It lasts and always will, because God loves it, and thus everything has being through the love of God.
>
> In this little thing I saw three properties. The first is that God made it, the second is that he loves it, the third is that God preserves it. But what is that to me? It is that God is the Creator and the lover and the protector. For until I am substantially united to him, I can never have love or rest or true happiness; until, that is, I am so attached to him that there can be no created thing between my God and me. And who will do this deed? Truly, he himself, by his mercy and his grace, for he has made me for this and has blessedly assured me.

Julian of Norwich, *Showings*, translated by Edmund Colledge and James Walsh, *The Classics of Western Spirituality* (1978), pp. 130–31.

b) *The Role of Worship in the Analogical Approach* – If God is the kind of God we find not only in storms but also in the still small voices of everyday life, then church (as in "going to church") cannot simply be a separate place where we go to find a God who isn't anywhere else. But if God is never far from any one of us, why do we "go to church"? The classic answer is that we go to "worship" God.

For Christians, God is present in the liturgy (public worship of the church) in a special and unique way. Catholics have emphasized the real sacramental presence of Christ in the eucharist. But liturgy or public worship is connected to the rest of life. The sacramental life of Catholicism, for example, is based on the incarnational or analogical perspective according to which the ordinary realities of creation—bread, wine, water, words, and the people who speak them—are all potential manifestations of God. The world is full of God.

Christians believe that in God's history with us some of that potential has become actual. Christians go to church because they believe God is manifested in the scriptural word proclaimed and preached in the assembly, in the fellowship with other believers, and in the eucharist. But, under modern conditions, going to church serves another crucial function. It is a kind of school in which Christians cultivate the analogical imagination and learn to experience the world sacramentally, i.e. as potentially full of God.

Under modern conditions, the liturgy provides a counter-cultural voice. It is an alternative to the chorus of dominant voices that teach us daily that God is absent from the world, and that we should not expect to find God there. The liturgy can reshape our expectations about God. From its biblical stories and its sacraments, we can learn to expect to find God in the still small voices of our everyday experiences of creation. Even in spite of suffering, the biblical stories teach, we can trust that the world remains full of the God in whom we live and move and have our being. Our culture teaches us that God is absent from the ordinary affairs of music, school, sports, and business. The liturgy teaches analogical patterns of perception and experience. It can teach people how to pay attention to the God who is never far from any one of us. This leads to praise and thanksgiving.

c) *Religious People in the Analogical Approach*—According to the analogical approach, the rare souls we recognize as saints and mystics are not the only ones who experience God. The long list of the "twice-born" includes St. Paul and St. Augustine, with their new-found and often oppressive certitudes. In the face of such religious prodigies, it is crucial to recall the multitude of less spectacular souls who walk daily along the way in which they have been nurtured.

The New Testament gospels offer to believers two other models of Christian faith and discipleship. Their religious postures seem more ordinary and everyday than Paul's. One is the steady, trusting faith of Mary the mother of Jesus. Her soul magnified the Lord who lifts up the humble. The other is the sometimes shaky but ever generous-hearted faith of Peter the apostle, an unlikely and near-comic "rock." His ineptitude and full measure of human weakness were matched only by his willing spirit. These two gospel figures, each embodying a different nuance of weakness, keep us from being overwhelmed by Pauline power and perfectionism.

In addition to the examples of Mary and Peter, I can think of many saints who have lived with God under modern conditions. I am reminded especially of St. Elizabeth Seton. My daily tasks in Emmitsburg often take me under the shadow of her memory. She lived her life with God as a wife and mother as well as a Christian teacher and founder of a religious community. In the midst of various monuments to her memory, I think often of her dancing shoes. She had danced in them as a young New York socialite and she kept them until her death. They are now on display in the museum at the Provincial House of the Daughters of Charity in Emmitsburg. They look incredibly small. Someone with a dialectical imagination might see in her having saved the shoes a sign that her conversion was less than complete. Someone with an analogical imagination might find in it a spiritual refreshment and consolation.

In the analogical approach, loving God with all one's heart and soul and strength appears as a way of living open to anyone. Even seemingly little souls who are not twice-born can experience God in the dancing shoes, hazelnuts, and other murmurs of daily life. But this experience is difficult for those who have not learned to expect God to appear in the world. A joke readers may have already heard provides a light-hearted illustration.

> In the middle of a severe flood, a man took refuge from the rising water on top of his roof. As the water continued to rise, he prayed to God and asked to be saved from the flood. A rescue boat appeared and tried to take him aboard. But the man declined, saying that he had faith that God would save him. As the water continued to rise, a rescue helicopter came and dropped the man a rope ladder. But again he declined. He knew God would save him and he sent the helicopter on its way. Eventually the water covered the house and the man drowned. When he got to heaven, he was quite upset with God for failing to save him. He asked God angrily, "Why didn't you save me when I prayed to you?" "Well, I tried," God replied. "I sent you a boat and a helicopter. Why didn't you use them?"

The man on the roof had an excessively dialectical imagination and an over-developed sense of God's separation from the world. He was expecting fire and storms and earthquakes instead of boats and helicopters.

THE ANGELS OF SUPER THRIFT

Having argued that the world is full of potential manifestations of God, and that ordinary people experience God in their daily lives, good faith impels me to provide at least one example from my own religious experience. I call it "The Angels of Super Thrift."

My wife is now a practicing physician. We have three children. During her years in medical school, as during my years in graduate school a decade earlier, we had to live apart for weeks at a time. This was often difficult and stressful. One particularly stressful night, we had a long-distance argument on the phone. It was an especially bad one. Mutual recrimination and guilt were flying in all directions. After I had hung up for the second time, I felt terribly alone. As often happens at such times, I felt my situation was impossible and I didn't see how I could go on. I had to get out of the house.

Depression draws me to food. So I got in my car and drove to the Super Thrift parking lot in Emmitsburg. I pulled into a parking space. "God," I said, "if you want me to keep doing this, you'd better send me some help." Then I put my head down on the steering wheel and cried.

After a while a wonderful thing happened. A red Escort pulled in beside me. The concerned and curious faces inside belonged to one of my closest friends and her daughter. They of course asked me if I was all right and I said NO. They stayed with me for a while and then went inside for their groceries. Soon I gathered enough energy to go inside too. I wanted to buy a one-pound box of Cheese-Its—my medicine for emotional and spiritual ills.

As I walked in the door, another wonderful thing happened. Another of my closest friends—we go back to college days—was standing in the checkout line near the door. I must have looked pretty awful. When she saw me, she came right over and said, "You look like hell." Then, right in the middle of the Emmitsburg Super Thrift, she gave me a big hug. This didn't make everything all right, but I no longer felt so alone and impossible.

Just as in the stories in the Bible, God had truly heard my prayer and sent not one but two angels to comfort me. I bought my Cheese-Its and went home and ate the whole box. My wife came home the next weekend, and we had our usual reconciliation.

To the cynical eye, this is not a story about God or angels at all. It's simply about a couple of supermarket coincidences. After all everyone in Emmitsburg goes to Super Thrift at least once a day. What makes it plausible for me to believe that God sent angels to comfort me?

This is how I expect God to act. From my earliest childhood, when my mother listened to my prayers each night and taught me to say "good night" to God, through all the years of reading and hearing the stories about God in the scriptures, I have learned from my inheritance, my tradition, what God is like. This is the kind of thing I expect God to do. It doesn't happen all the time, but it happens often enough that when it doesn't, I give God the benefit of the doubt. My sense of the story, however, leads me to expect that in the face of death, giving God the benefit of the doubt will be very difficult.

Was this a "supernatural intervention"? The theological name for what these first chapters are about is "fundamental theology." In discussions of fundamental theology, contemporary theologians often get very nervous about what they call "supernatural interventions." Interventions or interferences by God in the world's affairs are said to violate the autonomy of the world and of human beings. They offend the modern sense of how things work.

When used with reference to God, terms such as *intervention* and *interference* connote a certain inappropriateness. They imply that God is someone who lives outside of or separate from the world. This is a modern concept, given classic expression in David Hume's essay "Of Miracles." This essay will be treated at length in Chapter XIII below. For the present, it will be enough to say the following. If God is not someone who lives outside of or separate from the world, but rather is the Creator "who gives to everyone life and breath and everything" (Acts 17:25), then it would be preferable to speak of God's *manifestations* rather than God's *interventions*. In speaking of such manifestations, Christian theology has traditionally used the term *revelation*.

Questions for Review and Discussion

1. List and discuss three ways in which the modern American context shapes the practice and understanding of traditional religion.

2. What distinguishes religious experience from other extraordinary experiences?

3. How are Yahweh and Vishnu/Krishna similar? How are they different?

4. How are the experiences of Moses and Arjuna similar? How are they different?

5. Discuss the danger of using extreme cases to understand religious experience.

6. What is phenomenology of religion? Distinguish its *dialectical* and *analogical* moments.

7. Contrast the dialectical and analogical approaches to religious experience. What are the differences in how each approach conceives God and the people who have religious experience? Give biblical examples of each approach.

8. How is speaking about God's action as *manifestation* different from speaking of God's action as *intervention*? Why is the difference religiously important?

For Writing and Reflection

1. Both Moses and Arjuna were, in a sense, at crisis points in their lives. In both cases, in some mysterious ways, the God of their mothers and fathers—a God they were already familiar with or had learned about—made a self-revelation to them and had an impact on what they decided to do.

    Write an essay about any event in your life that might be termed a "crisis" or a "problem," in which religious faith has had either a positive or a negative effect.

    In writing this essay, give serious thought to the possibility that religious experience isn't just something that happens to others. You might actually have your own religious experiences. One of the purposes of theology is to learn to reflect on them. With the possible exceptions of burning bushes and kaleidoscopic light shows, perhaps you are more like Moses and Arjuna than you think.

2. Using the text from *Showings* by Julian of Norwich and Pascal's "Memorial" as examples, write an essay comparing and contrasting the analogical and dialectical approaches to religious experience. Use the texts to support your claims.

For Further Reading

Mircea Eliade, ed., *Encyclopedia of Religion* (New York: Macmillan Publishing Co., 1987). An excellent general reference guide to the history of religions. Articles on *Bhagavadgita* (Vol. 2), *Mahabharata* (Vol. 9), and Moses (Vol. 10) provide background for this chapter.

Ninian Smart, *The World's Religions* (Englewood Cliffs, NJ: Prentice-Hall, 1989). Provides an excellent college-level survey of the religions of the world. The problem of defining religion is discussed on pp. 10–21. The chapters on Judaism and the religions of India are also pertinent to this chapter.

R.C. Zaehner, ed. and trans., *Hindu Scriptures* (London and Toronto: J.M. Dent & Sons Ltd., 1966). The source for the translation of *Bhagavadgita* used in this chapter.

Declaration on the Church's Relationship to Non-Christian Religions in Norman P. Tanner, S.J., *Decrees of the Ecumenical Councils*, 2 vols (London and Washington, DC: Sheed & Ward and Georgetown University Press, 1990), Vol. II, pp. 968-71.

William James, *The Varieties of Religious Experience* (New York: Mentor Books, 1958).

Sigmund Freud, *Moses and Monotheism*, trans. by Katherine Jones (New York: Vintage Books, n.d.). This book first appeared in 1939, the year of Freud's death.

Rudolf Otto, *The Idea of the Holy* (New York: Sheed & Ward, 1958).

Mircea Eliade, *The Myth of the Eternal Return* (New York: Pantheon Books, 1965).

John Shea, *Stories of Faith* (Chicago: Thomas More Press, 1980). Helps the reader to identify and reflect upon less dramatic forms of religious experience. In Chapter 1 the author explains them as "revelation-faith experiences."

David Tracy, *The Analogical Imagination* (New York: Crossroad, 1980). The source for the typology of analogical and dialectical used in this chapter.

Nicholas Lash, *Easter in Ordinary* (Charlottesville: University of Virginia Press, 1988). Provides an in-depth, fundamental-theological account of religious experience.

Alfred North Whitehead, *Religion in the Making* (Cleveland and New York: Meridian Books, 1965; original edition 1926).

Cheikh Hamidou Kane, *Ambiguous Adventure*, translated from the French by Katherine Woods [1963], African Writers Series (London: Heinemann International, 1972), first edition 1962. In this novel a Muslim youth from colonial Senegal travels to France to go to school and encounters the conflicts between his traditional culture and modernity.

Terms To Identify

Yahweh

Vishnu

Krishna

Moses

Arjuna

monotheism

polytheism

modernity

enlightenment

separation of church and state

the holy or the sacred

Hindu

twice-born soul

mysterium tremendum et fascinans

theophany

Bhagavadgita

phenomenology of religion

analogical

dialectical

reductionism

Chapter IV

Christian Revelation

"RELIGIOUS EXPERIENCE" AS AN AMBIGUOUS TERM

In the previous chapter, the term *religious experience* was used ambiguously or in two different senses. One sense was descriptive, the other engaged or evaluative.

a) *"Religious Experience" as a Descriptive Term* — In the context of phenomenology of religion, and with reference to the stories of Arjuna and Moses, *religious experience* was intended as a primarily descriptive term. Used in this sense, the term has two implications. First, it means that we recognize in the accounts of Arjuna and Moses a certain conformity to patterns of behavior that we have learned to call religious. We recognize that these accounts should be filed under "religion." Second, referring to the stories of Arjuna and Moses as "religious experiences" doesn't necessarily commit one to the position that Arjuna and Moses really did meet God. This question is left open. With these two qualifications, the term *religious experience* can be used in psychology, sociology, and philosophy. Religious behavior is a fascinating human phenomenon and can be studied from a variety of methodological perspectives. In a general way, we can say that the term *religious experience* is associated with the cross-disciplinary area of study in North American colleges and universities known as "Religion" or "Religious Studies."

b) *"Religious Experience" as an Engaged Term* — In discussing the dialectical and analogical approaches to religious experience, and in my story about the angels of Super Thrift, the term *religious experience* was intended in a primarily evaluative or engaged way. In talking about my Super Thrift experience, I wanted to claim, first, that the people I met really were God's angels, and, second, that on that night God had taken my own little story up into the larger story of salvation.

It is important to emphasize that both senses of the term *religious experience* can be used to refer to the same event, Exodus 3–4, for example. In each case, however, something different is meant. The difference is one of perspective. Each sense of the term implies a different attitude on the part of the speaker. When used primarily for description, *religious experience* puts the speaker in the disengaged posture of an observer, more or less interested, of someone else's religious life. William James, for example, is extremely sympathetic to the accounts he treats in *The Varieties of Religious Experience*. He never closes off the possibility that what he calls "religious experience" might include experience of a reality other than the self and the world. On the other hand, one never gets the sense that James considers any of the texts he studies religiously relevant to him, except in a most general way.

By contrast, the person who uses the term *religious experience* in the second, or engaged, sense assumes a posture more like that of a participant-observer. This engaged posture implies some degree of self-involvement with the claim, a commitment to its consequences as religiously relevant here and now.

In the modern context, the ambiguity of the term *religious experience* appears deliberate. *Religious experience* is a political term. It functions as a silent peace treaty between "non-believers" and "believers" in the religiously pluralist English-speaking world. In its descriptive sense, it allows non-believers to talk about religious claims and put them on hold without offending believers. The descriptive sense also serves to put the study of religion into a form acceptable to state-supported colleges and universities in the United States. On the other side, the term's ambiguity allows religious people to use it in its engaged sense. "Believers" can talk publicly about their religious commitments without offending "non-believers."

But the very ambiguity required by the political uses of the term renders it unsuitable for theology. When one hears the term *religious experience*, one never knows for sure whether those who use it are intending to talk about God, or simply about what goes on in someone's consciousness apart from any reference to God. "Talking about God" is the literal meaning of the term *theology*.

In theology, therefore, when one wishes to talk about religious experience in our second or engaged sense, the term *revelation* is usually used. *Revelation* makes clear that those who use it are intending to talk about God. The term *revelation* brings the tension between traditional Christianity and modernity into full view. The term *religious experience* appears designed to obscure it. Traditional Christianity is most offensive to modernity precisely at the crucial point where it claims to have been given a revelation from God at a particular time and place. This connection to a particular time and place is often called the "scandal of particularity." The scandal, it should be emphasized, is not only intellectual but also political. To enlightened perceptions, the particularity of religious claims appears exclusionary and, in fact, has often proved threatening to individual political liberty.

In western Christian theology since the enlightenment, therefore, the category of revelation has assumed a pivotal and contested place. Revelation is the key category needed to get any modern Christian theology off the ground. *Revelation* is a technical theological term. Readers should therefore expect it to involve various distinctions and nuances of meaning. This chapter's purpose is to explore the various senses of the term *revelation* in Christian theology.

REVELATION IN GENERAL IN THE WORLD RELIGIONS

While it would be exaggerating to claim that every major religion of the world has a recognizable and central doctrine of revelation, many religions, especially the scriptural ones, do have some operative and significant notion of revelation. Literally *revelation* means drawing back a veil, the disclosure of what was hidden. In a general sense, revelation is the appearance of the sacred or the self-manifestation of the transcendent. Many religions have holy scriptures (writings) that describe or testify to divine self-disclosures and teachings. In these scriptural religions, the sacred texts are bound up with the sense of divine revelation. The three great western religions, Judaism, Christianity, and Islam, all originated in the near east and are centered on the revelation of Abraham's God. The various Hindu scriptures mentioned

in the previous chapter communicate a similar, through not identical, sense of divine self-disclosure.

CHRISTIAN REVELATION IS CHRIST-CENTERED

What makes Christian revelation unique is its Christ-centered
nature. God can be known from creation, and spoke, as we profess
in the creed, through the prophets. But for Christians, God's self-
disclosure comes primarily through Christ. The Christian understanding of revelation is, therefore, a Christ-centered one. This
Christocentric nature of revelation is well expressed in the opening
lines of the New Testament book known as the letter to the Hebrews:

> In times past, God spoke in partial and various ways to our
> ancestors through the prophets; in these last days, he spoke to
> us through a son, whom he made heir of all things and through
> whom he created the universe (Heb 1:1–2).

This passage goes on to call the Son "the effulgence of God's
splendor and the stamp of God's very being" (Heb 1:3). The great
hymn to Christ in the first chapter of the Pauline letter to the
Colossians calls him the "image of the invisible God" (Col 1:15).
The hymn which begins the fourth gospel calls Jesus God's
"word" (Jn 1:1–14). "No one has ever seen God; but God's only
Son, he who is nearest to the Father's heart, he has made him
known" (Jn 1:18). In Jesus' life and teaching, according to this
understanding, we find God revealed. We find what God has to
say to us.

Christianity's emphasis on a Christ-centered understanding
of revelation is almost a matter of definition. It is Christ who
specifies Christianity and differentiates it, both empirically and
theologically, from other religions. If God's self-disclosure or revelation in Christ is full and sufficient, then we need not expect any
new revelation. The revelation of God that took place in Christ
becomes normative, i.e. it provides the terms, for future Christian
experience of God. Thus Vatican II's *Dogmatic Constitution on
Divine Revelation* calls Christ "both the mediator and the fullness
of all revelation" (Paragraph 2).

The Christian dispensation is the new and definitive covenant. It follows that it will never pass away, and that no new public revelation is to be expected before the glorious manifestation of our Lord Jesus Christ (see 1 Tm 6, 14 and Tt 2, 13). (Paragraph 4)

CHRISTIAN REVELATION IS GOD'S OWN SELF-COMMUNICATION

It has pleased God, in his goodness and wisdom, to reveal himself and to make known the secret purpose of his will (see Eph 1,9). This brings it about that through Christ, God's own Word made flesh, and in his Holy Spirit, human beings can draw near to the Father and become sharers in the divine nature (see Eph 2, 18; 2 Pt 1, 4). (Paragraph 2)

This text underscores the idea that it is God's very self that is communicated in Christ. During one of the farewell discourses that appear in the second half of St. John's gospel, the apostle Philip is said to interrupt Jesus with the request, "Lord, show us the Father and we ask no more." Jesus answers that "Anyone who has seen me has seen the Father" (Jn 14:9). The word God spoke in Christ is quite literally a living word, God's own self-expression. Jesus' revelation of the Father is not just in his teaching but in his very being, in everything he says and does. Citing John 14:9, Vatican II's *Dogmatic Constitution on Divine Revelation* goes on to say:

To see Jesus is to see his Father (see Jn 14, 9). This is why Jesus completes the work of revelation and confirms it by divine testimony. He did this by the total reality of his presence and self-manifestation—by his words and works, his symbolic acts and miracles, but above all by his death and his glorious resurrection from the dead, crowned by his sending the Spirit of truth. (Paragraph 4)

God's revelation in Christ, therefore, is not simply a transfer of information, but deeply personal. Revelation involves that "existential," or self-involving, kind of knowing spoken of in Chapters 1 and 2. In knowing and experiencing Jesus of Nazareth, his followers came to know and experience God. Those who would know God in later generations must make Jesus' life and teaching their own, steeping their imaginations in his image to such an extent that their very structures of experience are reshaped. So transformed, they are prepared to meet Jesus in the scriptural word, proclaimed or read in private; in the church's sacraments, especially the eucharist, or the breaking of the bread; in Christian fellowship; and in corporal and spiritual service to those in need.

CHRISTIAN REVELATION IS A "UNITY OF WORD AND DEED"

As Christian theology has developed in the modern west, various ways have arisen for conceiving and talking about the basic doctrine that God has made a definitive self-communication in Christ. Some Christian theologians, both Catholics and Protestants, have treated revelation as primarily a body of truths or doctrines.

As something of a reaction to this modern view, an alternative understanding of revelation as event or history developed in the twentieth century. According to this interpretation, the emphasis in speaking about revelation would be on what God has done, rather than on what God has said. We find examples of God's saving deeds in the exodus or the life of Christ.

Refusing to accept one of these positions to the exclusion of the other, the Second Vatican Council insists on balancing the two. The *Dogmatic Constitution on Divine Revelation* speaks of God's plan of revelation as being realized "through deeds and words bound together by an inner dynamism." This inner unity is described in the following way:

> . . . God's works, effected during the course of the history of salvation, show forth and confirm the doctrine and the realities signified by the words, while the words in turn proclaim the works and throw light on the meaning hidden in them. (Paragraph 2)

All of this is said in the context of the opening affirmation that God's revelation to us communicates God's own self. Speaking of revelation as primarily word or primarily event, or an inner unity of both, illustrates the felt human need to elaborate on the bare assertion that God has made a self-communication to us. Recalling what was said about analogy in Chapter II, it is clear that the meaning of "God speaks to us" or "God acts in history" is not immediately self-evident. Such language cries out for interpretation. Does God have a voice or a body? Perhaps so, but if not, then we have to admit that God neither speaks nor acts in precisely the way that we do. In any case, the scriptural and confessional (worship) statements about God speaking and acting require some interpretation. Theologians must therefore do more than simply repeat them.

The question of how God makes the self-disclosure to us, how the common ground is established on which the divine and the human can meet, is most difficult. In the end it will elude a completely intellectually satisfying answer. The attempt to get at what the phrases "God speaks" and "God acts" refer to involves much biblical and philosophical reflection. The preference expressed in the previous chapter for conceiving of God's action as manifestation rather than as intervention indicates the direction of my own reflections on the matter. In his excellent survey, *Models of Revelation*, Avery Dulles has mapped out the territory very clearly. Dulles' "symbolic" model of revelation is closely akin to what has been called above an "analogical" approach to religious experience.

CHRISTIAN REVELATION IS APOSTOLIC

The creed that Catholics and other Christians use to profess their faith refers to the church as "apostolic." *Apostolic* is a term that recurs in statements about Christian self-understanding. Christians describe their faith as in some sense the faith of the apostles. The term can be applied to revelation in a similar way. Jesus' twelve apostles and the others who were the first Christian missionaries and evangelists play a key role in the Christian understanding of revelation. They are the ones who received God's saving self-communication in Christ and who preached the "gospel," or good news, about it. The New Testament, called in the beginning the "apostolic writings," bears witness to the faith of this apostolic generation and is closely bound up with the Christian understanding of revelation. In the next chapter, on the Bible and the church, we will consider how the apostolic faith in God's saving revelation in Christ is communicated to later generations.

It has been a common Christian claim that revelation ended with "the death of the last apostle." This is true enough as long as we stipulate that future generations must appropriate for themselves God's self-communication in Christ. For Catholics, this usually implies a sense that revelation unfolds and develops in the life of the church. But saying that revelation ended with the apostolic generation could imply that God is no longer active among us. This line of thought raises some questions that usually go along with the Christ-centered, apostolic understanding of revelation.

TWO QUESTIONS AND THREE DISTINCTIONS

If Christian revelation is understood in the Christ-centered way explained above, two questions usually arise. First, if revelation ended with the passing of the apostolic generation, does that mean that God is no longer revealed to us except in testimony from the past? Does God no longer work among us? Do we no longer experience God? Second, if revelation is Christ-centered, what about the unevangelized who have never heard of Christ? Does a Christ-centered understanding of revelation imply that those who are without an explicit knowledge of Christ cannot know God in a saving way? The tendency to generate distinctions is typical of the general process of questioning and reflection. Christian theologians have often approached these two questions by distinguishing among various senses of the term *revelation*.

REVELATION AND revelation

To begin we can distinguish REVELATION (upper case) from revelation (lower case). REVELATION refers to God's self-disclosure in Christ or REVELATION in the strict or proper Christian theological sense. Revelation (lower case) refers to our own Spirit-led personal and historical appropriation of REVELA-

TION. This is our unfolding and developing understanding of what God has made known to us in Christ.

In this loose or extended sense, we can speak meaningfully of God's ongoing self-manifestation to us even now in the events of our lives. This is revelation too. The point of this distinction between upper and lower case revelation is to remind us that daily Christian experience takes place in the categories provided by the foundational Christian story of Jesus' life, especially the cross and resurrection. Our contemporary Christian experience is in some way dependent upon or derived from the apostolic experience.

My "Angels of Super Thrift" story is a good example of such dependence. The biblical story of God's involvement with Israel and with Jesus has shaped my sense of what God is like and my expectations about the kinds of things God will do. My experience took place, therefore, in the context of the biblical tradition. It provided the terms in which my experience made sense. My own little personal story was taken up into the Big Story of salvation.

The distinction between the Big Story of salvation and our little personal stories is another way of illuminating the difference between REVELATION and revelation. REVELATION is the Big Story, the biblical story. Revelation (lower case), our own present "religious experience," is what happens when our own stories become part of the Big Story. Christians are people who have, by grace, been taken up into the story of Jesus and who actually experience life in the terms provided by his story.

Public Revelation and Private Revelation

Catholic theology has a related distinction that pertains to the church's devotional life. This is the distinction between public revelation (REVELATION) and private revelations (a more dramatic form of revelation in the loose or extended sense above). From time to time, people claim more dramatic revelations than normal mediations of Christ in daily life. These include religious visions involving Christ, Mary and the saints, claims to prophetic inspiration, and other ecstatic phenomena such as we find described in the Pauline letters to the Corinthians.

Although Christians have often argued over whether such ecstatic phenomena or dramatic religious experiences ceased with the end of the apostolic age, Catholic theologians have generally agreed that in principle such revelations are possible. They have nevertheless approached them cautiously and with some of Jesus' reserve toward those who demanded a sign. (See *Dogmatic Constitution on the Church*, paragraph 12.) Claims about such experiences are usually referred to as "private revelations." *Private* doesn't imply that they are not in some way ordered to the service of the community. But they are not "public" because they are not intended in principle or necessary for all Christians. They are not an original part of the Big Story. They are instances of the Holy Spirit's ongoing guidance of the church. They are examples of people being taken up into the Big Story in particularly dramatic ways.

Christian mystics such as St. Hildegarde of Bingen (1098–1179), St. Bridget of Sweden (1303–1373), and St. Teresa of Avila (1515-1582) have often claimed to have had revelatory visions. In recent times, *Showings*, written by the medieval mystic Julian of Norwich, has become increasingly popular as a source of contemporary spirituality.

The best-known or most popular examples of private revelations are the Marian apparitions or reported appearances of Mary the mother of Jesus. From medieval Walsingham to contemporary Medjugorje, Christian people, often children, have claimed that the Blessed Mother appeared to them. Many of these apparitions occurred during the great devotional revival of Catholicism in nineteenth century France. Among the most famous Marian apparitions are the one to St. Catherine Labouré (1830), involving the so-called "miraculous medal," LaSalette (1846), Lourdes (1858), and Fatima, Portugal (1917). These apparitions usually involve a call to repentance and prayer. In many cases, local bishops or other church authorities have, upon investigations, found these claims to revelation to be obvious frauds. In other cases, such as the ones mentioned above, church authorities have encouraged such devotions in various ways. As in the cases of Catherine Labouré and Bernadette Soubirous of Lourdes, some claimants have been canonized as saints. Some of the recommended devotions have been subsumed into the liturgical calendar. Sometimes such devotions are encouraged by official declarations that nothing in these revelations is contrary to faith or morals and that information about them can be published without harm to the faith. When private revelations teach spiritual principles that we do not find in scripture or church teaching, or when they seem to pander to the kind of popular craving for the sensational upon which supermarket tabloids thrive, they have been rejected.

Private revelations cannot add anything to the fullness of God's revelation in Christ. No new church doctrines can be taken from them, for example. They cannot be forced on any Christian. Nevertheless, in addition to their fascination as cultural phenomena, the Marian apparitions have contributed significantly to the devotional lives of many Christians. Those who might be inclined to scoff at them ought to choose carefully the grounds on which they choose to do so. An objection in principle to such phenomena logically involves a rejection of the unusual phenomena associated with the originating Christian revelation described in the New Testament. If private revelations encourage morbid curiosity, a desire for signs and wonders associated with religious sensationalism and magic, they are religiously useless. If they lead people to Christ, they are of the Spirit of God. In any case, they are not REVELATION. Like their more ordinary counterparts in daily life, they occur in terms of the basic Christian story. Mary is Jesus' mother. As we are his disciples and the church is his mystical body, Mary is in some sense the mother of Christians.

General and Special Revelation or Natural and Revealed Religion

The second question deals with the ramifications of a Christ-centered understanding of revelation for the way we think about those who have never heard of Christ. Christian theologians in the modern period have generally approached this question by distinguishing special revelation (REVELATION) from general revelation, or revealed religion (REVELATION) from natural religion. Since scripture clearly teaches that God can be known from creation, e.g. Romans 1:20, and the human heart, e.g. Romans 2:14–15, it is not difficult to argue that in the near universal human religious practice we find, mixed with error, various human responses to "general revelation." This would be "natural religion." Religions based on symbols drawn from the

natural world (nature religions) could be seen as responses to
God's revelation in creation. Ethical or prophetic religions could
similarly be interpreted as responding to God's revelation in the
human heart or conscience. Modern Christian theologians,
whether Catholic or Protestant, have generally been hesitant to
say that natural religion or general revelation could be sufficient
for a saving relationship with God. This had to come explicitly
through Christ.

Contemporary discussion of Christ and the world religions
has moved beyond the previous modern discussion of revelation
in terms of natural and revealed religion. Vatican II's *Declaration
on the Church's Relationship to Non-Christian Religions* offers the
beginnings of a framework for this new discussion. Reaffirming
the church's mission to preach Christ as "the way, the truth, and
the life" (Jn 14:6), it also pledges the church's openness to what is
"true and holy" in other religions, and urges Catholics to dialogue
and cooperation with those of other faiths. Hinduism, Buddhism,
Islam, and Judaism are mentioned explicitly (paragraphs 2–4).

At this time in history, honest and hopeful openness to in-
terreligious dialogue is preferable to abstract theories, Christian
or otherwise, about how all the religions and their respective
saviors might be related. Until some fuller time, Vatican II's documents (those on the church, religious freedom, the church's relationship to non-Christian religions, and the church in today's
world) have made some important Christian theological statements about those who have never heard the gospel.

> Since Christ died for everyone, and since the ultimate calling
> of each of us comes from God and is therefore a universal
> one, we are obliged to hold that the holy Spirit offers every-
> one the possibility of sharing in this paschal mystery [Christ's
> redemption] in a manner known to God. *Pastoral Constitution
> on the Church in Today's World*, paragraph 22. See also the
> *Dogmatic Constitution on the Church*, paragraph 16.

FAITH

In Christian theology, revelation and faith are correlative
terms. There can't be revelation without someone to believe in it.

VATICAN II ON ISLAM

The church also looks upon Muslims with respect. They worship the one God living and subsistent, merciful and almighty, creator of heaven and earth, who has spoken to humanity and to whose decrees, even the hidden ones, they seek to submit themselves whole-heartedly, just as Abraham, to whom the Islamic faith readily relates itself, submitted to God. They venerate Jesus as a prophet, even though they do not acknowledge him as God, and they honor his virgin mother Mary and even sometimes devoutly call upon her. Furthermore they await the day of judgement when God will require all people brought back to life. Hence they have regard for the moral life and worship God especially in prayer, almsgiving and fasting.

Although considerable dissensions and enmities between Christians and Muslims may have arisen in the course of the centuries, this synod urges all parties that, forgetting past things, they train themselves toward sincere mutual understanding and together maintain and promote social justice and moral values as well as peace and freedom for all people. *Declaration on the Church's Relationship to Non-Christian Religions,* paragraph 3.

There can't be faith without a disclosure of God to believe in. Faith, therefore, is our believing response to God's self-communication. As the *Constitution on Divine Revelation* puts it:

> In response to God's revelation our duty is "the obedience of faith" (see Rm 16, 26; compare Rm 1.5; 2 Cor 10, 5–6). By this, a human being makes a total and free self-commitment to God, offering "the full submission of intellect and will to God as he reveals," and willingly assenting to the revelation he gives. (Paragraph 5)

Since the terms *revelation* and *faith* are interrelated, what we say about revelation also applies to faith. Faith can be described, therefore, as: a Christ-centered, personal response to God's self-communication, a unity of word and deed, and apostolic.

FAITH AS A CHRIST-CENTERED, PERSONAL RESPONSE TO GOD'S SELF-COMMUNICATION

God's revelation in Christ appeals not only to the head but also to the heart. It is addressed to the complete person. As the above citation from Vatican II affirms, therefore, Christian faith involves "a total and free self-commitment to God." Since revelation is God's own self-communication, our faithful response must involve our own deepest selves. It must be personal. Christian faith, therefore, involves one in a personal relationship with Christ. Christians love and trust Jesus. A faith that is personally believed will also be lived out in daily imitation of Jesus' example. This doesn't mean that Christians are perfect. But if Christ is really alive in them, his example will have some effect on the way they live. Christian faith, like revelation, will reflect an inner unity of word and deed.

FAITH AS APOSTOLIC

If Christian faith has what we might term a strong affective dimension, we cannot deny to it a cognitive or intellectual dimension as well. One cannot have any sort of personal relationship with someone about whom one knows nothing. As a result of God's revelation in Christ, Christians generally believe that there are some truths that can be affirmed and others that have to be denied. This concern for the truths of "the faith" is seen in the creedal fragments, perhaps from baptismal liturgies, that we find in the New Testament, and in the emphasis of the pastoral epistles (1 and 2 Timothy and Titus) on keeping the apostolic faith intact. "Take as your norm the sound words that you heard from me, in the faith and love that are in Christ Jesus. Guard this rich trust with the help of the holy Spirit that dwells within us" (2 Tim 1:13–14). We can therefore speak of "assenting to the truths God has revealed" as long as this assent is not, in the spirit of modern rationalism rather than in accordance with tradition, mistaken for the kind of assent we give to the theorems of Euclidian geometry.

Further, in its original sense, the term *apostle* refers to one who is sent. In this sense, the apostolic faith is by nature contagious. Those who live in Christ will want to share with others what they have found in him. This leads to the missionary or evangelical aspect of Christian faith. Christians have different approaches to the missionary task in the twentieth century.

FAITH AND QUESTIONING

In the long history of Christianity, the term *faith* has often been abused. Young people questioning what they are taught have been told that they must accept it "on faith." Faith functions here as a kind of magic, substitute source for knowledge, completely discontinuous with reasoning. Many modern Christians have unwittingly accepted the dripping sarcasm with which the eighteenth century philosopher David Hume ended his essay "Of Miracles":

> Our most holy religion is founded on *faith*, not on reason; and it is a sure method of exposing it to put it to such a trial as it is by no means fitted to endure.

This passage should be an insult to any intelligent Christian. If it is true, then "faith" can be used to paper over obvious absurdities and one must abandon one's intelligence in order to "have faith." If it is true, one must choose between faith and reason, religion and science. The Catholic tradition, by contrast, is committed to the belief that faith and reason cannot in the end conflict because they come from the same God.

Faith and reason cannot be so easily separated. Faith is not knowledge, but it is not irrational. It is especially not like geometrical or mathematical knowledge. It is a personal commitment that one can come to and hold intelligently, even if it involves matters that can't be proven or logically demonstrated.

Faith is the lifelong process of learning to trust God. It is very much like being married. Like a commitment to another human being, the decision of faith has highs and lows, moments of consolation and desolation. It grows, is sometimes sorely tested, and is not immune to questioning.

If the biblical story is any indication, the process of learning to trust God is usually a struggle. As we have seen, the great biblical heroes of faith—Abraham, Moses, Jacob—all argued with God. They questioned God's ways. The story of Jacob's struggle with the angel (Gn 32:23–31) indicates that the very name Israel embodies the idea of struggling with God. Mary questioned the angel of the annunciation, and her question was quite an intelligent one. Though their questions were not always so intelligent, the disciples questioned Jesus regularly. Peter struggled to follow him. Though he rarely let on, perhaps Paul did too.

If faith did not admit of the struggle of intelligent questioning, then faith would be theoretical knowledge or some magical substitute for it. It may as well have been invented by people who were afraid that Hume was right, and that faith could not stand being exposed to the reasoned arguments of its critics. When struggling reason finally gets down on its knees in faith, the decision need not be irrational. Pascal, paraphrasing St. Augustine, has put it well: "Reason would never submit unless it judged that there were occasions when it ought to submit. It is right, then, that reason should submit when it judges that it ought to submit" (*Pensées*, 174).

The act or assent of faith, the decision truly to believe in God and God's saving work in Christ, is an "existential" or self-involving one. It commits those who make it to certain personal positions on the ultimate questions. It means that the last reality with which we have to deal is not the indifferent universe but the living God of Jesus Christ, that human nobility and human suffering cannot in the end simply not matter, that death does not have the last word. To live in Christ by faith is to begin to experience life in terms of the story of Jesus and to act accordingly.

Questions for Review and Discussion

1. Clearly explain the difference between the descriptive and engaged senses of the term *religious experience*.

2. How does the term *religious experience* function in a modern English-speaking context to avoid conflict?

3. Apply both the descriptive and engaged sense of *religious experience* to the story of Moses and the burning bush in Exodus 3–4.

4. What is unique and different about the Christian understanding of revelation?

5. What does Vatican II's *Dogmatic Constitution on Revelation* mean by calling God's revelation a "unity of word and deed"?

6. "Revelation ended with the death of the last apostle." Discuss.

7. Explain the difference between:
   a) REVELATION and revelation;
   b) public revelation and private revelations;
   c) general revelation and special revelation.

8. In each of the above pairs (a, b, c), one of the terms refers to the same thing. Identify the three terms that mean the same and explain the common reality they all refer to.

9. What is the role of questioning or struggle in faith?

For Writing and Reflection

Read Chapter 1 of John Shea's *Stories of Faith*. Write an essay about a "revelation-faith experience" that you have had or could imagine.

For Further Reading

Dogmatic Constitution on Divine Revelation in Norman P. Tanner, S.J., ed., *Decrees of the Ecumenical Councils*, Vol. II, pp. 971–81. This is one of the council's key documents, essential for understanding the Catholic Church's authoritative teaching on the matters discussed in this chapter.

Avery Dulles, *Models of Revelation* (Garden City, NY: Doubleday & Co., Inc., 1983). Provides a clearly written and comprehensive survey of contemporary theological literature on the topic of revelation.

P. De Letter, "Revelations, private," *New Catholic Encyclopedia*, 12, 446–48.

Dogmatic Constitution on the Church, Chapter 8, entitled "The Role of the Blessed Virgin Mary, Mother of God, in the Mystery of Christ and the Church" in Tanner, ed., *Decrees of the Ecumenical Councils*, Vol. II, pp. 891–98.

John Macquarrie, *Mary for All Christians* (Grand Rapids, Mich.: Eerdmans, 1990).

Declaration on the Church's Relationship to Non-Christian Religions, in Tanner, ed., *Decrees of the Ecumenical Councils*, Vol. II, pp. 968–71.

Dogmatic Constitution on the Church, Chapter 2, entitled "The People of God," paragraphs 15 & 16 in Tanner, ed., *Decrees of the Ecumenical Councils*, Vol. II, pp. 860–62. This text discusses the Catholic Church's understanding of those who are outside of visible communion with it.

Terms To Identify

REVELATION	faith
revelation	public revelation
rationalism	general revelation
apostolic	special revelation
religious experience	natural religion
private revelations	revealed religion
scandal of particularity	

Chapter V

The Bible and the Church

WHAT IS THE BIBLE?

No discussion of Christian revelation can omit the Bible. For Christians it is the record of God's revelation. Not only does it bear witness to God's self-disclosure in the history of Israel and of Jesus but also Christians believe that, when they read or proclaim the scriptures in faith, God's own word addresses them. That is why lectors conclude each liturgical scripture reading with the proclamation, "The word of the Lord."

We can go into almost any bookstore and buy one of the various translations or versions of the Bible. It is a taken-for-granted part of our cultural furniture. Though some readers may own Bibles and use them regularly, others may have never even seen or opened one. Before discussing the Bible theologically in terms of God's revelation, therefore, we must first describe what the Bible is.

The word *Bible* comes from the Greek *ta biblia* and means simply "the books." This meaning indicates that the Bible is not a book in the ordinary sense. It was not written by one author or group of authors at one particular time in history. The writings that we find in the Bible—we call them *books* too—were produced by many different human authors over a long period of time. These writings originated out of the religious life of the people Israel and of the first Christian communities or churches. Their authors did not speak as isolated individuals but as members of a religious body. Their writings were likewise preserved in their religious communities, where they were used for such purposes as worship, instruction, and personal and communal prayer. Eventually the various individual writings were gathered together into the one collection that we call the Bible.

When speaking of the Bible's origin from an historical point of view, we must distinguish two separate processes:

1) the actual composition of the individual books, the production of the text;

2) the process of gathering these books into a sacred collection of scriptures, the formation of the canon.

Canon is the word used to refer to the eventually agreed-upon list of scriptural books. In its simplest meaning the canon is the Bible's table of contents.

The Bible is a literary classic of western culture and could be studied for its value as literature. But Christians give it a further significance and regard it as in some sense from God. It is "God-breathed" (2 Tim 3:16) or inspired by the same Spirit whom the creed confesses as having "spoke[n] through the prophets."

The Christian Bible is divided into two parts: the Old Testament, or the Hebrew scriptures, and the New Testament, or Christian-specific part of the Bible. There are two different canons or lists for the Old Testament. The Hebrew canon, used by Jews and Protestants, has thirty-nine books. The canon used by Catholics is based on the contents of the Septuagint. The Septuagint is a Greek translation or version of the Hebrew Bible, with some additions of works originally in Greek. It originated among Greek-speaking Jews in Egypt in the third and second centuries B.C. and became the most commonly used Bible among the early Christians, a majority of whom spoke and wrote in Greek. The Septuagint-based canon, used by Catholics, has forty-six books. This difference in the number of Old Testament books distinguishes so-called Protestant and Catholic Bibles. The seven books contained in the Septuagint but not in the later Hebrew canon are called "apocryphal" (hidden) or "deuterocanonical" (second canon). They are: Sirach, Wisdom, Baruch, Tobit, Judith, and 1 and 2 Maccabees, as well as additions to the books of Esther and Daniel.

THE OLD TESTAMENT

The term *Old Testament* dates from the second half of the second century A.D. Some Christian scholars prefer to replace it with the term *Hebrew scriptures*. Though there are some good reasons to recommend this change, this book will retain the traditional term *Old Testament*. First, the term *Hebrew scriptures* is not an entirely accurate designation for the Catholic Old Testament with its basis in the Greek Bible or Septuagint used by most New Testament authors. But beyond the level of mere description, the term *Hebrew scriptures* is fundamentally misleading as a reference to the Old Testament. From the beginning, the communion of early Christian churches rejected proposals to abandon, along with its God, what came to be called the Old Testament. This rejection of Marcion, a second century Christian from Asia Minor, and others who wished to separate Christianity entirely from its parent Judaism, represented a conscious decision by early Christians to make the sacred writings of Judaism their own.

This momentous choice entailed a christological or Christ-centered reading of the Hebrew scriptures. The centuries-old history of this tradition of interpretation means that, although *Hebrew scriptures* and *Old Testament* refer to roughly the same set of books (allowing for the seven book difference), the religious reality to which these terms refer is far from the same. A glance at some of the messianic psalms, e.g. Psalm 110, or the book of Isaiah, e.g. Isaiah 52:13–53:12, is sufficient to establish the force of this point. To the Christian eye, these texts, as they have been interpreted from New Testament times to the present, are references to Jesus Christ. To the Jewish eye, they can only refer to some other figure or to various of God's promises as yet unfulfilled. The term *Old Testament* should not be interpreted to imply that Judaism is obsolete. As St. Paul puts it, "For the gifts and the call of God are irrevocable" (Rom 11:29).

THE CONTENTS OF THE OLD TESTAMENT

The Old Testament books have their original context in the life and history of the people known as Israel. Some of the oral

THE OLD TESTAMENT CANON

The Law (Torah)/The Pentateuch

Genesis
Exodus
Leviticus
Numbers
Deuteronomy

The Prophets

Major Prophets:
Isaiah, Jeremiah,
Ezekiel, Daniel

Minor Prophets:
Hosea, Joel, Amos,
Obadiah, Jonah,
Micah, Nahum,
Habakkuk,
Zephaniah, Haggai,
Zechariah, Malachi

The Writings

Historical Books

Joshua
Judges
1 & 2 Samuel
1 & 2 Kings
1 & 2 Chronicles
Ezra
Nehemiah
Ruth
Esther
Lamentations
Judith
Tobit
Baruch
1 & 2 Maccabees

Wisdom Books

Job
Psalms
Proverbs
Ecclesiastes
Song of Songs
Sirach
(Ecclesiasticus)
Wisdom

"Catholic" OT—46 books
          (Septuagint canon)

"Protestant" OT—39 books
          (Hebrew canon)

OLD TESTAMENT HISTORY

oral traditions

1800 ┬ Abraham

1290 ┼ exodus, desert experience
        Moses

formation of
    narratives

        conquest of Canaan
        judges
        Saul
1000 ┼ David's kingdom
        Solomon
            kingdom divided
            (north & south)

writing

722 ┼ north falls to Assyrian empire

587–538 ┼ south falls to Babylonian empire
            exile, or Babylonian captivity

redaction and
more writing

323–142 ┼ Israel ruled by Alexander the
            Great's successors
            (Ptolemies & Seleucids)

Septuagint (LXX)
    Greek OT

167 ┼ Maccabean, or Hasmonean, revolt
        against Greeks

63 ┴ Roman rule of Palestine
        Herod family

and written sources upon which these books are based date as far back as the second millennium B.C. In referring to its scriptures, Jewish tradition distinguishes three groups of books:

1) the law (Torah), traditionally attributed to Moses;

2) the prophets;

3) the writings

The entire collection is sometimes referred to as *Tanak*, a term which comes from abbreviations for the Hebrew words for the three divisions. The Septuagint, the pre-Christian Greek version of the Hebrew scriptures, distinguishes the historical books from the prophetic books, thus yielding the fourfold division we find in Christian Bibles: 1) the Pentateuch, or "five books" of the law or Torah, 2) the historical books, 3) the wisdom writings, 4) the prophets.

The Pentateuch — The five books of the Pentateuch are Genesis, Exodus, Leviticus, Numbers, and Deuteronomy. Many of our best-known Bible stories come from Genesis, especially its first eleven chapters: Adam and Eve in the garden, Cain and Abel, Noah and the flood, and the tower of Babel. Abraham the patriarch appears in chapter 12. Abraham's son Isaac and his grandson Jacob come later. It is from Jacob or Israel that the people take their name. Genesis ends with the story of Jacob's son Joseph, the dreamer to whom his father had given the many-colored coat. Joseph's brothers sell him into slavery in Egypt. When a famine brings the brothers to Egypt, they are reunited and Joseph forgives his brothers.

The book of Exodus picks up here and tells how Jacob's descendants (the Israelites) came to be enslaved in Egypt. The God of Abraham, Isaac, and Jacob reveals the divine name, Yahweh, to Moses. Moses, the heroic lawgiver of Jewish tradition, leads the Israelites out of Egypt, crosses the Red (or Reed) Sea to the forty years of wanderings in the Sinai deserts, and receives the laws of the covenant from God.

Leviticus spells out the Mosaic law in great detail. Here, for example, we find traditional Jewish dietary restrictions (cf. Lv 11) and rules for animal sacrifice. Numbers continues the narrative of Israel's wanderings in the desert wilderness and adds to the law. The book of Deuteronomy, or second law, probably written in the seventh century B.C., brings the story up to Moses' death just prior to Israel's entrance into Canaan.

The Historical Books—Joshua, Judges, 1 & 2 Samuel, 1 & 2 Kings, and 1 & 2 Chronicles tell the story of Israel's conquest of Canaan under the judges, the rise of the monarchy under David and Solomon, the division of the kingdom after Solomon into Israel (north) and Judah (south), the fall of Israel in 722 B.C. and finally the exile, or Babylonian captivity, of Judah in 587 B.C. The remaining historical books chronicle the exile, the return to the land of Israel, and the Maccabean revolt against Greek rule in the second century B.C.

The Wisdom Literature—The wisdom writings include the psalms, traditional sources of Jewish and Christian prayer, and the books of Job, Proverbs, Ecclesiastes, the Song of Songs, Sirach, and Wisdom. These books show their authors meditating on the meaning of God's covenant with Israel, sometimes in dialogue with the Greek or Hellenistic culture, which came to the ancient near east with the conquests of Alexander the Great in the fourth century B.C.

The Prophetic Books—Christians divide the prophetic books between major and minor prophets. The former include Isaiah, Jeremiah, Ezekiel, and Daniel (in the Septuagint). They are followed by the twelve minor prophets.

The Old Testament story is vast, spanning nearly 2,000 years. It is important to note that the individual books were not necessarily written in the order in which they appear in our Bibles. Many of them were put into their final form long after the events they purport to describe. This raises questions about the Old Testament's historical reliability and literary intent. The Reading Guide in the *Catholic Study Bible* (Oxford University Press, 1990) and the bibliographies it contains provide readers with an excellent introduction to these questions and the resources used to answer them. The information on the Old Testament's contents provided here is intended primarily as context for the New Testament.

THE NEW TESTAMENT CANON

Fourfold Gospel	Pauline Collection	
Matthew	Romans	
Mark	1 Corinthians	
Luke/Acts of the Apostles	2 Corinthians	
John	Galatians	
	Ephesians	
	Philippians	
	Colossians	
	1 Thessalonians	
Catholic Epistles	2 Thessalonians	
James	**1 Timothy**	
1 Peter	**2 Timothy**	**pastoral epistles**
2 Peter	**Titus**	
1 John	Philemon	
2 John	Hebrews	
3 John		
Jude		

Apocalypse
(*Revelation*)

THE CONTENTS OF THE NEW TESTAMENT

The New Testament is considerably smaller than the Old Testament. Most of its twenty-seven books were completed during the second half of the first century A.D., between Jesus' death (ca. A.D. 30) and A.D. 100. Compared with the sweep of the Old Testament, this is a relatively brief period.

The process of canonizing or gathering these books together into a Christian collection with "scriptural" authority comparable to that of the Hebrew scriptures took much longer. Not until the mid-second century do we find a New Testament work cited as "scripture" ("it is written"). The term *New Testament*

NEW TESTAMENT AND LATER HISTORY

	30 or 33	Jesus' death & resurrection
	50–62	St. Paul's letters
	100	individual NT "books" complete
end of composition stage		
	220	NT canon (list) stabilized
end of canonization stage		
	c.400	St. Jerome's Vulgate (translation from Hebrew [OT] and Greek [NT] to Latin)
	1450	Bibles printed
	1516	First edition of Erasmus' Greek New Testament
	1534	Luther's German Bible
	c.1550	Council of Trent on canonical scriptures
	1582	Douai NT
	1609	Douai OT
	1611	King James Version
	1749	Douai revised
	1946	Revised Standard Version NT
	1952	Revised Standard Version OT
	1970	New American Bible
	1973	New International Version
	1986	NAB Revised NT
	1990	New Revised Standard Version

also dates back to the second half of the second century A.D.,
as does the first list of books. By the beginning of the fifth
century A.D., the present list of twenty-seven had been widely
accepted.

Like the Old Testament books, the twenty-seven New Testament books can be divided into groups. Twenty-one of the
twenty-seven have been traditionally designated as letters or epistles. Many of these (the exact number is a matter of scholarly
dispute) were written by the great Christian missionary St. Paul.
Paul became a follower of Jesus a few years after the Lord's
death. Paul himself died in the mid-60s A.D. in the first Roman
persecution of Christians under the emperor Nero. Other New
Testament letters are attributed to the apostles John (3), Peter
(2), James (1), and Jude (1).

Though none of the four gospels mentions its author by
name, they have been traditionally called the gospels according to
Sts. Matthew, Mark, Luke, and John. The four gospels tell in
narrative form of Jesus' ministry, death, and resurrection. Because of their similarities, the gospels of Matthew, Mark, and
Luke are called "synoptic," from the Greek for "seeing together"
or "with one view." The fourth gospel, that of the "beloved disciple," is traditionally attributed to the apostle John. The Pauline
letters and the four gospels form the core of the New Testament
canon.

The Acts of the Apostles is the second part of St. Luke's
gospel. It tells the story of the beginnings of the church of Jesus
from his ascension up until just before Paul's death. The main
character in the first half is St. Peter. St. Paul dominates the
second half of Acts.

Finally, there is the Apocalypse or book of Revelation.
Apocalypse means *revelation* in Greek. This is the last book of the
Christian Bible. The author identifies himself as John, but he is
probably not the John who was Jesus' disciple. The Apocalypse is
a strange book, filled with visions and symbols about the end of
the world as we know it and the final triumph of Christ. It is one
of the most controversial biblical books. Early Christians debated
its scriptural status and contemporary Christians argue about its
prophetic meaning.

THE NEW TESTAMENT TEXT

Before Johann Gutenberg (ca. 1400–1468) began the process of printing with movable type, books had to be copied by hand from handwritten originals. Over long periods of time the copying process could lead to corruptions in the text. When reading ancient texts such as the Bible, therefore, it often occurred to intelligent people to question whether the copies they were reading were faithful to the original. The easiest way to answer this question would be to compare the copy with the original. But usually, by the time the question arises, the originals have already been lost. If this is the case, as it is with ancient documents in general, then in order to answer the question about the text, it is necessary to assemble all the existing copies and compare them. This is the work of the textual critic, who must be skilled not only in ancient languages but also in the art of handling and deciphering the handwriting of ancient manuscripts. The goal of textual criticism is to reconstruct from the surviving copies a text that comes as close as possible to the original. Ancient Alexandrians practiced textual criticism with the manuscripts of Homer and Plato, as did the Egyptian Christian Origen, with Hebrew manuscript copies of the Old Testament texts.

Since the New Testament survives only in manuscript copies, it was necessary to establish a critical reconstruction of the original. The Christian humanist scholar Erasmus of Rotterdam (1467–1536) pioneered the textual criticism of the New Testament and is recognized as having begun the modern process of reconstructing the New Testament's Greek original. Erasmus published his Greek New Testament in 1516.

The work of the New Testament textual critic is first to locate all existing manuscript copies and compare them, noting variant readings. On the basis of these comparisons, the critic determines the number of independent sources or manuscript families. The original is then reconstructed on the basis of the most ancient and/ or reliable manuscript witnesses. This hypothetical reconstruction is called the critical text. It should be free of copying errors or editorial interpolations that might have built up during the course of the text's transmission. Any truly scholarly work in any discipline must be based on a critical text. Such texts are usually accompanied by apparatuses such as notes and commentary that note variant readings and sometimes explain why one reading has been chosen over another. Such notes often appear in study editions of the Bible.

Because of the comparatively large number of copies (more than 5,000) and the high quality of some of the manuscript copies upon which it is based, the critical text of the New Testament is considered to have an extremely high degree of reliability. The two oldest complete manuscripts of the New Testament, the Codex Vaticanus and the Codex Sinaiticus, date back to the fourth century. The most ancient New Testament fragment we now have dates from the beginning of the second century and contains five verses from John 18.

The mention of chapter and verse points to an unusual feature of the Bible. When we talk about books, we usually refer to passages in them by citing the page number. But when we refer to the Bible and other ancient works, we use chapter and verse. This convention developed because of the irregular page sizes of manuscript copies or the scroll form. It enabled people with different copies to talk or write publicly about what they had read and know that others would be able to find the passage being referred to.

BIBLE TRANSLATIONS

People often wonder which one of the numerous English translations of the Bible they should use. Most translations are done by reputable scholars trained in the original languages. They base their translations on the critical text. The Bible translation you choose depends on what you want to use it for and whether you feel comfortable with it. People use Bibles for personal prayerful reading, for scholarship, for group Bible study, and the like. The readings that Catholics in the United States hear in church on Sunday are taken from the New American Bible. This translation will therefore have a familiar and even intimate ring for church-going Catholics. Protestants from the so-called "mainline" denominations (Episcopalians, Lutherans, Methodists, Presbyterians) have a similar experience with the Revised Standard Version (RSV). Older Protestants might prefer the venerable King James Version upon which the RSV is based. The New International Version is popular among Protestants of a more Evangelical bent.

Translations differ in how literal they are and in the literary quality of the language. Often literal translations cannot succeed in capturing the tone and nuance of language in the original. On the other hand, freer translations sometimes sacrifice accuracy to eloquence. In spite of the variety of translations, there is no substitute for reading the Bible in Hebrew and Greek, the original languages of the Old and New Testaments, respectively.

CHURCH AND CANON

We have briefly considered the contents of both the Old and New Testaments and problems related to the text and translation of the Bible. But all of this has assumed that the Bible is already there. It doesn't really explain how we got the Bible. Since this is a book about Christian theology, it is appropriate to focus on the New Testament and ask where it came from. At first the answer seems obvious. Paul, the evangelists, and the others wrote the New Testament under the inspiration of the Holy Spirit. But even this appeal to the Holy Spirit only gets us as far as the individual books. Previously we distinguished two phases in the process of the Bible's coming to be: 1) the production of the texts, 2) the formation of the canon. We will now focus on the question of the New Testament canon.

The scriptures used by Peter and Paul and the other early Christians were the Hebrew scriptures, usually in the Septuagint version, interpreted in a Christ-centered way. Paul, the evangelists, and the others give us no indication that they were writing for a future New Testament. Nor is there any indication that their works were immediately thought of as scripture in the same sense as the Hebrew scriptures. The evangelists don't even seem to be aware that their works will become a set of four. We don't find the four canonical gospels together until the mid-second century when a Syrian Christian named Tatian tried to harmonize them in a work called the *Diatessaron*. Nowhere in the gospels does Jesus tell his disciples to write down his life and teaching in four gospels that will be included in a collection with early Christian letters and other writings to form the New Testament. Even if we believe that the individual New Testament works were composed under the inspiration of God's own Spirit, that still doesn't tell us anything about how they got in the New Testament. The New Testament canon cannot be explained without reference to the church.

From an historical point of view, it is impossible to avoid the conclusion that the New Testament comes to us from out of the life of the church, the communion of Christian churches, for whom the individual writings were religiously important. The New Testament canon does not come directly from the Holy Spirit to individuals bypassing the experience of the church. Nor does it come down from some authority in the church. The New Testament canon comes not "from above" but amid controversy and development from the Spirit-led inner workings of the church. Scripture and canon are deeply related to church. They are ecclesial concepts. Later in the chapter, we will have to become clearer about the meaning of the term *church*. For now we will look briefly at the process by which the New Testament canon was formed in order to see what this process tells us about the nature of the church for which the New Testament canon is scripture.

THE FORMATION OF THE NEW TESTAMENT CANON

Two passages in the New Testament letters provide some clues about the beginnings of the process by which the canon was formed. They appear in Colossians and 2 Peter. Some scholars question Paul's authorship of Colossians. In any case, the letter can be safely dated in the seventh decade of the first century between 62 and 70 A.D. After the closing greeting, the author, probably Paul, instructs the readers in the following terms:

> And when this letter is read before you, have it read also in the church of the Laodiceans, and you yourselves read the one from Laodicea (Col 4:16).

A STATEMENT FROM THE U.S. CATHOLIC BISHOPS

The basic characteristic of biblical fundamentalism is that it eliminates from Christianity the Church as the Lord Jesus founded it. That Church is a community of faith, worldwide, with pastoral and teaching authority. This non-church characteristic of biblical fundamentalism, which sees the Church only as spiritual, may not at first be clear to some Catholics. . . .

It is important for every Catholic to realize that the Church produced the New Testament, not vice-versa. The Bible did not come down from heaven, whole and intact, given by the Holy Spirit. Just as the experience and faith of Israel developed its sacred books, so was the early Christian Church the matrix of the New Testament.

From "Pastoral Statement for Catholics on Biblical Fundamentalism," National Conference of Catholic Bishops, March 26, 1987. *Origins,* 17 (Nov. 5, 1987), p. 377.

This passage indicates that the author intended or presumed that the churches would read his letters in public and exchange them. The phrase "in the church" suggests a liturgical context. Thus the impetus for a collection of Pauline letters may have come from Paul himself. Paul's letters, however, show no sign that he regarded them as on a par with "scripture," which for him would have been what we call the Old Testament. Paul's letters are intended to represent him and his divinely bestowed apostolic authority when he can't be there in person.

2 Peter is generally regarded as the last New Testament book to be written, perhaps from Rome to Asia Minor, and possibly as late as 125 A.D. In the context of reaffirming for his readers the teaching that there will be a day of judgment, the author of 2 Peter refers in passing to a collection of Pauline letters. He doesn't name any of the letters but could easily be interpreted as identifying them with scripture. The word he uses could be translated either as "the other scriptures" or simply "his other writings."

And consider the patience of our Lord as salvation, as our beloved brother Paul, according to the wisdom given to him, also wrote to you, speaking of these things as he does in all his letters. In them there are some things hard to understand that the ignorant and unstable distort to their own destruction, just as they do the other scriptures (2 Pet 3:15–16).

The exchange of letters and the congregational reading mentioned in Colossians 4 eventually result in the Pauline collection seemingly presumed in the passage from 2 Peter above. We can imagine a Christian merchant from Asia Minor, for example, traveling to Rome and exchanging copies of his church's Pauline letters for a copy of Paul's letter to the Romans. Eventually the letters would be copied together in a collection and circulated.

While nearly all of the New Testament books were probably completed before the end of the first century, the key phase in the formation of the canon must be located in the second century. By this time, the collection of Pauline letters and the four gospels, the core of our present canon, must have been circulating among the churches. But it is important to recall that these two collections would have circulated along with a slew of other Christian writings. These could be divided into three categories. First were the works of those we have come to call the "fathers of the church" because of their role in giving Christianity its decisive shape. Some of the early or "apostolic" fathers such as Ignatius of Antioch and Clement of Rome wrote works that pre-date some of the books in the canonical New Testament.

Second was a vast array of gnostic literature. Gnosticism is a name given to second century groups who a) viewed Jesus primarily as a bringer of secret and saving knowledge (*gnosis* means knowledge in Greek), and b) tended to devalue Jesus' humanity as well as the material world. Because Jesus' death could not be fitted into their view of him, the gnostics also tended to devalue Christian martyrdom. They produced acts, apocalyptic works, and gospels, all of which were attributed to apostles.

Third, the second century also produced popular works such as the apocryphal gospels and the *Protoevangelium of James*, imaginative reconstructions of details from the lives of Jesus and Mary that we do not find in the first century canonical gospels.

Works from each of these three groups would have circulated among second century Christians along with the works that eventually became part of the New Testament. The New Testament disengaged itself from these other Christian writings in the midst of great controversy.

Marcion

The process by which our twenty-seven New Testament books were separated out from the other Christian writings of the second century is complex and difficult to reconstruct historically. Our first example of a conception of Christian scripture with the basic gospel-Paul structure of the New Testament comes from the mid-second century heretic Marcion. He was a wealthy merchant and shipbuilder from Asia Minor. His father was a Christian bishop there. Marcion was a radical Paulinist who made a complete split between the Hebrew scriptures and its God and Jesus and his Father. He proposed a scripture that excluded the Old Testament and included a gospel, probably part of St. Luke, and a collection of Pauline letters. Marcion presented his idea, along with a large offering, to the church at Rome but was rejected there and by other Christians. He eventually began his own church.

Gnosticism and Persecution in the Second Century

The chief catalyst for the formation of the New Testament canon was probably the challenge posed by gnosticism in the second century. Roman persecution of the church was also a factor. These two forces, heresy and persecution, helped simultaneously to unify the churches and solidify their scripture.

Second century gnostic writings claimed to present teachings that Christ had given in secret to Peter, Mary Magdalene, Philip, Thomas, and other apostolic figures. The New Testament appears to have arisen in the struggle to disentangle the faith of the apostles and martyrs from heresy.

Irenaeus of Lyons and the Apostolic Tradition

A key figure in this struggle and in the formation of the New Testament canon was the church father Irenaeus (ca. 130–200).

The bishop of Lyons in Roman Gaul (contemporary France), Irenaeus was the leader of the Christians in the Rhone valley. A cosmopolitan figure, he had contact through his travels and personal acquaintances with the churches and leaders in the major Christian centers of the second century Roman world: Asia Minor, Rome, Alexandria, Syria, and Gaul. In his work, *Against Heresies*, Irenaeus articulated the notion of "apostolic tradition," which would help to distinguish the true faith of the apostles and martyrs from the alleged secret apostolic teaching of the gnostics.

It is important to be clear on the nature of the struggle from which the New Testament canon emerged. It was about how to identify, amid the rather vast field described above, those writings that were truly apostolic and thus witness to the faith of the apostles and martyrs. The challenge Irenaeus posed to the gnostics was simple and quite ingenious. If Jesus had really revealed all of what you say to Peter, Mary Magdalene, Thomas, and the others, why aren't your faith and your writings preserved and handed down in the great apostolic churches of Rome, Alexandria, Antioch in Syria, and Asia Minor? Thus Irenaeus appealed against the gnostics to the apostolic tradition that lived in the apostolic churches. Pre-eminent among those churches for Irenaeus was the church of Rome where Peter and Paul had witnessed to Christ by laying down their lives. *Martyr* means witness. Irenaeus' Rhone valley church had been persecuted severely and his collection of apostolic writings was a martyrs' canon which cherished the memory of Jesus' real suffering and death in the gospels as well as the apostolic testimony of Paul and Peter.

For Irenaeus, the truly apostolic writings taught the living faith of the apostolic churches. The apostolic writings, or canonical books, functioned in turn as norms within the churches for Christian faith and practice. *Canon* literally means reed or measuring rod. The truly apostolic writings would help bishops (*a bishop is literally an overseer*) like Irenaeus, pastors, and people to distinguish the true apostolic faith from the false claims of the gnostics. Irenaeus' list of apostolic writings includes almost all the books in the canonical New Testament.

In Irenaeus' understanding, the "apostolic tradition" includes not only the gospel of salvation in Christ but also basic minimal church structures, namely the canon and the episcopacy, by which that gospel is handed on and preached. The apostolic writings and the apostolic church are thus in a reciprocal, mutually reinforcing relationship that Irenaeus calls the "apostolic tradition." In his view, the scriptures and the church are not pitted against one another. To those confused by gnostic teachings, Irenaeus counseled:

> It behooves us, therefore, to avoid their (the Gnostics') doctrines, and to take careful heed lest we suffer injury from them; but to flee to the Church, and be brought up in her bosom, and to be nourished with the Lord's scripture (*Against Heresies*, 5, 20, 2, as cited in Kelly, 95).

THE NEW TESTAMENT CANON AND THE CHURCH

Second century Christianity is noteworthy for its striking concern for communion in the apostolic faith among the various churches of the Roman world. The Christians of Asia Minor, Rome, Syria, Alexandria, and Gaul kept in close touch and understood themselves as one body. The canonical New Testament gathers together writings that are traditionally associated with all of these centers, Paul and John from Asia Minor, for example, and thus bears witness in its very composition to their understanding of their communion in faith. As the second century came to a close, however, the canonical New Testament itself had begun to function as a way of ensuring that unity. The apostolic churches of the second century were not idyllic islands of concord, immune from serious division. Amid struggle and controversy, the scriptures and the church came in the second century to have a mutually constitutive relationship. In our attempts to understand what the church is, this primordial second century situation might serve as a model.

While we have not taken the story of the New Testament canon and the church beyond Irenaeus, we can conclude that the historically vague process from which the New Testament emerged would be equally displeasing to both Protestant and Catholic polemicists. It is clear that before there was a New Testament or a Christian Bible, there was the apostolic Christian church, a communion of local churches. It is equally clear that the New Testament canon came into being precisely to serve as a norm or a measure for the church's apostolic faith. Though the New Testament is the church's scripture and needs to be read and interpreted in her bosom, as Irenaeus puts it, the New Testament is not subordinate to the church.

Nor is the New Testament a magical book, appearing out of nowhere and interpreting itself without a context. Its proper context is the apostolic tradition out of which it comes and to which it gives decisive shape. We can neither separate the scriptures from the church nor arbitrarily subordinate them to the church.

THE CHURCH OF CHRIST AND THE SCANDAL OF CHRISTIAN DIVISION

In speaking of the Bible as a witness to God's saving revelation in Christ, it has been impossible to avoid speaking about Christ's church. But in the setting of twentieth century Christian pluralism, it is not immediately clear whose church we are talking about. Is it the Southern Baptist Convention, the Greek Orthodox Church, the United Church of Christ, to name only a few contemporary Christian denominations? In contemporary speaking about the church of Christ, therefore, it is difficult to avoid what Vatican II's *Decree on Ecumenism* (paragraph 1) calls the "scandal" of Christian division.

Americans generally experience Christian pluralism in the United States as a healthy manifestation of religious freedom. In the American political context, how could Christian pluralism be viewed as anything but a positive good? How could so many Christians have come to experience it as a painful scandal or stumbling block?

John 17 offers a taste of the experience of Christian division as a scandal. In this text, we find Jesus concluding his farewell discourse at the last supper. He prays to the Father for the disciples gathered with him in the upper room and for future disciples.

> I pray not only for them, but also for those who will believe in
> me through their word, so that they may all be one, as you,

Father, are in me and I in you, that they may also be in us, that
the world may believe that you sent me (Jn 17:20–21).

But instead of the unity for which Jesus prays, we experience
hundreds of Christian denominations, broken communion in faith
and worship, and a fractured body of Christ. This is the scandal of
Christian division. At the beginning of this century, the Protestant
missionaries who began the contemporary ecumenical movement
experienced this scandal in a dramatic way. Shocked by the confusing witness their divided churches presented to the people they
hoped to evangelize, they began the work of promoting greater
unity among all Christians. This work is known as ecumenism.

For Christians who take seriously Jesus' prayer for unity and
who recognize Christians in other communities of faith, contemporary division in Christian faith and worship can't simply be
religious pluralism as usual. Rather, and especially in family settings, being prevented from sharing faith and worship with those
we love is an experience of great pain. Using the particular theological resources they have inherited, Christians from various denominations have begun to dialogue about the questions of faith
and order that divide them. Often even the participants have been
surprised by the positive results. The Lutheran-Roman Catholic
dialogue in the United States has been especially successful.

At Vatican II, the Catholic Church turned in a dramatic way
to face the scandal of Christian division. Though the council intended to affirm its faith that the fullness of what is necessary for
Christ's church dwells in the Catholic Church, it recognized, at
the same time, that true Christians live in churches outside of
visible communion with the Catholic Church. The council also
recognized outside the visible boundaries of the Catholic Church
the presence of divine gifts that are essential to Christ's church.
These include sacramental baptism, the scriptures, true Christian
faith, hope and love, and the gifts and fruits of the Holy Spirit.
This does not mean that Christians outside of communion with
the Catholic Church are really Catholics without knowing it or in
spite of themselves. Rather they truly experience the gifts of
Christ's church in their own churches (*Dogmatic Constitution on
the Church*, paragraph 15; *Decree on Ecumenism*, paragraph 3).

The reality and extent of Christian division lends a certain ambiguity to the term *church* in contemporary Christian discourse. Theologically, the term *church* should refer simply to the "one, holy, catholic and apostolic" church that many Christians profess in the creed. But Christian division complicates the matter. Because it recognized other Christians, not merely as individuals, but as members of churches or communities of faith, Vatican II did not simply (i.e. absolutely and without qualification) identify the church of Christ with the Catholic Church. It taught rather that the church of Christ "subsists in" the Catholic Church. This careful language leaves room for the position that the church of Christ may subsist, in varying degrees, in other churches (*Dogmatic Constitution on the Church*, paragraph 8; compare *Decree on Ecumenism*, paragraph 4 and *Decree on Religious Freedom*, paragraph 1).

Except when it refers clearly to some specific Christian denomination, e.g. the Catholic Church, Christian readers of this book should read *church* theologically as referring to the church of Christ, confessed in the creed and now presently divided, but whose reality they truly experience in their own communities of faith. They can also pray that the Holy Spirit will lead Christians out of their present disunity, and that, through prayer, dialogue, and common effort, Christians may realize more fully, and in forms yet to be made known, the unity that Jesus prayed for them to have.

In the meantime, Christian theology in the contemporary United States needs to be consciously ecumenical. Speakers in the Christian theological conversation must be critically aware of their own location in a particular church tradition. Further, they must attend, in an ecumenical spirit, to the various traditional locations of other Christian speakers in the conversation.

In all of this, the Bible itself stands as a hopeful ecumenical sign. Along with baptism, it is one of our most treasured, shared Christian possessions. Biblical scholars have succeeded to a large extent in creating a common Christian conversation about the Bible. Scholars from any denomination can take part in it. Ordinary Christians from different denominations can study and pray the scriptures together.

The New Testament canon offers a special insight into Christian unity. From the great Christian centers of the ancient world, the New Testament canon gathers together quite a diverse collection of Christian witness and tradition. Like an icon it reflects the communion in faith and worship of the local Christian churches throughout the ancient Mediterranean world. The rich and often complementary diversity of theologies and practices in the various books is striking. And yet each different Christian voice is a witness to the fullness of Christ, and each is included in the canon as a sign of what the church's unity should be like.

Questions for Review and Discussion

1. What is the difference between the Bibles used by Catholics and those used by Protestants?

2. What is the significance of calling the Hebrew scriptures the Old Testament?

3. How many books are there in the Old Testament and how are they divided up?

4. How many books are there in the New Testament and how are they divided up?

5. What is textual criticism? Why is it necessary and what is its goal?

6. Discuss the influence of a) Marcion, b) gnosticism, and c) the Roman persecutions of Christians on the formation of the New Testament canon.

7. The Bible is the church's book. Discuss.

8. Explain the theological meaning of the phrase "the scandal of Christian division."

9. In an ecumenical setting, explain the meaning of *church* as a theological term.

10. How does the Bible itself, especially the New Testament, serve as a sign of Christian unity?

For Further Reading

Donald Senior, General Editor, *The Catholic Study Bible* (New York: Oxford University Press, 1990). The Reading Guide, extensive notes, maps, and other reference tools make this a very useful Bible.

Lawrence Boadt, *Reading the Old Testament, An Introduction* (New York: Paulist Press, 1984).

Pheme Perkins, *Reading the New Testament, An Introduction*, Revised edition (New York: Paulist Press, 1988).

Joseph F. Kelly, *Why Is There a New Testament?* (Wilmington, Del.: Michael Glazier, 1986). Provides a clearly written account of the New Testament's origins. It is geared specifically for a college-level audience.

Hans von Campenhausen, *The Formation of the Christian Bible*, translated by J.A. Baker (Philadelphia: Fortress Press, 1972) is a standard scholarly treatment of this chapter.

William R. Farmer and Denis M. Farkasfalvy, *The Formation of the New Testament Canon, An Ecumenical Approach* (New York: Paulist Press, 1983).

Eusebius, *The History of the Church*, translated by G.A. Williamson (New York: Penguin Books, 1965). Eusebius' Books IV and V make considerable use of Irenaeus.

Cyril C. Richardson, editor, *Early Christian Fathers*, Vol. I in *The Library of Christian Classics* (Philadelphia: The Westminster Press, 1953). Contains an English translation of parts of Irenaeus' *Against Heresies*. Book III on the apostolic tradition is especially helpful.

F.F. Bruce, *History of the Bible in English* (Third edition; New York: Oxford University Press, 1978).

Decree on Ecumenism in Norman P. Tanner, S.J., ed., *Decrees of the Ecumenical Councils*, Vol. II, pp. 908–920.

Questions for Research and Writing

1. Here are some biblical passages that have influenced the history of theology. Below them is a list of standard Bible commentaries. Pick a scripture passage. Find it in your Bible. Use at least three books from the list of commentaries to help you interpret the passage. Summarize your findings in a paragraph. You are free to use commentaries other than those listed here.

1. Gn 1:1	16. Mk 6:5–6	31. Rom 16:1–2
2. Ex 3:14	17. Mk 10:42–45	32. 1 Cor 11:23–27
3. Is 53:4–5	18. Mk 14:34–36	33. 1 Cor 14:6
4. Jer 7:4–7	19. Lk 1:1–4	34. 1 Cor 15:3–7
5. Jos 10:12–13	20. Lk 8:2–3	35. Gal 3:27–28
6. Job 42:2–6	21. Jn 1:1–5	36. Eph 5:32–33
7. Ps 22:2	22. Jn 3:5	37. Phil 2:9–11
8. Ps 110:1	23. Jn 8:57–58	38. Col 1:15
9. Sir 24:1–3	24. Jn 17:20–23	39. Jas 2:26
10. Wis 7:21–26	25. Acts 7:59–60	40. Jas 4:13–16
11. 2 Mac 12:42–45	26. Acts 9:3–9	41. Rev 12:1
12. Mt 5:31–32	27. Acts 16:14,40	42. Rev 20:1–10
13. Mt 5:38–39	28. Rom 1:17	43. Jn 20:28–29
14. Mt 11:25–27	29. Rom 1:20	44. Lk 2:1–2
15. Mt 16:17–19	30. Rom 7:21–25	45. Lk 2:52

Single-Volume Commentaries (usually found in Library Reference Section).

The New Jerome Biblical Commentary (Englewood Cliffs, NJ: Prentice-Hall, 1990).

Peake's Commentary on the Bible (revised edition; London: 1962).

Multi-Volume Commentaries (series including commentaries on all the biblical books).

Old Testament Message: A Biblical Theological Commentary (Wilmington, Delaware: Michael Glazier, 1982–84).

New Testament Message Series: A Biblical Theological Commentary (Wilmington, Delaware: Michael Glazier, 1979–81).

The Anchor Bible (New York: Doubleday, 1964ff).

Collegeville Bible Commentary (Collegeville, Minnesota: Liturgical Press, 1983).

2. Write an essay about some occasion, e.g. a wedding or other family event, when you have experienced the pain and scandal of Christian division in a dramatic way. Explore your feelings at this time and try to reflect theologically on your experience.

3. The *Gospel of Thomas*, discovered in the twentieth century, is a collection of Jesus' sayings. You might go to the library and look at it. A significant body of scholarly opinion considers many of these sayings very old, reflecting the stage prior to the composition of the canonical gospels. Assuming for the sake of discussion that this is true, write an essay arguing for or against contemporary Christians deciding to include the Gospel of Thomas in the New Testament. Use your historical and theological knowledge about the formation of the New Testament canon to support your argument.

Terms To Identify

Bible	*Tanak*
canon	synoptic
Old Testament	critical text
New Testament	Codex Vaticanus
Hebrew scriptures	Codex Sinaiticus
Septuagint	*Diatessaron*
apocryphal	apostolic fathers
deuterocanonical	gnosticism
Torah	*Protoevangelium of James*
Pentateuch	*Against Heresies*

martyr

bishop

apostolic tradition

church

scandal of Christian division

ecumenism

pope

Marcion

Origen

Erasmus

Tatian

Ignatius of Antioch

Irenaeus of Lyons

Clement of Rome

Chapter VI

Inspiration and Tradition

Chapter V treated the Bible. It explained what the Bible is and something of its, especially the New Testament's, historical and religious origins. Chapter VI will continue to treat the Bible, but in a more explicitly theological way. This chapter addresses two questions. First, what do people who accept the Bible as a religious book believe about it? Second, how does the Bible actually function as a religious book, or how do people in fact read it as a religious book or scripture?

A brief answer to the first question is that Christians believe the Bible to be God's inspired word. Continuing the emphasis of the last chapter, a brief answer to the second question is that Christians, with more or less awareness, read the Bible religiously as members of a living community of faith, or as part of what Vatican II's *Dogmatic Constitution on Divine Revelation* calls "the living tradition of the whole Church."

The chapter expands on these brief answers in three parts. Part I treats author-centered theories of biblical inspiration. Part II treats church or tradition-centered theories of inspiration. Part III develops *tradition* as a theological category and uses it to talk about interpreting the Bible religiously as the church's inspired scripture.

Because the discussion of inspiration and inerrancy among contemporary Evangelical and Fundamentalist Protestants holds such a prominent place in American religious culture, this chapter borrows from it the terms *strict* and *limited inerrancy*. The opening chapters of Genesis serve throughout as a kind of case study in interpreting the Bible religiously, i.e. as scripture.

THE GENERAL MEANING OF BIBLICAL INSPIRATION

Christians have used the term *inspiration*, apparently taken from 2 Timothy 3:16, to express the idea that the Bible is more than just another literary classic. It is from the Spirit of God in a special way. By the doctrine of inspiration, Christians have understood God as, in some true sense, the author of scripture. The scriptures are from God in a special way that the words of Augustine, Aquinas, or the greatest of authoritative Christian teachers are not. In matters that have to do with faith and life, Christians can give them unwavering trust. As the author of 2 Timothy exhorts his readers to remain steadfast in the truths they have learned, he writes:

> . . . from infancy you have known [the] sacred scriptures, which are capable of giving you wisdom for salvation through faith in Christ Jesus. All scripture is inspired by God and is useful for teaching, for refutation, for correction, and for training in righteousness (2 Tim 3:15–16).

This particular scripture emphasizes the practical or religious meaning of inspiration. It is neither a magical idea nor some abstract theological construction. Inspired scripture is to be used in Christian life. It gives Christians trustworthy instruction in the truth, providing a norm for faith, as well as for the needed daily reform of our lives. It is assumed to have its context in one's personal life, and by implication in a Christian family and community of faith. ". . . from infancy you have known [the] sacred scriptures, which are capable of giving you wisdom for salvation through faith in Christ Jesus" (2 Tim 3:15).

Believing in the doctrine of inspiration makes a practical difference. It means that through the scriptures God continues to nourish and address Christians. As Vatican II's *Dogmatic Constitution on Divine Revelation* (paragraph 21) emphasizes, this is especially true in the setting of the church's liturgy or public worship. When Christians hear the word proclaimed, they know that the Spirit of God is near, teaching and instructing them, judging and convicting them of sin, and consoling them with the offer of God's grace. In the context of an appeal for charity and concord within the church at Rome, St. Paul wrote with reference to the Old Testament: "For whatever was written previously was written for our instruction, that by endurance and by the encouragement of the scriptures we might have hope" (Rom 15:4).

PART I

AN AUTHOR-CENTERED THEORY OF INSPIRATION

While believing in the doctrine of inspiration, Christians have not usually ignored the literary evidence that the biblical writers continued to act as free human agents. Both Luke and John, for example, clearly acknowledge their role in the composition of their gospels (cf. Lk 1:1–3; Jn 20:30–31). Both used their intelligence and judgment in selecting and arranging the material from their sources.

Using Aristotle's causes, medieval theology spoke of the sacred writers as "the instrumental efficient cause" of scripture and of God as the "principal efficient cause." In his book on *Biblical Inspiration*, Bruce Vawter puts it this way, emphasizing that biblical inspiration in general was thought of on the model of prophetic inspiration:

> God, the principal cause, had moved the instrumental cause, the Prophet, to speak, to act, to write. The effect produced is the word of God: it is God who uttered it through the Prophet, who of himself would have been incapable of it. Yet it is a word into which the Prophet also has truly entered, for it is the work of his mind and will and other faculties that the principal cause utilized and 'elevated' in the process. The words are Jeremiah's, wrung from his heart and experience; and the word is God's. (48–49)

This is a theological theory, based on the respected human wisdom of its time, and intended to help people who are familiar with Aristotle understand what divine inspiration of the Bible might mean and how it might work. As a theory it has served the church well, enabling Catholics to affirm both the real human authorship of the Bible and analogous divine authorship. Thus Catholics and some other Christians have grown accustomed to speaking of the Bible as the "word of God in the words of men."

BIBLICAL INERRANCY: A COROLLARY OF INSPIRATION

Behind traditional theories of inspiration lay a corollary deduced from the analogy of divine authorship. This is called *inerrancy*. The term *inerrancy* has unfortunately dominated most modern discussion of biblical inspiration. The reasoning goes something like this. The Bible is God's word in a true and proper sense. The Bible is intended for our instruction. God would certainly not lie to us or deceive us, nor would God make a mistake. Therefore the Bible must not have any errors in it. If it did, we would have to attribute errors to God and we wouldn't be able to trust the Bible as a guide.

STRICT INERRANCY

Within the framework of the author-centered or prophetic understanding of inspiration, one could locate God's inspiration in one of three places: 1) in the author, 2) in the written words, or 3) in the content, the message or teaching of the book. Content is understood as the words illuminated by the literary intent. One's view of inerrancy is related to whether one locates inspiration in 1, 2, or 3. If one understood inspiration as located in the words, one could assign a maximum role to God such that the very words of scripture became God's own, as if by mechanical dictation. The result would be a very strict understanding of biblical inerrancy. Every word would have to be factually true.

This tended to be the view adopted by Protestant theologians during the modern period or the seventeenth and eighteenth centuries. Its contemporary proponents call it the theory of "plenary verbal inerrancy." Inspiration understood as factual errorlessness or inerrancy extends to every single word. Its scope includes what we would call scientific or historical assertions. The 1978 "Chicago Statement on Biblical Inerrancy" provides a clear contemporary statement of this position.

LIMITED INERRANCY

The history of theology shows that strict inerrancy or "plenary verbal inerrancy" is only one of many ways to understand the traditional author-centered theory of inspiration. We saw above that inspiration need not be located in the words themselves. Instead it could be located in the content or the words illuminated by literary intent. Rather than focusing on the words, this approach tries to determine what the affirmations of scripture are intended to teach. This requires investigation into the historical context and literary form of the particular book or passage under consideration.

During the twentieth century, Catholics and mainline Protestants have tended to a broader understanding of biblical inspiration than the "plenary verbal inerrancy" approach of their Evangelical contemporaries. They focus on the content rather than the words. The God upon whom we can rely has given us a scripture that teaches without error the religious truths that we need for salvation. The primary purpose of the Bible is not to make assertions about science and history. In the process of religious instruction, however, the scriptures might speak of historical matters. Some of the Bible's historical assertions, e.g. that Jesus died, are an essential part of its religious teaching.

Vatican II's *Dogmatic Constitution on Divine Revelation* provides a clear statement of what is meant here by "limited inerrancy." Without using the modern term *inerrancy*, the council makes a positive statement about inspiration.

> In the process of composition of the sacred books God chose and employed human agents, using their own powers and faculties, in such a way that they wrote as authors in the true sense, and yet God acted in and through them, directing the content entirely and solely as he willed. It follows that we should hold that whatever the inspired authors or "sacred writers" affirm, is affirmed by the Holy Spirit; we must acknowledge that the books of Scripture teach firmly, faithfully and without error such truth as God, for the sake of our salvation, wished for the biblical text to contain. (paragraph 11)

Rather than on scientific or historical accuracy, the focus here is on the errorlessness of what is taught for the sake of our salvation. The central concern is to find out what the biblical writers wanted to assert or teach.

The Example of Genesis 1–3
A Strict Inerrantist Interpretation

The controversy over inerrancy gives rise to the strict and limited approaches. The controversy itself is closely linked to the ongoing debate about how to interpret the first three chapters of Genesis. Genesis 1–3 contains the biblical account of creation and fall. The application of both the strict and the limited theories of inerrancy to Genesis 1–3 will provide a good illustration of how they work.

In the mid-seventeenth century, the Irish archbishop James Ussher (1581–1656) calculated that the creation described in Genesis 1–2 had occurred in 4004 B.C. Ussher arrived at this date by adding up the generations he found in the Old Testament's genealogical tables, e.g. Genesis 10–11. According to Ussher, the earth was approximately 6,000 years old. Ussher's chronology had long appeared in the King James Version of the Bible and was taken for granted among English-speaking Protestants.

By the nineteenth century, geologists had discovered that the age of the earth stretched back incalculably into the past. The science of geology provided the common-sense reading of Genesis 1–2 with its first challenge. Charles Darwin's (1809–1881) *The Origin of Species* (1859), with its theory of evolution by natural selection, intensified the challenge.

Genesis became the battlefield where the nineteenth century's great conflict between science and religion was waged. The sciences of geology, with its staggering estimate of the age of the earth, and biology, with the theory of evolution by natural selection, seemed to mean that the opening chapters of Genesis could no longer be read in what had appeared to be their "natural" or plain sense, namely, that God had created the world, including the separate species, in seven days some 6,000 years ago.

The point here is not so much the insistence by strict

inerrantists that every word in the Bible be taken "literally."
Proponents of strict inerrancy freely acknowledge that there is
poetry in the Bible. They were simply not accustomed to including the opening chapters of Genesis, so crucial to our understanding of the biblical vision of life, among the Bible's poetic sections. They read Genesis as a factual account of how the world
began.

In the United States the controversies over evolution galva-
nized the commitment of many conservative Protestants to strict
inerrancy and gave rise to the fundamentalist movement of the
1920s. In defense of biblical inerrancy, fundamentalist Christians
launched a crusade against evolution, attempting to exclude it
from biology courses in public schools. The crusade reached its
height in 1925 when John Scopes, a high school biology teacher
from Tennessee, was prosecuted and convicted for violating a
Tennessee law which forbade the teaching of evolution in the
schools. Despite Scopes' conviction, the adverse publicity from
the trial tended to discredit the fundamentalists and their strict
inerrantist interpretation of Genesis.

Those Protestants who remained committed to strict inerrancy tended to separate themselves from the traditional Protestant denominations that they denounced as too "liberal." Eventually the religious heirs of the fundamentalists of the 1920s would
retreat somewhat from this separatist posture and call themselves
"Evangelicals." Fundamentalist Christians and some Evangelicals
insist that those who reject their theory of plenary verbal inerrancy also reject the Bible as inspired by God. *The Battle for the
Bible*, the title of a 1976 book on the topic, continues to divide
many Protestant denominations in the United States. Strict inerrantists have surfaced with renewed strength and have exercised
increasing influence in the Lutheran Church Missouri Synod and
the Southern Baptist Convention.

Strict inerrantists continue to insist that Genesis 1–3 provides us with factual information about the origin of our world.
Some are willing to admit that "day" can be interpreted as a
period of time, thus defusing the age of the earth issue. But
most remain unwilling to budge on the issue of the separate
creation of the species by God. The concept of natural selection
poses for them a radical challenge to the biblical understanding

of a provident God. Strict inerrantists at southern California's Institute for Creation Research argue for "scientific creationism" and the scientific legitimacy of the belief that God created the species separately.

The Example of Genesis 1–3
A Limited Inerrantist Interpretation

Those whose understanding of inspiration limits inerrancy to what the Bible intends to teach for the sake of our salvation take a different approach in their interpretation of Genesis 1–3. Genesis, they argue, is not a science book. Its purpose has nothing to do with providing factual answers to scientific questions about the origin of the world. It has a religious purpose and a religious message that can be learned from a contextual analysis of its literary form and intent.

Most interpreters begin by contrasting Genesis 1–3 with the Babylonian creation epic, the *Enuma Elish*. The contrast helps the interpreter to focus in on the teaching that is specific to Genesis. The purpose of Genesis 1–3 is to teach in poetic form what we have come to know as the biblical doctrine of creation.

According to Genesis, God is the ultimate source of all that is. God's creation is good. Human beings bear God's image even in their sexual differentiation. The world of which we are a part has both a physical and a moral order. Creation is not an accident. God has a purpose for us. Human beings are portrayed, in a rather psychologically insightful way, as endowed with free choice. Genesis attributes the various forms of disorder we find in God's creation to the abuse of human freedom.

This is a powerful vision of religious truth that has provided generations of Jews and Christians with a basic vision of God, the world, and human beings. It provides a framework for our experience and helps us to deal with the questions that we considered in Chapter I. This vision is not without its problems, but they have little to do with science. Rather they have to do with human purpose and the meaning of human suffering. To focus on such questions as the age of the earth, the length of the days of creation, and the origin of the separate species is to misinterpret Genesis at the most basic level. The point is not simply that now we believe that God created the world by evolution by natural selection, but rather that, from a historical and literary perspective, Genesis has nothing to do with such questions.

PART II

A CHURCH-CENTERED THEORY OF INSPIRATION

In the previous chapter, we drew attention to the role of the church in the formation of the New Testament canon. We saw that an author-centered understanding of inspiration doesn't really account for the New Testament but only for the individual books. A church-centered understanding of inspiration would explicitly acknowledge the intimate relationship between the Bible and the church in both historical origin and present Christian practice.

In 1964 Karl Rahner (1904–1984) wrote an essay on *Inspiration and the Bible*. Its context was the debate at Vatican II over the *Dogmatic Constitution on Divine Revelation*, which we have already cited several times. Rahner proposed that since God brought the apostolic church and the New Testament into being together, we might also think of inspiration as a gift to the church. Scripture is one of what Rahner calls the constitutive elements of the church. Inspiration of the scriptures "is but simply the causality of God in regard to the Church, inasmuch as it refers to that constitutive element of the Apostolic Church which is the Bible" (51). Rahner's theological reflections are here directed to the second century history that we reviewed in the last chapter. His idea of biblical inspiration as part of the constitution or formation of the church has been developed by others into what I have called a "church-centered" understanding of inspiration. The understanding of inspiration as a gift to the church and not just to individuals corrects some of the inadequacies of the traditional author-centered view in three areas: 1) the composition of the New Testament books, 2) the formation of the New Testament canon, 3) the New Testament's continued functioning as a living word within the church.

THE COMPOSITION OF THE BOOKS

The author-centered view of inspiration presumes an image of an individual writer writing a book the way a modern author would. God inspires the author the way God inspired the Old Testament prophets. But scholarship reveals a quite different picture. Ancient writers worked with already existing traditions, both oral and written, and reshaped and reinterpreted them to suit new situations. Rather than writing as a form of self-expression, literary production here was conscious of speaking on behalf of a community, of handing on its traditions. This doesn't make biblical writers faceless mouthpieces of community consciousness. No one could deny that Paul, Luke, and the author of the fourth gospel have their own ideas and literary styles. They used their traditions to critique their communities and call them to be converted again. But the process of tradition transmission by which much of the New Testament came to be justifies an emphasis on the fact that Paul and the others wrote as members of the community of faith. Their witness not only expressed but helped to constitute the faith of the apostolic church.

THE FORMATION OF THE NEW TESTAMENT CANON

From our historical knowledge of the canon's second century origins, it is difficult to conceive it solely in terms of the decisions of individuals. The formal decisions of local church gatherings at the end of the fourth century recognized an already completed process. Individuals such as Irenaeus and Origen contributed significantly to the process by which the apostolic writings were recognized as scripture. But they certainly didn't claim to be establishing the canon on their own authority. They were very much the spokespersons who witnessed to and defended the writings used in their churches. In its teaching on the canon, the sixteenth century Council of Trent simply accepted as canonical the books that had been translated in Jerome's Vulgate, namely the contents of the Septuagint. The closing of the canon occurred for Protestants at the time of the reformation when the deuterocanonical books were rejected. There has never been any formal fixing of a Protestant canon.

While an author-centered view of inspiration explains, with some difficulty due to the role of tradition, the origin of the individual books, it doesn't begin to account for the formation of the canon. In order to do justice to our historical knowledge about how the canon came to be, we must broaden our understanding of inspiration to include some reference to the church.

THE NEW TESTAMENT AS A LIVING WORD

The author-centered view of inspiration makes it difficult to imagine, except in individualistic terms, how the New Testament continues to function as a living word in the church. This ignores our experience of hearing and reading the scriptures not simply as isolated individuals but as Christians who live in a community of faith. In talking about the New Testament's present functioning in the church, we leave behind the apostolic or formative church and so cease to speak of inspiration in any strict sense. Nevertheless, the derived "inspiration" by which the Spirit teaches Christians the present meaning of the scriptures requires an ecclesial dimension as well as a purely individual one.

PART III

TRADITION

In Catholic theology, the name for the historical relationship between the Bible and the church is *tradition*. In the previous chapter, we considered the relationship between the Bible and the church in a more historical way. The "church-centered" understanding of inspiration reflects on this relationship in a more theological way. The church-centered view of inspiration sketched above could just as easily be called a tradition-centered view. It corresponds in many ways to an understanding of tradition as a living process.

In the second chapter of Vatican II's *Dogmatic Constitution on Divine Revelation*, under the heading "the transmission of divine revelation," we find the council's discussion of tradition. It comes between an opening chapter on revelation itself and the chapter on the inspiration and interpretation of scripture. This arrangement reflects the view of scripture as a unique, privileged moment in the tradition process. As did Irenaeus, whose *Against Heresies* it cites in paragraph 7, the constitution understands scripture in terms of apostolic tradition.

Tradition in its literal sense means "handing over" or "handing on." In its common-sense meaning, it is what one generation in a nation or a culture passes on to the next. From a theological point of view, tradition might be described as a living process in which the revelation of God in Jesus Christ is given and received, handed on, reflected upon, and interpreted anew. Such an understanding of tradition is very similar to a church-centered understanding of biblical inspiration.

The *Dogmatic Constitution on Divine Revelation* divides the process of Christian tradition into three moments: 1) the preaching and teaching of Jesus, 2) the apostolic preaching, and 3) the preaching and teaching of the apostles' successors or the bishops of the church. The first two moments of the process are constitutive of the apostolic faith and the apostolic church. Scripture belongs to the second moment. The third moment is not constitutive of the church but preserves and develops what was established in the apostolic church.

The constitution places great emphasis on the role of the church's bishops as "successors of the apostles," a term first used by Clement of Rome at the end of the first century. It cites Irenaeus' description of the apostles as "handing over their teaching role" to the bishops. The teaching and preaching function of bishops in the church is genuinely "conservative," much as it is described in the New Testament's pastoral epistles, 1 and 2 Timothy and Titus. The constitution provides assurance that the church's teaching office is "not above the Word of God, but serves it, teaching only what has been handed on . . ." (paragraph 10).

INTERPRETING THE BIBLE AS THE CHURCH'S INSPIRED SCRIPTURE

How do Christians know when to take the Bible literally, or in what appears to be its plain sense, and when to assume that the Bible is teaching religious truth in figurative or poetic form? To put it another way, how do Christians know what scripture intends to assert or teach?

As we have seen in the example of Genesis, a limited inerrancy approach encourages an appeal to historical context and literary form to illuminate meaning. But for Christians, the question of what the Bible asserts is of more than historical and literary interest. When Christians bring their experiences and questions to the scriptures, they do not merely want to know what the words meant back then. They want to know what they mean or say now. This is where an appeal to the reader's location in a living tradition can be most helpful.

Vatican II's *Dogmatic Constitution on Divine Revelation* (paragraph 12) draws attention to three interrelated levels of interpretation involved in reading the Bible as a religious book or an inspired scripture. We can call these levels of interpretation the traditional, the historical-literary, and the canonical.

THE TRADITIONAL LEVEL OF INTERPRETATION

We can begin by distinguishing two senses of tradition as a living process. The first is tradition as an assumed, shared context of Christian common sense. I want to suggest that Christians of whatever denomination generally read the Bible religiously from such a context. It is communicated to them through such experiences as going to church or praying together. Tradition in the second sense is the historical record, made available largely through scholarship, of the church's interpretation of the Bible. This record includes sermons and conciliar and papal teachings.

These two aspects of tradition are never completely separated. The second is always influencing the first, e.g. through preaching and liturgy. The point of the distinction is to draw attention to the fact that Christians normally use tradition in the first sense to read the Bible, and they don't even think about it. Only when common-sense readings break down, as in the case of Genesis, do readers become aware of their shared assumptions and perhaps feel the need to consult some form of tradition in the second sense for clarification.

An appeal to tradition in this first sense implies that interpreting the Bible, discerning what it asserts or teaches, may be, like reading and writing in general, a much less private activity than it might at first appear. Questions about when to take the Bible literally bring to mind the image of an individual reading a Bible in abstraction from both the history of the individual and the history of the Bible. The author-centered, and by implication reader-centered, framework for thinking about biblical inspiration encourages us in this picture. So does the individualistic ethos of our society. We tend to view religious beliefs as private and personal rather than as the common possession of a community of faith. It is probably no accident that the most extreme forms of the author-centered view of inspiration flourish in the midst of this individualistic ethos.

In this context, appeals to tradition, especially when they are made by Catholics, are often greeted with suspicion. They are interpreted as appeals to authority, as references to the Catholic claim that the church teaches authoritatively through its bishops of whom the pope is the head. But the Catholic Church's authoritative interpretations of scripture are rather rare. More often the church exercises judgment in other ways, much as it did, for example, in the matter of the New Testament canon. This is primarily what it means to say that the Bible is the church's book and should be interpreted in terms of the church's living tradition. Rather than an appeal to authority, this claim is a recognition of the church-centered nature of biblical inspiration.

In order to illustrate what is meant by tradition as Christian common sense, I want to draw attention to a relatively obscure New Testament passage, verse 9 of the letter of Jude, and imagine a Christian common-sense response to it.

The Example of Jude

Nestled between 3 John (the third epistle of John) and the Apocalypse in the New Testament is a brief writing (25 verses) known as the letter of Jude. Jude has had minimum impact on the shape of Christianity, certainly no influence comparable to that of the gospel of John or Romans. Jude urges Christians to defend the faith against false teachers. In the process, it cites a passage from what appears to be the partially preserved "Assumption of Moses." The passage makes reference to a dispute between the archangel Michael and the devil over the possession of Moses' body. Even Christians who are regular Bible readers have probably never heard of this dispute between Michael and the devil.

Suppose a non-Christian were reading the New Testament privately for the first time and came across verse 9 of Jude. Suppose further that our hypothetical reader asked the average Christian of whatever denomination whether the story about the dispute between Michael and the devil over Moses' body is intended to be taken literally. Most Christians, strict inerrantists excepted, would probably answer with a certain hesitation. They might say they didn't know, but that it really didn't seem to matter, or they might just answer in the negative.

If, however, after reading about Jesus' resurrection appearances, the non-Christian were to ask whether the New Testament accounts intend a bodily resurrection, most Christians would probably answer affirmatively without much hesitation. How do we explain this? Why is what the New Testament says about what happened to Jesus' body after his death taken with much more seriousness than what it says about what happened to Moses' body?

A comprehensive answer to these questions would involve both historical and canonical considerations. A more accessible answer would lie in an appeal to what Vatican II calls "the living tradition of the whole church." Most Christians would not need an authoritative pronouncement of the church to know that Jesus' resurrection is central to Christian faith and Moses' assumption is not.

Christians would know this as if instinctively from their experiences as members of a community of Christian faith. They would know from years, perhaps decades, of celebrating Easter, singing the hymns about Jesus' resurrection, listening to the scriptures and preached word proclaimed in church, saying the creed, having some familiarity with the classics of Christian painting and music. Christian common sense, the context for Christian interpretation of the Bible, is shaped by countless instructions, sermons, liturgical hymns, and celebrations that have drawn the attention of Christians to the centrality of the resurrection. Even scholars enter into this living process as their ideas get filtered down or tested in sermons and books. This process, experienced in some way by all Christians, is what is meant by "living tradition."

Breakdowns in Christian Common Sense

Like ordinary common sense, Christian common sense can break down. In the example of Genesis, interpretation at the historical-literary level helped to correct Christian common sense amid divisive conflict. For Catholics, the church's teaching office is part of living tradition. It has the task of providing pastoral guidance and leadership in such situations of conflict. Though Catholics believe that God assists bishops through the grace of their office, even bishops must, from a human perspective, use the same means available to other Christians when they form the positions through which they will lead and guide. In short, they too must read the Bible at the traditional, historical-literary, and canonical levels.

When Christian common sense breaks down in a situation of conflict, one of the available means is to consult tradition in the second sense as the historical record of how the Bible has been interpreted in the church. For example, reference to the history of the interpretation of Genesis, especially St. Augustine's commentary, would have illuminated nineteenth century conflicts about Genesis and evolution and the age of the earth. In disputed questions between Catholics and Protestants, a common and fruitful approach, e.g. in the Lutheran/Roman Catholic dialogue in the United States on the topic of "justification," has been to review carefully the pre-reformation history of biblical interpretation on the disputed question. Like a living legal tradition, the history of biblical interpretation is not monolithic. Scholarship reveals competing patterns of interpretation and responses to changing historical circumstances. Historical prece-

dents provide catalysts and direction for continuing reinterpretation in new circumstances.

THE HISTORICAL-LITERARY LEVEL OF INTERPRETATION

As we have seen in the example of Genesis, when Christian
common sense was challenged during the modern period, many
Christian interpreters turned for clarification to the historical-
literary level of interpretation. They used archaeology, the history
and literature of the ancient near east, and their knowledge of
ancient languages to bring to light the original meaning of Genesis
1–3 in its historical context. Since the enlightenment, the historical and literary search by scholars for original meanings of the
biblical texts has shown the capacity to enrich Christian understanding of the Bible in a religious way. We could, for example,
apply historical-literary analysis to the book of Jude and try to
figure out the meaning of the reference to the assumption of
Moses in its original setting.

In spite of its usefulness, the historical-literary level of interpretation has definite limits. Because the Bible must function
religiously within a living community, i.e. it must still speak to
Christians in their situations, its present meaning can never be
limited to some form of authorial intent. A reinterpretation of
Genesis 1–3, for example, should both respond to the present
questions raised by modern science and be consistent with what
we know of the authors' intent.

THE CANONICAL LEVEL OF INTERPRETATION

If the historical-literary level of interpretation appeals to the
original meaning of a text in its context, canonical interpretation
appeals to the intent of those who canonized or collected the
individual books and the Spirit who led them. Original meanings
of canonical works are not sufficient. As parts of an inspired
canon, biblical texts are read religiously with serious attention to
the "content and unity of the whole of scripture." The presence of
a work in the canon might alter its original meaning. The Old
Testament Song of Songs is perhaps the best example of that. In a

canonical setting, difficult texts should be read in light of scripture as a whole. Different passages on a similar theme should be expected to provide mutual illumination.

To choose an example with ecumenical significance, both the Pauline collection of letters, with its emphasis on faith alone, and the fourfold gospel, with its emphasis on the daily following of Christ, were included by the early church in the New Testament canon. Christians who accept the New Testament as scripture should not expect these two emphases to be at odds. Rather they should look for interpretations which allow both emphases to stand and mutually enrich one another. Far from being contrived, such interpretations acknowledge the canonical status of each New Testament work.

CATHOLIC AND PROTESTANT DIFFERENCES ON SCRIPTURE AND TRADITION: AN ECUMENICAL VIEW

While Catholics and Protestants might both in fact interpret the Bible in what Catholics would call a "living tradition," they have historically disagreed over the relationship of scripture and tradition in the church. In Protestant theology, tradition has been only a human and historical category and not a theological one. The Protestant reformers of the sixteenth century were responding to what might be termed a crisis of religious authority. They sought a trustworthy religious authority by which believers could know with certainty what God had revealed for their salvation. Martin Luther (1483–1546) and others eventually concluded that "scripture alone" is a reliable religious authority, not tradition or the church's teaching office, whether it be in conciliar, episcopal, or papal form.

In his famous appearance before the emperor at the Diet of Worms, Luther challenged his accusers to prove him wrong from scripture. He is said to have described himself in this instance as "captive to the word of God." *Sola scriptura*, scripture alone, became a reformation rallying cry and one of the pillars of reformation theology. This did not mean that Luther had no place for tradition in the form of the councils, creeds, and papal teaching of the past. Rather, he regarded them as merely human. Scripture, by contrast, came from God. Since Gutenberg, it also had the great advantage of the unchanging and easily available form of the printed word.

The modern Protestant scholastics who followed the reformers spoke of the "material sufficiency" of scripture. This meant that all God had to reveal to us could be found in scripture. Catholic controversialists answered with the familiar argument that the church came before the Bible. We only know that there should be a Christian Bible through the testimony of the tradition. Protestant controversialists used texts such as 2 Timothy 3:16 to show that the Bible testified to itself. After the Council of Trent in the sixteenth century, Catholic scholastics of the modern period tended to treat oral tradition as a second and separate source of revelation. To it they attributed all sorts of historically unverifiable practices and beliefs as having come down from the apostles.

Scripture alone *versus* scripture and tradition: this summarizes the state of post-reformation Protestant-Catholic controversy. In the instincts and sensibilities of ordinary Christians, these controversial positions are still alive and well. With the exception of the most conservative scholars on both sides, it would be fair to say, however, that, through ecumenical dialogue, the Christian theological conversation in the United States has moved beyond these controversial positions.

ECUMENICAL CONVERGENCE ON SCRIPTURE AND TRADITION

Both the reformers and their Catholic opponents were relatively ignorant of the history of Christian origins. What has changed is that both Catholic and Protestant scholars have come to a better understanding of history. As a result, the second half of the twentieth century has witnessed significant ecumenical convergence in the disputed area of scripture and tradition as constitutive of the church.

One of the most important convergences is a turn toward tradition as a broad category for understanding the life of the church. The history of Protestant biblical scholarship since the nineteenth century has convinced all but strict inerrantists that the individual scriptural books, as well as their collection into the canon, are part of a process of the transmission of traditions. This turn toward tradition was articulated clearly at the World Council of Churches' Fourth World Conference on Faith and Order at Montreal in 1963.

The greatest Catholic theologian of the twentieth century, Karl Rahner, argued that a Catholic could defend the thesis of the "material sufficiency" of scripture, with one proviso. The proviso is that the one revealed truth that must necessarily come from tradition is the canon, the church's testimony to the New Testament itself and the Bible as a Christian scripture. Significantly, "the canon of the sacred books" is the one specific mentioned as coming from tradition in the *Dogmatic Constitution on Divine Revelation* at Vatican II. This document spoke of one source of revelation instead of the counter-reformation two sources. 2 Timothy 3:16 is rarely any longer used by Protestants to argue for the New Testament's testimony to itself. From what we now know about the formation of the New Testament canon, most interpreters agree that 2 Timothy 3:16 refers to what would eventually be called the Old Testament, and probably in its Septuagint version.

On the related and important disputed question of authority in the church, Catholic theologians remain committed to the teaching office (*magisterium*) of the church in its episcopal, conciliar, and papal forms. They hold that this teaching office originates in the apostolic tradition, along with the scriptures, and that it has the trust of interpreting the word of God for the sake of the church's unity in faith. This trust is to be exercised in service and not arbitrarily.

While most Protestant theologians do not view the church's teaching office as essential to its constitution, many support a reformed episcopal *magisterium* and/or Petrine ministry (papacy) as a pastoral necessity, with important historic precedent, for the sake of the church's unity. The Lutheran/Roman Catholic USA dialogue on "Authority and Infallibility in the Church" is the best source for finding such positions carefully articulated. This and other important ecumenical dialogues have highlighted the need to explore further tradition as a theological rather than a merely historical category, and to develop approaches for disengaging human tradition from apostolic tradition.

Questions for Review and Discussion

1. From what you've read, compose a general definition of biblical inspiration.

2. What does the term *inerrancy* mean when applied to the Bible? Distinguish "strict" from "limited" inerrancy. Use the example of the interpretation of Genesis 1–2 to show how strict and limited views of inerrancy differ.

3. Explain why limited inerrantists think they are justified in separating the Bible's trustworthiness or religious value from the accuracy of its apparent statements about what we in the twentieth century would call "science" and "history."

4. Explain why strict inerrantists do not think they can justify the separation or distinction in Question 3 above.

5. Distinguish a church- or tradition-centered theory of inspiration from an author-centered one. What are the advantages of regarding biblical inspiration as a gift to the church rather than simply to individual authors?

6. What was the great conflict between religion and science in the nineteenth century? How have modern sciences affected the degree to which one can accept the apparently "natural" meaning of Genesis 1–2?

7. What is the meaning of *tradition* as a theological term in Vatican II's *Dogmatic Constitution on Divine Revelation*? Explain the three "moments" of tradition and the role of bishops.

8. According to Vatican II's *Dogmatic Constitution on Divine Revelation*, what are the different levels of interpretation at which readers operate when they interpret the Bible as the church's inspired scripture?

9. How does the example of Jude illustrate the largely unrecognized role of the church's living tradition when Christians read the Bible as scripture?

10. How did Catholics and Protestants differ on scripture and tradition in the period after the reformation? How has the ecumenical movement changed those differences?

For Writing and Reflection

1. View the film *Inherit the Wind* (United Artists, 1960). It raises various questions about how to interpret the opening chapters of Genesis and other parts of the Bible. These questions are based on an apparent conflict between science and biblical religion. The film also draws this conflict in terms of the urban and the rural, the modern and the traditional. The film's various characters experience this conflict between modern science and traditional religion in different ways. Pick the character whose experience is most like yours and write an essay about how this conflict is illustrated in his or her approach to the Bible and to religion in general. Be specific and demonstrate your familiarity with the film.

2. From Old Testament scholars, we learn that an important part of the historical background or context for the creation stories in Genesis, especially Genesis 1, is the ancient Babylonian creation epic known as *Enuma Elish*. Go to the library and find Pritchard's *Ancient Near-Eastern Tests* (ANET). Read tablets IV–VI of *Enuma Elish* in ANET. Write an essay in which you compare and contrast the creation accounts in Genesis, especially chapter 1, and in *Enuma Elish*, tablets IV–VI. Make special note of their respective views on God, the world, and human beings. For the sake of your essay, assume that the final editors of Genesis came into contact with *Enuma Elish*, probably during the exile in Babylon, and composed Genesis 1 and edited Genesis 2–3 as a kind of answer or alternative to *Enuma Elish*. From comparing and contrasting the two texts, what can you conclude about the intended teaching or meaning of Genesis on the important questions of God, the world, and human beings?

For Further Reading

Dogmatic Constitution on Divine Revelation in Norman P. Tanner, S.J., ed., *Decrees of the Ecumenical Councils*, Vol. II, pp.

971–981. Chapter 2 deals with tradition and Chapter 3 with the inspiration and interpretation of Scripture.

Bruce Vawter, *Biblical Inspiration* (London: Hutchinson & Co., 1972).

Paul Achtemeier, *The Inspiration of Scripture, Problems and Proposals* (Philadelphia: Westminster Press, 1980). This work by a biblical scholar in the Reformed tradition is the source for most of what this chapter says about a "church-centered" theory of inspiration.

Karl Rahner, *Inspiration in the Bible* (New York: Herder & Herder, 1961). In this work Rahner puts forward his proposal that inspiration be understood as a gift to the church rather than to individual authors. It is part of God's activity in establishing the church.

Raymond F. Collins, "Inspiration," in Raymond E. Brown, S.S., Joseph A. Fitzmyer, S.J., and Roland E. Murphy, O.Carm., eds., *The New Jerome Biblical Commentary* (Englewood Cliffs, NJ: Prentice-Hall, 1990), pp. 1023–1033. This article presents an historical survey of Jewish and Christian thought on inspiration.

Glenn C. Stone and Charles LaFontaine, eds., *Exploring the Faith We Share: A Discussion Guide for Lutherans and Roman Catholics* (New York/Ramsey: Paulist Press, 1980). Published on the 450th anniversary of the Augsburg Confession (Lutheran), the editors intended this book to disseminate among ordinary Lutherans and Catholics the results of the first six rounds of the Lutheran-Roman Catholic dialogue in the United States. Chapter 6 deals with scripture. Pages 119–122 deal with revelation and tradition.

Mark D. Lowery, *Ecumenism, Striving for Unity Amid Diversity* (Mystic, Conn.: Twenty-third Publications, 1985). This is a popular introduction to ecumenism. Its annotated bibliography provides access to further works.

Terms To Identify

inspiration

inerrancy (strict and limited)

plenary verbal inerrancy

sola scriptura

Fundamentalist

Evangelical

Enuma Elish

tradition

magisterium

The Origin of Species

James Ussher

Charles Darwin

John T. Scopes

Karl Rahner

material sufficiency of scripture

Chapter VII

Defining Theology

THE PROBLEM OF DEFINITION

Having discussed both the depth-dimension of human experience and Christian revelation in some of their various aspects, we are now in a position to consider the definition of theology. In its literal sense, the word *theology* means talking about God. But this is not as simple as it sounds. We do not experience God directly, face to face as the Bible might put it, but through various worldly mediations of a personal, natural, historical, or cultural nature. "No one has ever seen God. Yet if we love one another, God remains in us, and his love is brought to perfection in us" (1 Jn 4:12). This means that when we talk about God, we are also talking about ourselves in our contexts in nature, history, and culture. Mention of history and culture draws attention to the fact that theology has a history like other disciplines. During the course of that history, people have understood theology in various ways.

The first Christian theologians were people like St. Paul. They reflected on the present meaning of what God had done in Christ. Paul, for example, was a missionary, or evangelist. He addressed his reflections to the questions and needs of the people of the Mediterranean cities of the Roman empire where he preached and founded Christian churches. Paul's reflections as we find them in his New Testament letters grew out of and fed back into the specifics of his life "in Christ." During the time of the early church fathers, theologians came most often from the ranks of bishops and pastors. Later, many theologians were monks. In a very general way, we can say that theology is a more or less disciplined form of reflection on Christian life. This reflection in turn influences Christian living and generates new questions.

During the period called the Middle Ages, from roughly 800 to 1500 A.D., European Christians, who had yet to divide into Catholic and Protestant camps, conceived and built up what we now know as universities. Here in the great medieval centers of learning like Bologna, Paris, and Oxford, theology became for the first time an academic discipline, or a "science," as the medieval scholars would have called it. Theology was no longer the pursuit of bishops and pastors, nor of monks and abbots, but of schoolmen or scholastics. They bore such titles as "master of the sacred page" or "doctor of sacred theology." These medieval doctors were the first to reflect on the nature of theology as a science or a discipline and to address the question of its definition.

This chapter is divided into two parts. The first examines two classical definitions taken from the medieval thinkers, Anselm of Canterbury (ca. 1033–1109) and Thomas Aquinas (ca. 1225–1274). The second part of the chapter considers three contemporary definitions, those of John Macquarrie, Bernard Lonergan (1904–1984), and Gustavo Gutierrez.

PART I

CLASSICAL UNDERSTANDINGS OF THEOLOGY

Anselm's Definition

FAITH SEEKING UNDERSTANDING: THEOLOGY AS PRAYERFUL-LITURGICAL

Perhaps the best-known definition of theology was never intended as a definition at all. It comes from the original title of one of St. Anselm's works, *Faith Seeking Understanding*. St. Anselm (ca. 1033–1109) was a monk and often wrote for the spiritual and intellectual benefit of his brothers in the monastic community. He was also involved in introducing Aristotle's logic into medieval thought, and is therefore a transitional figure in theology's move from the monastery to the university. *Faith Seeking Understanding*, or the *Proslogion*, as it eventually came to be called, is written in the form of a discourse that alternately addresses the reader and God. Anselm describes himself as having written "in the person of one who strives to lift his mind to the contemplation of God, and seeks to understand what he believes."

This idea of a prayerful attempt to understand what one believes is central to the classical understanding of theology. It is an intellectual activity. But it is an intellectual activity that takes faith for granted. Lest what Anselm presupposes be confused with a modern, rationalistic notion of faith as a list of beliefs, we should note that Anselm prefaces his argument with a long and passionate address to God, for which we find the model in St. Augustine's *Confessions*. The accompanying excerpt from Chapter I of *Faith Seeking Understanding* illustrates the extent to which Anselm's believing is an internal part of his thinking. His question is obviously deeply felt, but he doesn't try to construct an argument that will exert some kind of external coercion on his mind. Its purpose is rather to understand the God in whom he already believes and trusts.

> Permit me, at least from afar or from the deep, to look upwards toward Your light. Teach me to seek You, and reveal Yourself to me as I seek; for unless You instruct me I cannot seek You, and unless You reveal Yourself I cannot find You. Let me seek You in desiring You; let me desire You in seeking You. Let me find You in loving You; let me love You in finding You. O Lord, I acknowledge and give thanks that You created in me Your image so that I may remember, contemplate, and love You. But this image has been so effaced by the abrasion of transgressions, so hidden from sight by the dark billows of sin, that unless You renew and refashion it, it cannot do what it was created to do. Lord, I do not attempt to comprehend Your sublimity, because my intellect is not at all equal to such a task. But I yearn to understand some measure of Your truth, which my heart believes and loves. For I do not seek to understand in order to believe but

I believe in order to understand. For I believe even this: that
I shall not understand unless I believe (from St. Anselm's
Proslogion, Chapter I, translation by Jasper Hopkins and
Herbert Richardson, 93).

Thomas Aquinas' Definition

SACRED DOCTRINE OR THE SCIENCE OF FAITH:
THEOLOGY AS SCIENTIFIC

Nearly two centuries and the rise of the universities separate
Anselm from Thomas Aquinas. Thomas taught theology at the
University of Paris. His great work, begun eight years before his
death in 1274, is entitled the *Summa Theologica*, or summary of
theology. As the Prologue to the First Part explains, he intended
it for the "instruction of beginners." It is based on Thomas'
courses at the University of Paris and is divided accordingly into
questions that reflect the give-and-take of scholastic argument.
Question 1, for example, is devoted to the nature and extent of
sacred doctrine and subdivided into ten articles. Each article begins with a question followed by two or three objections to the
position that Thomas will eventually take. A brief statement of
Thomas' own position on the question is introduced with the
words "On the contrary . . . ." Then Thomas argues for his position in a longer answer beginning with the words "I answer
that . . . ." He follows this argument with a reply to each of the
original objections.

SACRED DOCTRINE AS SCIENCE

In the first article of Question 1, Thomas points out that, in
Book VI of his *Metaphysics*, Aristotle had treated "theology" as a
part of philosophy. Thomas, therefore, needed another term for
what in this book we are calling *theology*. The term he chose was
sacred doctrine. Sacred doctrine is different from Aristotle's theology, called "natural theology" by later scholastics, because it studies God's own wisdom or teaching (doctrine), which comes to us
through divine revelation. That is why it is called *sacred* doctrine.
The term is precise and not just a pious phrase. Thomas regards

sacred doctrine as a "science." It is the science of faith because, as he explains in article 2, it is "established on principles revealed by God."

We usually reserve the term *science* for disciplines such as chemistry, physics, or biology, which we regard as empirical, or based on facts. According to the second objection in article 2, sacred doctrine can't be a science because it deals with individual facts "such as the deeds of Abraham, Isaac, and Jacob." This exclusion of the factual from science indicates that people in the thirteenth century understood the term *science* quite differently than we do. Their understanding was based on Aristotle's, as explained, for example, in his work called the *Posterior Analytics*. Thomas regards sacred doctrine as a science in the sense that it is "knowledge through causes." There are reasons for what we believe. Even though these reasons are ultimately God's wisdom and not ours, we have a share in them through faith, and, therefore, theologians, or "masters of the sacred page," can talk about them.

THOMAS' MODEST CONFIDENCE

Thomas speaks with striking confidence of revelation as the basis for sacred doctrine. He believes that revelation comes from God. But he doesn't have the same confidence in arguments and conclusions that come from theologians. God's truth can only be received by us in a human way, and this lends a certain built-in modesty to all of Thomas' theology. While he is confident that, on the basis of revelation, Christian theology really does speak about God, he realizes that what it says is quite limited and far from exhaustive. In his reply to the first objection in article 7, he puts it this way:

> Although we cannot know in what consists the essence of God, nevertheless in this science we make use of His effects, either of nature or of grace, in place of a definition, in regard to whatever is treated of in this science concerning God; even as in some philosophical sciences we demonstrate something about a cause from its effect, by taking the effect in place of a definition of the cause (*Summa Theologica*, Pt. 1, Q. 1, art. 7, translated by the English Dominicans, Vol. I, 5).

SUMMARY

For Thomas, we can conclude, sacred doctrine, or sacred theology, is the science of faith. In our own context, it would make more sense to call theology an academic discipline—or even a fine art—rather than a science. In any case, it is clear that with Thomas and his medieval colleagues theology becomes an activity that is done in schools. And so it remains. Protestant reformers tried to make theology more scriptural and less dependent on Aristotle. Luther especially tried to make it more obviously personal, but the basic medieval model remained. "I would not exchange my doctor's degree for all the world's gold," the mature Luther declared (cited in Eric W. Gritsch, *Martin—God's Court Jester, Luther in Retrospect* [1983], 2).

Because St. Thomas Aquinas has been such an influential figure in Catholic thought, his understanding of theology has been emphasized. From St. Thomas we can learn many things: his rooting of theology in faith, his openness to inquiry in the question format, his confidence in public discussion, and his simultaneous modesty about his conclusions. We know that Thomas was a deeply religious person who devoted his life to the great movement of Christian renewal begun by St. Francis of Assisi and St. Dominic in the thirteenth century. From his writings this is not always clear. In the *Summa*, for example, Thomas writes rather with the abstract coolness of a scientist. The academic setting, moreover, readily lends itself to a preference for impersonal knowledge over personal knowledge, proof over argument, the abstract and quantitative over the concrete and individual. Following the model of science, theology tended to become more abstract and less connected to Christian living.

In the modern period, with its love for the universal and the geometric, this trend to the abstract became even more pronounced. After the middle ages, as many observers have pointed out, few theologians have been canonized or recognized by the church as saints. In both Catholic and Protestant Christianity, we find waves of popular devotionalism and pietism providing needed correctives to the dryness of modern theology. Contemporary theology's greatest challenge is to reunite head with heart and restore theology to its original foundation in Christian living.

ST. THOMAS, SUMMA THEOLOGICA, PART I

Question 1
Second Article
Whether Sacred Doctrine is a Science?
We proceed thus to the Second Article:—
Objection 1. It seems that sacred doctrine is not a science. For every science proceeds from self-evident principles. But sacred doctrine proceeds from articles of faith which are not self-evident, since their truth is not admitted by all: For all men have not faith (2 Thess. iii. 2). Therefore sacred doctrine is not a science.

Objection 2. Further, no science deals with individual facts. But this sacred science treats of individual facts, such as the deeds of Abraham, Isaac, and Jacob, and such like. Therefore sacred doctrine is not a science.

On the contrary, Augustine says (De Trin. xiv. 1), to this science alone belongs that whereby saving faith is begotten, nourished, protected, and strengthened. But this can be said of no science except sacred doctrine. Therefore sacred doctrine is a science.

I answer that, sacred doctrine is a science. We must bear in mind that there are two kinds of sciences. There are some which proceed from a principle known by the natural light of the intelligence, such as arithmetic and geometry and the like. There are some which proceed from principles known by the light of a higher science: thus the science of perspective proceeds from principles established by geometry, and music from principles established by arithmetic. So it is that sacred doctrine is a science, because it proceeds from principles established by the light of a higher science, namely, the science of God and the blessed. Hence, just as the musician accepts on authority the principles taught him by the mathematician, so sacred science is established on principles revealed by God.

Reply Objection 1. The principles of any science are either in themselves self-evident, or reducible to the conclusions of a higher science; and such, as we have said, are the principles of sacred doctrine.

> *Reply Objection 2.* Individual facts are treated of in sacred doctrine, not because it is concerned with them principally; but they are introduced rather both as examples to be followed in our lives (as in moral sciences), and in order to establish the authority of those men through whom the divine revelation, on which this sacred scripture or doctrine is based, has come down to us.
>
> *(Translated by the English Dominicans, Vol. I, 2.)*

PART II

SOME CONTEMPORARY UNDERSTANDINGS OF THEOLOGY

Macquarrie's Definition

THEOLOGY AS THE CLEAR EXPRESSION OF THE FAITH

At the Council of Trent in the mid-sixteenth century, the Catholic Church established its present seminary system. With this, theology moved out of the universities and into seminaries or "divinity" schools. Modern theology was often known as "divinity." Where Thomas had moved from God to creation and the return of creation to God, modern theology followed the tendency to academic specialization. Most seminaries or divinity schools divided the field of theology into four main areas of specialization.

1. *Sacred scripture*, or *Bible*, is devoted to the exposition of the meaning of the scriptures studied in their original languages of Hebrew and Greek.

2. *Dogmatic*, or *systematic, theology* presents in systematic form the various Christian beliefs such as those we find in the creed. Systematic theology treats basic Christian doctrines such as God, Christ, and the church.

3. *Moral theology*, or *Christian ethics*, studies the basic principles of Christian living and their application to various

areas of life, e.g. business, medicine, married life, and political life.

4. *Church history*, although it is not, strictly speaking, a theological discipline, is also usually found in the seminary or divinity curriculum.

In his widely used work *The Principles of Christian Theology* (1966), Anglican systematic theologian John Macquarrie presents a contemporary formulation of the classical understanding of theology. While Anselm and Aquinas would probably recognize themselves in it, Macquarrie's definition also shows some signs of having been influenced by the modern developments described above.

> Christian theology seeks to think the Church's faith as a coherent whole. It aims not only at showing the internal coherence of the Christian faith, that is to say, how the several doctrines constitute a unity, but also at exhibiting the coherence of this faith with the many other beliefs and attitudes to which we are committed in the modern world. Only if these tasks are accomplished can the faith be held intelligently and be integrated with the whole range of human life (v).

After this description, Macquarrie goes on to define theology as "the study which, through participation in and reflection upon a religious faith, seeks to express the content of this faith, in the clearest and most coherent language available."

Lonergan's Definition

MEDIATION BETWEEN A RELIGION AND A CULTURE:
THEOLOGY AS CONTEXT-BASED

Just as in the previous chapter, modern understandings of the Bible and its divine inspiration were criticized as too author-centered and individualistic, so we might ask if the three definitions we have considered so far might not be too theologian-centered or individualistic. Each definition of theology is framed in terms of faith and reason and each presumes that reason ought to proceed in a disciplined and coherent way. Macquarrie does mention the faith of the church, but apart from this, one could study these three definitions carefully without ever adverting to the fact that the theologian works within a community of discourse or a history. We could come away from our definitions with the quite modern idea of the theologian as solitary inquirer, apart from any community or conversation, seeking to understand his or her own isolated faith.

THE EXAMPLE OF HUMAN LANGUAGE

A good illustration of the point being made here can be found in the phenomenon of human language. Like our culture and our history, our language is there before we as individuals ever arrive on the scene. At the peril of being denied participation in the human community of subjects so essential to our being and becoming, we must simply learn to speak English or Arabic or whatever, or else find some suitable substitute for speaking. In a very real sense, our language becomes the vehicle for our thought and experience. We speak the language. When we do, the words and ideas are taken for our own, but in some real sense they belong as well to the language. Our language sets the boundaries for what is thinkable and what is do-able. Attempts to transcend these boundaries must be framed in terms of the language. More radical exponents of this view might say that the language speaks us. Or more simply, language speaks. Each of us speaks English with his or her own recognizable accent and style, but the language remains English, and this both enables and limits our communication. So it is with the history or tradition out of which theologians speak.

HISTORICAL SENSE AND HISTORICAL CONSCIOUSNESS

Nineteenth century thought, with its general tendency to emphasize history, provided a needed corrective to the enlightenment's emphasis on the solitary individual inquirer. The nineteenth century also saw the rise of a more historical approach to theology. In Catholic thought, the person with whom this approach is most often associated is John Henry Cardinal Newman (1801–1890). His *An Essay on the Development of Christian Doctrine*, first published in 1845, has been especially influential.

In speaking of a developmental view of Christianity and its doctrine and theology, one can distinguish the dawning realization that theology has a history from the further realization that we are a living part of it. We can call the first realization historical sense and the second realization historical consciousness. To have historical sense is to understand that the words of Anselm and Aquinas, for example, must be interpreted in their historical contexts. If we want to understand them, we cannot lift them out of their settings in history and treat them as if they were written by the person next door.

Historical consciousness is more complex. One could try to understand Anselm and Aquinas in their proper settings as if one were a completely neutral observer with no context of one's own. But this would ignore our own historical context and its influence on our interpretation of Anselm and Aquinas. When we begin to understand why we might or might not be inclined to bother with Anselm and Aquinas in the first place, and why some of their ideas make sense to us and others are much more difficult to appreciate, the strange thoughts of Anselm and Aquinas might even begin to challenge our ordinary ways of looking at things. Without historical consciousness, the awareness that we too are a living part of history, we might be naively inclined to mistake our own way of looking at things for some sort of fixed norm by which we judge Anselm and Aquinas as stupid, or worse, boring.

Interpreting any tradition, participating in it, and carrying its conversation forward, involves some sort of fusion or critical and mutually correcting interaction between the context of the past and the context of the present. This involves nothing more mysterious than what happens when we communicate successfully with one another. Historical distance and our awareness of that distance simply make communication more difficult, and we have to work harder to understand. This realization has led some theologians to reconceive theology in a less individualistic and more historically oriented way. Instead of faith and reason, they speak of religion and culture. The Canadian theologian Bernard Lonergan (1904–1984) will serve as an example.

Just as Anselm and Aquinas would have distinguished theology from the faith upon which it reflects, so Lonergan distinguishes theology from religion. Instead of defining theology in terms of faith and reason, however, he defines it in terms of religion and culture.

> [T]heology is not the same thing as religion. Theology is reflection on religion. It mediates between a religion and a culture. Its function is to bring to light the significance and value of a religion in any given culture. It follows that, even though the religion remains unchanged, still a theology will vary with cultural variations . . . While theology used to be defined as the science about God, today I believe it is to be defined as reflection on the significance and value of a religion in a culture. From this view of theology it follows that theology is not some one system valid for all times and places, as the Aristotelian and Thomist notion of system assumes, but as manifold as are the many cultures within which a religion has significance and value (*Philosophy of God and Theology*, 22, 33).

TWO PERSPECTIVES

In Lonergan's hands, theology has gone from being faith seeking understanding or the science of faith to being a mediation or a bridge between a religion and a culture. The change is one of perspective. The classical perspective is that of a given theologian at a given time and place without explicit reference to the fact that he or she is part of a history that happens to be one among a variety of actual and possible histories. Working out of this perspective, one might tend to take the common sense of one's own place and time for what is "normal." It was just such an erroneous assumption that led many Christians to think that Copernicus and Galileo were incompatible with the book of Joshua. Missionaries working out of such a perspective might tend to confuse Christianity with their culture and practice cultural imperialism in the name of evangelization.

The historically oriented perspective, or historical-mindedness as Lonergan calls it, has one great advantage going for it. Unless something like it is true, it is impossible to explain the undeniable fact of what Newman called "development." Theology has a history. Doctrines have a history. We have already seen the example of the New Testament canon. Newman cites many others, including the Trinity, the episcopacy, and the papacy. Missionaries with historical-mindedness would know that

TWO PERSPECTIVES ON THE INQUIRER LEAD TO	
TWO DIFFERENT APPROACHES TO THEOLOGY	
CLASSICAL/MODERN (Anselm, Aquinas, early moderns)	**POST-MODERN/ HISTORICALLY MINDED/ MULTI-CULTURAL** (Lonergan, Gutierrez)
1. begin from the abstract individual	1. begin from the concrete, embodied individual; language, history, sexuality, culture are part of person; built-in
2. strength-advantage: emphasis on what human beings have in common	
	2. strength-advantage: emphasis on what makes human beings different: history, culture, language, embodiment
HUMAN NATURE	
3. world and nature as given; we look at it; subject *vs.* object	
	3. human as part of nature; transforms it, makes history
4. theory (theology, for example), once you have it, tends to remain the same	
	4. theories vary with cultures
5. cultural "common sense" tends to be taken as *normal*	
	5. emphasis on many cultures; a pluralism
6. religion as doctrines to which individuals privately assent; doctrines are eternally valid statements; theology presents them in organized (systematic) form	6. emphasis on religion as an embodied or incarnate way of living in history; religious doctrines develop in history; theology as mediation between religion and cul-

7. weakness-disadvantage: oversimplification of human life in terms of OBJECTIVISM; focus on products of human thinking; numbers and statements have a certain magic quality as objective	ture has a history; there are many theologies within Christianity
	7. weakness-disadvantage: confusion about human life in the form of SUBJECTIVISM; skepticism and absolute historical relativism

prospective Christians in North Borneo ought to be instructed with materials in their own language and prepared by people familiar with their history and culture. Catechetical materials prepared in France or the United States would probably not work very well.

THE FAITH UNCHANGED

Lonergan claims that, while theologies might reasonably be expected to vary with cultural variations, the religion or faith itself "remains unchanged." Even though there have been many theologies in the history of Christianity, we can still say that it is the one Christian faith that they express. At this point, we might ask how this is so, if our only access to the one Christian faith is through its changing cultural forms such as theology, liturgy, and the like. We cannot just say that Christianity is whatever it happens to become, because then the term *Christianity* would be meaningless. There must be some internal dynamic that guides development. This was the question Newman faced. He used analogies from personal-psychological and organic growth and devised tests to help correlate the past and the present and to distinguish true developments from corruptions or false developments.

Within Christianity it is true that the Bible, the creeds, the liturgy, and the authoritative teaching of ecumenical councils remain unchanged. They are there in the black and white of the books that contain them. But in their very unchanging they remain dead letters, black marks on a printed page, until they are read or heard in faith and become real and living in particular human beings in particular times and places. This brings us back to history again. In the case of Christianity, it seems impossible, therefore, to speak of the religion remaining the same without some references to the living Christ and his quickening Spirit. These two are the true sources of living continuity in Christian experience and Christian doctrine. In an incarnational perspective, the living Christ and the Spirit must always be mediated in some visible form. The visible is never perfect and can always be improved.

PERSONAL FAITH AND THEOLOGY

Lonergan speaks of theology in very general terms and seems to do so on purpose. He knows that we live in a world with many different religions and cultures. Therefore he defines theology in such a way that his definition can have the widest possible application. In addition to Christian theology, we can have, on Lonergan's terms, Islamic theology, Mormon theology, Hindu theology, etc., as long as the one we call a theologian is engaged in mediating the living riches of a religious heritage to a present cultural situation.

Personal faith, or participation in the religious community, doesn't seem to have the same centrality in Lonergan as it does in the previous definitions. Though it might be difficult to imagine why one would want to, it is conceivable on Lonergan's terms that one could be a theologian of a religion in which one did not participate. In this way, for example, I could study Buddhism sympathetically and perhaps even contribute to the development of its theology.

While this is certainly undeniable, it is also true that theologians who actively participate in the faith they study might have a certain advantage in explaining it. Though not completely private and incommunicable, religious faith does involve a person more intimately than the study of, for example, geology. For this reason, theology should have room for the appeal of the evocative and persuasive, the witness of the personal voice. Theologians who are believers ought not to be restricted, for the sake of academic credibility, to speaking as if they were not. Nor, as we shall see below, is it fair to assume that those who share a religious faith are more biased in their study of it than those who do not.

Gutierrez' Definition

CRITICAL REFLECTION ON CHRISTIAN PRAXIS:
THEOLOGY AS PRAXIS-ORIENTED

We have already noted that theology in the modern period tended to become overly academic and separated from Christian living. One of the richest examples of contemporary theology that is close to Christian living comes from Latin America and parts of Asia and Africa. It also illustrates Lonergan's understanding of theology as reflection on the significance of a religion in a culture. This new and sometimes controversial form of theology is called "liberation theology."

Liberation theology begins with the suffering experienced by the extremely poor and illiterate in countries such as Brazil, Peru, El Salvador, and Nicaragua. Theologians of liberation seek both to analyze the political and economic causes of needless suffering, and to reflect, in the light of the scriptures and tradition, in a way that leads to loving action that will help alleviate suffering. They reflect in turn upon such action in a process leading continuously to new action and new reflection. In his 1973 book *A Theology of Liberation*, Peruvian theologian Gustavo Gutierrez defines theology as "critical reflection on praxis" (p. 6) "worked out in light of the Word" (p. 11).

The relationship between theory and its practical application, or practice, is usually conceived in such a way that scholars produce a body of ideas or a theory and someone else applies it. Thus theoretical physics is applied by aeronautical engineers to the practice of building airplanes. In contrast to *practice* as applied theory, the term *praxis* is meant to emphasize the mutual interplay between action and reflection. Action and reflection, theory and practice, feed into one another in a systematic way, so that *praxis* can never be the mere application of some abstract theory. This notion of praxis, or lived theory, has a lot in common with the biblical notion, found in St. John's gospel, for example, that truth is something we do.

We might expect liberation theologians to call what they do critical reflection on Christian experience. But *praxis* has further connotations that make it preferable to *experience*. Liberation theology doesn't simply take experience for granted and think about it. Rather it insists on the need to transform experience. Since the everyday experience of the people in Latin America is often one of intense suffering, the term *praxis* is meant to imply that the causes of such a distorted and dehumanized form of experience need to be changed. The word *praxis* refers to the effort to live out such Christian love. Liberation theologians find biblical support for their views in the story of the exodus or God's deliverance of Israel from slavery in Egypt, in the insistence of the Old Testament prophets on justice for the poor, the orphan, and the widow, and in Jesus' own suffering and death. Peruvian artist Edilberto Merida's sculpture of the Crucified One, which appears on the cover of Gutierrez' book, gives moving expression to this identification with the sufferings of Christ.

We can learn some important truths about theology from the theology of liberation.

1. The need for theology to be in close touch with Christian experience, or better, Christian praxis. Liberation theology is inseparable from the small communities of Christians struggling for justice in Latin America. Liberation theologians continue to teach and write books, but what they teach and what they write arise from their reflections on the struggle of the suffering people with whom they are in solidarity.

2. The need for theology to take up a critical posture toward culture and to speak on behalf of those who suffer. Liberation theology provides the means to nuance Lonergan's understanding of theology as reflection on the significance of a religion in a culture. Against modern individualism, we have emphasized the importance of language, history, and culture in the very coming to be of individuals. But liberation theology draws attention to the fact that culture and tradition might shape experience in distorted and inhuman ways. When it does, it needs to be criticized in light of the view of the human person we find in Christian revelation.

Reflecting on the meaning of a religious faith in a given culture is not simply or even primarily a matter of adapting Christianity to that culture. There is also a critical or prophetic moment, a call to repentance, in which Christians challenge distorted cultural values in the name of the apostolic faith. Christians around the world who experience suffering from the distorting influences of tradition have found a model in liberation theology. Thus in the United States black theology and feminist theology have reflected similarly on the struggle for justice by black people and women.

In his writings and addresses, Pope John Paul II has often used the term *inculturation* to refer to the process of bringing Christian faith and culture into a living relationship. Inculturation involves both translating the Christian message into forms that will be intelligible in the culture and transforming the culture in the light of the Christian vision. As reflection on Christian praxis in a given culture, theology is an important part of the inculturation process.

SUMMARY

In the early Christian generations, the link between Christian living and theological reflection was usually clear. In Anselm and Aquinas, we see that this reflection can take place in an academic setting and in a disciplined or systematic way in dialogue with contemporary forms of knowledge. But the academic environment has not always served theology well. In the modern period, theology becomes overly theoretical, and the connection with Christian living is less clear. By reminding us that we have no reason to expect theology to be the same everywhere, Lonergan brings us back to concrete history. We can expect theological reflection to occur in terms of a particular culture. Different cultures will most likely have different theologies. Liberation theology emphasizes that theology ought not to reflect culture uncritically. Rather it should adopt a prophetic or transformative posture toward those aspects of culture that cause people needless suffering. In short, theology is prayerful-liturgical, scientific, context-based, and *praxis*-oriented.

The understanding of theology from which we will work in this book borrows something from each of these perspectives. While we do not wish to fall into the abstract excesses of modern theology, we can retain the medieval idea that theological reflection can be done with profit in an academic setting. As did Anselm and Aquinas, we presuppose faith in God's revelation in Christ as we find it in scripture and tradition. From Lonergan and the liberation theologians, however, we learn that our understanding of scripture and tradition is hard to separate from our present experience as Christians. Once we realize this, we are no longer faced with a choice between a starting point in revelation or a starting point in contemporary experience. Our task is rather to sort out this relationship between religion and culture. Such reflection is geared not only to the exposition of the traditional faith in culturally meaningful terms but also to the transformation of culture in the light of Christ's message.

APPENDIX

THE DIFFERENCE BETWEEN THEOLOGY AND RELIGIOUS STUDIES

The discipline of religious studies has arisen relatively recently in the United States. State-supported universities, for example, if they study religion at all, usually have departments of religious studies or religion rather than departments of theology. The umbrella professional organization for scholars of religion in the United States is called the American Academy of Religion. The emergence of the discipline of religious studies represents an attempt to deal with the abiding human phenomenon of religion in an increasingly secular environment.

In contrast to theology, the disciplines of religion and religious studies take up a more professedly neutral or non-evaluative posture toward religious phenomena. They take various approaches to religion, ranging from the psychological and sociological to the literary. By far the most common approach is historical. Many scholars of religion or of the Bible and Christian origins, for example, consider themselves non-engaged historians of religion. In addition to this difference in posture, the disciplines of religious studies and theology also differ in scope, procedure, and intended audience.

Scope

The discipline of religious studies has a much broader field than that of theology. A good religion or religious studies department will include a variety of scholars whose primary fields of competence extend beyond western Christianity to the religions of the near east (Judaism, Islam, etc.), the religions of the far east (Hinduism, Buddhism, Taoism, Confucianism, etc.) as well as basic religions such as those of native Americans or Africans. Departments of theology, by contrast, are usually limited to specialists in the various areas of the particular religion they study.

Procedure

In terms of description and evaluation, we can say in general that religious studies is more descriptive than evaluative, and that theology, because of its religious commitments, tends to have a heavier dose of evaluation along with its descriptions. But this easy distinction between description and evaluation, between fact and interpretation, is sometimes difficult to maintain. Scholars of religion debate the question of how evaluative they ought to be toward their subject. Some think that they can go further than simply describing religion, either historically or in terms of types and categories. By exhaustively explaining religious claims in other than religious categories, those of history, psychology, or sociology, for example, they think they can sometimes prove religious claims false. Others, like William James and Mircea Eliade, are committed to letting religious phenomena speak for themselves as much as possible. While it is difficult to imagine that scholars of religion are not in some way personally involved in what they study, the engagement of theologians tends to be more obvious and explicit. Whether one chooses religious studies or theology often depends on a personal decision about how much distance one wishes to keep between oneself and the faith being studied.

Intended Audience

Religious studies is addressed to a primarily academic audience, and to those individuals among the general public for whom the art or history of Buddhism, for example, might be of personal interest. Theology is usually done within and addressed to a particular religious faith community such as Judaism, Christianity, or Islam, or one of their confessional subgroups. Examples of such subgroups in U.S. Christianity would include Lutherans, Methodists, and Roman Catholics, among others. Each has a distinctive and recognizable theological tradition within the broader Christian stream.

THE QUESTION OF BIAS

One ought not to conclude from this contrast, however, that theologians are biased and students of religious studies are not. This would be philosophically naive. Everyone comes to the inquiry about religion with pre-conceived ideas about what is to be studied. Philosophers have called these pre-conceived ideas pre-judgments (prejudices in a neutral sense) and pre-understandings. This is no less true of those who profess to describe someone else's religion than it is of those who profess to be reflecting on their own. We usually discover our pre-conceived ideas in dialogue with others or in dialogue with the material under study. They can be called biases only when people are completely unaware of them or refuse to admit their influence on the direction of the inquiry.

Two factors determine whether we ought to grant academic legitimacy to the study of religion either by theologians or by students of religious studies. We can put them in question form:

First, how comprehensive and faithful has this study been in its approach to historical and other forms of evidence? Has the evidence been allowed, for example, to correct pre-conceived ideas when necessary?

Second, how honest and critically aware has this study been about its own pre-conceived ideas? When, as it usually does, evidence admits of more than one interpretation, has this study admitted the legitimate influence of pre-understandings and pre-judgments on its conclusions?

Questions for Review and Discussion

1. How did theological questions arise for St. Paul?

2. Compare and contrast the definitions of Anselm and Aquinas. Think of at least two adjectives to describe the tone of each definition. How do the differences in these definitions reflect, or show the influence of, the different contexts or locations in which Anselm and Aquinas did theology?

3. Compare and contrast the definitions of Lonergan and Gutierrez. Think of at least two adjectives to describe the tone of each definition. How do the differences in these definitions reflect, or show the influence of, the different contexts or locations in which Lonergan and Gutierrez did and do theology?

4. How does "science" in the medieval or Aristotelian sense differ from our understanding of "science"? Does our understanding represent an advance over that of Aristotle and Aquinas?

5. What is the significance of the shift from defining theology in terms of faith and reason to defining it in terms of religion and culture?

6. What are the four main areas of specialization in modern theology? How do they reflect the culture in which they arose?

7. What is the difference between "historical sense" and "historical consciousness"? How does the example of human language illustrate historical consciousness?

8. What are the two sides or aspects of inculturation? Which of these aspects is closest to the emphasis of Lonergan's definition? Which is closest to the emphasis of Gutierrez' definition? Explain.

9. What does the term *praxis* mean? Why do liberation theologians prefer it to both *practice* and *experience*?

10. What is the difference between the disciplines of theology and religious studies? How does their co-existence in the

United States reflect our cultural and political context? Discuss the question of "bias" in the study of theology and religious studies and in academic inquiry generally. Briefly, what is the difference between "bias" in a negative and pejorative sense and the philosophical idea of pre-understanding or pre-judgment?

For Writing and Reflection

1. From the definitions in this chapter, and from your own reflections, write an essay in which you develop your own definition of theology. Include your reflections on how the definition you propose reflects or is influenced by your own historical context or social location.

2. In *Summa Theologica*, Part I, Question 1, article 2, St. Thomas uses two analogies to illuminate the relationship between theology and the principles from which theology proceeds. Identify and state the two analogies. What, according to Aquinas in this text, are the principles from which theology proceeds? Write an essay in which you develop the implications of these two analogies. If the analogies work, what do they say about the relationship of theology to the principles from which it proceeds?

For Further Reading

St. Anselm of Canterbury, *Proslogion*, Chapter I in *Anselm of Canterbury*, edited and translated by Jasper Hopkins and Herbert Richardson (Toronto and New York: The Edwin Mellen Press, 1974).

St. Thomas Aquinas, *Summa Theologica*, 3 Vols., translated by the English Dominicans (New York: Benziger Brothers, 1947).

Hans Urs von Balthasar, "Theology and Sanctity," in *Word and Redemption, Essays in Theology 2*, trans. by A.V. Littledale in cooperation with Alexander Dru (Montreal: Palm Publishers, 1965), 49–86. A programmatic essay on the modern split between theology and spirituality and von Balthasar's vision of a spiritual theology.

John Macquarrie, *Principles of Christian Theology* (second edition; New York: Charles Scribner's Sons, 1977).

John Henry Cardinal Newman, *An Essay on the Development of Christian Doctrine*, sixth edition, foreword by Ian Ker (Notre Dame, Ind.: University of Notre Dame Press, 1989).

Bernard Lonergan, *Philosophy of God and Theology* (Philadelphia: Westminster Press, 1973). Lonergan's *Insight* (1957) and *Method in Theology* (1972) provide the basis for his understanding of theology.

Gustavo Gutierrez, *A Theology of Liberation*, translated and edited by Sister Caridad Inda and John Eagleson (Maryknoll, NY: Orbis Books, 1973; first published in 1971). Simultaneously with Gutierrez in Peru, African-American theologian James Cone in the United States was developing a liberationist perspective on the black experience. His many subsequent works are representative of the continuing project of African-American theology in the United States. In 1990 Orbis Books published a twentieth-anniversary edition of Cone's *A Black Theology of Liberation*. The theology of Rosemary Ruether develops the liberationist perspective in a feminist context. Along with a Ruether bibliography complete to 1987, Mary Hembrow Snyder's *The Christology of Rosemary Radford Ruether, A Critical Introduction* (Mystic, Conn.: Twenty-Third Publications, 1988) provides access to Ruether's original and sustained project of feminist theology in the United States.

Gregory Baum, *Compassion and Solidarity* (New York/Mahwah: Paulist Press, 1990), reflects from a liberationist perspective on the experiences of middle class Christians in North America.

Peter Schineller, S.J., *A Handbook on Inculturation* (New York/Mahwah: Paulist Press, 1990).

Monika Hellwig, "Theology as a Fine Art," in Jane Kopas, ed., *Interpreting Tradition, The Art of Theological Reflection*, The Annual Publication of the College Theology Society, Vol. 29 (Chico, Cal.: Scholars Press, 1984), 3–10.

Avery Dulles, *The Craft of Theology, From Symbol to System* (New York: Crossroad, 1992). This is an important statement on theology from one of the most distinguished theologians in this country.

American Academy of Religion, "Liberal Learning and the Religion Major: A Report to the Profession" (Atlanta, Ga.: Scholars Press, 1990). This twenty-page report was completed by an AAR task force in conjunction with the Association of American Colleges national review of arts and sciences majors and is available as part of a larger study from the AAC. It is a current statement of how scholars and teachers of religion understand their disciplines.

Terms To Identify

Christian theology

sacred doctrine

science (Aristotle and Aquinas)

Proslogion

Faith Seeking Understanding

Summa Theologica

systematic theology

moral theology

praxis

liberation theology

American Academy of Religion

An Essay on the Development of Christian Doctrine

St. Anselm of Canterbury

St. Thomas Aquinas

John Macquarrie

John Henry Newman

Bernard Lonergan

Gustavo Gutierrez

historical sense

historical consciousness

inculturation

religious studies

PART TWO
INCARNATION

He is the image [*ikon*] of the invisible god . . .

(Col 1:15).

I should myself call the Incarnation the central aspect of Christianity . . .
John Henry Newman, *An Essay on the Development*
of Christian Doctrine (1878 edition)

What did the face of Christ look like? This point the Bible passes over in silence. You know well that the early Christians thought of Christ as a shepherd. The short mantle, the small tunic; one hand is holding the foot of the lamb while the other clasps a staff. This figure is familiar in our countries, for we see it reflected in many of the people whom we know. That was how the earliest Christians imagined the gentle face of Christ. And then in the eastern Church one finds the long nose, the curly hair, the black beard. All this was creating an oriental Christ. As for the medieval artists, many of them painted a face of Christ resplendent with the authority of a king. Yet tonight for me the face is that of the picture preserved in Borgo San Sepulchro. There still remains fresh in my memory the time when I saw this picture as a seminarian for the first time. Christ has one foot on the sepulchre and in his right hand he holds a crucifix. He is facing straight out and his face bears the expression of encouragement it had when he commanded his disciples three times, 'Feed my lambs, feed my lambs, feed my lambs . . .' It is a face filled with vigor and strength. I feel great love for

173

that face. I am always fascinated by the face of Christ just like a man fascinated by the face of his beloved.

Shusaku Endo, Silence (1966)

Suppose the Son of man had been dressed as the Son of God, recognizable, immediately identifiable, bearing on his person the insignia and the decorations—truly, he would have been misunderstood, for he would have betrayed himself, he would have been marked out too soon, on the basis of appearances: it was necessary that all should be able to hear the sound of a human voice, to see his works, so as to choose in their own hearts. When he wasn't escaping into the hills, he used to get lost in the crowds. Only once had he put it on, his garment of glory; he'd saved it for his three best friends. After the resurrection, Mary had taken him for the gardener; the apostles along the lake thought he was a fisherman. Perhaps it was certitude that tore him apart.

Jean Sulivan, The Sea Remains (1969)

Chapter VIII

Classical Christology:
The Doctrines of the
Incarnation and the Trinity

OVERVIEW OF THE CHAPTER

Each Sunday, as part of their public worship (liturgy), many Christian churches profess their faith by saying together what is popularly known as the Nicaean Creed. The name comes from the church council which met at Nicaea in modern Turkey in A.D. 325. This council composed the creed upon which the one now in use is based. The Nicaean Creed has a threefold, or trinitarian, structure:

> We believe in one God, the Father, the Almighty . . .
> in one Lord, Jesus Christ . . .
> and in the Holy Spirit . . .

The section of the creed devoted to the Son continues in part:

> the only Son of God, eternally begotten of the Father,
> God from God, Light from Light, true God from true God,
> begotten, not made, one in being with the Father.
> Through him all things were made.
>
> For us men and for our salvation he came down from heaven:
> by the power of the Holy Spirit he was born of the Virgin
> Mary, and became man.

The task of this chapter will be to examine this creedal confession that Jesus Christ is the incarnation (becoming human) of God, that he is truly God and truly human. We shall look briefly at the theological controversies from which the creed developed and at the creed's interpretation by later councils at Constantinople in 381, Ephesus in 431, and Chalcedon in 451. We shall also consider how the distinctive Christian belief that Jesus Christ is truly God shapes in turn the Christian understanding of God as the Holy Trinity. Like Jews and Muslims, Christians profess belief in one God (monotheism). Unlike Jews and Muslims, Christians are trinitarian monotheists, calling upon one God as Father, Son, and Holy Spirit.

Most of the issues treated in this chapter fall under the branch of systematic theology known as Christology, the study of the person and work of Christ. It is called *classical* Christology to distinguish it from various *modern* approaches which have arisen since the enlightenment's (ca. 1650–1800) radical challenge to the traditional understanding of Christ. This challenge will be considered in Chapter IX.

The emphasis of this chapter throughout is that classical Christology as exemplified in the creed is not an abstract theory. It begins from and returns to the two-sided Christian experience of salvation and worship in Christ. The early Christological controversies from which the creed emerged involve a massive complex of historical detail and theological speculation. Viewing these controversies from the perspective of their relationship to Christian living and worship necessarily oversimplifies them. But perhaps it will also convey some sense of what was at stake in these controversies, and why fourth and fifth century Christians took them so seriously. Before considering the councils and the controversies surrounding them, therefore, we shall look briefly at some of the New Testament witness to this twofold Christian experience of salvation and worship.

CHRISTIAN LIVING:
SALVATION AND THE DAILY FOLLOWING OF CHRIST

St. Paul's New Testament letters testify, both historically and religiously, to an experience of salvation in Christ that had already taken shape in the second decade after Christ's death. For Paul "life is Christ" (Phil 1:21). His sense of having been transformed in Christ or created all over again comes through with clarity and power in his letters. "I have been crucified with Christ; yet I live, no longer I, but Christ lives in me; insofar as I now live in the flesh, I live by faith in the Son of God who has loved me and given himself up for me" (Gal 2:19–20). This life in Christ is a "new creation" (Gal 6:15).

In Romans 7, Paul writes evocatively of his own previous inability to do under his own power what he thought was good. He felt God's law as an unbearable yoke imposed coercively from without. In Christ, however, he came to live in a new way. The exhortations to fellow Christians in his letters clarify the nature of this new way of living. Not only do those who live in Christ avoid the various forms of immoral behavior Paul lists, but most importantly, in Christ, whom Ephesians 2:14 describes as "our peace," they live in peace and charity in their own families and communities. In Christ old divisions are abolished and we are reconciled to God and one another. "For all of you who were baptized into Christ have clothed yourselves with Christ. There is neither Jew nor Greek, there is neither slave nor free person, there is not male and female; for you are all one in Christ Jesus" (Gal 3:27–28).

For Paul, putting on Christ meant especially experiencing his own present suffering in union with the sufferings and death of Christ, "always carrying about in the body the dying of Jesus" (2 Cor 4:10). Through faith, Paul became "conformed to his death" (Phil 3:10). Paul's own martyr's death at Rome would be his ultimate witness to his conformity to Christ. His union with Christ's death gave Paul a share in the hope for resurrection. Thus being in Christ through faith implies not only a transformation of the daily routine of the present life but also a hope for resurrection beyond death.

Paul urged his fellow Christians to imitate him (Phil 3:17). "Be imitators of me, as I am of Christ" (1 Cor 11:1). The parental metaphors he uses suggest that he expected this putting on of Christ to be a long process of transformation. He addresses the Christians of Galatia as "My children, for whom I am again in labor until Christ be formed in you!" (Gal 4:19). Ephesians speaks of the need for Christians to "grow in every way into him who is the head, Christ" (4:15).

In Paul, then, we find the earliest detailed example of a conception of Christian living as an inner conformity to or an imitation of Christ through faith. We find a similar emphasis on the following of Christ in the New Testament gospels. They are at one in presenting the fourfold New Testament gospel. It presents Jesus' life and death as the model for Christian discipleship. "Whoever wishes to come after me must deny himself, take up his cross, and follow me" (Mk 8:34). After the word *cross*, Luke 9:23 adds the adverb *daily*. The contemporary witness of liberation theology reminds us that disciples' identification with Christ's sufferings and death can take various cultural forms and need not entail passive resignation in the face of injustice.

CHRISTIAN PRAYER AND WORSHIP

"Thanks be to God through Jesus Christ our Lord" (Rom 7:25). Paul punctuates his letters with frequent bursts of spontaneous thanksgiving and praise. The Father and the exalted Lord Jesus Christ appear side by side as when Paul greets his correspondents with the peace of "God our Father and the Lord Jesus Christ." The need to offer appropriate praise and thanksgiving for the new life in Christ led to the rather remarkable development of Christian worship, the practice of addressing prayer to Christ himself or through him to the Father.

Without going into great detail, we can highlight the centrality of Christian worship in the formation of the New Testament. Contemporary scholars emphasize the worship setting of many gospel traditions. In the Pauline letters we find traces of various forms of worship: baptismal liturgies with their professions of faith in Christ as Lord, references to the singing of psalms and hymns and actual hymns to Christ as Lord, the Lord's supper, and references to the public reading of scripture and the apostolic writings. Christian liturgical practice clearly precedes and influences the formation of the New Testament.

Paul begins the first letter to the Corinthians with a matter-of-fact reference to disciples throughout the world as "all those everywhere who call upon the name of our Lord Jesus Christ"

(1:2). In the Old Testament, when one calls on the name of the Lord, one adores God, the Lord. Paul identifies Christians as those who "call upon the name of our Lord Jesus Christ." It is extraordinary that among these people were some who, like Paul and the twelve, were Jews, for whom strict monotheism was taken for granted. Many of Paul's converts were Gentiles, or non-Jews, but we can only assume that the experience of new life in Christ was so powerful for the Jews among them, that these strict monotheists could reconcile calling upon the name of our Lord Jesus Christ with the first commandment and its injunction to worship God alone.

The Acts of the Apostles offers some indication that it was just such a practice that led to the persecution and partial dispersion of the first church at Jerusalem. In Acts 7–8, we find signs of a division between those in the first Jerusalem community who spoke Greek, the Hellenists or Hellenistic Jews, and those who spoke Hebrew or Aramaic. The chief spokesperson for the Greek-speakers is presented as Stephen, the deacon whom Christians honor as the first martyr, the first to witness to his Christian faith with his life. Like our profession of faith, Stephen's apostolic preaching places Jesus the Lord "at the right hand of God" (7:55-56). According to Acts, Stephen's preaching about Christ as the exalted Lord precipitated his stoning, the punishment for blasphemy. Just as Christ did from the cross, Stephen prays that his executioners will be forgiven. In what can only be described as an extraordinary development, Stephen addresses his prayer to the exalted Lord Jesus at the Father's hand.

One of the most striking New Testament examples of the calling upon the name of our Lord Jesus Christ or worship addressed to Jesus appears in Philippians 2:6–11. This text is generally regarded as a liturgical hymn to Christ. Since it involves a profession of faith in his Lordship, some assign it a baptismal context. Paul wrote Philippians at the beginning of the first century's fifth decade, some twenty years after Christ's death. Paul's citing it indicates that the hymn had been in circulation prior to the letter's composition. This hymn offers evidence of a very early Christian belief that the same Jesus who had died on the cross "was in the form of God," presently exalted and deserving of the honor due to God's own name. The confession "Jesus Christ is Lord" indicates that God's own name has been given to Christ. Significantly, Paul uses the hymn in the context of an exhortation to the following or imitation of Christ.

> Have among yourselves the same attitude that is also yours in
>   Christ Jesus,
> Who, though he was in the form of God, did not regard equality
>   with God something to be grasped.
> Rather, he emptied himself, taking the form of a slave, coming in
>   human likeness;
> and found human in appearance, he humbled himself, becoming
>   obedient to death, even death on a cross.
> Because of this, God greatly exalted him and bestowed on him
>   the name that is above every name, that at the name of
>   Jesus every knee should bend, of those in heaven and on
>   earth and under the earth, and every tongue confess that
>   Jesus Christ is Lord, to the glory of God the Father (Phil
>   2:5–11).

We can conclude that the Christian confession of Jesus as truly God and truly human has deep connections to Christian living. To say that Jesus is truly human is to affirm that he is someone we can really imitate. To say that he is truly God is to affirm that when we call upon him and worship him, we do not dishonor God by idolatry. If Jesus is not truly human, if he did not take for his own our lot of suffering, temptation and death, then we cannot really take seriously the New Testament's injunctions to follow and imitate him. If he is not truly God, he lacks what it takes to transform us and to save us from death, and we would dishonor God by calling upon his name.

CHRISTOLOGY'S BEGINNINGS

While the scriptural witness speaks of God the Father and our Lord Jesus together, it does not clarify their relationship as clearly as we might expect. On the one hand, the gospels speak of Jesus in a way that makes clear that he was remembered as a human being. A key fact here is his death. He is "born of a woman" (Gal 4:4). He weeps, he gets angry, he shows compassion and he is deeply distressed at the prospect of his impending death.

On the other hand, the gospels communicate the clear sense that Jesus is more than a mere man. He speaks and acts with God's authority. He claims a unique relationship with the Father. He is charged with blasphemy and eventually executed. Further, scripture never gives the impression that there is more than one Jesus, or that Jesus is divided into parts, one part who suffers and dies, the other part who forgives sins and rises from the dead.

Early on some people got the idea that Jesus would be easier to understand if he had only appeared to be a human being and had not really suffered and died. They found the memory of the Lord's suffering and death embarrassing. This effort to explain away the New Testament's clear memory of Jesus as a human being is probably the oldest and most persistent of Christian heresies. It is called *docetism*.

This belief that Jesus only appeared to be human played havoc with the experience of Christian salvation based on union in faith with Jesus' death and resurrection. If Jesus didn't truly suffer and die, then he couldn't have risen from the dead. The apostolic faith as Paul preached it would have been false. Likewise attempts to better understand Jesus by treating him as a simple human being would have jeopardized both the experience of Christian worship and the need for a power that can transform us in this life and save us from death in the next.

The familiar profession of faith in Jesus as truly God and truly human has now become part of Christian common sense. In order to appreciate it more fully, we will look briefly at the process by which it came about. This involves attention to the first four "ecumenical," or universal, councils of the undivided church before it split into east and west in A.D. 1054. Ecumenical councils are assemblies that represent the whole church and make doctrinal and disciplinary decisions. The first councils came together to settle controversies about who Christ was. They established the ways of speaking about Jesus that we now take for granted in our worship, preaching, and instruction.

THE COUNCIL OF NICAEA, A.D. 325

The Council of Nicaea stands at the beginning of a process by which Christianity was transformed from an illicit, sometimes persecuted religion in the Roman empire to the empire's official or established religion. Crucial to this process was the Roman emperor Constantine (d. 337). Constantine came on the scene when the Roman empire, divided into eastern and western halves, was governed collegially by four tetrarchs, one of whom was Constantine's father. The latter's death began his son's rise to power. In 312 Constantine defeated his western rival, Maxentius, and by 324, the year prior to Nicaea, he had become undisputed emperor of a united empire embracing east and west.

Constantine's genuine fondness for Christianity grew in part from his attribution of his victory against Maxentius to the fact that his legions had fought under the sign of the cross. Tradition has it that he had seen a cross in the sky in a dream on the eve of the battle. Although he was not baptized until just before his death, he granted legal status to Christians, supported the church through massive building projects, and financed the copying of the scriptures.

Constantine dreamed of holding his vast and diverse domains together with the religious glue of Christian faith. At the time of his victory in the east, divisions that had arisen during the persecutions of the previous century continued to split the church. In the hopes of healing these divisions Constantine called the church's bishops together at Nicaea in modern-day Turkey near his capital. Constantine's new Rome, Constantinople, would not be ready for dedication until 330. Thus Constantine became the political occasion for Nicaea and its creedal statement about Christ.

Assuming the contemporary experience of separation of church and state and the purely spiritual and interior understanding of Christian faith that it fosters, contemporary readers may be offended at Constantine's involvement in religious affairs. Nevertheless, without reference to the politics of the Roman empire, and the complex of relationships among the political and mercantile centers of Alexandria, Constantinople, Antioch, and Rome, it is impossible to appreciate the cultural intensity of the fourth century Christological controversies.

Arianism

The first chapter of St. John's gospel contributed to Christian devotion and thought the ~~two dominant Christological images of Word (*Logos*) and Son of God~~. Commented upon by the great Alexandrian master, Origen (d. 254), the fourth gospel occupied a special place in eastern theology, especially at Alexandria.

In the Johannine approach, however, the relationship of the Word, or Logos, to the almighty, or Pantokrator, remained in need of clarification. In John 10:30, for example, Jesus says, "I and the Father are one." A few chapters later, he says, "The Father is greater than I" (Jn 14:28). In Alexandrian theology's fusion of the images of Word and Son, the relationship of the Logos to the Pantokrator, of the Son to the Father, remained somewhat fluid and open to an interpretation that subordinated the Logos/Son to the Father, as John 14:28 might suggest. In his teaching on the relationship of the Father and the Son, the Alexandrian pastor, Areios (hereafter Arius, the Latinized and more common form of his name), made this subordinationist tendency radical and explicit. As we shall see below, the Council of Nicaea responded to Arius' teaching with a strong affirmation of the Son's divine status.

Arius' teaching was the immediate occasion for the division Constantine found among Christians. But the roots of division reached back deeper into a controversy over the treatment to be accorded those who had denied the faith during the recently ended persecutions. Arius had softened his position on this question and his Christology gave his opponents an opportunity to attack him.

Near the center of the controversy stood the trinitarian baptismal formula of Matthew 28:19. "Go, therefore, and make disciples of all nations, baptizing them in the name of the Father, and of the Son, and of the Holy Spirit." In rejecting Arius' position, the Council of Nicaea used a trinitarian baptismal creed. Arius protested to Constantine his belief in the Trinity, appealing to Matthew 28:19 (Grillmeier, 222). Arius was a well-known pastor and this controversy had to do with how the trinitarian language of the church's public worship was to be understood.

Arius' chief theological concern was to preserve strict monotheism. His interpretation of scripture, however, was guided by categories derived from Middle Platonism, a form of Plato's philosophy current at this time. In his *Thalia*, or *Banquet*, a popular work partly in verse, as well as in a creed he wrote around 320, Arius calls the Father the *monad*, or the one. The Word or Son becomes the *dyad*, the twofold or second. In these philosophical categories, however, the Son must necessarily be radically other than and less than the Father. In Arius' verses from the *Thalia*:

> The Father is alien in being to the Son, and he
> has no origin.
> Know that the monad was, but the dyad was not,
> before it came into being.

In the confession of faith cited previously, he made the Son's subordination explicit:

> For he [the Son] is not eternal or as eternal and uncreated
> as the Father, nor does he have identical being with the
> Father . . . thus introducing two uncreated *archai*
> [beginnings].
> Rather, as monad and *arche* of all, he [the Father] is God
> before all . . .

Any more intimate relationship of the Son with the Father would render the Father "composite and divisible and changeable and corporeal." If by definition there can be only one monad, it is left for the dyad (the Son/Logos) to be something less, a creature with a beginning, an angelic, godlike being somewhere between the divine and the human. He is "God's perfect creature, but not as one of the creatures; brought forth but not as others are brought forth" (from the confession of faith). The dyad or Son functions for Arius as an intermediary between the Father and the world. He is like the Demiurge who fashions the world in Plato's *Timaeus*. The Father is so distant that even the Son can know him only with creaturely knowledge. "He [the Father] is inexpressible (even) for the Son" (*Thalia*).

The occasion for the Arian controversy at Alexandria was probably a public disputation over the exegesis of Proverbs 8:22–31, an Old Testament passage about wisdom applied to the Son and much commented upon at Alexandria (Pelikan, 193). The Hebrew of Proverbs 8:22 reads: "The Lord begot me, the first-born of his ways, the forerunner of his prodigies of long ago." Interpretation of the Greek (Septuagint) for *begot* is crucial for the controversy. The Nicaean Creed will offer an interpretation of it at odds with Arius'. On the basis of his Platonic understanding of monotheism, Arius interpreted this verse, along with the opening verses of John's gospel, to mean that the Logos had a beginning—even if it was before time. The main point is that the Logos is not eternal, but a special creature. As Arius put it in one of his verses: "Once God was alone, and not yet a Father, but afterwards he became a Father" (Pelikan, 195). With reference to the Son, Arius would say in his best known verses: "Before he was begotten he was not" or simply "There was when he was not."

The public dispute about the interpretation of Proverbs 8:22 made it clear that Arius did not believe the Son to be God in any true sense. For the sake of worship, the Son could be addressed as God. "He is not God truly, but by participation in grace . . . He too is called God in name only" (Kelly, 229).

Is the Son truly God or God in name only? This is the difference between Nicaea on the one hand and Arius on the other. Arius says the Son is God in name only. The creed says the Son is "true God of true God," "eternally begotten of the Father." What difference does it make? Why should Christians care?

What is at stake are the very experiences of Christian worship and Christian salvation with which we began the chapter. If the Son is a creature and not truly God, then the three centuries of Christian worship preceding Nicaea are a blasphemous fiction. If Arius is correct, Christians break the first commandment and commit idolatry every time they use God's name to call upon Jesus in prayer, every time they baptize in the name of the Son. Because they continued to address prayer and worship to Christ, and to baptize with the trinitarian formula of Matthew 28:19, Arius and his followers were accused of having fallen back into polytheism in spite of themselves. After the council, this argument would be made forcefully by Athanasius (d. 373), champion of Nicaean orthodoxy and bishop at Alexandria for nearly fifty years (Grillmeier, 271).

As for salvation, a creature who had a beginning could not save people from death and transform daily life. Only one who shared the status of the Pantokrator, the creator of all things, had the power to do this. Arius' doctrine, therefore, has the practical consequence of denying the possibility of Christian experience. Because his opponents were certain that this experience was available to them in the church, they rejected Arius' teaching. Apart from an appeal to the fundamental Christian experiences of salvation and worship, the rejection of Arius' doctrine at Nicaea is nothing but an arbitrary exercise of power, a preference for one literarily plausible reading of scripture over another.

Nicaea's Teaching

The bishops at Nicaea wanted to adhere strictly to the language of scripture. But the Arian controversy placed them in the position of having to clarify the sense in which the Logos or Son of John's prologue is "from God." They wanted to interpret "begot" of Proverbs 8:22 in such a way that Christian worship would still make sense. In composing their creed, or symbol of unity in faith, they began appropriately with a trinitarian baptismal creed from one of the local churches, perhaps that of Eusebius of Caesarea. A comparison of the creed with the prologue of John's gospel shows how closely the bishops adhered to the language of scripture. The titles ascribed to the one Lord Jesus Christ (God, light, [only] Son), reference to his role in creation, as well as to the incarnation, all appear in John 1. (See the accompanying chart.)

To this heavily scriptural language they added two clarifying expressions. The first is "only-begotten from the Father" with the clarifying phrase "from the substance of the Father." "Only-begotten" has a possible basis in a variant reading of John 1:18 that, in our present text, calls the Word "the only Son, God." The second clarifying expression is the controversial *homoousion*, translated as "one in being" or "consubstantial" with the Father. Its position after the phrase "begotten not made" indicates its role as clarifying the manner in which the Son is "begotten" or brought forth from the Father.

These two phrases are intended to emphasize against Arius that the Son was not made or created from nothing in the manner of creatures. Nor did he come from some material and divisible "stuff," such as a physical interpretation of *substance* might suggest. He is "begotten" (Proverbs 8:22) "not made" in such a way that he can be called *homoousion*, or one in being, with the Father. He is brought forth from the Father, "from the substance of the Father," "by a process comparable to natural generation, as opposed to some process of 'making,' like that of God's created works" (Stead, 233). Our present form of the creed further clarifies the manner in which the Son is "from God" by introducing the phrase "eternally begotten."

The combined effect of the two clarifying expressions involving the word *substance* (perhaps *reality* might serve as a synonym), along with the further addition of "eternally begotten," is to lend support to the confession of the faith that the Son is truly God. The Son/Logos is not merely "God from God," as Arius would have been willing to accept, but "true God from true God." The teaching of Nicaea is that the Son is truly God.

Nicaea and the Doctrine of the Incarnation

The doctrine of the incarnation (Jn 1:14) means that God became human in Jesus Christ. The Nicaean Creed establishes the framework in which the incarnation, the Word made flesh of John 1:14, will be subsequently understood. It does this by the way in which it speaks about the "one Lord Jesus Christ." Its language has two important features. First, only *one* Lord Jesus Christ is being confessed in the creed. The second important feature is that two different kinds of things are said about him. On the one hand, he is confessed as "true God" and his role in creation is acknowledged. He is the one "through whom all things came to be." On the other hand, it is this same one Lord Jesus Christ who is said to have become human and to have suffered. Of this one Lord Jesus Christ the creed makes both divine and human claims. This simultaneous presence of unity (one Lord Jesus Christ) and difference (both human and divine activities) will require further elaboration in the councils of Ephesus and Chalcedon.

The controversies leading up to Nicaea's affirmation of the divinity of Christ raged among Alexandrian Christians and involved the interpretation of the legacy of Origen, Alexandria's

John 1:1–5, 10–11, 14, 18

In the beginning was the
   Word,
   and the Word was with
      God,
   and the Word was God.
He was in the beginning with
   God.
All things came to be through
   him,
   and without him nothing
      came to be.
What came to be through
   him was life,
   and this life was the light
      of the human race;
the light shines in the darkness,
   and the darkness has not
      overcome it. (1–5)

He was in the world,
   and the world came to be
      through him,
   but the world did not
      know him.
He came to what was his
   own,
   but his own people did not
      accept him. (10–11)

And the Word became flesh
   and made his dwelling
      among us,
   and we saw his glory,

*Nicaean-Constantinopolitan
Creed*

We believe in one God, the
Father, the Almighty, maker
of heaven and earth, of all
that is seen and unseen.

We believe in one Lord, Jesus Christ the only Son of
God, eternally begotten of
the Father, God from God,
Light from Light, true God
from true God, begotten not
made, one in Being with the
Father. Through him all
things were made. For us
men and for our salvation he
came down from heaven: by
the power of the Holy Spirit
he was born of the Virgin
Mary, and became man. For
our sake he was crucified
under Pontius Pilate; he suffered, died, and was buried.
On the third day he rose
again in fulfillment of the
scriptures; he ascended into
heaven and is seated at the
right hand of the Father. He
will come again in glory to
judge the living and the
dead, and his kingdom will
have no end.

the glory as of the Father's
only Son,
full of grace and truth.
(14)

No one has ever seen God.
The only Son, God, who is at
the Father's side, has revealed him. (18)

We believe in the Holy
Spirit, the Lord, the giver of
life, who proceeds from the
Father and the Son. With
the Father and the Son he is
worshiped and glorified. He
has spoken through the
Prophets.

We believe in one holy catholic and apostolic Church. We
acknowledge one baptism for-
the forgiveness of sins. We
look for the resurrection of
the dead, and the life of the
world to come. Amen.

greatest theologian. Subsequent controversies would bring into play the diverging perspective of Christians from Antioch in Syria. Their Christological tradition had a strong sense of the human freedom of the one Lord Jesus Christ and of his importance as a moral model for Christians. When they talked about him, they used terms such as *person* and *nature* differently than they were used at Alexandria. These two terms would be at the center of future controversies. Before looking at these developments, however, we must pause and consider the contribution of the Council of Nicaea and its creed to the Christian understanding of God as Trinity.

Nicaea and the Doctrine of the Trinity

The Arian controversy illustrates that one's answer to the question of whether the Lord Jesus Christ is truly God has a profound impact on one's understanding of God and God's relations with the world of which we are a part. To Arius' Platonic monotheism the creed proposes an alternative of Christian trinitarian monotheism with its basis in the liturgical or worship life of the church. Distinctively Christian prayer does not call upon God as an Arian monad or a deist clockmaker. It calls upon God as Father, Son, and Holy Spirit. As the traditional doxology, or prayer of praise, would have it: "Glory be to the Father and to the Son and to the Holy Spirit, as it was in the beginning, is now and ever shall be, world without end. Amen."

We have seen how Nicaea's response to Arianism used a canonical approach to scripture within the context of the liturgical life of the church where God is called upon in trinitarian terms, e.g. Mt 28:19. Indeed, the Nicaean Creed, in its trinitarian structure, is drawn from the liturgical life of the church. It is an excellent illustration of the relationship between prayer and doctrine. As you pray, so you believe. One of the most powerful arguments against Arius was that his doctrine (the way he believed) contradicted the way he prayed. He could not accept that the latter has a certain priority. As modern people we might be inclined to agree with him.

As you pray, so you believe. In reflecting on this theological maxim, I am reminded of something my eldest daughter said many years ago, just after she had received her first communion. I was reading Hans Küng's *Does God Exist?* (1980) and had left it on the seat of the car. One morning as we got into the car to go off to school, Thea saw the book and read aloud the title's three words. Then she looked up and said something like, "Well, of course God exists. We receive him in communion every Sunday." Though this answer might never satisfy a contemporary, secular inquirer, I remember being struck at the time by its patristic-sounding logic. Beginning from liturgical experience, it is the sort of logic used at Nicaea. When faced with the question of whether the Son was truly God, the council answered something like, "Well, of course the Son is truly God; we have always worshiped him."

Because of our political experience as religiously free people in a denominational pluralism, we tend to think that beliefs are the crucial aspect of religion. The order proposed here (prayer/liturgy precedes and founds formal doctrine) probably strikes the reader as backward. Nevertheless, on the basis of centuries of Christian experience, I make bold to urge the contrary. Formal doctrines such as the Trinity, as well as our theological reflections on them, have an inevitably secondary or derived character. If this is true, the move from the primary level of worship to the secondary level of doctrine can best avoid drowning in a sea of theological abstraction by clinging mightily to the worship experiences where trinitarian language has its true home.

With all of this in mind, we can consider briefly Nicaea's contribution to the development of the doctrine of the Trinity. The council's chief contribution turns out to be its use of the term *homoousion*. As we have seen, its primary purpose was to intensify the claim that the Son is "from God" in a completely unique way, i.e. that the Son is truly God. Having confessed that, however, we must add that the term has implications about the Son's "ontological" status. If the Son is "one in being" with the Father, he is whatever the Father is. In the secondary order of reflection, it didn't take long to become clear that the Holy Spirit had to share the same ontological status and be *homoousion* with the Father and the Son as divine.

The Nicaean Creed had ended simply with "And in the Holy Spirit." A little more than fifty years later, the Council of Constantinople in 381 added the article on the Holy Spirit to Nicaea's brief statement. We have it as preserved in the records of the Council of Chalcedon and it is part of our present "Nicaean Creed."

> We believe in the Holy Spirit, the Lord, the giver of life, who proceeds from the Father [and the Son]. With the Father and the Son he is worshiped and glorified. He has spoken through the prophets.

This affirms the divinity of the Holy Spirit understood as "one in being" and coeternal with the Father and the Son. In the creed accepted at Constantinople in 381, the Spirit is said to proceed from the Father. Later in the west, the phrase "and the Son" (*filioque* in Latin) was added. It remains in the creed now in use among Catholics and Protestants. This addition of the *filioque* has been a source of contention between western Christians and the Greek Orthodox.

In his work *On the Trinity*, St. Augustine developed western thinking on the Trinity. He contributed three analogies comparing the Trinity as one in three to the inner life of the human mind. In the best known of these, the Father is compared to the mind, the Son to the mind's knowledge of itself, and the Spirit to the mind's love of itself.

The insight that ultimate reality is communal rather than individualistic has far-reaching implications for our understanding of ourselves and our relations with the world and God. It offers a relational alternative to a modern view of persons as isolated individuals, separated from one another, from the world, and from the God of deism (more on this God in the next chapter). But even this is relatively abstract.

All such speculative language presupposes the originating experience of Jesus as the Father's Son who sent his Spirit so that disciples would not be orphaned. It further presupposes the witness to this experience in scripture, and its celebration and continuation in the liturgy and life of the church.

In explaining new life in Christ to his disciples in Galatia, Paul spoke in trinitarian terms of the possibility of a new relationship with God that would mean the end of slavery and fear.

> As proof that you are children, God sent the Spirit of his Son into our hearts, crying out "Abba, Father!" So you are no longer a slave but a child, and if a child then also an heir, through God (Gal 4:6–7; compare Rom 8:14–17).

Paul intends this as good news about salvation. Abstractions such as the formula of "three persons in one God" and our simultaneous insistence that the unity of persons is not numerical but one of nature (the doctrine does not absurdly claim that three integers are one integer) lend a small measure of coherence to our reflections about the kinds of experiences Paul describes and the divine reality that makes them possible. But apart from reference to such experiences and their celebration in worship, trinitarian language remains empty and abstract. It is simply a way of teaching that, on the basis of our experience with Jesus, the one God is, and is best spoken of as, Father, Son, and Holy Spirit. Perhaps the best pastoral presentation of the Trinity remains the creed itself. Recognizing its confessional or worship posture, John Calvin urged that the creed always be sung rather than spoken.

THE COUNCIL OF EPHESUS, A.D. 431

Nestorianism

The controversies leading up to the Council of Ephesus had their theological roots in the diverging approaches of Alexandria and Antioch to the mystery of the union of God and the human in Christ. To oversimplify, Alexandrians after the Council of Nicaea tended to emphasize Christ's true divinity. Antiochenes tended to emphasize Christ's true humanity. Each emphasis grew out of a concern with salvation. The Alexandrian side stressed the need for a divine Savior, the Antiochene side stressed the principle that "what is not assumed [by Christ] is not saved." In Antiochene thought, Christ could function much more easily as a moral model. In this controversy, Nestorius, archbishop of Constantinople, represented the Antiochene approach. The Alexandrian approach found its spokesperson in Cyril, archbishop of Alexandria and a follower of St. Athanasius (d. 373).

The controversy's immediate occasion was Nestorius' approval of a sermon by his chaplain in Constantinople in November of 428. Nestorius refused to grant Mary the mother of Jesus the title *theotokos*, or God-bearer. For Cyril this signaled a serious breach of Nicaean orthodoxy. According to the *homoousios*, the creed affirmed that Jesus is whatever God is, one in being with the Father. If this is true, then Jesus' mother Mary must be in some sense the mother of God or *theotokos*. The alternative is some sort of deep division or duality in Christ by which Mary would be the mother of the man Jesus, the Son of David, but not of the divine Word, the Son of God.

In a series of three letters to him, Cyril criticized Nestorius' approach as implying two sons and set forth his own position on the unity of Christ. For Cyril the unity had to be there from the beginning. The human and the divine could not be set next to each other and then united. "For he was not first begotten of the holy virgin, a man like us, and then the Word descended upon him; but from the very womb of his mother he was so united and then underwent begetting according to the flesh . . ." (Cyril's Second Letter to Nestorius in Tanner, I, p. 42).

Nestorius was no match for Cyril either theologically or politically. He could not defend successfully the characteristic Antiochene concern for a free response from the man Jesus to the Christological union. In Cyril's favor, both Origen of Alexandria and Eusebius of Caesarea had used *theotokos* of Mary. Cyril had the support of both Pope Celestine (d. 432) and most of Nestorius' fellow bishops in Asia Minor.

Nestorius was condemned at Ephesus and replaced as bishop. The council formally decided that Cyril's second letter to Nestorius was in conformity with the Nicaean creed. This meant that giving Mary the title of *theotokos* was consistent with the creed. As Cyril's letter explained of his predecessors:

> So have they dared to call the holy virgin, mother of God [theotokos], not as though the nature of the Word or his godhead received the origin of their being from the holy virgin, but because there was born from her his holy body rationally ensouled, with which the Word was hypostatically united and is said to have been begotten in the flesh (Tanner, I, p. 44).

With the *theotokos*, Ephesus made explicit the oneness of Christ implied in the language of the creed. Cyril and the Alexandrians understood this as a real or "hypostatic" (personal) union of the Logos and the humanity of Christ. The Antiochenes continued to speak of two natures. Since Alexandrians often used this term *nature* to refer to Christ's oneness, the potential for future controversy remained.

BETWEEN EPHESUS AND CHALCEDON, A.D. 431–451

In 433 Cyril and John of Antioch agreed to the "Formula of Reunion." It had been worked out by Antiochene theologians and spoke of Christ as "consubstantial with the Father in respect to his divinity and at the same time consubstantial with us in respect of his manhood. For a union of two natures has been accomplished" (Kelly, 329). Earlier we noted that, following scripture, the Nicaean Creed had spoken of *one* Lord Jesus Christ doing two different kinds of activities, those proper to God and those proper to us. The "Formula of Reunion" uses the terms *person* and *nature* to make sense of the way the gospels and the creed speak about Christ. It attributes to him a "unity of person" and a "duality of natures." Alexandria and Antioch were moving closer in their uses of the terms *person* and *nature*. In many ways the "Formula of Reunion" anticipates the Christological definition of Chalcedon. In the meantime, there would be one more serious dispute between the two camps. It arose with a reassertion of Alexandrian (one nature) Christology, which, in its most radical form (monophysitism), virtually ignores the humanity of Christ.

In fifth century Egypt, the patriarch of Alexandria—after Ephesus the archbishops of Alexandria, Constantinople, Rome, and Antioch came to be known as patriarchs—had acquired a stature that has been compared to that of the ancient pharaohs. Cyril's influence attests to this. When Cyril died in 444, he was succeeded by Dioscorus, an ambitious patriarch, intent on stamping out Antiochene influence in the upstart imperial city of Constantinople. In his reassertion of Alexandria's "one nature" formula, Dioscorus found an ally at the imperial court in Eutyches, an aged monk who presided over a large monastery in Constantinople. This "aged and muddle-headed archimandrite" (Kelly, 331) represented Alexandrian Christology in its most extreme form. As a radical monophysite, Eutyches had great difficulty acknowledging the true humanity of Christ. He refused to accept the "Formula of Reunion's" confession that Christ is *homoousios* (consubstantial or one in being) with us. He is said to have compared Christ's humanity to a drop of honey in the sea of his divinity. Eutyches' virtual denial of the true humanity of Christ has come to be called *monophysitism* from the Greek *monos* (one) and *physis* (nature).

In 448 Flavian, patriarch of Constantinople and a supporter of the "Formula of Reunion," presided over a synod that condemned Eutyches' views. A confession of faith that Flavian read at the proceedings marked an important advance in the conflict between Alexandria and Antioch and helped prepare the way for the definition of Chalcedon. Flavian's confession used the *prosopon* of Antioch and the *hypostasis* of Alexandria synonymously to refer to Christ's oneness. "We acknowledge that Christ is from two natures after the incarnation, in one *hypostasis* and one person, confessing

one Christ, one Son, one Lord" (Grillmeier, 534). Eutyches succeeded in turning Flavian's formula into a monophysite slogan: "I
acknowledge that the Lord was 'from two natures' before the
union, but after the union I acknowledge only 'one nature' "
(Grillmeier, 524).

Eutyches' appeals of his condemnation brought Pope Leo the
Great, bishop of Rome, into the controversy. When Emperor
Theodosius realized the extent of Eutyches' popular support,
Flavian found himself out of favor. The emperor wanted a second
council at Ephesus, presided over by Dioscorus, to settle this new
controversy over Eutyches. Pope Leo responded to the summons
to this council with his *Tome to Flavian*, a letter that defended the
true humanity of Christ in "two natures" terminology as understood in the west. Using scriptural examples from the story of
Jesus' raising of Lazarus in John 11, Leo illustrated how the language of two natures can clarify our understanding of the two
different kinds of statements scripture makes about the one
Christ. "It does not belong to the same nature," Leo argued, "to
weep for a dead friend with emotions of pity and to recall the
same friend from the dead with a word of power" (Frend, 767).

Leo also defended the "communication of idioms" or proper-
ties by which what belongs to the one Christ in his human nature,
e.g. having a mother, can be predicated or said of the Logos and
vice versa. Thus we can say that Mary is *theotokos* or mother of
God. But Leo's belated intervention was not enough to prevent
Flavian's banishment by this "robber council" (Leo's term) of 449
and its rehabilitation of Eutyches.

In July of the next year, Emperor Theodosius was thrown
from his horse in a hunting accident and died. Under the influence
of Theodosius' sister, Pulcheria, the new emperor, Marcian, was
more favorable to Leo. This set the stage for the Council of
Chalcedon.

THE COUNCIL OF CHALCEDON, A.D. 451

The new council met at Chalcedon in October and November
of 451 under the emperor Marcian. The council produced a definition that has guided western Christianity's understanding of the

incarnation ever since. The four great Christian centers of Alexandria, Antioch, Rome, and Constantinople each contributed something of their Christologies to the definition. The definition uses the terms *person* and *nature* to bring together the *one* of Alexandria and the *two* of Antioch. It brought some limited conceptual and linguistic clarity to future understanding of the one Lord Jesus Christ confessed in the creed, but spoken about in two ways. The definition excludes both Nestorian and monophysite interpretations of the Christological union.

The definition's basic wording is taken from the "Formula of Reunion." This makes sense. The Formula had been composed by Antiochenes and heartily approved by Cyril of Alexandria. The "two nature" language of the Formula is echoed in the Roman contribution to the definition, Leo's *Tome to Flavian*. The definition also adopts Flavian's use of *prosopon* and *hypostasis* as synonyms, which we translate as *person*. Nestorius had used *prosopon* in a quite different way. Flavian's identification of the terms makes a significant gesture in the direction of Alexandria. Finally, since Eutyches had given a monophysite interpretation to Flavian's "from two natures," the definition speaks of the one Christ as made known "in two natures."

The definition reaffirms the faith of Nicaea and the *theotokos* of Ephesus. Chalcedon, like Ephesus before it, can be read as a commentary on the Nicaean Creed. The definition confesses "One and the same Christ, Son, Lord, Only-begotten, to be acknowledged in two natures." To this are added four qualifying adverbial phrases. The first two, "without confusion" and "without change," exclude the monophysitism of Eutyches, which would have swallowed up Christ's humanity in his divinity. The second two, "without division" and "without separation," exclude the kind of radical duality in Christ which Nestorius was accused of teaching. With the adverbial phrases, the excesses of Alexandria and Antioch are rejected.

The one Lord Jesus Christ is acknowledged "in two natures." One nature is divine. The other is human. The one Christ is confessed to be *homoousios* with the Father respecting his divine nature. Thus, to return to Leo's example, he could raise Lazarus from the dead. He is confessed to be *homoousios* with us, respecting his human nature. Thus he could weep for his friend with emotions of pity. These two natures are preserved in "one Person and one subsistence [*hypostasis*] not as if Christ were parted or divided into two persons."

SUMMARY

The conciliar process we have just reviewed produced an ecumenical consensus by which the one Lord Jesus Christ was confessed as divine (Nicaea), one (Ephesus), and human (Chalcedon). Arianism (the denial of Christ's true divinity), Nestorianism (the division of Christ in two), and monophysitism (the denial of Christ's true humanity) serve as types of three fundamental Christological errors.

To put it as simply as possible, we can say that in the Chalcedonian definition the term *person* or *hypostasis* answers

Council	Said	Against	Which said
Nicaea I (325)	The Word of God is one in being (*homoousios*) with the Father	Arianism	The Word is a creature; "There was when he was not"
Ephesus (431)	Jesus is one; Mary is *theotokos*	Nestorianism	Mary is the mother of the human Jesus but not of the divine Word
Chalcedon (451)	Jesus is one person in two natures, human and divine	Monophysites	Jesus had one nature only, his divine nature, into which his humanity was absorbed

the question *who?* with regard to Christ. The term *nature* answers the question *what kind of?* or simply *what?* These modest conceptual and linguistic boundaries have guided the church in its subsequent preaching, worship, and theology.

THE LIMITS OF CREED AND DOCTRINE

What, then, are we to make of these abstract-sounding creedal formulas that come to us as proclamations about God? All that has gone before suggests that, despite their sometimes abstract form, the primary return we should expect from them is religious rather than intellectual. Creeds and doctrines were not written to answer theoretical philosophical questions nor to carry the weight of the life and worship they presuppose. They were written to be proclaimed—even sung—and taught in assemblies of believers. Apart from this environment, they are like fish out of water.

This is not to deny their cognitive value but to locate it properly. The terms *person* and *nature* from Chalcedon, for example, have little or no value as independent contributions to philosophy. Rather their cognitive value arises out of a particular context and lies in their capacity to clarify the meaning of the Nicaean Creed. The latter, for its part, is intended as a faithful reflection of scripture's language.

Mindful of all of this, as well as of Calvin's insight that the creed is best proclaimed when it is sung, I offer the following four guides. They provide a perspective or context in which creedal confessions can be appropriately approached and doctrines fruitfully interpreted.

1. *Creedal confessions about Christ ought to be interpreted in the context of the experience of Christian salvation*. The Chalcedonian definition is not a theoretical explanation of the incarnation and how it is possible. It is a public confession of faith, worked out in a situation of conflict, and framed so that members of each contending group could recognize their faith in it. The formula of one person in two natures is a way of expressing the foundations in reality for the experience of Christian salvation and Christian worship described at the beginning of the chapter. Apart from this concrete historical context, the idea of an incar-

nate god is simply one among the many examples of a common pattern in the history of religions. If one is living "in Christ," difficulties with "person" in the Chalcedonian sense, however disturbing, will most likely not be enough to dislodge one from the Christian way of life.

2. *Creedal language has an appeal that transcends the appeal to the imagination*. The Chalcedonian confession is framed in abstract-sounding language. Appreciating Cyril's Logos-centered view of Christ, for example, requires operating at a high level of abstraction that conceives the union taking place prior to Christ's human history. This is difficult in part because our images of the flesh and blood figure of Jesus from the gospels keep intruding. This is the very point of the incarnation, Jesus Christ as the *ikon* or "image of the invisible God" (Col 1:15).

It is difficult to use the Chalcedonian language of one person in two natures without imagining one of three images: 1) the bright angelic effulgence of the Alexandrian Logos, 2) the bearded, dusty Palestinian Jew who bled and died on the cross, 3) these two figures somehow united, almost two people. Yet imagining Christ for many Christians is a central part of religious living, indispensable for ordinary forms of prayer and moral living. Imagine the figures of the crucified Christ you have seen, some emphasizing pain and suffering, others emphasizing peace and glory.

As Christian iconoclasts (image breakers) from patristic times to the reformation have realized, there is a certain built-in tension between imagining and the confession of one sovereign God in Christ. More precise or less paradoxical technical language is not likely to dissolve this tension. As iconoclasts have failed to grasp, such tension goes along with our being less than angels. Most contemporary reinterpretations are no less easy to imagine than the formula itself. The creeds offer some direction for our religious imaginings and help to discipline the tendency to proliferate images promiscuously. This sentence from Augustine captures the legitimate discrepancy between what we confess in the creed and what we imagine. "The image of the Trinity is one person, but the supreme Trinity Itself is three persons" (Kelly, 278).

3. *Creedal statements such as Chalcedon's are best understood as confessional or worship language*. There comes a point in religious life when we must give up imagining and confess the ultimate

inadequacy of our images. When we reach this point, when we move from the posture of imagining or questioning to the posture of worship, creedal language comes into play. While mystery ought not to be invoked lightly or prematurely to stifle questioning, Christians must at some point simply confess their belief in the incarnation as a saving mystery of faith rather than as a technical piece of theoretical knowledge. Though we do not use the Chalcedonian confession in our liturgy or public worship, we do use the western version of the earlier Constantinople creed. Here amid the proclamation of the word and the eucharistic prayer, Nicaea's *homoousios*, however abstract, is at home in a worship context. When we are in church, our primary task is not to ask what it means but to confess it. It gives a certain tone or shape, nuanced by the liturgical context, to the profession of our faith in God.

4. *Creedal language is to be distinguished from technical philosophical language*. From the point of view of philosophical reason, the greatest difficulty with Chalcedon comes if we assume that we already know what God is and what a human being is. We place them next to each other and then ask how they can possibly be joined in Christ as Chalcedon confesses. This is to miss the point of revelation's claim that in Christ God has made clear to us what God and human beings really are. In order to believe in the incarnation, we must allow it to reshape our ideas of what God is and what a human being is. These two sets of ideas (ours and revelation's) cannot be unrelated. On the other hand, God's good news should surprise us.

THE GOOD NEWS OF THE INCARNATION

One of the surprises implied in the "one person, two natures" formula is that the bodily condition of humanity, with all that embodiment implies, is not so base and worthless that God would not assume it. Even though we are selfish and cruel, though we suffer and die, we are salvageable. Another surprise is that God salvages us not by rescuing us from our bodily or incarnate condition but by taking it on in Christ. Our very condition of being embodied becomes the way God saves us. After the incarnation, we know that we are to look for God not in timeless glimpses of

God can become human
Human can be God

an angelic eternity, but at particular moments in particular places with their smells and sights, even places like Golgotha.

The image of the Logos or Word from the hymn in John 1 has tended to dominate eastern Christology. Western Christology by contrast has been deeply marked by the image of Christ from the hymn in Philippians 2. Christ "empties himself," fully embracing the human condition. Death on a cross is not excluded from but drawn into this embrace, and God knows the depths of human suffering.

The birth and death of Christ, the mother and child, the crib and the crucifix, with their liturgical counterparts in Christmas and Easter, have been dominant themes in western Christian art. This art has helped to shape unawares our images of Christ. Such images, along with devotional practices such as the stations of the cross and the mysteries of the rosary, have kept alive our sense of Christ's humanity, the reality of the incarnation and all it promises. This sense of the incarnation must be a crucial part of the context for our abstract Christology of person and natures. The incarnation of God in Christ has been one of the most powerful religious symbols in human history. It is the religious center of Christianity, especially in its Catholic form. In its light, other people, our bodies, our history, and every aspect of our world, all become potential icons or manifestations of God. In the sacraments and in the scripture viewed by analogy with the incarnation, this sense is alive in a special way.

Questions for Review and Discussion

1. How is the creedal confession that Jesus Christ is truly God related to the early experience of Christian worship for which we find so much evidence in the New Testament?

2. How is the creedal confession that Jesus Christ is truly God related to the experience of Christian salvation, as we see it, for example, in St. Paul?

3. How is the creedal confession that Jesus Christ is truly human related to the experience of Christian salvation as new life in Christ (day-to-day Christian living), as we see it, for example, in St. Paul?

4. How did Arius and his followers understand the relationship between the Father and the Son/Logos? Explain.

5. Why did those who opposed Arius find his teaching (doctrine) about the relationship between the Father and the Son inconsistent with Arius' own experience of Christian worship? Do you think they were correct?

6. If Arius' theological understanding of the Son/Logos (his Christology) was correct, how would that affect Christian possibilities for new life now and salvation from death?

7. Identify what you think are the four most important words or phrases in the Nicaean Creed and explain how they provide an alternative to Arius' view of the relationship between the Father and the Son.

8. What is the chief contribution of the Council of Nicaea and its creed to the development of the doctrine of the Trinity?

9. What does the title *theotokos* mean? Why didn't Nestorius want to grant it to Mary the mother of Jesus? How was his refusal related to his understanding of Christ's role in the Christian experience of salvation?

10. Why did Nestorius' opponents think that the Nicaean Creed required that Mary be called *theotokos*?

11. Using examples, explain the difference between the approaches of Alexandrian and Antiochene Christians to the Christological union (the union of human and divine in Christ).

12. How did Eutyches understand the Christological union? Why would an Antiochene oppose his understanding? What aspect of the experience of Christian salvation did the monophysitism of Eutyches endanger?

13. What did each of the following contribute to the definition of Chalcedon: Cyril of Alexandria, "Formula of Reunion," Pope Leo the Great, Flavian of Constantinople? Explain.

14. How does the definition of Chalcedon:
    a) build on what came before it,

   b) balance the advantages of both Alexandrian and Anti-
     ochene approaches,

   c) remain faithful to both the experience of Christian wor-
     ship and the experience of Christian salvation?

15. State in simple form the doctrines of the incarnation and the
Trinity.

16. If the Nicaean Creed and the definition of Chalcedon are
neither theoretical philosophical positions nor appeals to the
imagination, how are we to understand them? Where, when,
and how are they supposed to work?

For Writing and Reflection

1. The Arian controversy was in many ways an argument about
how to interpret scripture. Given Arius' understanding of the
Word's (Jn 1) relationship to the Father, write an essay in which
you explain how Arius would interpret John 1:1–3 and Proverbs 8:22–23, and how these same two texts would be interpreted from the perspective of the Nicaean Creed. Do you find
Arius' interpretations of these passages plausible? Why did the
bishops at Nicaea think Arius should accept their interpretations? What were their arguments? What do we learn from the
Arian controversy about interpreting scripture at the canonical
and traditional levels? (Recall Chapter VI above.)

2. Read Chapter 7 of the Old Testament (deuterocanonical)
book of Wisdom. Concentrate primarily but not exclusively on
verses 24–26. This was a passage frequently applied to the
Son/Logos and commented upon at Alexandria, where the
Septuagint version was originally produced. Identify the metaphors in this passage. Write an essay about how these metaphors could be applied to the question of the Father's relationship to the Word/Logos, and to the question of whether the
Father's generation of the Word was material or non-material.

For Further Reading

Norman P. Tanner, S.J., ed., *Decrees of the Ecumenical Councils*,
Volume I. The first 103 pages of this volume contain all the

primary documents, in translation and in the original languages, of the councils discussed in this chapter.

Aloys Grillmeier, S.J., *Christ in Christian Tradition*, Volume I of *From the Apostolic Age to Chalcedon (451)*, translated by John Bowden (second revised edition; Atlanta: John Knox Press, 1975). This is an indispensable but difficult and technical work. Unless otherwise indicated, all the quotations from Arius in the chapter are from pp. 224–228 of this work.

Jaroslav Pelikan, *The Emergence of the Catholic Tradition (100–600)*, Volume I of *The Christian Tradition, A History of the Development of Doctrine* (Chicago and London: University of Chicago Press, 1971). This initial volume of Pelikan's now complete great work is clearly written with generous citations from primary sources.

J.N.D. Kelly, *Early Christian Doctrines* (revised edition; San Francisco: Harper & Row, 1978). A book much like Pelikan's above. It is very clearly written and integrates the primary sources very well into the text.

W.H.C. Frend, *The Rise of Christianity* (Philadelphia: Fortress Press, 1984). This is a history of Christianity rather than of Christian doctrine. It is very valuable for contextualizing the three councils treated in this chapter. It reads very well, and Frend is quite comfortable with the theological aspects of Christian history.

Christopher Stead, *Divine Substance* (Oxford: Clarendon Press, 1977). This is the most technical and inaccessible of the works listed here. It is an important and thorough study of how the key term *substance* was understood and used in the centuries before Nicaea. Chapter XIII deals with the word *homoousios* and Chapter IX with the phrase "from God's substance" from the creed.

Robin Lane Fox, *Pagans and Christians* (New York: Alfred A. Knopf, 1987). This work is included primarily because of its interesting, revisionist portrayal of Constantine as both Christian and even theologian. Compare Grillmeier's portrayal of Constantine in Chapter III.

Gerald O'Collins, *Interpreting Jesus* (New York/Ramsey: Paulist
   Press, 1983). A clearly written survey of classical and contemporary Christology.

Terms To Identify

Christology

Arius (Arianism)

Nestorius (Nestorianism)

ecumenical council

Trinity

docetism

Constantine

Nicaean Creed

homoousios (on)

theotokos

Pantokrator

Eutyches

monophysitism

incarnation

Flavian (Constantinople)

Pope Leo the Great

"Formula of Reunion"

Tome to Flavian

Cyril of Alexandria

Dioscorus

Athanasius

Chapter IX

The Historical Jesus

MODERN SUSPICION OF CLASSICAL CHRISTOLOGY

Until the beginning of the age of reason (ca. 1650), Christology retained the classical form described in the previous chapter. Theologians interpreted scripture and conducted their discussions in the light of the creedal confessions of Nicaea, Ephesus, and Chalcedon. Most leaned more to the Alexandrian than to the Antiochene side. Protestant reformers correctly urged renewed stress on Christ's saving work rather than a narrow focus on abstract questions about his identity. Popular devotion kept alive a strong sense of Christ's true humanity. The modern period brought to western civilization a massive cultural and intellectual shift. It would challenge the very idea of revealed religion and subject the historical foundations of Christianity's claims to searching and often hostile scrutiny.

In this chapter, we will consider some of the cultural changes that gave rise to "critical history" in general and to the "historical criticism" of the New Testament in particular. Dramatic changes occurred almost simultaneously in the cultural areas of politics, science, philosophy, historical study, and religion. A new spirit came upon the elites of Europe. After a brief taste of that spirit, we will review the results of its application to New Testament study in what has come to be called the "quest for the historical Jesus." Finally, we will consider the difficult situation into which this quest had placed educated Christians at the beginning of the twentieth century.

THE RELATIONSHIP BETWEEN FAITH AND HISTORY

The Example: Jesus died "for our sake"

An example will clarify modernity's difficulty with traditional Christology. In the present form of the Nicaean Creed, Christians confess that Jesus suffered and died "for our sake." He died for us. This last statement contains both an historical affirmation about Jesus (he died) and a religious confession of faith (his death was for us).

As the four gospels illustrate, Christian preaching has always taken a similar twofold form. The message of salvation is proclaimed in the telling of the story of Jesus. The plausibility of Christian religious claims is linked, therefore, to the plausibility of its historical claims about Jesus. This relationship between faith and history can be put simply using our example. If we could show that Jesus had never existed, and therefore never died, then the claim that he died for us would be silly and not worthy of our respect. But establishing the historical claim that Jesus died is not in itself sufficient to establish the religious claim. Nevertheless, in order to take the religious claim seriously, we must be convinced of the plausibility of the historical claim. Though historical study can conceivably falsify such religious claims as "Jesus died 'for our sake,' " it cannot prove them, but only render them more or less plausible. During the modern period, the plausibility of Christianity's historical claims about Christ was radically questioned.

CRITICAL HISTORY AND ITS POLITICAL DIMENSION

The attempt to investigate the past in as scientific a way as possible is called critical history or historical criticism. Critical history's key distinguishing characteristic is its reliance on sources. Critical or scientific claims about the past must be made on the basis of sources that are contemporary with, or as close as possible to, the events in question. In addition to written sources of various kinds, historical sources also include the material results of archaeological research, e.g. coins, building inscriptions, and the like. The more independent, contemporary sources historians can find to attest to past events, the more seriously will others have to take their account of them. Traditions about the past that cannot be supported with multiple, independent, contemporary sources will be taken less seriously or regarded with suspicion.

It would be a mistake to regard the rise of critical history as a purely intellectual event. It only appears that way to us because we view it from the perspective of separation of church and state. The ideal of critical history is profoundly political and motivated by a drive for political emancipation. A chief source of modernity's suspicion of Christianity was the position of privilege or establishment it had occupied since Constantine. Enlightened historians wanted to free the telling of the story from the control of authorities who benefited from its traditional form. They wanted to let the sources speak. Eventually, in the late or second enlightenment, the "masters of suspicion," Marx, Nietzsche, and Freud, would turn the critical spirit back on modernity's own naive faith in its unbiased rationality.

Critical history, therefore, is difficult to separate from the deep and politically motivated distrust and resentment of tradition in which it originated. Biblical criticism, or New Testament criticism in our case, is what happens when the critical spirit, the modern drive for emancipation or enlightenment, encounters the Bible. We can no longer simply carry on the conversation of classical Christology as before. Someone in the congregation or the classroom will inevitably begin to wonder how we know that Jesus even existed, not to mention that he did all the marvels the New Testament attributes to him.

THE CRITICAL OR ENLIGHTENED SPIRIT

In the vocabulary of modern western thought, being "critical" doesn't mean saying something uncomplimentary about another. Rather it refers to the ability to use one's mind or critical faculty. It involves the ability to make distinctions (its literal meaning) and to ask questions. Above all, however, *critical* means thinking for oneself, thinking independently. A critical mind is suspicious of arbitrary authorities and questions them systematically.

Some modern thinkers would have us believe that the time prior to the seventeenth century was the age of faith. The critical spirit was dead and only came to life in the age of reason (1650–1800), as the enlightenment or modern period is often called. The very term *enlightenment* presumes the darkness that preceded it. But we have seen that patristic and medieval thinkers asked difficult questions about the Bible. Before the closing of the canon, Christian writers debated the apostolic authorship of Jude, James, the fourth gospel and the Apocalypse. Textual critics such as Origen suspected the scriptural texts they had received and worked to establish critical texts. Tatian in the second century and Augustine in the fifth noticed the variations in the gospel narratives and tried to harmonize them. It was widely recognized that literal interpretation alone would render scripture unintelligible at many points. Allegorical interpretation and the appeal to various other-than-literal senses of scripture abounded in the pre-modern church. All of these are examples of a critical or questioning approach to traditional sources.

But the modern critical spirit goes deeper. The above examples of pre-enlightenment criticism presuppose a basic posture of trust toward tradition. The enlightened spirit, by contrast, is characterized by its posture of radical doubt or skepticism toward the tradition. It is this attitude toward tradition that separates classical and medieval from modern criticism or reason.

In 1648 the Treaty of Westphalia ended the more than one hundred years of religious wars that had followed upon the reformation. The model of medieval Christendom with an established church was still assumed. Just as Protestants and Catholics disagreed about what God had revealed, so the warring princes disagreed about which church should be established. By 1648 they had grown weary of the fighting. They divided Europe up into a multiplicity of miniature Christendoms or confessional states.

Weariness with public strife over religious faith pointed to the need for a religious authority open to all. It would not have to appeal to a special revelation. Christianity could be made into a rational religion based on the cultivation of each individual's ability to think independently. This independent, internal authority is reason. The age of reason declared reason's independence from all forms of arbitrary external authority. Reason's mortal enemy was tradition conceived as an arbitrary, externally imposed restraint on the individual. The critical ideal of the age of reason is eloquently expressed in Immanuel Kant's (1724–1804) essay "What Is Enlightenment?" with its motto "dare to think." In its excesses, the critical spirit leads to the image of the solitary inquirer seeking the light without regard for community, history, culture, or language.

THE "NEW SCIENCE" EMBODIES THE CRITICAL SPIRIT

The rise of the "new science," already begun in the sixteenth century, gave both expression and impetus to the critical spirit. Medieval universities had accepted the ancient Greeks, Aristotle (384–322 B.C.) in physics and Ptolemy (ca. A.D. 100–170) in astronomy, as scientific authorities. Ptolemy's earth-centered or geocentric theory explained the motions of the observable heavenly bodies. The sun, the moon, and the moving stars (planets) moved around the earth. Ptolemy posited a network of wheels in the heavenly vault to explain the planetary wanderings. To the senses, the sun appeared to rise and set over a flat earth.

With their new telescopes, Nicholas Copernicus (1473–1543), Galileo Galilei (1564–1642), and Johannes Kepler (1571–1630) challenged the Ptolemaic view. They replaced it with a simpler, sun-centered or heliocentric theory. Eventually Isaac Newton's (1642–1727) physics, with its view of motion as mechanics based on laws of nature in a space-time framework, would replace Aristotle's physics with its assumption of rest as the natural state and the need for an unmoved mover to explain motion.

Aristotle had been the representative of the received wisdom as well as the philosophical partner of medieval theology. The Copernican revolution discredited him. More importantly, it discredited the common-sense view of the world according to which the sun rises and sets. Not only had tradition misled us, but our very senses had conspired in the deceit. What seemingly obvious or cherished beliefs would be the next to fall before the advances of the new science?

The Copernican revolution had both exhilarating and profoundly disquieting effects. In his so-called "methodic doubt," René Descartes (1596–1650) gives classic expression to this paradox of enlightened thought. In the common-sense posture, learning comes about through basic trust in what the tradition and the senses propose. In Descartes' contrary posture, learning comes through doubting. The methodic doubt means that an inquirer ought to doubt whatever appears until presented with a truth whose clarity and distinctness cannot be doubted.

The erection of doubt into a method for finding the truth constitutes a radical break with the past. As the term *enlightenment* implies, modern thought begins with the assumption of its radical discontinuity with tradition. It is therefore preoccupied with questions of method. Descartes' *Meditations* (1641) combines a deep suspicion of appearances with a simultaneous and paradoxical confidence in critical reason's ability to probe beneath appearances to find a better account of what is really going on. Even in those most suspicious of modern doubters, Marx and Freud, this confidence survives.

ENLIGHTENED RELIGION: REASONABLE CHRISTIANITY AND DEISM

Before considering what happened when the critical spirit applied the corrosive acids of suspicion to the figure of Jesus in the New Testament, we need a clearer picture of what is religiously distinctive about modernity. Three general tendencies characterize the enlightened approach to religion:

1. the rejection of particular, revealed (supernatural) religions in favor of an abstract approach to religion (deism) with a heavy ethical emphasis;

2. skepticism about supernatural (miraculous) claims;

3. religious tolerance and a split between faith and reason.

The spectacle of the religious wars that followed the reformation helped to discredit in the eyes of many the very idea of a special revelation from God. It seemed too particular, too limited to the concrete history of a rather backward and insignificant people. The fact that God's revelation had not been universal or given to everyone seemed offensive. It was after all over what God had revealed that Protestants and Catholics fought.

The alternative to such a supernatural or revealed religion would be a natural religion, one that did not require God's special intervention into human affairs. This natural religion, or religion of reason, has come to be known as deism. In their works *Christianity Not Mysterious* (1696) and *Christianity as Old as Creation* (1730), the English deists John Toland (1670–1722) and Matthew Tindal (1655–1733) proposed a sanitized, "rational" version of Christianity nearly identical with the practice of virtue. The French popularized deism in a form more explicitly hostile to Christianity. For Voltaire, the pen name of François Marie Arouet (1694–1778), positive religion or historical Christianity was reducible to priestcraft. According to Voltaire, the first theologian or divine was "the first rogue who met the first fool." Voltaire was one of the first to compare God to a watchmaker, the distinctively deist analogy.

> When I see a watch whose hands mark the hours, I conclude that an intelligent being has arranged the springs of this machine so that its hands will mark the hours. Thus when I see the springs of the human body, I conclude that an intelligent being has arranged these organs to be received and nourished for nine months in the womb . . . (*Treatise on Metaphysics*, 1734 in Livingston, 25–26).

It was no accident that deism began in England. Newtonian physics with its laws of nature lent itself well to a watchmaker God. The image of the machine had yet to acquire the negative tone we might now be inclined to give it. Newton's nature could congenially be viewed as a finely wrought watch. But the logic of the watchmaker analogy moved unavoidably forward. The deist God appeared increasingly remote from nature. Like the watch, the world could run by itself according to its own laws. Like the critical inquirer, it was autonomous. The thought that God would interfere with the world seemed unfitting, even offensive. In any case, nature's regularity made it unnecessary.

Some proponents of rational Christianity had argued that biblical miracles and prophecies distinguished Christian claims to special revelation from amid the competing voices of the history of religion and enabled us to regard them as true. In the chapter "Of Miracles," in his 1758 *Inquiry Concerning Human Understanding*, the Scottish philosopher David Hume posed the enlightenment's most radical challenge to Christianity as a revealed religion. Presupposing the closed and rather mechanical view of Newtonian nature, Hume defined miracles as "violations of the laws of nature." He argued that by definition the regularity of our experience of nature will always force the reasonable person to discount miraculous claims. No testimony to the miraculous could ever outweigh our own experience of the regularity of nature's laws. He concluded, therefore, that a religion could never be founded on the basis of testimony to miracles and prophecies. In the closing paragraph, he drove a wedge deep between faith and reason and concluded that the reasonable person, proportioning belief to the evidence, could never take the way of faith.

With the belief that competing religious claims could not be decided on rational grounds, positive or revealed religions appeared as instances of "enthusiasm," or "fanaticism," as we might now call it. As long as the various churches were stripped of legal power, the enlightened thought it best to tolerate these opposing enthusiasms. They assumed that without state support, the churches would probably die out eventually.

Where established churches still held political power, in France for example, the emancipative drive of enlightened reason generated an intense hostility to Christianity, especially in its Catholic form. Voltaire's slogan, "Crush the infamous thing," sums it up well. This opposition between faith and reason appeared in dramatic form during the French revolution of 1789 when a Paris mob enthroned the "goddess of reason" on the high altar at Notre Dame Cathedral.

ENLIGHTENED RELIGION AND THE LIFE OF JESUS

The methodic doubt extended to all areas of critical inquiry. Traditional historical accounts were abandoned, often rightly, in favor of the search among the sources for the real story. For example, historians sought evidence in historical sources for Homer's claims about Troy and the Trojan war, or for Livy's account of the founding of Rome by Romulus and Remus.

A critical historian would tend to be unhappy with the gospels on at least three counts. First, the Bible, along with Homer and other ancient works, was an example of the kind of traditional history that needed to be revised on the basis of sources. Second, the gospels represented the supposed basis in reality for the legal privileges and political and economic power enjoyed by Christian churches in Europe. Rare is the westerner who would disown Jesus. But the link between Jesus and institutional Christianity, the "infamous thing" of Voltaire, had to be broken. Third, many enlightened deists were committed to at least the offensiveness, if not the impossibility, of miracles as "violations of the laws of nature." The New Testament was filled with supernatural claims about Jesus. Resurrection from the dead was only the most spectacular example. In "Of Miracles," Hume had made a special point of mentioning it more than once.

Applying the wider split between faith and reason to the case of Christology, people began to distinguish between the church's supernatural Jesus and the real or natural Jesus. The assumption of such a split led to the attempt to tell the story of Jesus as it must have really happened, that is, without the supernatural. Lives of Jesus began to appear. Apart from a few scattered references to Jesus and his execution in Roman historians such as Tacitus, Suetonius, Josephus, and a letter of Pliny the Younger (we shall review these references in Chapter XI below), the gospels remain the only source for the life of Jesus. Out of this attempt to use the gospels as sources for critical history, contemporary New Testament criticism has developed. The term "historical Jesus" refers to our best possible historical reconstruction of his life.

THE QUEST FOR THE HISTORICAL JESUS

H.S. Reimarus

In 1906 Albert Schweitzer (1875–1965) wrote the history of the attempt, from the enlightenment to the beginning of the twentieth century, to write a critical biography of Jesus. In English translation, it was entitled *The Quest for the Historical Jesus*. The story begins with a German deist, Hermann Samuel Reimarus (1694–1768). "Before Reimarus," Schweitzer wrote, "no one had attempted to form a historical conception of the life of Jesus" (13). Guided by his deist assumptions, Reimarus sought to discover the purely natural Jesus behind the supernatural Jesus of the gospels. His work provides the model for all subsequent efforts in the "life of Jesus" genre.

Reimarus drew attention to Jesus' emphasis on the kingdom of God in his preaching and on its future-oriented nature. Reimarus interpreted this kingdom of God in a purely secular way. Jesus would be the political savior of Israel. Reimarus took this to be the obvious meaning of *messiah* and argued that Jesus' followers understood him this way prior to his death. Reluctant to give up their brief taste of notoriety and financial gain, the apostles decided to steal Jesus' body shortly after his burial. They waited a while and then proclaimed Jesus as risen and ascended. The political messiah of Israel had become the suffering Savior of all. Reimarus interprets their motivation and that of the early Christians largely in terms of the financial gain to be had from the "community of goods" described in Acts 2:42–44 and 4:32–35. His lengthy work, entitled "Defense of the Reasonable Worshipper of God," appeared posthumously and only in edited fragments. The views described above were presented in the most controversial fragment entitled, "The Goal of Jesus and His Disciples."

Three of Reimarus' themes have continued to preoccupy New Testament scholars, even those who don't share his naturalistic assumptions. First, he drew attention to the kingdom of God and its future-oriented nature. Second, he emphasized the difference between the message of Jesus and the proclamation of his disciples. Third, he realized that the disciples had shaped the story of Jesus to suit their own purposes. They tell us as much. They were not enlightened historians.

D.F. Strauss

In 1835 David Friedrich Strauss (1808–1874) published *The Life of Jesus Critically Examined*. Between the tradition, which looked to the gospels as supernatural history, and the rationalists, who sought a purely natural history, Strauss proposed a "mythical" interpretation. "Myth" was a necessary part of religion that Strauss explained as "the perception of truth, not in the form of an idea, which is the philosopher's perception, but invested with imagery . . ." (George Eliot's translation of Strauss' *Life*, 80, in Livingston, 177). In Schweitzer's terms, religious myth "is nothing else than the clothing in historical form of religious ideas, shaped by the unconsciously inventive power of legend and embodied in a historic personality" (Schweitzer, 79).

Strauss' quest for the historical Jesus, therefore, took the form of trying to disengage Jesus from the New Testament's imaginative or mythic perceptions of him. Unlike Reimarus, he does not charge the first Christians with conscious deceit. Mythical thinking came naturally to the pre-scientific mind. Strauss develops a set of criteria for identifying mythical elements in the gospel stories. First and most importantly, we are in the presence of myth, "when the narration is irreconcilable with the known and universal laws which govern the course of events" (in Livingston, 177).

Strauss is the first scholar to have systematically applied the category of myth to the study of Jesus' life. He stirred great controversy even in the United States, where the Brook Farm transcendentalists devoured *The Life* even before its translation into English by George Eliot. Strauss' mythical interpretation of the sources presented a radical challenge to any understanding of traditional Christology as having a basis in history. Strauss' contemporary, Bruno Bauer (1809–1881), went so far as to deny that Jesus and Paul had ever existed. But most life of Jesus researchers took another path and turned Jesus into an enlightened moral teacher.

T. Jefferson

Nearly twenty years before Strauss, in 1816, the third president of the United States, Thomas Jefferson, had anticipated this path with his little-known work, *The Life and Morals of Jesus of Nazareth*. Like Reimarus, Jefferson drew a sharp distinction between the doctrines of Jesus and those of traditional Christianity.

Leaving out the supernatural elements, Jefferson cut Jesus' words from the four gospels verse by verse and pasted them into another book to form a sort of gospel harmony. As he wrote to John Adams in 1813, Jefferson assumed that what was "evidently his [Jesus']" was "as easily distinguished as diamonds in a dunghill." The president fancied his harmony as holding "the most sublime and benevolent code of morals which has ever been offered to man" (Jefferson, 20).

Jefferson's Jesus was an enlightened teacher of sublime ethical doctrine. Such a view would have increasing popularity as the nineteenth century produced a whole series of lives of Jesus. The best of these coffee table volumes was Ernst Renan's French *Life of Jesus* (1863). Many of the later lives were based on the hypothesis that Mark rather than Matthew was the first gospel and that it represented the "historical core" of Jesus' life.

A. Harnack

In 1900 Adolf von Harnack, the great Lutheran historian of dogma, published a popular essay called *The Essence of Christianity*. It gave classic expression to what has come to be called the liberal Protestant view of Jesus as a sublime ethical teacher. Rather than Reimarus' future-oriented kingdom of God, Harnack's Jesus taught a more culturally palatable doctrine: the fatherhood of God, the brotherhood of man, and the infinite worth of the human soul. "The Christ that Harnack sees," a Catholic critic wrote, "looking back through nineteen centuries of Catholic darkness, is only the reflection of a Liberal Protestant face, seen at the bottom of a deep well" (George Tyrrell, *Christianity at the Cross-roads* [1909], 44).

A. Schweitzer

Schweitzer criticized Harnack in a similar vein. He concluded that the quest for the historical Jesus had failed and had only succeeded in domesticating him. The attempt to squeeze Jesus into the categories of the modern world had turned him into a reflection of that world. Each life of Jesus took on the character of the historian who had written it. Schweitzer ends his book with a moving reflection on how out of place and how much of a challenge Jesus is in the modern world. "He comes to us as One unknown, without a name, as of old, by the lake-side, He came to those who knew Him not" (Schweitzer, 401).

Although Schweitzer showed that the sources were not sufficient for a complete life of Jesus, he did conclude that the historical Jesus, as Reimarus had argued, must be understood in the context of Jewish eschatology, the messianic hope for God's decisive future intervention on behalf of Israel. But Schweitzer gave an "apocalyptic" rather than a political interpretation to Jesus' preaching about a future kingdom of God. *Apocalyptic* refers to a mindset, expressed in literary works such as the New Testament Apocalypse, that expects God's imminent intervention, amid catastrophe and cataclysm, to end this present age and usher in a new one. In Schweitzer's reconstruction, Jesus went to his death on the cross, mistakenly expecting it to bring the end of this age and the beginning of the kingdom of God.

SUMMARY

At the beginning of the twentieth century, what was regarded as advanced gospel criticism, based on "scientific" methods, had reached a series of conclusions at drastic odds with traditional Christology. First, it radically questioned the historical reliability of the gospel witness. The New Testament's claim to be based on eyewitness testimony was de-emphasized in favor of a stress on the creative activity of the evangelists. Second, aspects of the gospel witness that failed to accord with the enlightenment worldview were attributed to the creative activity of the early church. Third, this creative activity of the first Christians was interpreted along the lines of what Strauss had called myth.

THE HISTORY OF RELIGIONS SCHOOL

A fourth conclusion was added by scholars belonging to what came to be known as the "history of religions school." They reached the height of their influence in the first part of the twentieth century. In their view, the first Christians borrowed most of their Christological elements such as a dying and rising Savior

God, a heavenly Redeemer, and sacramental rituals of washing and eating from Greek, Oriental, or Hellenistic patterns. All of these were applied to the earthly Jesus in a process of Hellenization by which he became a supernatural or mythological figure.

Richard Reitzenstein (1861–1931) in *The Hellenistic Mystery Religions* (1910) and Wilhelm Bousset (1865–1920) in *Kyrios Christos* (1913) applied the methods of comparative religion to the study of the New Testament and Christian origins. Their method is distinguished by its treatment of Christianity as one among the many religions in the ancient Hellenistic world. The adjective *Hellenistic* designates the fusion of Greek and Oriental culture made possible by the conquests of Alexander the Great three centuries before Christ.

The Hellenistic religions to which Christianity was most often compared and related were the "mystery religions" that became prominent in the Roman empire at the end of the second century after Christ. They centered on the mysteries, i.e. rites and doctrines, associated with agricultural gods of the ancient near east and the natural cycles of vegetable life. Figures such as Attis, Dionysus, Adonis, Serapis, Osiris (from Egypt), and Mithras were interpreted typologically as dying and rising savior gods who served as models for the deification of Jesus of Nazareth. St. Paul is "credited" with having turned the following of Jesus into a Hellenistic mystery religion. A sharp dichotomy is drawn between Jesus and Paul and between early Palestinian Christianity and Hellenistic Christianity. The Christ we find in the New Testament is not the historical Jesus but a mythical Hellenistic savior figure.

CONCLUSION

At the beginning of this chapter we discussed the relationship between faith and history using the example "Jesus died for us." We saw how foolish it would be to confess that Jesus died for us if we knew that he had never died. By the beginning of the twentieth century, many educated Christians had been led to suspect, in the name of history and reason, that they might be in a similarly foolish position. If our traditional confessions of faith in Jesus are true, then we ought to be able to interpret history in a way that is consistent with their intent. In the first decades of the twentieth century, Christians faced the claim from numerous respected authorities that history could not honestly be read in a way that is consistent with traditional Christology. In the next chapter, we will survey the responses that twentieth century Christians have made to this challenge and the various approaches they have taken to the historical-critical study of the gospels.

Questions for Review and Discussion

1. How does the creedal confession that Jesus suffered and died "for our sake" illustrate the relationship between faith and history in Christianity?

2. Describe the "modern critical spirit." What distinguishes it from pre-modern uses of reason? Use examples from pre-modern study of the Bible.

3. What is the "new science"? Who are some of its chief representatives and what are their achievements? How did the "new science" both reflect and contribute to or intensify the "modern critical spirit"?

4. Define "critical history" or "historical criticism." What distinguishes modern or "critical" accounts of the past from the more traditional or heroic histories that preceded them?

5. With an emphasis on deism, describe the enlightened or modern approach to religion. What distinguishes it from pre-modern approaches to religion?

6. Explain how the "quest for the historical Jesus" (the nineteenth century attempt to write the life of Jesus) grew out of the enlightened approach to religion and the ideal of critical history. In other words, what made the modern critics so skeptical of the New Testament gospels that they thought they had to start all over again to write Jesus' life?

7. What were the results of the "quest for the historical Jesus"?

8. What are Hellenistic mystery religions? Examples? How do they figure in the history of religions school account of Christian origins?

9. Describe the situation faced by educated Christians at the beginning of the twentieth century with regard to historical knowledge about Jesus' life.

For Writing and Reflection

1. Write an essay in which you discuss the following. Using examples, explain the enlightenment ideal of "critical history." Using specific examples from modern "lives of Jesus," explain what happens when the ideal of critical history is applied to the gospels prior to the twentieth century. What was the "political" intent of applying historical criticism to the gospels at this time?

2. Because he feared the reaction of authorities, Reimarus never published his work on Jesus during his lifetime. Though D.F. Strauss did publish his, it spelled the virtual ruin of his academic career. Hume too jousted with government censors and delayed the inclusion of "Of Miracles" (Section X) in the *Inquiry* until long after he had written it. All of these authors lived under established churches in their respective countries. How do their situations illustrate the "political" dimension of the enlightenment or age of reason? With them in mind, argue for or against the thesis: The enlightenment was primarily a political rather than an intellectual event.

For Further Reading

James C. Livingston, *Modern Christian Thought from the Enlightenment to Vatican II* (New York: Macmillan Publishing Co., 1971). This work begins with an excellent overview of the enlightenment and goes on to treat modern religious thought with heavy emphasis on primary sources.

For reading in primary sources, the reader should consult current editions of Kant's "What Is Enlightenment?"; also see Descartes' *Meditations*, and Hume's *An Inquiry Concerning Human Understanding*, especially Section X. If you can only read one, pick "What Is Enlightenment?"

John S. Kselman, S.S. and Ronald D. Witherup, S.S., "Modern New Testament Criticism," in Raymond E. Brown, S.S., Joseph A. Fitzmyer, S.J., and Roland E. Murphy, O.Carm., eds., *The New Jerome Biblical Commentary* (Englewood Cliffs, NJ: Prentice-Hall, 1990), pp. 1130–1145, especially pp. 1131–1133.

Hans-Georg Gadamer, *Truth and Method*, pp. 235–341. Gadamer discusses the philosophical issues involved in the enlightenment's critique of tradition. He treats the Bible specifically as well as the general issue of the interpretation of tradition.

Albert Schweitzer, *The Quest for the Historical Jesus* (London: Adam and Charles Black, 1954). This remains one of the most important religious books of the twentieth century. Not only does it survey the nineteenth century but it charts many other paths to be taken by twentieth century New Testament scholarship.

Charles H. Talbert, ed., *Reimarus Fragments* (Philadelphia: Fortress Press, 1970). Reimarus' work remains the archetype for many contemporary reconstructions of the historical Jesus.

Thomas Jefferson, *The Life and Morals of Jesus of Nazareth*, ed. by Henry Wilder Foote (Boston: Beacon Press, 1951). This brief work epitomizes the modern tendency to turn Jesus into a sublime ethical teacher. It has the added interest of coming from one of our most important presidents.

Jaroslav Pelikan, *Jesus Through the Centuries* (New York: Harper & Row, 1985). Pelikan's work contains two excellent chapters on the modernization of Jesus in the eighteenth and nineteenth centuries, "The Teacher of Common Sense" (Ch. 15) and "The Poet of the Spirit" (Ch. 16).

Terms To Identify

critical

enlightenment

geocentric/heliocentric

Copernican revolution

methodic doubt

critical history/historical criticism

deism

historical Jesus

Hellenistic

mystery religions

apocalyptic

history of religions school

Dionysus

Osiris

Mithra

René Descartes

Immanuel Kant

David Hume

Albert Schweitzer

Adolf von Harnack

Bruno Bauer

David F. Strauss

H.S. Reimarus

Thomas Jefferson

Voltaire

Isaac Newton

Galileo

Johannes Kepler

Ptolemy

John Toland and Matthew Tindal

Chapter X

Twentieth Century Gospel Criticism

A SPECTRUM OF POSITIONS

We could approach the study of gospel criticism in the twentieth century from a variety of perspectives. Each perspective might generate a different spectrum of positions. The treatment of gospel criticism in this chapter organizes positions according to diverging attitudes toward modernity or the enlightenment heritage. On a linear spectrum, this perspective generates three ideal-typical positions: 1) fundamentalism, 2) skeptical historical criticism, 3) moderate historical criticism.

These three positions emerged during the course of the first six decades of the twentieth century. In response to new historical and archaeological discoveries, and to the shifting trends of the academy, they have continued to undergo adjustments and shifts of emphasis. After a brief account of fundamentalism as a rejection of historical-critical study of the Bible, this chapter's discussion of New Testament criticism will focus on the towering scholarly figure of Rudolf Bultmann, and to a lesser degree on his contemporary and counterpart, Joachim Jeremias.

FUNDAMENTALISM

The term *fundamentalism* is difficult to define. Some Christians apply it to themselves. Others apply it to those whose interpretations of the Bible are more literal than their own. In this chapter we will use the term to refer to the strict inerrantist position described in Chapter VI. It is based on a considered decision to reject historical-critical method and exclude modernity absolutely from biblical interpretation. Despite its claim to represent tradition, fundamentalism is quite modern. Its rejection of modernity is deliberate and self-conscious. Fundamentalism's chief historian in the United States, George Marsden, defines it as "militantly anti-modernist Protestant evangelicalism" (4). Fundamentalism is thus a modern anti-modernism. It reached the height of its influence during the first quarter of the twentieth century and has undergone a dramatic resurgence during the 1980s.

As their name suggests, fundamentalists' chief concern is to protect the "fundamentals" of traditional Christian faith. As evangelical Protestants, they believe that the Bible is the sole authority in matters of Christian doctrine and practice. It can serve as this authority only if it is completely without error. The Bible's errorlessness must extend to every word in its natural sense. This belief in the absolute errorlessness of the Bible is called "plenary verbal inerrancy." In the words of Jerry Falwell, a leader in the fundamentalist revival of the 1980s: "The Bible is absolutely infallible, without error in all matters pertaining to faith and practice, as well as in areas such as geography, science, history, etc." (*Listen America*, [1981], 63).

While it doesn't necessarily imply literalism, the commitment to historical inerrancy excludes the methods of historical investigation of oral and written sources and analysis of literary form developed since the enlightenment. Such methods are usually dismissed as the "so-called higher criticism." Historical criticism inevitably leads scholars to, as Harold Lindsell puts it, "deny things that the Bible clearly affirms" (Lindsell, 21).

The Mosaic authorship of the Pentateuch, the historicity of Jonah, and the single authorship of Isaiah are prominent controversial examples. Each of these so-called biblical affirmations is denied by most scholars, on the basis of source and form criticism in the case of Moses and Isaiah and literary analysis in the case of Jonah. Fundamentalist "plenary verbal inerrancy" appears in its most strident form in Harold Lindsell's *The Battle for the Bible* (1976), and in more measured tones in the 1978 "Chicago Statement on Biblical Inerrancy."

The Evangelical Christians for whom Lindsell claims to speak, however, are also committed to textual criticism of the New Testament, sometimes called "lower criticism." Through familiarity with the Greek Old Testament text, one finds that the New Testament often cites the general sense of the Old Testament rather than its exact words. Further, it cites frequently from the Septuagint or Greek Old Testament, which often differs considerably from the traditional Hebrew text. In the face of such difficulties, some Evangelical scholars have found it necessary to abandon the obvious sense of plenary verbal inerrancy. They have moved cautiously into forms of historical criticism. George Ladd is a good example.

Affirming that the Bible is the inspired word of God, but produced by men in history, Ladd argues that historical-critical methods "must be used because of the obvious fact that the Bible is not a magical book, but a product of history written in the words of men" (Ladd, 22). Ladd recognizes that in its origins and development, historical-critical method "has been, and frequently still is, the foe of any supernaturalistic understanding of the Bible as the inspired word of God" (Ladd, 41). Accordingly, Ladd and like-minded Evangelical New Testament scholars such as Ralph P. Martin and Robert Gundry attempt to use historical-critical methods without accepting the skeptical and naturalistic assumptions of the enlightenment worldview (described in the previous chapter). This attempt to disengage historical-critical methods from enlightenment assumptions distinguishes moderate from skeptical historical criticism, and locates Ladd and his colleagues in the moderate position on the spectrum. Before further considering the diverging attitudes of moderate and skeptical critics toward modernity, it is important to clarify the common frame of reference within which all gospel critics work.

COMMON ASSUMPTIONS OF SKEPTICAL AND MODERATE GOSPEL CRITICS

Source Criticism

Both moderate and skeptical critics share a commitment to an historical approach to the sources of the biblical books. Since we are concerned with the figure of Christ, we will concentrate on gospel criticism. The historical-critical approach to the gospels begins with what is called the "synoptic problem." Because of their similarities, Matthew, Mark, and Luke are known as the "synoptic" gospels. They can be placed in columns and "seen" together. In spite of their similarities, however, Matthew, Mark, and Luke are also different. Explaining these differences within the general context of similarity is the synoptic problem. Historical critics seek the explanation of the simultaneous similarities and differences of the synoptics in the written sources used by the evangelists. Pre-enlightenment scholars often dealt with these differences of content, structure, or chronology by writing harmonies.

A strong but not unanimous consensus holds that Mark and not Matthew was the first gospel. This is the basis for the "two-source theory" as an explanation for the synoptic problem. As the first complete gospel, Mark is the first source. A second source is a hypothetical collection of the sayings of Jesus reconstructed from the non-Markan material that Matthew and Luke have in common. This second source is called "Q" from the German word *Quelle*, or *source*. According to the two-source theory, Matthew and Luke use Mark and "Q" as sources. Both Matthew and Luke also have material from sources unique to them. Thus the simultaneous similarities and differences in the synoptics are explained by an appeal to their sources.

Form Criticism

Such source criticism, however, is limited to an investigation of the gospels' written sources. In the early twentieth century, scholars began to apply to the gospels the methods historians had used to study the oral sources of ancient literature and the Old Testament. This approach is called form criticism. It presupposes that the sayings of Jesus and narratives about him that we now find in the gospels were originally handed down by word of mouth. Recall that Jesus left us no known written work. He preached to the people and taught his disciples in oral form. His disciples imitated him in this.

The work of source criticism provides form critics with the beginnings of a view of the gospels as wholes composed of identifiable parts. Form critics attempt to break down the various written sources into the little pieces of oral tradition out of which they were composed. These pieces or individual units of Jesus tradition are called *pericopes*. An example of a pericope is the "Our Father" or the "Lord's Prayer." We find the short form of it in Luke

11:2–4 and a longer form in Matthew 6:9–13. Because it is shorter, the Lukan version is often considered to be older.

Contemporary gospel criticism, therefore, presupposes a three-stage process of transmission and attempts to trace the units of Jesus tradition back through the three stages. Working backward, the three stages are: 3) the written gospels, 2) the apostolic preaching, 1) Jesus' own preaching and teaching. According to this three-stage framework, a thirty to forty year period of oral transmission preceded the actual composition of the four gospels. During that time Jesus traditions were passed on in the form of individual units.

One of form criticism's key ideas is that the form in which Jesus traditions were passed on was shaped by their use or "setting in life" (*Sitz im Leben*) in the apostolic church. As explained by a pioneer form critic, setting in life is "a typical situation or occupation in the life of a community" (Bultmann, *History of the Synoptic Tradition*, 4). Examples are worship, work, hunting, or war. The literary form in which a particular piece of oral tradition will be handed on is, therefore, related to what the saying or story is used for by members of a living community. Form follows function.

This means that Jesus traditions were remembered because they were used by early Christians. How they were used influenced the form in which they were handed on. The term *literary form* is not primarily aesthetic, literary in the strict sense, but sociological, i.e. related to the life of the community. A saying of Jesus with an instructional setting in stage 1 might be used in the setting of worship in stage 2. A parable used by Jesus in one setting might appear in another in the apostolic preaching or the written gospels.

By comparing the written gospels, form critics try to isolate the individual units of tradition and trace them back from stage 3 to stage 1. Some material in the gospels will be attributed to the editorial activity of the evangelists, some to the apostolic church, and some to the "historical Jesus." The goal of form criticism as described by Rudolf Bultmann in his classic work, *The History of the Synoptic Tradition*, is "to rediscover the origin and the history of the particular units and thereby to throw some light on the history of the tradition before it took literary form" (4). Reconstructing from written sources the hypothetical

history of hypothetical units of tradition is, it should be emphasized, a highly speculative activity. One need not be a skeptic to
practice form criticism. Skeptical and moderate critics use the
method with differing results. The latter are distinguished from
the former by their greater confidence that stage 3 is faithful to
stage 1.

More Recent Methods of Gospel Criticism

At the mid-point of the twentieth century, form criticism
gave rise among the generation of Bultmann's students to a related approach called "redaction criticism," or editorial criticism.
A redactor is an editor. Redaction criticism, therefore, studies the
influence of the evangelists as editors on the traditions they trans-
mitted. Where form critics tend to be more interested in the
component pieces of the gospels, redaction critics begin by viewing each of the four gospels as wholes, but wholes composed of
parts. The evangelist is not simply a passive compiler of or con-
duit for the community's Jesus traditions. Rather he participates
actively in the community's questions and struggles and seeks to
make the memory of Jesus present to them.

By identifying the individual pieces of Jesus tradition, form
criticism set the stage for redaction criticism's view of the evangelists as active editors. When confronted with the concrete situations of the churches in which they lived, the evangelists had
available to them a whole body of Jesus traditions collected in
various forms. Why, ask the redaction critics, did the evangelists
select these traditions, leave out others, or modify them in this
way or that? Why did Matthew arrange the traditions he chose in
one way and Luke in another? Questions such as these presuppose a view of the evangelists as theologians with pastoral concern
in a church community.

Analysis of the structure of a gospel, i.e. the way the material
is arranged, can lead to conclusions about the evangelist's religious purpose. What problems and questions did Matthew's
church community have? How does his selection and arrangement of traditions about Jesus address these questions? What
does Matthew want to teach? It is easy to see that such emphasis

on the literary intent of the gospel as a whole is much easier to integrate into the life of the contemporary church than the more fragmented results of form criticism.

While form criticism had concentrated on the second stage of the transmission process, redaction criticism includes a renewed interest in the historical Jesus of stage 1. Schweitzer had long ago distinguished a life of Jesus from a picture of his public ministry. It is to just such a picture or portrait of Jesus that many redaction critics have turned their efforts.

In its treatment of each gospel as a literary whole, redaction criticism illustrates the rich possibilities of a narrative or more strictly literary approach to the gospels. Some recent New Testament scholars have noted that historical-critical method's concern to break down the story in order to reconstruct its historical basis does a certain violence to the gospels as narrative. They have therefore sought to supplement historical-critical method with more properly literary methods of analysis drawn from contemporary literary theory. One area where this approach has been effective is in the study of Jesus' parables.

In addition to an increasing emphasis on literary analysis, New Testament scholars have become more aware of the social setting of the New Testament writings and of our picture of Jesus. The use of social theory in New Testament study has provided a needed corrective to the characteristic individualism of modern thought, and to the narrowly psychological emphasis of much scholarly treatment of Jesus and Paul.

Summary

Twentieth century practitioners of historical-critical method are committed to an investigation of the gospels in terms of their literary and oral sources. They work out of the commonly assumed framework of the three-stage process of the transmission of Jesus traditions. They use the methods of source, form, and redaction criticism along with more recent methods that supplement the historical approach. Having considered what skeptical and moderate critics share in common, we will now distinguish them.

SKEPTICAL HISTORICAL CRITICISM

The Example of Rudolf Bultmann (1884–1976)

Two factors distinguish skeptical historical critics from their moderate colleagues. First, skeptics doubt the ability of historical-critical method to penetrate beyond stage 2 and the apostolic church to the historical Jesus of stage 1. Second, their commitment to the enlightenment worldview makes skeptics radically suspicious of the gospels' supernatural claims.

This position is best illustrated by the example of Rudolf Bultmann, who is both a biblical scholar and a philosophical theologian in the Lutheran tradition. Bultmann is probably the most influential New Testament scholar of this century. Even those who disagree with his conclusions must use his work and present alternatives to his radical positions. Bultmann's thought combines two characteristic emphases: 1) a stress on the limitations of human language for speaking about God and God's acts, 2) extreme skepticism about the value of the gospels as sources for historical knowledge about Jesus. These two emphases lead him to view faith as almost completely discontinuous with reason. He dismisses attempts to show rational grounds for faith by appealing to the historical continuity between the historical Jesus and the church's faith as useless grasps at worldly security in the form of objective knowledge. We will briefly survey Bultmann's thought under the two headings of "The Enlightenment Worldview" and "The Historical Jesus."

THE ENLIGHTENMENT WORLDVIEW

Like many German theologians in the wake of World War II, Bultmann wanted to make Christian faith a living option for modern people. His influential post-war essay "New Testament and Mythology" picked up a line of enlightened thought that we have seen previously in David Hume and D.F. Strauss. Hume's essay "Of Miracles" had appealed to the regularity of the laws of nature in its rejection of testimony to miracles. As his first criterion for distinguishing the mythical from the historical in the gospels, Strauss had appealed to "the known and universal laws which govern the course of events" (Strauss, *Life of Jesus*, 87–89, in

Livingston, 177). Bultmann makes a similar appeal, but instead of rejecting faith in Christ, he wants to reinterpret it.

> It is impossible to use electric light and the wireless and to avail ourselves of modern medical and surgical discoveries, and at the same time to believe in the New Testament world of spirits and miracles. We may think we can manage it in our own lives, but to expect others to do so is to make the Christian faith unintelligible and unacceptable to the modern world ("New Testament and Mythology," 5).

Bultmann presented his views to an American audience in a series of lectures at Yale in 1951, later published as *Jesus Christ and Mythology*. Modern science, he claimed, "does not believe that the course of nature can be interrupted or, so to speak, perforated, by supernatural powers" (15). "Modern man" acknowledges as real "only such phenomena or events as are comprehensible within the framework of the rational order of the universe." Miracles "do not fit into this lawful order" (37–38). To speak as if they do, to speak as if God were one among the various causes of things who sometimes intervenes in the causal chain, is to speak "mythologically." Like Hume, Bultmann rejects miracles as violations of the laws of nature. Like Strauss, he defines myth in terms of the laws of nature.

Must we then conclude that Bultmann's thought is entirely captive to the enlightenment worldview? This is not so easy. On the basis of the above, we might expect Bultmann to abandon his faith that God acted in Christ and continues to act today through the word that proclaims Christ. Instead he retains his faith in a paradoxical form. The eyes of faith identify what appears natural with God's action. Thus Bultmann claims to challenge the enlightenment worldview precisely in its obsession with objectivity, certitude, and proof in terms of the laws of nature. The proclamation of salvation in Christ is for Bultmann a kind of sacrament in which God calls forth the response of faith. "The invisibility of God excludes every myth that tries to make God and His action visible; God withholds Himself from view and observation. We can believe in God only in spite of experience, just as we can accept justification only in spite of conscience" (83–84).

THE HISTORICAL JESUS

Luther had distinguished faith from works and taught that we are saved by faith alone and not by our works. As the last quotation suggests, Bultmann gave his own personal interpretation to Luther's teaching on justification by faith alone. The less support it has in the human "works" of historical argument, the purer is our faith in Christ. In this idiosyncratic interpretation of Luther's faith-works distinction, our lack of historical knowledge about Jesus appears almost providential. It frees us from the temptation to think that our faith rests on some sort of objective proof.

In his treatment of the synoptic tradition, Bultmann thinks he has identified sets of laws or regular patterns that govern the transmission of oral tradition in its various forms. Oral transmission almost requires distortion. A faithful passage from the written gospels of stage 3 back to the historical Jesus of stage 1 is scarcely possible. From an historical point of view, the form critical study of the transmission of Jesus tradition tells us primarily about the early church rather than about Jesus. His book *Jesus and the Word* (1926) presents Bultmann's views on what little we know about the historical Jesus. He holds it as "certain that Jesus did not speak of his death and resurrection as redemptive acts" (214). "Greek Christianity's" attribution of a divine nature to Jesus "introduced a view of his person as far removed as possible from his own" (216).

The Jesus traditions were Hellenized, distorted by the influence of Greek religions. Bultmann accepts the history of religions school's sharp dichotomy between early Palestinian Christianity and later Hellenistic Christianity. In the Hellenization process, the language of incarnation, redemption, and resurrection has been borrowed from such Hellenistic religions as gnosticism and the mystery religions. Bultmann's application of the category of myth to the New Testament is relentless. His controversial program of "demythologizing" reinterprets the present personal meaning of what the New Testament proclaims in mythological form. His treatment of the New Testament's central claim that Jesus rose from the dead will serve as a good example.

From the perspective of reason or historical knowledge we are left with Jesus' death on the cross. This is the most certain fact we know about him. With regard to the resurrection, Bultmann asks in "New Testament and Mythology," "Is it not a completely mythical event?" (44). To demythologize the claim that Jesus rose bodily from the grave is to speak about the present meaning of the cross as God's act for us. "Faith in the Resurrection is really the same thing as faith in the saving efficacy of the cross" (41). The demythologized meaning of the mythological proclamation of the resurrection, therefore, is that God is offering us the present possibility of "new life" in Christ—a new kind of existence. About the resurrection as an event that happened to Jesus we can say nothing.

Difficulties

Although some find his resolute faith in the face of skepticism attractively heroic, Bultmann's skepticism about the historical Jesus and his radical interpretation of Christian faith make his theological position a difficult one for most believers to hold. Bultmann's position presents difficulties in the areas of faith and history, the enlightenment worldview, and an incarnational approach to Christianity.

FAITH AND HISTORY

Bultmann's emphasis on the discontinuity between faith and reason helps correct the modern fascination with objective proof. To appreciate his point, we need only recall that not all who witnessed the facts of Jesus' life became believers. Faith is personal and witnesses are not necessarily disciples. But in his concern to emphasize this, Bultmann needlessly exaggerates the separation between faith and reason. While faith moves beyond the merely historical, Christian preaching begins there. Unless the connection between Jesus as he actually was and as the church presents him is clearer than Bultmann would allow, it is difficult to understand how an intelligent person could be moved, even by God, to believe in the gospel.

THE ENLIGHTENMENT WORLDVIEW

In a chapter on gospel criticism, we have wound up talking about Bultmann's theology of faith. Historical investigation is difficult to separate from the assumptions of historians. Despite his desire to challenge modernity with the real gospel rather than an antiquated worldview, Bultmann's interpretation of the gospels as history has been unduly guided by a now outdated enlightenment view of the laws of nature. The universe of quantum physics and relativity is much more open and mysterious than was the universe of Newton and Hume. The history of theoretical science shows their "laws of nature" approach to be overly mechanical, overly confident, and overly closed. We are in a position to make room for more dramatic "acts of God," better interpreted as signs from or manifestations of God than as violations of nature's laws. The New Testament claim that God has done something unique and wonderful in Jesus Christ can be taken more seriously than Bultmann takes it. He is correct in pointing to our difficulty in imagining, conceiving, or speaking about how a truly transcendent, spiritual God might "act" or "do" things. But if it means anything to call God "Creator," we should allow God more room to move than Bultmann does.

INCARNATIONAL CHRISTIANITY

Bultmann's extreme iconoclasm minimizes any incarnational understanding of Jesus himself and of Christianity as a faith. Rather than Word made flesh, there is only Word. The point of Jesus as the "image of the invisible God" (Col 1:15) is dismissed as Hellenization. Despite the role of sacrament in Pauline and Johannine Christianity, there is little room in Bultmann's theology for the belief that God deals with us sacramentally in a consistent way that is suited to our bodily or incarnate condition.

MODERATE HISTORICAL CRITICISM

New Testament critics I have called moderates tend 1) to have a less drastic view than Bultmann of the distance separating reason from faith. It is important for them to be able to show a plausible connection between what the church believes and our historical knowledge about Jesus. This involves 2) a more critical approach to the enlightenment view of nature as a closed system of laws. Moderate critics, therefore, tend to be more open to the gospels' supernatural claims. And these critics are less committed to the view that the transmission of Jesus traditions necessarily involves Hellenizing distortions. Their use of form criticism emphasizes the solid base of the gospels in traditions that reach back faithfully to stage 1. In general moderate critics are concerned to disengage conclusions required on strictly historical grounds from conclusions required by the enlightenment worldview. The contemporary scholar who epitomizes moderate, or centrist, criticism, as he calls it, is Raymond E. Brown.

In Bultmann's own generation, scholars such as Joachim Jeremias (1900–1979) in Germany, Oscar Cullmann (1902–) in Switzerland, and Vincent Taylor (1887–1968) and C.H. Dodd (1884–1973) in England used form criticism to arrive at conclusions about the historical Jesus that challenged Bultmannian skepticism. Jeremias, in particular, has worked to show that the written gospels preserve some of Jesus' own words, in his own native language, and, further, that they hand on to us in reliable form his message and the basic ideas of his preaching. Jeremias' *New Testament Theology* (1971) provides a mature statement of his position.

Jeremias is a specialist in Aramaic, an ancient near eastern language akin to Hebrew and spoken in first century Palestine. When Jesus preached and taught by word of mouth, he would have spoken his words in Aramaic. Jeremias has searched the gospel traditions for residues of Aramaic vocabulary, word order, grammatical structure, etc. His many books on the words of Jesus, Jesus' prayers, parables, the eucharistic words, and the sermon on the mount present a convincing case for the faithfulness of the written gospels to the message of Jesus. One of his most controversial arguments is that the idea of Jesus' death as redemptive sacrifice in terms of Isaiah 53 should be attributed to Jesus himself, and not to the primitive community (*New Testament Theology*, 286–299).

One of Jeremias' most striking contributions to our knowledge about the historical Jesus is his work with the Aramaic term *Abba*. *Abba* appears in Mark 14:36 as the name Jesus uses to address the Father in prayer. It is an informal and intimate form of address whose meaning is similar to *Daddy* as it would be used by an adult child to address his or her father. Jeremias translates it as "dear Father."

Though his claims for the absolute uniqueness of Jesus' use of this term to address God have to be softened in light of recent research, his claims for its significance remain valid. If not unique, *Abba* is Jesus' distinctive way of addressing the Father in prayer. This Aramaic word, preserved in the gospel tradition, still bespeaks Jesus' sense of what the Father is like, as well as his own sense of intimacy with the Father. It remains important to know that he spoke to the Father "as a child to its father: confidently and securely, and yet at the same time reverently and obediently" (*New Testament Theology*, 67).

Another significant challenge to the skeptical application of form criticism comes from two Scandinavian scholars, Birger Gerhardsson and Harold Riesenfeld. They argue for the role of memorization as a rabbinic teaching device in the oral transmission of Jesus' words. Rabbis taught their disciples by word of mouth and the disciples were expected to remember the master's teaching. While they do not deny that the early church shaped the Jesus traditions, as form criticism has shown, they insist that the oral tradition of Jesus' words began during his ministry. Jesus' parables and sayings would have been memorized by his disciples. The literary structure of much of the material in the gospels, repetition, and parallelism would seem to lend itself to oral transmission.

In an accessible series of lectures published in 1977 as *The Origins of the Gospel Traditions*, Gerhardsson concludes that "in the synoptic Gospels we hear not only a whisper of the voice of Jesus, but are confronted with faithfully preserved words from the mouth of Jesus and reports which in the *end* go back to those who were with Jesus during his ministry in Galilee and Jerusalem" (90). While the position of Gerhardsson and Riesenfeld remains controversial, it offers a welcome corrective to mainstream views. It regards the process of transmission leading to the gospels as primarily preservative rather than creative.

The hypothesis of a sharp dichotomy between Palestinian and Hellenistic forms of Christianity has not fared as well in the second half of the twentieth century as it did in the first. It has been replaced by an emphasis on the diversity of first century Judaism in Palestine and the importance of Hellenistic Judaism as a medium for the spread of Christianity. Hellenistic Judaism rather than gnosticism or mystery religions is seen as the context for the early New Testament Christology found in Philippians 2, Colossians 1, John 1, and so on. In these texts, the Christological significance of Jesus is described in Greek terminology drawn from the Septuagint versions of Isaiah and the wisdom literature rather than from Hellenistic religions.

Earlier global hypotheses about the linear evolution of belief in Jesus' divinity have given way to an emphasis on the great diversity of New Testament Christology, the antiquity of some of its most exalted forms, and a growing consensus on at least an implicit Christology during Jesus' ministry. Aramaic studies have made significant contributions to our knowledge of early Palestinian Christianity. *Maranatha*, probably the first known Christian prayer, indicates that Palestinian Christians prayed to Jesus as Lord (*Maran*) in Aramaic. Archaeological discoveries such as the Dead Sea Scrolls have also enriched our knowledge of the diversity of first century Palestinian Judaism. Aspects of the Jesus tradition that were previously regarded as Hellenization have emerged as part of Jesus' own milieu.

Some scholars still treat the resurrection in a manner closer to Bultmann than to the Christological tradition. Others, such as the Lutheran theologian Wolfhart Pannenberg and the Catholic New Testament scholar Raymond E. Brown, have argued, on the basis of New Testament evidence, for the reality of Jesus' bodily resurrection as a primitive Christian belief.

THE CATHOLIC POSITION ON GOSPEL CRITICISM

Protestant scholars pioneered and developed the application of the historical-critical method to the Bible and to the gospels in particular. At the beginning of the twentieth century, the Catholic Church's teaching office tended to view such methods with suspicion. In 1902 Pope Leo XIII created the Pontifical Biblical Commission. Many hoped that it would help lead Catholic scholarship to a responsible appropriation of the new methods.

But between 1905 and 1915, the new commission issued precautionary decrees on such topics as the authorship of Genesis, Isaiah, and the gospels. Their conclusions had what we would now describe as a distinctively fundamentalist cast. With Pope

Pius X's condemnation of "modernism" in 1907, the leading Catholic biblical scholar, Alfred Loisy, was excommunicated. In the first decades of the twentieth century, the church's official magisterium seemed to have turned its back on the historical-critical study of the Bible.

But the magisterium's position on biblical criticism has changed and developed over the course of the century. The major turning point came when Pope Pius XII's 1943 encyclical, *Divino Afflante Spiritu*, opened the way for Catholic scholars to use historical-critical methods. Something very much like what I have described as moderate historical criticism represents the church's authoritative teaching on the subject of gospel criticism.

The Pontifical Biblical Commission's 1964 "Instruction on the Historical Truth of the Gospels" makes this clear. Interpreters of the gospels are encouraged to use historical methods of study, but the Instruction notes that form criticism is often found together with certain "rationalistic prejudices" that deny in principle the possibility of God's revelation. What is meant by this is the extreme form of what we have called the "enlightenment worldview," as represented by Hume, Strauss, and in some respects Bultmann.

The 1964 Instruction goes on to bid interpreters of the gospels to "take careful note of the three stages of tradition by which the teaching and life of Jesus have come down to us." The three stages are then described with emphasis placed on attention to the selection and arrangement of material by the "sacred authors." The key to the Instruction's approach is its insistence that the use of historical-critical method can be disengaged from the enlightenment worldview. This is the same position we have seen in Evangelical scholar George Ladd's book *The New Testament and Criticism*, and in the work of Raymond E. Brown, himself a former member of the Pontifical Biblical Commission. Brown's book *Biblical Exegesis and Church Doctrine* (1985) lays out in popular form his "centrist" position on the use of historical-critical method within the context of a believing church.

Vatican II's *Dogmatic Constitution on Divine Revelation* summarized the 1964 Instruction's approach to the gospels, citing the document itself in a footnote. After solemnly affirming the historical fidelity of the gospels to what Jesus did and taught, the council goes on to speak of the apostolic preaching, and then of the composition of the gospels.

> Next, inspired writers composed the four gospels, by various processes. They selected some things from the abundant material already handed down, orally or in writing. Other things they synthesized, or explained with a view to the needs of the churches. They preserved the preaching style, but worked throughout so as to communicate to us a true and sincere account of Jesus [here appears the footnote reference to the 1964 Instruction]; for whether they wrote from their own memory and recollections, or from the evidence of "those who from the beginning were eyewitnesses and ministers of the word," their intention was that we might know "the truth" concerning the things of which we have been informed (see Lk 1:2–4). Paragraph 19 (Tanner, II, 978–979).

CONCLUSION

None of this means that we have now proven that the historical Jesus is exactly what the tradition has always claimed him to be. But the initial rush of enlightened fervor has cooled down over the course of the twentieth century. Scholars can no longer responsibly dismiss the incarnation and the resurrection as Greek myth. The fact that Jesus was worshiped in a Palestinian setting, for example, is widely acknowledged. At the beginning of the twentieth century, it was easy to pit faith against reason, Jesus against Paul, Palestinian Christianity against Hellenistic Christianity, the Jesus of history against the Christ of faith. It is no longer so. Intelligent people can no longer be told, in the name of science and history, that it is intellectually dishonest to take the way of faith.

The key is to base historical conclusions about Jesus on historical evidence rather than on prior assumptions. Good historical critics must try to disengage their use of historical-critical method from the worldview in which that method originated. But the differences between conclusions based on the naturalistic assumptions of a David Hume and the solid results of historical investigation are not always easy to see. No scholar is deliberately uncritical.

Over the course of the twentieth century, moderate historical criticism has gained increasing respect on historical grounds. Many New Testament scholars have abandoned the grand schemes and scientific pretensions of the century's earlier generations. Assured results of historical investigation are often inconclusive, especially when working with such ancient sources as the gospels. Solid historical conclusions are often modest and limited. The more global speculations based on such conclusions have been increasingly recognized as related to prior assumptions, whether the latter be traditional or modern assumptions. The further we move from the closed, mechanical Newtonian universe of David Hume's natural laws, the less clear are the reasons for preferring modern secular assumptions to traditional Christian ones.

Questions for Review and Discussion

1. What is the characteristic religious belief of twentieth century fundamentalists? How does this belief distinguish fundamentalists from both skeptical and moderate historical critics?

2. Describe the common framework in which twentieth century New Testament critics (both skeptics and moderates) do their work.

3. What is the "synoptic problem" and what is the most commonly accepted solution to it?

4. Define and distinguish among source, form, and redaction criticism.

5. What two factors distinguish skeptical from moderate critics of the New Testament gospels?

6. What is the "enlightenment worldview" (recall the previous chapter)? What does it mean to say that someone is "committed" to it? Give at least two examples from the text of how Bultmann's commitment to the enlightenment worldview influenced his interpretation of the New Testament.

7. At what points in his thought does Bultmann challenge the enlightenment worldview?

8. How did Luther's distinction between faith and works and his teaching on justification by faith alone influence Bultmann's understanding of the religious value of historical research, i.e. the relationship between faith and history discussed at the beginning of the last chapter?

9. What are some of the difficulties with Bultmann's thought?

10. Contrast the approaches of Bultmann and Jeremias to the words of Jesus as they are reported in the gospels.

11. What are some of the arguments used by Jeremias, and by Gerhardsson and Riesenfeld, to defend the basic faithfulness of the gospels to Jesus' preaching? Do their arguments have as much plausibility as Bultmann's? Explain. What might incline you to accept one rather than the other?

12. Discuss the significance of the Aramaic word *Abba*.

13. What is the Catholic Church's official position on the application of historical criticism to the Bible and to the gospels in particular? How has this position developed over the course of the twentieth century? What is its attitude toward the enlightenment worldview?

For Writing and Reflection

1. Using examples, write an essay that compares and contrasts skeptical and moderate historical criticism of the gospels. Explain how skeptical and moderate criticism, taken together, differ from fundamentalism. Argue for or against the thesis: One can apply the ideal of critical history to the gospels without accepting completely, or in all of its consequences, the enlightenment worldview.

2. At the beginning of *Jesus and the Word*, in the process of dismissing interest in Jesus' "personality," Bultmann remarks almost offhandedly, "I do indeed think we can know almost nothing concerning the life and personality of Jesus . . ." (8). (The book is an historical study of Jesus' teaching rather than his life.) Read either, 1) the sections on miracle, prayer and

faith in *Jesus and the Word* (172–191), or 2) the section on "The Meaning of God as Acting" (60–85) in *Jesus Christ and Mythology*. Then write an essay on how Bultmann maintains his intellectual and religious balance as both an historical skeptic and a very serious Christian believer.

For Further Reading

J.S. Kselman and R.D. Witherup, "Modern New Testament Criticism," in R.E. Brown et al., eds., *New Jerome Biblical Commentary*, pp. 1130–1145. Excellent historical overview of the material in this chapter, includes explanations of the various kinds of criticism.

George Marsden, *Fundamentalism and American Culture, The Shaping of Twentieth-Century Evangelicalism, 1870–1925* (New York: Oxford University Press, 1982). The standard history of fundamentalism.

Harold Lindsell, *The Battle for the Bible* (Grand Rapids, Mich.: Zondervan, 1976). A lively contemporary defense of strict inerrancy or "plenary verbal inerrancy."

J.I. Packer, *God Has Spoken* (Downers Grove, Ill.: Intervarsity Press, 1979). The Appendix contains "The Chicago Statement on Biblical Inerrancy" (1978), pp. 138–153.

George Ladd, *The New Testament and Criticism* (Grand Rapids, Mich.: Eerdmans, 1984). An Evangelical scholar's clearly written defense of and introduction to New Testament criticism.

Rudolf Bultmann, *Jesus and the Word* (New York: Charles Scribner's Sons, 1958). Bultmann's own historical account of Jesus' teaching. Originally published in 1926. Pages 172–191 are especially worthwhile on the religious topics of miracles, prayer and faith.

————, "New Testament and Mythology," in Hans Werner Bartsch, ed., *Kerygma and Myth by Rudolf Bultmann and Five Critics* (New York: Harper Torchbooks, 1961). This is a symposium featuring Bultmann's programmatic essay on de-mythologizing the New Testament.

————, *Jesus Christ and Mythology* (New York: Charles Scribner's Sons, 1958). This is a series of popular lectures delivered by Bultmann on his program of demythologizing. The last lecture on "The Meaning of God as Acting" provides a glimpse into Bultmann as an insightful and paradoxical religious thinker.

————, *The History of the Synoptic Tradition* (New York: Scribner's, 1963). While the three previous works of Bultmann are popular presentations of his thought, this one shows Bultmann the form critic at work. His judgments on the historical reliability of the traditions he studies in this work provide justification for classifying him as a "skeptical" critic.

Joachim Jeremias, *The Prayers of Jesus* (Philadelphia: Fortress Press, 1978). The first half of this book contains a long essay on *Abba*, an excellent entry into the work of Jeremias.

————, *New Testament Theology* (New York: Charles Scribner's Sons, 1971). This is a systematic presentation of Jeremias' historical assessment of the reliability of the traditions about Jesus.

Raymond E. Brown, *Biblical Exegesis and Church Doctrine* (New York/Mahwah: Paulist Press, 1985). A popular presentation of biblical scholarship for a Catholic audience by a distinguished New Testament scholar.

Joseph A. Fitzmyer, S.J., *A Christological Catechism, New Testament Answers* (New York/Ramsey: Paulist Press, 1991). This book contains the 1964 "Instruction on the Historical Truth of the Gospels" from the Pontifical Biblical Commission along with Fitzmyer's detailed commentary.

Raymond E. Brown, S.S. and Thomas Aquinas Collins, O.P., "Church Pronouncements," in R.E. Brown et al., eds., *New Jerome Biblical Commentary*, pp. 1166–1174. A useful survey of church pronouncements on biblical study. They are concentrated mostly in the twentieth century.

Terms To Identify

synoptic problem

setting in life (*Sitz im Leben*)

pericope

Abba

form criticism

source criticism

redaction criticism

myth (Bultmann)

"Instruction on the Historical
Truth of the Gospels"

Rudolf Bultmann

Joachim Jeremias

Aramaic

demythologize

literary form

plenary verbal inerrancy

fundamentalism

two-source theory

Q

Chapter XI

An Historical-Theological Portrait of Jesus
Part I: Jesus in Context

JESUS AND JUDAISM: CONTINUITY OR DISCONTINUITY

Treatments of Christology often begin with what is described as a consensus on our historical knowledge about Jesus. The spectrum of positions in New Testament scholarship, however, often makes such claims about consensus controversial. Because of the limited nature of our sources for knowledge about the historical Jesus, and because of the rich diversity of first century Palestinian Judaism, the historical conclusions upon which such claims for consensus are based are often highly speculative.

In explaining the consensus, theologians usually refer to the various criteria New Testament scholars have developed for identifying authentic sayings of Jesus. One of the most commonly used is the criterion of discontinuity or dissimilarity. According to this, when traditions about Jesus cannot be derived from or are discontinuous with either what we know of first century Palestinian Judaism or of the beliefs and practices of the early church or both, they are taken to be authentic. This is because Jesus' own originality is the most plausible historical explanation for their presence in the tradition.

Another significant criterion, however, is the criterion of coherence or continuity. According to this criterion, the coherence or continuity of the gospels in general or of particular traditions with what we know about first century Palestine on other grounds lends them a certain historical plausibility. Though scholars formulate these two criteria with differing shades of emphasis, they agree that these and other criteria must be applied convergently

247

rather than in isolation. The books by Ben F. Meyer, John P. Meier and Edward Schillebeeckx listed at the end of this chapter provide discussions of the criteria used in making historical judgments about the sayings of Jesus.

The obvious tension between the criterion of discontinuity or dissimilarity and the criterion of coherence or continuity reveals the basic question involved in trying to reach a consensus about the historical Jesus: How are we to understand Jesus' relationship to Judaism? To what extent is he continuous with the Jewish environment of first century Palestine? To what extent is he discontinuous with this context? If we add to this the rich diversity of first century Palestinian Judaism, these questions become more complex. We must ask about the specific forms of Palestinian Judaism to which the questions of continuity and discontinuity apply.

When one sets out to sketch Jesus' historical portrait, one can exaggerate from either side of the crucial question about Jesus and Judaism. First, Christians who wish to emphasize what is unique about Jesus, and by implication about Christianity, often do so at the expense of Judaism. The portrayal of Judaism as a merely external ritualistic or mechanical religion sets the stage for Jesus to play Martin Luther to first century Palestine's prototype of Roman Catholicism, the much-maligned Pharisees. The fact that the gospels portray Jesus as an observant Jew is lost.

On the other side, Christians who wish to emphasize the "Jewishness of Jesus," or his continuity with his Jewish heritage and environment, have greater difficulty explaining some of the more obvious facts about Jesus and the early church, namely, Jesus' death by execution and the early conflicts that led to the separation of Christians from Judaism. Within the basic context of continuity, therefore, tension or discontinuity must be sufficient to explain Jesus' execution and the separation of church and synagogue.

As if this complexity were not enough, new discoveries and scholarly perspectives have brought to late twentieth century work on the historical Jesus an emphasis on the diversity of first century Palestinian Judaism. As various scholars have emphasized different aspects of that context, the effort to situate Jesus in his Jewish context has produced diverse results. Thus the latter decades of the twentieth century have witnessed books on Jesus as zealot, magician, rabbi, Essene, eschatological prophet, and peasant Jewish cynic. Each of these portraits focuses on a different aspect of the diverse forms of Judaism that existed prior to the virtual destruction of Palestinian Judaism by the Romans between A.D. 70 and A.D. 136.

Consensus on the historical Jesus comes to grief on the question of Jesus' relationship to the diverse Judaism of his day. This chapter, therefore, refrains from presenting any so-called consensus of New Testament scholarship on the historical Jesus. Given the limited nature of the sources, any author's version of the "consensus" would no doubt reflect his or her own theological views. This is not bad, however, as long as one doesn't try to clothe the speculative aspects of any interpretation of New Testament scholarship with the mantle of pure objective history. Nor does it mean that we can't have reliable knowledge about the historical Jesus. Rather, it means that one's historical reconstruction, i.e. how one organizes this knowledge, how one shades and focuses the portrait, will be influenced by other than purely historical considerations. One's own religious history and commitments are prime examples of such other than purely historical considerations. Rather than being entitled "An Historical Portrait of Jesus," therefore, this chapter is called "An Historical-Theological Portrait of Jesus." The designation of Jesus as God's Son-Servant-Wisdom is a limited attempt to take account of various locations within Judaism with which historically reliable traditions about Jesus can be associated.

Chapter VIII has presented the church's faith about Jesus as the Christ, the Son of God. Modern suspicions that classical Christology cannot be reconciled with history have been surveyed in Chapter IX. The present chapter will present a historical-theological portrait of Jesus. It has four goals:

1) to take seriously modern suspicions about the historical reliability of the New Testament sources;

2) to interpret the sources in a way that is both historically plausible and defensible, as well as

3) compatible with the traditional expressions of the church's faith about Jesus;

4) to present a religiously compelling portrait of Jesus capable of functioning religiously in the lives of contemporary people.

FIRST CENTURY PALESTINE

The Palestine of Jesus' day was a small strip of land about the size of the state of New Jersey. It included most of the territory now controlled by the contemporary state of Israel. It is located on the southeastern shore of the Mediterranean Sea, its natural western boundary. To the north and inland is the Sea of Galilee. The Jordan River, which begins in the mountains north of Palestine, flows into the Sea of Galilee. The Jordan continues its southward flow into the Dead Sea, a large salt lake at the lowest point on earth.

Between the Mediterranean and the north-south water network of the Sea of Galilee-Jordan River-Dead Sea, Palestine was divided into three parts: Galilee to the north, Samaria in the middle and Judea in the south. Galilee had fertile farmland and the Sea of Galilee or Lake Gennesareth supported a significant fishing industry. Further south the land becomes more rugged and desert-like.

Within this relatively small area Jesus spent his life. The names of its towns and regions dot the gospels. Chief among them is the religious, commercial, and political center of ancient Israel, the city of Jerusalem. Jerusalem was built on a group of Judean hills not far from the northern banks of the Dead Sea. Galilee to the north was the site of Jesus' hometown of Nazareth, as well as most of his ministry. Many of his first disciples were Galileans. Its landscape and social and commercial structure provide the background for most of Jesus' parables. The land between Galilee and Judea was called Samaria. In the post-exilic period, the Samaritans had developed their own form of Judaism. It centered on their temple at Mount Gerizim near ancient Shechem. The journey from northern Galilee to Jerusalem, which Jesus made at least once, approximates the length of the New Jersey Turnpike, some hundred miles.

In the time of Jesus, even as it does today, Palestine occupied a strategic location in the Near East. Commercial and military traffic between Egypt and the various empires of Mesopotamia, site of present-day Iran and Iraq, had to cross Israel. Later it would serve as a buffer between the competing Greek centers of Alexandria and Antioch.

CULTURE

From Alexander to the Hasmoneans

Jesus or Yeshua was a first century Palestinian Jew. We begin with the supposition that any historically informed religious interpretation of him must place him in the context of first century Palestinian Judaism. The Jewish encounter with Greek culture in the centuries before Jesus helped determine the shape of the Judaism into which he was born. This encounter began nearly three centuries before Jesus under the Macedonian conqueror and apostle of Greek culture, Alexander the Great (d. 323 B.C.).

The Alexandrian conquest and its aftermath presented Judaism with a cosmopolitan culture. They responded by reinterpreting such traditional beliefs as Jewish election and covenant in a more self-consciously universal perspective. In the encounter with Greek culture, development of traditional Jewish beliefs about Torah, wisdom, and God's role in history helped to provide the basic categories, e.g. wisdom and resurrection, that would eventually be used to explain Jesus' significance to the Greek-speaking peoples to whom the New Testament was addressed. The Jewish encounter with Greek culture made it humanly possible for Jesus to take on a broader, more universal meaning, grounded religiously in Judaism, but extending beyond what we might call ethnic and national boundaries.

One of the most important developments at this time took place in the area of eschatology. *Eschatology* literally means talking about the last things. It refers to the religious view of history found in the prophetic tradition of Israel, e.g. in Isaiah. An eschatological view of history is future-oriented, looking forward in hope to a decisive revelation of God. Under Greek persecution and the fierce struggle for independence from the Seleucids, Jews who were the forerunners of the Pharisees of Jesus' day went to the resources of their prophetic tradition. Their expressions of eschatological hope took the form of apocalyptic (see Chapter IX, p. II) as we find it in the book of Daniel.

It is important to emphasize that Greek influence on Judaism need not be interpreted as a corruption or distortion of the ancient faith. As a living faith tradition, Judaism had encountered world empires before and had responded with religious developments of its own traditions. Attention to the Jewish response to the Hellenistic worldview helps to explain the particular form Judaism took in Jesus' day. His contemporaries and those who came before them were divided according to their diverse responses to the challenges posed by Greek culture. People can respond to the cultural influence of a foreign conquest in two ways: resistance (separatism) and accommodation (assimilation). In the centuries before Jesus, Judaism experienced a dialectic of Hellenization and separatism.

With Alexander's death at the age of 32, his generals divided up the lands he had won. Chief among them were Ptolemy, whose base of power was in Alexandria in Egypt, and Seleucus, whose base was in Antioch in Syria. The Ptolemies, with their capital city at Alexandria, ruled Israel. Greek influence or Hellenization came first to the educated and those involved in commerce or political administration. All of these affairs were conducted in a dialect of Greek known as *koinē*, which became the chief vehicle of Greek influence. During this period, the Hebrew scriptures were translated into Greek at Alexandria (the Septuagint). The Old Testament books of Ecclesiastes (Qoheleth), Wisdom, and Sirach (Ecclesiasticus) reflect a spectrum of responses to Judaism's encounter with the Hellenistic worldview.

The Hasmonean Revolt

In 198 B.C. the Seleucids took control of Israel. The intensified pressure to Hellenize was symbolized by the building of a Greek gymnasium in Jerusalem in 175. Some among its elite would have made Jerusalem into a Greek city-state in the Seleucid empire. Antiochus IV was a Seleucid king who took his divine pretensions seriously and tried to put an end to traditional Jewish worship and observance in his kingdom. By 167 he had abolished the Jewish law. In his efforts at "abolishing traditional laws and customs" (1 Macc 3:30), he was probably aided by a group of Jewish reformers at Jerusalem. They had achieved influence in the previous decade and favored radical accommodations to Hellenistic civilization, including the abandonment of the law (Torah) and the sacrifices it prescribed.

The situation is reflected in this general description from the first chapter of 1 Maccabees, a strongly anti-Greek source.

> In those days there appeared in Israel men who were breakers of the law, and they seduced many people, saying: "Let us go and make an alliance with the Gentiles all around us; since we separated from them, many evils have come upon us." The proposal was agreeable; some from among the people promptly went to the king, and he authorized them to introduce the way of living of the Gentiles. Thereupon they built a gymnasium in Jerusalem according to the Gentile custom. They covered over the mark of their circumcision and abandoned the holy covenant; they allied themselves with the Gentiles and sold themselves to wrongdoing (1 Macc 1:11–15).

Antiochus had hoped that religious unity might help him raise the revenue he needed for his wars against the Ptolemies and the Romans. But on his return from a campaign in Egypt, upon hearing of a Jewish insurrection in Jerusalem, Antiochus plundered the temple and set up a statue of Zeus, "the abomination of desolation" (1 Macc 1:54), on the altar in its inner sanctum, the holy of holies. This happened in 167.

Rather than offer the prescribed pagan sacrifices in their hometown, the priest Mattathias of Modin and his five sons began a guerrilla resistance to the Seleucid armies and mercenaries who had been sent to enforce the king's Hellenizing policies. "Zeal for the law" is the phrase 1 Maccabees uses repeatedly to characterize Mattathias and his sons. Mattathias died in 166 B.C. and his son Judas Maccabeus (the hammer) took command of the resistance. With his brothers Simon and Jonathan, who eventually became high priest, Judas successfully led the Jewish resistance to the Seleucids. Their family was known as the Hasmoneans. Within two years the statue of Zeus was removed and the temple rededicated (1 Maccabees 4). Hanukkah commemorates this event. By 142 B.C., the Seleucids granted Israel's independence. The Hasmoneans had won.

"Zeal for the law" generated a broad coalition of support for the Hasmoneans. The priestly core was joined by the Hasidim, or "assembly of the pious" (1 Macc 2:42), known for their devotion to the law. The break-up of this coalition against the radical Hellenizers of the second century gave rise to the parties or division in the Palestinian Judaism of Jesus' day. These are the three "sects" or "philosophical sects" spoken of by the historian Josephus (A.D. 37–ca. 100) in his *Antiquities of the Jews*, 13.6 and *Jewish War*, 2.8: the Pharisees, Essenes, and Sadducees.

Pharisees, Essenes, and Sadducees

Pharisees: The Pharisees, who occupy a prominent place in the gospels, are descended from the Hasidim, or "pious ones," of the Maccabean period. Their reinterpretation of the prophetic tradition of Israel in the context of the Seleucid persecution and the Maccabean resistance gave rise to Jewish apocalyptic as we find it in the book of Daniel, especially chapters 7–12. With the exception of the earlier Isaiah 26:19, the book of Daniel (12:2–3) contains the first scriptural reference to the characteristic Pharisaic belief in the resurrection of the dead (Hengel, I, 196). In addition to their reinterpretation of the prophetic tradition into an epochal vision of universal history with Israel at the center, the Hasidim expressed their devotion to the law by their efforts to carry the holiness of the temple over into everyday life. The Pharisees, therefore, tried to live the law as perfectly as possible, according to a spirituality especially suited to those who were not priests. Their teachers built up a formidable body of oral commentary on the law.

The Pharisees of Jesus' time had two characteristic religious beliefs. The first was intense "zeal for the law." This zeal committed them not only to the written Torah but to the body of oral commentary that had grown up around it. The second was belief in the resurrection of the dead involving some degree of commitment to an apocalyptic interpretation of salvation history.

Far from being synonymous with hypocrisy, Pharisaism was a serious religious commitment that stood for the best of popular Jewish piety or religious devotion. After the Romans destroyed the temple at Jerusalem in A.D. 70, Pharisaism became the major vehicle for the survival of Judaism as a living faith.

Essenes: Mentioned by both Philo, a first century Alexandrian Jewish philosopher, and the historian Josephus, the Essenes remained something of a mystery until the 1947 discovery of their community's library at Qumran near the Dead Sea. The Dead Sea Scrolls show that the community's leader was known as the Teacher of Righteousness, probably a Zadokite, or member of the priestly nobility. A central part of his "zeal for the law" involved devotion to the priesthood. It is probable that the Teacher of Righteousness and his followers withdrew their support from the Hasmoneans and the temple at Jerusalem when the Hasmonean Jonathan, one of Mattathias' sons, became high priest. The Essenes rejected the worship of God at the temple of Jerusalem.

The core of this group lived a community- or monastic-style life in the caves around the Dead Sea at Qumran. They were celibates who practiced frequent rituals of washing and sacred meals and took in orphans and widows. Their interpretation of the history of salvation tended to be apocalyptic. They emphasized the need for repentance and lived in expectation of Israel's deliverance from the Hasmonean betrayal. The Essenes represented the most extreme form of separatism as a response to the encounter with Greek culture.

Sadducees: The third "sect" mentioned by Josephus, and probably the one to which he belonged, was the Sadducees. The radical Hellenizers of second century Jerusalem had been crushed in the Hasmonean revolt. But once the Hasmoneans themselves came to power, they became increasingly Hellenized within the context of continued commitment to the written Torah, which the radical Hellenizers had rejected. As their experience brought them closer to political "realism," their view of history became increasingly secularized and distanced from the apocalyptic views of the Hasidim, who became the Pharisees and the Essenes. In addition to Jonathan's becoming high priest, the Hasmoneans made alliances with Greek rulers and added Gentile territories to the kingdom of Israel, further alienating their support among the Hasidim. The priestly families who remained loyal to the Hasmonean kingdom developed into the Sadducee party. Centered on the temple at Jerusalem, the Sadducees regarded both

Pharisaic devotion to oral tradition as well as the Pharisaic and
Essene tendency to view history apocalyptically as innovations.
As illustrated by Mark 12:18–25, Sadducees tended to ridicule
belief in the resurrection of the dead. They regarded the Pharisees as superstitious. Though the Pharisees regarded them as
worldly and skeptical, the Sadducees remained faithful to the
practice of Torah. Annas and Caiaphas (Lk 3:2; John 18) would
have been Sadducees.

In explaining to a Hellenistic audience, Josephus, himself a
member of the priestly aristocracy, emphasized the difference in
their attitude toward "fate." The tendency of the Pharisees and
the Essenes to view God's sovereignty over history in apocalyptic
terms appears in the Hellenistic worldview as belief in fate. By
contrast the more educated and urbane Sadducees attributed evil
to human folly rather than to divine chastisement (*Antiquities*,
12.5). Josephus' own histories can be read as an alternative or
corrective to apocalyptic interpretations of Jewish history of the
sort we find in Daniel.

Romans and Herods

To fill in the picture of Palestinian culture in Jesus' time, it
remains to explain the Roman presence and the role of Herod the
Great (d. 4 B.C.) and his family. In 64 B.C. the weakened
Hasmonean dynasty suffered a crisis of succession. Both Pharisees and Sadducees were in communication with the Roman
leader Pompey, whose military forces constituted a formidable
presence in the eastern Mediterranean area. In 63 B.C. Pompey
occupied Jerusalem and Israel's brief century of independence
came to an end.

By 37 B.C. the Romans had chosen Herod as local ruler of
Palestine. Herod came from Idumea, a territory to the south of
Judea that the Hasmoneans had annexed to Israel. Herod's educa-
tion had thoroughly imbued him with Hellenistic culture. Because
of this and his ethnic background, the Pharisees and their support-
ers opposed him, and he never achieved popular support in Israel.
He began the rebuilding of the temple at Jerusalem as well as
many other architectural projects including fortresses and pagan

shrines. Josephus, whose sources were not particularly sympathetic to Herod, portrayed him as ruthlessly cruel (*Antiquities*, 14–17).

Herod died around 4 B.C., and his kingdom was eventually divided among three of his sons. Archelaus ruled Judea and Samaria as Roman representative for Palestine. In A.D. 6 the Romans deposed and exiled him for cruelty and incompetence. Philip ruled the areas to the east of Galilee. Herod Antipas was tetrarch of Galilee during the time of Jesus. Antipas beheaded John the Baptist (Mk 6:17–29; Mt 14:3–12; Josephus, *Antiquities*, 18.5). Because Jesus was a Galilean, Pontius Pilate sent him to Herod Antipas before condemning him to death (Lk 23:6–12). In the gospels, Jews loyal to the Herod family are called "Herodians." In Mark 12:13, they are seen asking Jesus if it is lawful to pay taxes to the Roman emperor. While the Herods were indeed stand-ins for the Romans in Palestine, their wily ruthlessness in defense of their own interests belies their common designation as Rome's "puppets."

After the Romans exiled Archelaus, the emperor sent a prefect to govern Judea and Samaria. This explains the presence of Pontius Pilate in Judea at the time of Jesus' trial. Josephus (*Antiquities*, 18.3–4; *War*, 2.9) provides an account of Pilate's tenure in Judea, including a reference to Jesus' execution under him. The sanhedrin, a council composed of both Pharisees and Sadducees, priests and laity, and presided over by the high priest, represented the limited autonomy the Romans allowed in Judea and probably dated back to the days of Ptolemaic rule. Taxes were heavy and went to support the Romans as well as the temple and the Herods. Publicans or tax collectors, those who took money from their own people to give to the conquerors, were looked down upon as disloyal and dishonest.

Though not exhaustive, historical sources about Jesus' world are quite substantial. They include the deuterocanonical books and intertestamental literature, Josephus and other historical works as well as the Dead Sea Scrolls. The gospels portray a first century Palestine that is consistent with what we know from other sources. In addition, these sources help us to understand what the gospels say.

Summary

1) The Judaism of Jesus' day was divided between pious separatists like the Pharisees and the Essenes and worldly-wise assimilationists like the Sadducees and Herodians. Since the radical challenge to Torah that preceded the Hasmonean revolt, Jews of whatever party or sect were united in their support for Torah. Those who even appeared to attack it would not be tolerated.

2) Since the Hasmonean revolt, a popular vision of eschatology or salvation history had arisen. Exemplified by the book of Daniel, where we find the mysterious Son of Man figure, this apocalyptic reinterpretation of the prophets tended to see the world history that included Greek and Roman conquerors as under God's sovereignty and divided up into epochs. In figures such as the Teacher of Righteousness and John the Baptist, these views included the traditional prophetic call for repentance.

3) Beneath all of this lingered the subversive memory of Judas Maccabeus and the hundred years of Jewish independence under the Hasmoneans. In the context of the new reinterpretation of salvation history, those who suffered under the Romans continued to name their children Judas and Simon (see Mt 13:55) and hoped that God would anoint another deliverer. In the decades after Jesus' death, such sentiments would give rise to the nationalist Zealot movement and their unsuccessful revolts in A.D. 67 and 132.

WHERE DOES JESUS FIT?

Despite his devotion to the law, his use of apocalyptic language, and other points of contact, attempts to locate Jesus on this religious spectrum encounter his resistance to easy categorization. Interpreting him solely as a rabbi or as an apocalyptic prophet like the Teacher of Righteousness or John the Baptist accounts neither for all the data about him nor for his powerful impact on history. Jesus' Galilean origin helps to account for some of the difficulty in placing him. Galilean Judaism, while devoted to both the law and the temple, was not generally as strict as that of the Judean Pharisees or the Essenes.

In the midst of all this continuity and discontinuity, one of the most striking things about Jesus is the way he talks about God. God is the merciful Father who clothes the lilies of the field and the birds of the air, who numbers the hairs on our heads and who makes the sun to rise and set on both the good and the bad alike. Since his unique relationship with the Father is also the focus of classical Christology, the following brief historical-theological portrait of Jesus will have as its theme Jesus and the Father.

DID JESUS REALLY EXIST?

In this chapter so far we have spoken about Jesus in a way that assumes his historical existence. If modern suspicions about the historical worth of the New Testament sources are to be taken seriously, we must now briefly address the question of Jesus' historical existence. Is there sufficient historical evidence outside the Bible for an otherwise intelligent person to conclude that there really was a Jesus of Nazareth? That such evidence exists is clear to most people who have examined the sources available. In addition to the writings of Flavius Josephus already mentioned, we can also consult a number of Roman writers who mention Jesus in passing.

The Testimony of Josephus

Josephus, who was born around A.D. 37, wrote the *Antiquities of the Jews* during the reign of the emperor Domitian (A.D. 81–96). *Antiquities*, 18.3 contains a well-known and controversial reference to Jesus. Most commentators agree that it has been tampered with by the hand of a Christian interpolator. Later in the same work, in his account of the death of James of Jerusalem, Josephus refers to James as "the brother of Jesus the so-called Christ" (*Antiquities*, 20.9; cf. Acts 15:13; 21:19; Gal 2:12 on James). This throw-away reference to Jesus the so-called Christ strongly suggests that Josephus had mentioned him earlier. On the other hand, the passage about Jesus describes him in terms an unbelieving writer would not use. This leads to the conclusion that Josephus' original reference to Christ was tampered with by a Christian scribe.

A listing of some of the troubles that beset Pontius Pilate's procuratorship provides the context for Josephus' reference to Jesus. This passage is sometimes known as the *Testimonium Flavianum*. The third chapter of Meier's *A Marginal Jew* is devoted to a discussion of Josephus as a source for historical knowledge about Jesus. The burden of the discussion deals with the controversial *Testimonium Flavianum*. Meier removes what he takes to be the recognizable Christian interpolations in the passage. He then offers a widely accepted reconstruction of the original text. He concludes that Josephus provides us with a late first century Jewish witness to some basic facts about Jesus' life. Here is the *Testimonium Flavianum* in Meier's reconstructed translation:

> At this time there appeared Jesus, a wise man. For he was a doer of startling deeds, a teacher of people who receive truth with pleasure. And he gained a following both among many Jews and among many of Greek origin. And when Pilate, because of an accusation made by the leading men among us, condemned him to the cross, those who had loved him previously did not cease to do so. And up until this very day the tribe of Christians (named after him) has not died out (Meier, 61).

The Testimony of Suetonius and Tacitus

Writing around A.D. 120, in a series of works on the *Lives of the Caesars*, the Roman historian Suetonius mentions in his *Life of Claudius* that emperor's expulsion of the Jews from Rome in A.D. 49. Widespread rioting (probably between Jews and Christians) occasioned this measure. Suetonius mentions "the instigation of Chrestus," probably a variant spelling of Christus. Acts 18:2 mentions St. Paul's meeting at Corinth with a husband and wife team of Christian missionaries, "a Jew named Aquila, a native of Pontus, who had recently come from Italy with his wife Priscilla because Claudius had ordered all the Jews to leave Rome." These two references combine to indicate a relatively early Christian presence in the Jewish community at Rome.

Claudius died in A.D. 54. Within a decade Jews and Christians again flourished at Rome. In A.D. 64 a great fire broke out in the city. Writing around A.D. 115, the Roman historian Tacitus tells the story of the fire and of how Claudius' successor, Emperor Nero, tried to blame the fire on the Christians. At this time, Nero began the first police action or persecution against the Christians at Rome. During it both Peter and Paul died. Tacitus' reference to Christ appears in the context of his identification of the Christians as the group on to which Nero tried to shift the blame for the fire. Rumor had it that Nero had started the fire himself. In the *Annals*, 15.38 (Loeb edition), Tacitus wrote:

> Christus, the founder of the name [Christians], had undergone the death penalty in the reign of Tiberius, by sentence of the procurator [*sic*] Pontius Pilate, and the pernicious superstition was checked for a moment, only to break out once more, not merely in Judaea, the home of the disease, but in the capital itself [Rome], where all things vile or shameful in the world collect and find a vogue.

Tacitus went on to describe the cruel details of the punishment the Roman Christians received.

The Testimony of Pliny the Younger

During the reign of Emperor Trajan (98–117), Pliny served as imperial legate in Bithynia, a part of what is now northern Turkey. The Romans looked upon the growing Christian movement much as we might look upon cults. Tacitus, as we have seen, called Christianity a "disease." Pliny called it a "depraved and excessive superstition." The Romans feared and persecuted groups such as the early Christians because, in the words of Emperor Trajan: "Any organization which brings men together, whatever its original and ostensible purpose may be, sooner or later develops into a secret society with subversive political aims" (cited from one of Trajan's replies to Pliny by F.F. Bruce, *Jesus and Christian Origins*, 24).

Due to this suspicion of what we might call free associations, the Romans engaged in periodic police actions against Christians. The Christian population of Bithynia was growing and Pliny wrote a letter to Emperor Trajan seeking his instructions on how to handle the police measures designed to stop Christianity's growth and reclaim the people for more traditional religious practices. At the end of his letter, Pliny notes that, as a result of his persecution, people have returned to the abandoned temples and neglected religious services, and the sale of sacrificial animals is on the rise. Perhaps it was the aggrieved merchants who sold animals and their fodder who posted the anonymous list of Christians Pliny mentions at the beginning of his letter.

He went on to describe the police measures he took against the Christians. He had them interrogated—women deacons were interrogated under torture—to learn about the activities of the Christians. He required them to curse Christ and burn incense before images of the emperor and Roman gods, "none of which acts, it is said, those who are really Christians can be forced into performing." Pliny goes on to report what he had learned about Christian activities and it is in this context that he mentions Christ in passing, just as he had when he talked about requiring accused Christians to curse Christ.

> They affirmed, however, the whole of their guilt, or their error, was, that they were in the habit of meeting on a certain fixed day before it was light, when they sang in alternate verses a hymn to Christ, as to a god, and bound themselves by a solemn oath, not to any wicked deeds, but never to commit any fraud, theft or adultery, never to falsify their word, nor deny a trust when they should be called upon to deliver it up; after which it was their custom to separate, and then reassemble to partake of food—but food of an ordinary and innocent kind. Even this practice, however, they had abandoned after the publication of my edict, by which, according to your orders, I had forbidden political associations. I judged it so much the more necessary to extract the real truth, with the assistance of torture, from two female slaves, who were styled *deaconesses*: but I could discover nothing more than depraved and excessive superstition (*The Letters of Pliny*, Loeb Edition, II, Letter XCVI).

Conclusions about Jesus from Extra-Biblical Testimony

While there are references to Christ in other early extra-biblical literature, those mentioned above are significant and from them we can draw some modest conclusions.

1. Jesus is remembered in the context of the church. He would have had no significance at all to the Romans were it not for the Christian movement. As early as the fourth decade of the first century, it had already spread to the capital city. Josephus, Tacitus, and Pliny all use the term *Christians*. From their point of view, Christ is only worthy of mention as "the founder of the name" (Tacitus) or the one from whom "the tribe of Christians" took its name (Josephus).

2. Christ was executed under Pontius Pilate during the reign of Emperor Tiberius. Both Tacitus and Josephus mention his execution. From a purely historical point of view, it is the most certain fact we can affirm about him.

3. Jesus was remembered as a teacher and a wonder-worker. Josephus calls him "a wise man," a "doer of startling deeds."

4. Finally, we know something of how the Romans perceived the religious claims Christians made for Christ. For Tacitus and Pliny, *Christus* has become a name that refers to the founder of the Christian movement executed under Pilate. By his reference to "Jesus the so-called Christ," Josephus shows his awareness as a Jew that the name *Christus* involves a religious claim. From Pliny we learn something about Christian life and worship in northern Turkey at the beginning of the second century. In a striking passage, Pliny matter of factly describes Christian antiphonal singing of "a hymn to Christ as to a god."

If the tribe of Christians had eventually become extinct, we in the twentieth century would not hesitate to conclude that there had been a teacher from Palestine named Jesus, called Christ, remembered as a wonder-worker, who had been crucified under Pontius Pilate sometime between A.D. 26 and 36. We would also have little trouble accepting Tacitus' designation of him as the "founder of the name." We might wonder how an obscure teacher who had clearly been executed had occasioned after his death the rise of such a widespread religious movement, and how he had even become, at least in one obscure corner of the empire, the object of worship. Josephus, Tacitus, and Pliny, though they certainly did not call upon his name, had no reason to doubt the existence of the one called Christ and neither do we in the twentieth century.

JESUS AND JOHN THE BAPTIST

When we turn to the New Testament as a possible source for further historical information about Jesus, the familiar "Christmas story," found in the opening chapters of Matthew and Luke, seems the most obvious place to start. But the literary form and construction of what New Testament scholars call the "infancy narratives" make it very difficult to draw from them any but the most speculative historical conclusions. (See Walter Kasper, *Jesus the Christ*, 65.)

Outside of the infancy narratives, there seem no good reasons for doubting the gospel traditions that associate Jesus with Galilee, and particularly with the towns of Nazareth and Capernaum. Jesus apparently lived in Galilee long enough to be recognized as a Galilean and even mocked as a Nazarean (Jn 1:46).

Despite his close connection with Galilee, all four gospels have Jesus in Judea at the beginning of his public ministry. Specifically they locate him in an area near the Jordan River not far from Qumran where John was baptizing. Mark describes the stark prophetic figure of the Baptist this way: "John was clothed in camel's hair, and wore a leather belt around his waist. His food was grasshoppers and wild honey" (Mk 1:6). Josephus (*Antiquities*, 18.5) provides independent testimony to the life, work, and execution of John the Baptist. All four gospels tell us that John the Baptist baptized Jesus. "In those days," says Mark, "Jesus came from Nazareth of Galilee and was baptized by John in the Jordan" (Mk 1:9).

To the historical conclusions derived from extra-biblical sources, we can add Jesus' baptism by John the Baptist. Why is this such a certain conclusion? The answer to this question provides a good example of how New Testament scholars sometimes reason when trying to estimate the value of gospel traditions as historical sources. For the sake of discussion, let us assume the most skeptical possible posture and ask why we should believe the gospels when they tell us that John baptized Jesus. How do we know that the early church didn't just make it up? The answer is simply that when we examine the issue we find that the gospel writers would have no reason to invent such a story. The simplest and most reasonable explanation for the presence of

Jesus' baptism by John in the gospel traditions is that it really happened. It was probably a significant event in Jesus' life and his followers remembered it. How do we know this?

If Christians had invented the claim that John baptized Jesus, they would have gained nothing by it. Far from adding to Jesus' stature, such a claim seems to threaten it. According to Christian belief, Jesus was without sin (Heb 4:15). John's baptism is described as "a baptism of repentance for the forgiveness of sins" (Mk 1:4). Why then did Jesus agree to be baptized by John? Generations of Christian preachers and commentators have spoken of how he was giving us an example to imitate. It is also possible, however, that Jesus was a disciple of John the Baptist. According to John 1:36–37, some of Jesus' first disciples had been former disciples of John. Luke's infancy narrative portrays John and Jesus as cousins (1:36ff). Since it would have made little sense for the evangelists to invent it, we can reasonably conclude that the strong and well-attested association between Jesus and John in the gospel traditions is based on an authentic memory of their historical association. We can therefore safely regard it and Jesus' baptism by John as historical facts.

By itself this conclusion doesn't take us very far. While we know that John baptized Jesus, we don't really know why. We don't know what that immersion in water meant to John and to Jesus. Here we must interpret. Inevitably such interpretation will be guided not only by undeniable historical evidence, but also by the interpreter's prior knowledge and beliefs. Here an interpreter's own religious commitments can come into play. It is legitimate to look for an interpretation that will be faithful not only to the facts as known, but also to Christian faith as believed. Theological speculation will begin to run together with historical conclusions. That is why this chapter is called "An Historical-Theological Portrait of Jesus."

JOHN, QUMRAN, SECOND ISAIAH, AND JESUS

The Jordan wilderness where John baptized could not have been far from Qumran. Jeremias estimates "less than eight miles as the crow flies" (*New Testament Theology*, 43). The use of ritual washing was a common practice in the Dead Sea community. According to the gospels, John promised another baptism to follow his own. The Qumran community held a similar eschatological hope. These and other facts raise the question of John's possible connection with the community at Qumran. This is a question that we cannot answer with certainty, but it makes for interesting and possibly fruitful speculation.

One of the Dead Sea documents known as "The Manual of Discipline" uses a messianic text from Isaiah 40 to explain why the original members of the Qumran community had thought it necessary to withdraw into the wilderness. This text comes from the part of the book of Isaiah known as Second or Deutero-Isaiah (chapters 40–55). All four gospels use this same text to explain the significance of John the Baptist. Many readers will recognize it as a commonplace from the church's Advent liturgy.

> A voice cries out: in the desert prepare the way of the LORD!
> Make straight in the wasteland a highway for our God!
> Every valley shall be filled in, every mountain and hill shall be
>   made low;
> the rugged land shall be made a plain, the rough country a broad
>   valley.
> The glory of the LORD shall be revealed and mankind shall see it
>   together;
> for the mouth of the LORD has spoken (Is 40:3–5).

In addition to being the basis for Christianity's understanding of John as Jesus' forerunner, this text arguably represents John's own understanding of what he was doing in the Jordan wilderness. The fourth gospel puts it on John's own lips (Jn 1:23). He had gone there to prepare the way for the Lord, for the revelation of the glory of the Lord.

It is at least historically plausible to regard John's mission as a development and transformation of the Qumran community's understanding of its own role as a purifying agent preparing the way for the messianic age. Given Jesus' association with John in the gospel traditions, it is likewise plausible to interpret Jesus' ministry, from an historical point of view, as a possible development and transformation of John's. The early chapters of the fourth gospel speak of a baptizing mission by Jesus and his disciples simultaneous with that of John (Jn 3:22, 26; 4.1) and prior to the latter's imprisonment by Herod Antipas (Josephus, *Antiquities*, 18.5) and eventual death (Mk 6:17–29). John's question to Jesus from prison (Mt 11:2–6; Lk 7:18–23), Jesus' own high praise of John (Mt 11:7–19; Lk 7:24–35), and the gospel report that some people mistook Jesus for John the Baptist returned from the dead (Mk 6:14–16; 8:28) are all consistent with the view that there is a certain continuity between John and Jesus. And yet they are quite different.

The most obvious differences between them are captured in a saying from the hypothetical Q source reported in Luke 7:33–35. "For John the Baptist came neither eating food nor drinking wine, and you said, 'He is possessed by a demon.' The Son of Man came eating and drinking and you said, 'Look, he is a glutton and a drunkard, a friend of tax collectors and sinners.' But wisdom is vindicated by all her children." Playing on the parallel passage in Matthew 11:16–19, Schillebeeckx likens John to a "dirge" and Jesus to a "song" in their effects on people (Schillebeeckx, 139). Both John and Jesus are wisdom's children, but Jesus' greater inclusiveness, as illustrated by the reference to his association with tax collectors and sinners, contrasts with John's emphasis on the wrath to come with his images of the ax laid to the root of the tree and the winnowing fan to separate the grain from the chaff (Mt 3:7–12). Apparently Jesus thought that when the glory of the Lord was revealed, the tax collectors and sinners would be there to see it along with the righteous. In his *A Life of Jesus* (1973, ET 1978), the Japanese novelist Shusaku Endo contrasts the barren Judean wilderness with springtime in the Galilean countryside. He finds in this contrast a metaphor for the difference between the respective images of God of John and Jesus (28, 34).

The broad association of the missions of Jesus and John helps to provide a point of entry for our location of Jesus in the milieu of first century Palestine. It helps to locate Jesus in a particular sector of the widespread eschatological hopes of his day. He is involved in preparing Israel for its restoration in the messianic age as understood in the promises of Deutero-Isaiah. Sinners and Gentiles will be included in the revelation of God's glory. Significantly, Deutero-Isaiah provides New Testament writers with many of the categories used most frequently to explain who Jesus is and what his life means.

When we turn to the gospel accounts of Jesus' baptism, we find the evangelists using Isaiah to explain its meaning. They present Jesus' baptism in Isaian terms as the manifestation of his identity and role as Son-Servant. In the gospel accounts of Jesus' baptism by John, we pick up the first threads of the theme of Jesus and the Father upon which this historical-theological portrait is based.

JESUS' MANIFESTATION AS SON-SERVANT

After the simple statement that Jesus was baptized by John in the Jordan, Mark continues:

> On coming up out of the water he saw the heavens being torn open and the Spirit, like a dove, descending upon him. And a voice came from the heavens, "You are my beloved Son; with you I am well pleased" (Mk 1:10–11 & parallels).

This theophany, or manifestation of God, involves three moments: 1) the heavens open, 2) the Spirit descends, 3) a heavenly voice speaks. In reflecting prayerfully on this passage, it is possible to find in it numerous hints of literary allusion to the Old Testament, especially to the book of Isaiah, this time mostly from its third section (chapters 56–66). For example, we find the rending of the heavens (Is 63:19) and the Spirit's outpouring and leading Israel up out of the water (Is 63:11, 14). These allusions place Jesus' baptism by John in the context of Israel's hope for a new salvation from God, a new exodus. "Oh that you would rend the heavens and come down," pleads Isaiah 63:19. These apparent allusions to Isaiah identify Jesus' baptism as a decisive event in salvation history. In Jesus' baptism God's salvation is made known.

The clearest and most dramatic allusion to the Old Testament comes in the words of the voice from heaven. Some scholars have heard in them an echo of God's words to his "anointed" in Psalm 2:7, "You are my Son; this day I have begotten you." The heavenly voice says, "You are my beloved Son; with you I am well pleased" (Mk 1:11). The opening lines of the first of the songs of the "servant of the Lord" in Deutero-Isaiah go like this: "Here is my servant whom I uphold, my chosen one with whom I am pleased, upon whom I have put my spirit; he shall bring forth justice to the nations" (Is 42:1). The similarity is striking.

The Servant of the Lord is a mysterious figure who appears in four moving and beautifully composed oracles or hymns from Deutero-Isaiah, or the Book of Consolation. The servant is chosen and anointed with God's spirit. He is destined for both the restoration of Israel and "as a light to the nations, that my [God's] salvation may reach to the ends of the earth" (Is 49:6 from the second servant song). He will establish God's justice (Is 42:4) but not by military power. He does not cry out or shout in the street, nor does he break even a bruised reed or quench a smoldering wick (Is 42:2–3). God has given his servant to speak to the weary a word that will rouse them (Is 50:4). In spite of derision and disgrace, he doesn't turn back from his mission. His trust in the Lord is complete. He walks in the darkness without any light. By the suffering he endures, he "shall take away the sins of many" (Is 53:12), and the Lord will lift him up (Is 52:13).

To the Christian ear, trained by years of participation in the Lenten liturgy, these songs of God's suffering servant from Isaiah refer unmistakably to Christ. To a Jewish ear it would be otherwise. In any case, the New Testament uses these passages, perhaps more than any others in the Old Testament, to communicate the religious meaning of Jesus' life and death. The gospel accounts of Jesus' baptism portray it as a revelation to Jesus, and perhaps to John as well, of his identity as Son-Servant of God. In the midst of allusions to the exodus (Isaiah 63), the Davidic messiah (Psalms 2), and the Isaian servant (Isaiah 42), Jesus' decisive role as God's agent in the history of salvation is made known in Father-Son terms. He is anointed by the Spirit as the Father's Son-Servant.

However literally or figuratively we decide to interpret the details in the accounts of Jesus' baptism (would a television crew have been able to record the voice and photograph the dove?), the evangelists clearly want to tell us that when Jesus was baptized, God and his intentions for Israel and the nations were revealed. This revelation concerns Jesus' identity and decisive role in salvation history. It manifests his identity in terms of sonship. The meaning of this sonship is fleshed out in terms of Israel's eschatological hopes as drawn from Isaiah.

HOW DID JESUS INTERPRET HIMSELF?

If the gospels are any indication, the early church interpreted Jesus' baptism as a manifestation of his special sonship understood in a particular Old Testament context. We must ask if this particular understanding of Jesus' mission and identity, in terms of the Isaian servant theme combined with other Old Testament motifs, represents Jesus' own interpretation of himself. Jeremias, for example, has argued that Jesus interpreted his own death in terms of the suffering servant (*New Testament Theology*, 286–299). Even if Jeremias is wrong about this, we can hold as probable that Jesus fused elements from the prophetic and wisdom traditions of Israel to form his own interpretation of himself. As Walter Kasper has written in discussing the question of Jesus' titles, "Why should we attribute less originality to Jesus than to some hypothetical post-Easter prophet whose name we don't even know?" (*Jesus the Christ*, 107). Nevertheless, any attempt to move beyond this very general conclusion must remain highly speculative.

It is tempting, for example, to conclude that in Jesus' own personal growth and development he realized his identity and calling at his baptism. At the same time, we must admit that such a view remains as speculative as the one that comes from the other end of the Christological spectrum and holds that Jesus knew "he was God" from the very moment of his conception. The question of the "self-consciousness of Christ," as it is often called in Catholic theology, requires strong doses of both historical and theological modesty.

From an historical point of view, Bultmann warned many years ago that the gospel sources show no interest in Jesus' personality and that what has been written about the development of his inner life is often "fantastic" (*Jesus and the Word*, 8–9). In the end it is probably best to admit that, however fascinating they may be, questions about how Jesus interpreted himself or how it felt to be Jesus of Nazareth simply cannot be answered with anything more than educated theological speculation. In all such speculation about Jesus' interior life, it is well to recall this thought from C.S. Lewis: "I do not think anything we can do will enable us to imagine the mode of consciousness of the incarnate God" (*Miracles*, 114). Though Lewis is doubtless correct, this has

not stopped generations of Christians, from early Christian literature to contemporary cinema, from imagining about his hidden
life. Given Christ's incarnational stature in Christianity as God's
own "image" or "icon" (Col 1:15), this is neither surprising nor
inappropriate.

Questions for Review and Discussion

1. Describe the problem of Jesus' relationship to Judaism. What
   facts do we know about Jesus and about early Christians that
   require a certain degree of discontinuity with or tension between Jesus and the Judaism of his day?

2. What problems does the diversity of Palestinian Judaism in
   Jesus' day pose for an historical understanding of him?

3. Why is this chapter called an "historical-theological portrait"
   of Jesus rather than simply an "historical portrait"?

4. Describe first century Palestine: its size, divisions, and
   location.

5. Describe the spectrum of Jewish responses to the Hellenization of Palestine that followed the conquests of Alexander
   the Great and intensified under Antiochus IV.

6. Describe the circumstances leading up to the Hasmonean revolt. What were its results?

7. How did the aftermath of the Hasmonean revolt influence the
   subsequent divisions in Judaism that we find during the time
   of Jesus, e.g. the division into parties such as Pharisees, Essenes, and Sadducees? What were the characteristic religious
   beliefs of each of these parties?

8. What is the origin of the Pharisaic belief in the resurrection of
   the dead? In what does this belief consist?

9. If there were no New Testament gospels, what would we be
   able to conclude from historical sources outside the Bible
   (extra-biblical sources) about Jesus' life and teaching?

10. Compare and contrast Jesus and John the Baptist. Why would
    John be compared to a dirge and Jesus to a song?

11. How is the text of Isaiah 40:3-5 connected to both Qumran (the Essene community) and John the Baptist?

12. How do the gospel accounts of Jesus' baptism by John use the Old Testament to explain the meaning of Jesus' baptism?

For Writing and Reflection

1. Construct a chart that locates the various divisions within Palestinian Judaism in Jesus' time on a line moving from extreme separatism from Hellenistic influence on the right to extreme accommodation on the left. Your chart should include: Pharisees, Sadducees, Essenes, Zealots, Herodians, tax collectors.

2. Daniel 7 relates a dream about four beasts that symbolize four succeeding world kingdoms to be followed by the kingdom of God. Using the notes and commentary (Reading Guide) in the *Catholic Study Bible*, or some other biblical reference works such as those listed at the end of Chapter V, write an essay explaining the meaning of Daniel 7 at the historical level of interpretation. Answer the following questions: Who are the four beasts? How are the kingdoms they represent related to Jewish history? What kind of hopes would this chapter arouse in Jewish readers during the period of persecution under Antiochus IV?

For Further Reading

Daniel, 1 & 2 Maccabees—These biblical books are valuable as background for understanding Palestine in the time of Jesus. The deuterocanonical 1 & 2 Maccabees describe the attempt to Hellenize Palestine under the Seleucids and the Hasmonean revolt under Judas. Daniel was written during the persecution under Antiochus IV.

Flavius Josephus, *Antiquities of the Jews* and the *Jewish War*. A valuable, independent source for the history of first century Palestine. References to Josephus in this chapter are from Books 12–18 of the *Antiquities* and Book 2 of the *Jewish War*. They can be found in Volumes VII–IX (*Antiquities*) and Volume II (*War*) of the Loeb Classical Library edition of Josephus' works.

F.F. Bruce, *Jesus and Christian Origins Outside the New Testament* (Grand Rapids, Mich.: Eerdmans, 1982). A survey of extra-biblical testimony about Jesus by one of the most distinguished Evangelical New Testament scholars of this century.

Martin Hengel, *Judaism and Hellenism, Studies in Their Encounter in Palestine During the Early Hellenistic Period*, translated by John Bowden, 2 volumes (Philadelphia: Fortress Press, 1974). A history, aptly described by its subtitle, by a scholar noted for his expertise in the area of Hellenistic Judaism.

Raymond E. Brown, S.S., Pheme Perkins, Anthony J. Saldarini, "Apocrypha; Dead Sea Scrolls; Other Jewish Literature," in R.E. Brown, et al., eds., *New Jerome Biblical Commentary*, pp. 1055–1082. A survey and bibliographical guide to the various forms of Jewish literature relevant to understanding the New Testament.

John P. Meier, *A Marginal Jew, Rethinking the Historical Jesus* (New York: Doubleday, 1991). An excellent resource that lays the groundwork (e.g. treatment of methodology, exhaustive review of available sources, discussion of criteria of authenticity, preliminary background) for the author's own portrait of the historical Jesus in a promised second volume.

Ben F. Meyer, *The Aims of Jesus* (London: SCM Press Ltd, 1979). One of the most accessible contemporary historical studies of Jesus, very readable and very scholarly. Its discussion of method, criteria of authenticity, and Jesus and John the Baptist are relevant to this chapter.

Edward Schillebeeckx, *Jesus, An Experiment in Christology*, translated by Hubert Hoskins (New York: Seabury Press, 1979). An extremely important but very difficult work. Provides detailed discussion of the methodological issues discussed in this chapter: sources, criteria, etc.

Walter Kasper, *Jesus the Christ*, translated by V. Green (New York/Ramsey: Paulist Press, 1977). An historically informed Christology.

Terms To Identify

criterion of discontinuity

criterion of coherence

Galilee

Jordan River

Dead Sea

Sea of Galilee

Samaria

Judea

Jerusalem

Alexander the Great

Ptolemy

Seleucus

Hellenization

koinē

Antiochus IV

Hasmoneans

Zealots

Testimonium Flavianum

Flavius Josephus

Suetonius

Tacitus

Priscilla and Aquila

Mattathias of Modin

Judas Maccabeus

Hanukkah

Antiquities of the Jews

Jewish War

Pharisees

Essenes

Sadducees

Philo

Qumran

Dead Sea Scrolls

Teacher of Righteousness

eschatology

apocalyptic

hasidim

Pompey

Herod the Great

Archelaus

Philip

Herod Antipas

Pontius Pilate

Pliny the Younger

Emperor Claudius

Chapter XII

An Historical-Theological Portrait of Jesus
Part II: Jesus and the Father

As we saw in Chapter X above, the gospels have been composed from previously existing oral and written traditions about Jesus. Josephus had described Jesus as a wise man, a teacher, and a worker of startling deeds. Thus there are traditions about Jesus' teaching and traditions about his works. In this chapter we will look at some of the better attested gospel traditions about Jesus' words and examine them from the point of view of the theological theme of Jesus' relationship to the Father. For purposes of organization, traditions about Jesus' words can be divided into three groups: prayers, parables, and teachings about the law. Finally, we will consider how the gospels portray Jesus' disciples.

WAS IT POSSIBLE FOR JESUS TO PRAY?

Before beginning with the theme of Jesus and the Father in Jesus' gospel prayers, we will address briefly a theological question that often comes up in discussing Jesus' life of prayer: Was it possible for Jesus to pray? The gospels preserve a clear memory of Jesus at prayer. Some Christians are shocked by this because it seems to offend their sense of respect for his divinity. Why would he pray to himself? Here we must recall that Christian professions of faith in the divinity of Christ have never simply identified Jesus with God without qualification. The one Lord Jesus Christ of the creed is not only confessed to be truly God but also truly human. The Trinitarian language of scripture and the councils is much preferable to unqualified statements such as "Jesus is God." In John's prologue, the Logos or Word is identified with God, but then we are told that this Word "became flesh" (Jn 1:14). The mystery of the incarnation means that we never find Christ as divine apart from Christ as human.

As the early Christological controversies and ecumenical councils attest, "the Word become flesh" requires some interpretation. This is the point of Christology. Whatever Christological framework we use, it ought to be possible to interpret the confession of faith in Jesus' divinity in such a way that we leave room in our understanding of Jesus' humanity for the gospels' clear and consistent testimony that Jesus prayed to the Father from the heart. In the terms of Nicaea and Chalcedon, we can say that the one Lord Jesus Christ prayed in his human nature.

As in the case of Jesus' baptism by John, the gospel testimony that Jesus prayed to the Father adds nothing to his stature. In fact, it threatens to confuse the clear New Testament profession of faith in his divinity. We have no reason to doubt that Jesus really did pray. When we examine the traditions about his prayer in the gospels, we find the same Father-Son theme we saw in the baptism.

THE JEWISH CONTEXT FOR JESUS' PRAYER

As Joachim Jeremias has put it, "Jesus came from a people who knew how to pray" (*The Prayers of Jesus*, 66). If we follow the supposition that any historically informed religious interpretation of Jesus must place him in the context of first century Palestinian Judaism, we can further suppose that Jesus prayed as an observant Jew of his day would have. In his attempt to reconstruct the daily patterns of prayer in the Palestine of Jesus' day, Jeremias finds a twofold basic structure of prayer. First would be the morning and evening recitation of the creedal Shema from Deuteronomy 6:4–5: "Hear, O Israel! The LORD is our God, the LORD alone! Therefore, you shall love the LORD your God, with all your heart, and with all your soul, and with all your strength." In addition, a pious Jew would have observed the three hours of prayer: morning, afternoon, and evening. Jeremias finds indications in the gospels that Jesus observed these times of prayer (*Prayers*, 72–75).

We can also assume that, as an observant Jew, Jesus was in the habit of attending the synagogue on the sabbath (Lk 4:16). Here he would have heard the scriptures proclaimed and interpreted. As the gospels attest, he also went up to Jerusalem for the passover at least once and took part in temple worship at Jerusalem.

Each of the evangelists fits the memory of Jesus at prayer into the structure and purpose of his gospel. When we examine what the gospels have to say about Jesus' prayer, we find three different kinds of testimony: 1) general descriptions of Jesus at prayer, 2) reports of the words Jesus used in prayer, and 3) Jesus' instruction to his disciples on prayer. We will consider each of these in turn.

JESUS AT PRAYER

Each evangelist testifies to Jesus' habit of prayer. Already in Mark 1:35, after a long evening with the afflicted, we find Jesus at prayer. "Rising early the next morning, he went off to a lonely place in the desert; there he was absorbed in prayer." After the feeding of the five thousand, this time in the evening, he left his disciples and "went off to the mountains to pray" (Mk 6:46). The night of the last supper found him in the garden at prayer (Mk 14).

In addition to the customary times of prayer, Jesus was also apparently in the habit of spending the night hours in prayer: "Then he went out to the mountains to pray, spending the night in communion with God" (Lk 6:12). Commenting on this passage, Jeremias speaks of "a firmly established tradition about Jesus' prayer in solitude by night" (*Prayers*, 76). Sometimes, as at Gethsemane or the episode of the transfiguration, Peter, James, and John are invited to accompany him.

Luke's gospel emphasizes the need to pray constantly (18:1; 21:36), and Jesus provides the model for this. "He often retired to deserted places and prayed" (5:16). Luke portrays Jesus as praying especially at important times in his life and ministry (9:18, 28).

While the evangelists tell us that Jesus prayed habitually, they rarely tell us what he said when he spoke to the Father. The gospel passages that report his words of prayer are, therefore, significant and revealing. The theme of the intimate relationship

between Father and Son suffuses the traditions about the words of
Jesus' prayer.

Reports of the Words Jesus Used in Prayer

Perhaps the most significant and revealing such tradition is
Jesus' use of the Aramaic "Abba" to address the Father. We have
discussed this term above in Chapter X. It signifies the informal,
familial intimacy of children with their parents. It could be used
by children of any age to address their fathers in an intimate way,
much as we might use "Daddy" in English. Jeremias translates it
as "dear father." Although the term appears only once in the
gospels (Mk 14:36), Jeremias' arguments that Jesus habitually
used this word to address the God of Israel have been widely
accepted. That would mean that where the Greek word for *Father*
appears in authentic traditions, it is most likely a translation of the
Aramaic "Abba" (Mt 11:25–26; 26:39, 42; Lk 10:21; 11:12; 22:42;
23:34, 46).

Some contemporary scholars who emphasize Jesus' continuity
with Judaism have criticized Jeremias' emphasis on Abba's uniqueness. They see Jesus' use of "Abba" as his personal variation on a
new attitude of trusting intimacy toward God emerging among the
pious of Jesus' day (Swidler, *Yeshua*, 56, 59, 71). Doubtless Jeremias has exaggerated in claiming that Jesus' use of "Abba"
"break[s] through the limits of Judaism." While Jesus' use of
"Abba" may not be as striking as Jeremias thought, it remains one
of the most distinctive facts we can know about him. It tells us how
Jesus felt toward the God of Israel. It speaks of his radical sense of
trusting intimacy with the Father, which influenced everything he
said and did. The Catholic theologian Edward Schillebeeckx has
called this Jesus' "Abba experience" (*Jesus*, 256–271). He locates
its distinctiveness in its "unconventional style" of prayer, its "unaf-
fected and natural simplicity" (*Jesus*, 261).

If contemporary Jewish scholars should succeed in showing
that a few of Jesus' Pharisaic contemporaries may have used the
word "Abba" in prayer, Christians need not be disturbed. Its
temporary retention by early Christians (Rom 8:15; Gal 4:6) attests to their recognition of its distinctiveness. With Jeremias,

Christians can still conclude that Jesus "spoke with God as a child speaks with his Father, simply, intimately, securely" (*Prayers*, 97).

Another instance where the synoptic tradition reports the words of Jesus' prayer appears in Matthew 11:25–26.

> I give praise to you, Father, Lord of heaven and earth, for although you have hidden these things from the wise and the learned you have revealed them to the childlike. Yes, Father, such has been your gracious will.

Here again we see the Father-Son theme at the heart of a tradition about Jesus' prayer. In this text from the hypothetical Q source, Jesus appears as Wisdom's child or agent. Like Wisdom herself, Jesus knows God intimately and reveals God to those he chooses (Havener, *Q: The Sayings of Jesus*, 80, 131). Earlier in the Q document, John the Baptist and Jesus are identified as Wisdom's children (Lk 7:35 and parallels). The opening formulas of chapters 2, 3, 4, 5, and 10 as well as verses 1:8 and 6:20 of the Old Testament book of Proverbs express the view of Wisdom applied to Jesus in this text from Matthew 11 either by himself or by the early Q tradition (see Schillebeeckx, *Jesus*, 264).

In this Q text from Matthew, the New Testament uses resources from the Jewish wisdom tradition to show Jesus' decisive role in salvation history. The Father-Son theme, expressed in similar terms from the wisdom tradition, is expanded upon in the great prayer for unity of John 17. In John's last supper prayer, Jesus asks that the unity of his disciples in love would be a faithful reflection or imitation of the intimate union between Father and Son.

Jesus Teaches His Disciples To Pray

John the Baptist had apparently taught his disciples a special prayer. Jesus' disciples accordingly asked him, "Lord, teach us to pray, as John taught his disciples" (Lk 11:1). The prayer Jesus taught them in response, the "Our Father" or the "Lord's Prayer," comes down to us in two different forms. The longer is Matthew 6:9–13; the shorter is Luke 11:2–4. Though substantially the same, these two forms differ in some details.

With the "Our Father," Jesus invites his disciples to share in the intimate communion with God at the center of his own life and being. Disciples are to pray as Jesus does, addressing God with the familial "Abba." As the ancient liturgies have it, Christians can now "dare" to say "Our Father." The Pauline passages that retain the Aramaic "Abba" capture the spirit of this instruction: "All who are led by the Spirit of God are sons of God. You did not receive a spirit of slavery leading you back into fear, but a spirit of adoption through which we cry out, 'Abba' (that is, 'Father')" (Rom 8:14–15).

The first part of the "Our Father" centers on God as "Abba" and echoes familiar characteristics of Jesus' ministry, especially the eschatological concern to advance God's will and kingdom. The second part centers on human need and exhibits the simple trust in God and his forgiveness so typical of Jesus. The prayer for forgiveness reminds us of Jesus urging his disciples to imitate the Father's limitless forgiveness.

In both Matthew and Luke, the "Our Father" appears in the context of a larger instruction to the disciples on prayer. Jesus emphasizes trusting confidence in prayer to a God who is near and who knows us intimately. As Bultmann has pointed out, Jesus urges prayer of petition in the true sense. We are not simply to ask for resignation to God's unchanging decrees. Prayer as Jesus teaches it seeks "to move God to do something which he otherwise would not do" (*Jesus and the Word*, 185). As Mark's passion account illustrates, Jesus' own prayer was not above the lament.

Jesus' disciples are to ask for anything in prayer. He explains this with a reference to the image of a human parent: "Would one of you hand his son a stone when he asks for a loaf, or a poisonous snake when he asks for a fish? If you, with all your sins, know how to give your children what is good, how much more will your heavenly Father give good things to anyone who asks him!" (Mt 7:9–11).

As with all Jesus' instructions to the disciples in the gospels, the evangelists intend these instructions on prayer for later generations of disciples, too. Because "Abba" is near, Jesus' disciples can pray from the heart with trust and confidence. As in Mark's account of Gethsemane, it is when the disciples fail to watch and pray that they fail Jesus.

We can conclude that in the instances where the gospels give us the words of Jesus in prayer, we find an emphasis on the intimate union between Father and Son. Emphasis on this theme is not here intended to give a narrow psychological or subjective interpretation of either Jesus' prayer or of his relationship to the Father. The gospels make it very clear that Jesus' intimate relationship with the Father has an eschatological context. He brings a decisive moment in salvation history. Jesus' role in bringing about the revelation of God's glory and salvation for Israel and the nations is variously expressed in the New Testament. Sometimes Jesus is placed in a prophetic context, as at his baptism. Sometimes he is seen as Wisdom's child and agent as in his prayer. In any case, his communion with God in prayer is inseparable from his mission as God's Son-Servant-Wisdom.

"ABBA" IN THE PARABLES

If Jesus' prayer is any indication, we can locate what Schillebeeckx has called Jesus' "Abba experience" at the heart of his life. He is in constant intimate communion with the Father. But reports of Jesus' prayer and gospel instruction on prayer say little about what Jesus thought "Abba" was like. How did Jesus imagine "Abba"? Turning to the gospel parables, Jesus' most characteristic form of instruction, we find a consistent portrayal of a figure, variously a shepherd, a woman looking for a lost coin or kneading dough, a householder, a king, a human father, who seems to embody what Jesus imagined the Father to be like. By attention to this figure of God in the parables, we get an idea of how Jesus understood the Father. We will look at two parables: the "laborers in the vineyard" (Mt 20:1–16) and the "prodigal son" (Lk 15:11–31).

What Is a Parable?

In the languages of Jesus' day, the term *parable* could be used in a very broad way to refer to any sort of comparison. The gospel traditions preserve the memory that Jesus taught in parables. We can use the term "story parable" to refer to the some thirty-odd story-length comparisons used by Jesus in the gospels. The literary form of the story parable, as used by Jesus in the gospels, seems to have been a unique development of the Jewish tradition out of which he came. Rabbis found the story parable an inspiring way to teach about the law. Later rabbinic literature contains many examples of parables that sound very much like Jesus'.

Jesus' story parables usually begin with a simple comparison, sometimes a simile, or comparison using *like* or *as*. The beginning of the parable of the "laborers in the vineyard" is a good example. "The kingdom of heaven is like a landowner who went out at dawn to hire laborers for his vineyard" (Mt 20:1). This comparison is then extended into a story.

Patristic and medieval theologians practiced an allegorical method of biblical interpretation. When they read the parables, they looked for symbolic meanings in the stories' various details. Against traditional allegorizing interpretations of the parables, contemporary interpreters have emphasized that Jesus' story parables were teaching devices. Rather than complex networks of allegory or symbolism, therefore, we should expect to find simple lessons in Jesus' story parables. Though a few parables have allegorical elements, e.g. the parable of the sower in Matthew 13, this is not generally the case.

The lessons of the parables are simple in the sense of non-complex, but they are not banal or simplistic. In fact, the disciples found them quite challenging. Jesus used his story parables to teach his disciples about what he called the reign or kingdom of God. This phrase, perhaps original with Jesus, appears hundreds of times in the gospels. It refers to Jesus' particular understanding of the restoration of Israel that he had begun with his mission of preaching and healing.

According to the parables, God's reign or kingdom comes suddenly and unexpectedly and is in the process of growing, like a mustard seed or leaven (Mt 13:31–33), to completion. As an observant Jew, Jesus would have been conscious that God always reigns. But he led his disciples to expect a future revelation of God's glory, as in the text from Isaiah 40. He taught them to pray for this and to be willing to sacrifice anything for it. In contrast to the fiery cataclysms in the eschatology of some of his contemporaries, Jesus' parables emphasize the gratuitous inclusiveness of the Father and the folly of the self-righteous who would exclude sinners and Gentiles. Like the prodigal son's patient father, Abba is willing to wait. He gives sinners time to repent and those outside the fold time to come in (see Kasper, *Jesus the Christ*, 78; Jeremias, *New Testament Theology*, 140).

A key element of the parables seems to be their intent to surprise. They challenge listeners to a new and unexpected perspective, that of Abba, whose reign Jesus uses the parable to explain. Jesus sets his parables in a situation characterized by the ordinary details of everyday life. Into this ordinary setting, he introduces an element of distortion, e.g. exaggeration or inversion. He jolts the listeners out of the ordinary and brings them up short. He challenges them to see things in a new way, with God's eyes rather than their own. In the parables of the "laborers in the vineyard" and the "prodigal son," Jesus challenges his listeners to imagine God and God's relations with people in a new way that emphasizes the difference between God's perspective and a limited human one. In the process, they give us some idea of Jesus' understanding of God.

The Laborers in the Vineyard (Mt 20:1–16)

This parable appears only in Matthew. It seems to reflect the economic conditions of Jesus' time. Writing of a later time, Josephus (*Antiquities*, 20.9) recounts an instance of unemployed workers receiving full pay for an hour's work. In Jesus' parable, the owner of an estate goes out at dawn and hires a group of workers for his vineyard. He agrees to pay them "the usual daily wage" (Mt 20:2). At mid-morning, noon, and again at mid-afternoon, the owner returns to the marketplace and hires other groups of workers for his vineyard. At the end of the day, he pays the workers. Nothing unusual so far.

The jolt comes in the way the owner of the estate goes about paying the workers. He begins with the last workers he had hired. They had only worked an hour, but he pays them a full day's wage. The workers who had been at it since dawn expect some sort of bonus. But the owner pays them the same usual daily wage as those who had worked only an hour. They become angry. They think it unfair that workers who had only worked an hour should receive the same wage as they. They complain to the eccentric owner. He replies that he is free to spend his money as he pleases and asks them, "Are you envious because I am generous?" (20:15).

What are we to make of the owner's strange behavior? This is certainly no way to run a business. The parable's context in Matthew probably has to do with the defense of including Gentiles in the churches to which the gospel is addressed. A possible context for this parable in the life of Jesus is his well-known ministry to the outcasts of his society, "Here is a glutton and a drunkard, a friend of tax collectors and sinners" (Lk 7:34). Perhaps his disciples or others expressed resentment, similar to that of the first group of laborers, at his inclusion of sinners. The parable would explain Jesus' conduct.

In any case, the parable is about the Father's mercy. It extends even to the latecomers. The parable gives Jesus' listeners both a picture of what God is like and an apology for Jesus' own behavior as friend of tax collectors and sinners. The Father is extravagant and inclusive with his gifts. He does not appear to measure them out by ordinary human standards. The owner's behavior offends the first group of workers just as Jesus' behavior probably offended even some of his disciples. The first group of workers speaks with the voice of common sense. Most readers can probably identify with the first group's sense that the owner had in some sense treated them unfairly. The expectations of the first group of workers in the parable are very much like our own would be. The owner wasn't fair. Jesus' first century challenge to ordinary ideas about God still sounds contemporary.

The Prodigal Son (Lk 15:11–32)

This is one of Jesus' best-known parables. It appears only in Luke. Its context in Luke (15:1–2) reflects in a general way its probable context in the ministry of Jesus. The parable illustrates God's love for the sinner and by implication defends Jesus' ministry to the outcasts. In this parable Jesus provides us with a touching, imaginative representation of what he thinks the Father is like.

Jesus compares God to the father in the parable. "A man had two sons," he begins. The first part of the parable (vv 11–24) deals with the father and the younger of the two sons. The latter asks his father for his inheritance. In a surprising burst of generosity, the father simply gives it to him right there on the spot. According to the social customs of the time, after the father had made such a gift, the elder son would then be assured of inheriting the father's land and the remaining property. The father's action seems to be a way of trying to be fair to both sons (Pheme Perkins, *Love Commands in the New Testament*, 51–57).

The younger son takes his inheritance and leaves home for "a distant land." He squanders his inheritance and winds up in a pig sty. He sinks so low that he would even have eaten the slop for the pigs, but "no one made a move to give him anything" (15:16). He decides to return to his father's house. He hopes at least to regain the status of a hired hand in his father's household. Instead of rejection, or even a grudging conditional acceptance, the returning prodigal receives from his father a royal welcome complete with music and dancing.

The second part of the parable (vv 25–32) shows the reaction of the elder son who describes himself as having "slaved" for his father for years (15:29). He refuses to join in the celebration or even to go in the house. He becomes angry with his father and responds to his extravagant forgiveness of the younger son with the same kind of bitterness exhibited by the first group of workers in the previous parable. His father said to him, "My son, you are here with me always; everything I have is yours. But now we must celebrate and rejoice, because your brother was dead and has come to life again; he was lost and has been found" (Lk 15:31–32). Jesus does not tell us whether the father succeeded in softening the heart of his eldest son.

Much could be said by way of commentary on this parable. Clearly the father, who awaits the prodigal's return and welcomes him with unexpected warmth and joy, is the parable's central figure. To call this the parable of the "prodigal son" is something of a misnomer. Again Jesus has pictured the father as extravagant in his mercy. The father's behavior goes far beyond the elder son's sense of what is fair. Given the parable's context, we can conclude that Jesus modeled his own behavior on his image of what the Father is like. In this parable he defends his ministry to the outcasts by an appeal to the Father's example.

Most people would find it hard to listen honestly and carefully to these parables without concluding that they are more like the first group of workers and the elder brother than they are like Jesus and his Abba. This is the challenge of the parables. Are those who hear them happy with the perspective of the elder son and first workers or do they need something more? This is what the gospels offer. In learning to see with God's eyes, in learning to live from God's perspective as embodied in the Father's Son-Servant-Wisdom, one becomes a disciple. The gospels portray this as a difficult daily process, but one that is not without the joy of the celebration that marked the prodigal son's return.

"Abba" as Compassionate and Inclusive

Distinctive among the characteristics of Jesus' ministry are the related features of compassion and inclusiveness. Based on his "Abba experience" and the understanding of God that derives from it, Jesus welcomed sinners and ate with them, included women among his disciples, and generally directed his ministry to the outcasts as well as to the mainstream. The God who sends rain and sun on both the good and the bad, the God who knows when sparrows fall, and who hears the cries of the afflicted, is the most likely model for Jesus' universal offer of the kingdom.

The present chapter has dwelt at length on Jesus' use of "Abba" or Father. But the use of the theme of Jesus and the Father as the focal point of this historical-theological portrait ought not to be misunderstood. It is essential to recall that the primary emphasis of "Abba" and the "Abba experience" is precisely on God's nearness and all-embracing compassion. To turn either Jesus' use of "Abba" or the Trinitarian language based on it against women by excluding their experiences from contributing to our understanding of God would be at odds with what is distinctive and significant about Jesus' use of "Abba" (Johnson, 79–82).

CHRISTIANITY AND JUDAISM

We have looked at the theme of Jesus and the Father in his prayers and in his parables. It remains to consider this theme in Jesus' teaching about the law or Torah. Christians often assume that Jesus did away with Torah and made Judaism obsolete. This is simply not true. Amid a mutual hostility reflected in the final stage of the gospel tradition, the communities of Jesus' disciples eventually separated from Judaism. This separation did not occur until after Jesus' death. Though the seeds for this separation were doubtless present in the implicit claims of Jesus during his ministry, these claims too were made in the context of the traditions of Israel. The relationship between Judaism and Christianity is therefore highly complex. Were this not true, Paul would never have had to write Romans, which is perhaps the best scriptural commentary on the question. Before we can consider the theme of Jesus and the Father in his teaching, therefore, it is necessary to clarify his relationship to the law or Torah.

Jesus as Prophet or Sage?

As the gospel traditions attest, the questions of Jesus' identity and of how his words and deeds were to be interpreted already challenged his contemporaries. While we in the twentieth century can locate him within the general outlines of first century Palestinian Judaism, it is very difficult to get a read on his precise coordinates. This is due in significant part to the limited nature of the available historical sources about Jesus and to the diversity of first century Palestinian Judaism. We should not discount Jesus' own originality and character as contributing to his historical elusiveness.

When trying to locate Jesus more precisely in his historical context, contemporary interpreters have appealed to both the prophetic and wisdom traditions of Israel. The obvious eschatological context of his ministry has led some to interpret Jesus primarily in prophetic categories. He is the "eschatological prophet" (Schillebeeckx) or "eschatological charismatic" (Martin Hengel).

Jesus also seems to be heir to Jewish wisdom tradition with an eschatology based on the final revelation of God's wisdom. Both models could involve teaching and interpreting the law. We have already seen that Jesus taught in parables. Josephus calls him a "wise man." He is often addressed as "rabbi" or teacher in the gospels. Though it would be anachronistic to call Jesus a "rabbi" in any technical sense, it is clear that he was an itinerant teacher with a band of disciples. He commented on the law. A contemporary Jewish scholar has called Jesus "a proto-rabbinic halakhist as well as a charismatic prophet." A "halakhist," often through the use of stories, helps people apply God's instruction in the law to their daily lives (Swidler, 49).

From the prophetic and wisdom traditions of Israel, Jesus appears to have forged his own understanding of what he was about. In view of what Christians believe about Jesus, his originality should surprise them least of all. For Christians, Jesus cannot be limited by any of these categories. He is more than a prophet, more than a wise teacher. Though it is carried by categories such as these, Jesus' claim had to exceed them in order to account for his death and the separation of Christianity from Judaism. However we sort out the categories to understand Jesus' claim about himself, it is clear that the theme of intimate communion with the Father will be part of the picture along with the fact that Jesus' teaching included instruction on and interpretation of the law.

Jesus Never Repudiates Torah

In an effort to find what is unique about Jesus and his teaching, many scholars have proposed various ways in which he breaks with Judaism and supersedes its law. But with regard to the law, it is difficult to find a case where Jesus clearly breaks or opposes it, let alone abolishes it (Sanders, *Jesus and Judaism*, Chapter 9).

The gospel traditions about what Jesus taught his disciples bear striking similarity to that strain of Jewish tradition that, after the destruction of Jerusalem and the dispersion, would develop into rabbinic Judaism. In short, Jesus appears much like the Pharisees. Doubtless the gospels reflect a real situation of conflict between Jesus and the teachers or sages of his day. But this tension and conflict had the nature of an intramural argument among people who shared the same basic frame of reference, namely, the law and the traditions surrounding it. It is probable that the more extreme denunciations of the Pharisees reflect the later conflicts between church and synagogue during the period when the gospels were being put together. In Luke 16:17 Jesus says, "It is easier for heaven and earth to pass away than for the smallest part of a letter of the law to become invalid." We can take this saying, as well as Matthew's apparent expansion of it in the sermon on the mount, as faithfully representing Jesus' attitude toward the law.

> Do not think that I have come to abolish the law or the proph-
> ets. I have come not to abolish but to fulfill. Amen, I say to
> you, until heaven and earth pass away, not the smallest letter
> or the smallest part of a letter will pass from the law, until all
> things have taken place. Therefore, whoever breaks one of
> the least of these commandments and teaches others to do so
> will be called least in the kingdom of heaven. But whoever
> obeys and teaches these commandments will be called greatest
> in the kingdom of heaven (Mt 5:17–20).

The Pauline letters give undeniable evidence that in the de-cades after Jesus' execution, a deep division arose in the early church. Were Gentile disciples bound to observe Torah as the first generation of disciples had continued to do after Jesus' death? As Sanders has argued so persuasively, if Jesus had clearly claimed to abolish the law, or if he had stopped observing it himself, this controversy never would have arisen. The fact that it did is our surest indication, from an historical point of view, of Jesus' own deep rootedness in the law. This fact should guide our interpreta-tion of the gospel traditions. Sanders concludes that Jesus gave his disciples no clear teaching repudiating the Mosaic law. Neverthe-less, because of his eschatological sense of acting on behalf of the Father, he apparently did not regard the Mosaic dispensation as final and absolute (Sanders, 267).

Jesus' Distinctive Interpretation of Torah's Love Commands

If Jesus did not abolish the Mosaic law, what then was distinc-tive about his teaching? His sense of the nearness of the Father and his kingdom apparently led Jesus to a radical interpretation of Torah's love commands. He does not abandon the law, but urges his disciples to go beyond it. He does this both in parable form, e.g. the "good Samaritan," and in more direct teaching. His prohi-bition of divorce, allowed by the Mosaic law, is a good example of the latter (Mt 19:3–9).

The view that Jesus taught grace and love and mercy and his Jewish contemporaries did not has been unmasked as an historical caricature that has served to demonize Jews in western culture. Rather than this caricature, Jesus' originality and distinctiveness as a teacher had to do with the interpretation he gave to the love commands of the law. In the matter of love, he consistently urged his disciples to go beyond what was strictly required of them (Swidler, 52–53, 57). This is how we are to understand the previously quoted saying that the disciples' holiness must "surpass that of the scribes and Pharisees" (Mt 5:20). The latter "have taken their seat on the chair of Moses. Therefore, do and observe all things whatsoever they tell you . . ." (Mt 23:2–3). The Pharisees' reverence for the law is to be both imitated and surpassed. Here again Jesus seems best interpreted in light of his understanding of the Father and the theme of his intimate communion with the Father. "So be perfect, just as your heavenly Father is perfect" (Mt 5:48).

What did Jesus teach about love? Each of the synoptic gospels preserves the episode in which another teacher questions Jesus about the law (Mt 22:34–40; Mk 12:28–31; Lk 10:25–28). In each case, the twofold commandment of love of God and love of neighbor is presented as the heart of the law. In Luke's version, the scribe himself gives the answer and Jesus merely affirms that he has interpreted the law rightly.

> You shall love the Lord your God with all your heart, with all your being, with all your strength, and with all your mind, and your neighbor as yourself (Lk 10:27).

That the "two great commandments" should come from the mouth of the scribe in Luke should not surprise us. They are citations from Torah. The first great commandment comes from the *Shema*, the daily creedal prayer of pious Jews (Dt 6:5). The command to love your neighbor as yourself comes from Leviticus 19:18. The verse that precedes it begins, "You shall not bear hatred for your brother in your heart."

Jesus insists on the inner bond between love of God and love of neighbor. This is captured most eloquently in a Johannine saying:

We love because he first loved us. If anyone says, "I love God," but hates his brother, he is a liar; for whoever does not love a brother whom he has seen cannot love God whom he has not seen. This is the commandment we have from him: whoever loves God must also love his brother (1 Jn 4:19–21).

In addition to insisting on the inner bond between love of God and love of neighbor, Jesus also extended the prevailing understanding of neighbor. This expansion is so radical that it remains Jesus' deepest challenge to our common-sense way of understanding our relations with other people. Jesus expresses it beautifully in narrative form in his parable of the "good Samaritan" (Lk 10:30–36). In Luke, Jesus tells this parable in direct response to the scribe's question, "Who is my neighbor?" According to Jesus, a neighbor is anyone in need whom we are able to help. Gospel love of neighbor is expressed in what have traditionally been called the corporal (Mt 25:31–46) and spiritual works of mercy.

Jesus expands the understanding of neighbor to embrace even enemies. This is striking. There can be no doubt that Jesus taught, "Love your enemies . . ." (Mt 5:44). In the last of the so-called "five antitheses" of the sermon on the mount, Jesus says, "You have heard that it was said, 'You shall love your neighbor and hate your enemy' " (Mt 5:43). This kind of exclusivism reflects the party divisions and sectarian attitudes of Jesus' day (Perkins, 28–30). In contrast Jesus completes the antithesis, "But I say to you, love your enemies, and pray for those who persecute you" (Mt 5:44). This is the most dramatic example of his taking what is in the law (Lv 19:18) and instructing his disciples to go beyond it from the heart.

What Does Jesus Mean by Love?

Our culture has overused the word *love* to such an extent that it is nearly empty of meaning. As an aging songwriter once put it, "Love Is Just a Four-Letter Word." Obviously Jesus means to take us beyond the lyrics of third-rate popular songs. But the connotations the word *love* has acquired make the task of understanding Jesus difficult. It requires interpretation. What does Jesus mean by *love*?

From the well-known hymn to love in 1 Corinthians 13:4–7 to the Johannine "God is love" (1 Jn 4:16), there is no lack of expansion on the meaning of gospel love in the New Testament. The love that Jesus teaches is expressed in countless everyday actions, especially acts of forgiveness.

> Love is patient, love is kind. It is not jealous, [love] is not pompous, it is not inflated, it is not rude, it does not seek its own interest, it is not quick-tempered, it does not brood over injury, it does not rejoice over wrongdoing but rejoices with the truth. It bears all things, believes all things, hopes all things, endures all things (1 Cor 13:4–7).

If what passes for love among us is more impatient, unkind, jealous, or snobbish than not, then it cannot be the love that 1 John 4:8–16 identifies with the very reality of God. "God is love, and whoever abides in love abides in God and God in him." When Jesus says we should love others, he means that we should treat them the way God treats us, the way the prodigal son's father treated him, the way the good Samaritan treated the man by the roadside, the way Jesus and the early Christian martyrs treated their executioners.

Jesus' instruction to love is rooted in his understanding of God as Abba. We are to love in a non-exclusive way because the Father, who makes the sun to shine on the good and the bad, has first loved us. This image of the Father is the basis of Jesus' ministry to the sinners and the outcasts, of his teaching that even sinners would be included in the kingdom, and of the eventual inclusion of the Gentiles in the church.

Jesus' sense of Abba's nearness is the basis for his distinctive interpretation of the law's commands to love. Immediately following the injunction to "love your enemies, and pray for those who persecute you" in Matthew comes an appeal to the Father's example. The Father's example should impel disciples to go beyond the ordinary standards of human decency by which we are "nice" to people we "like."

> That you may be children of your heavenly Father, for he makes his sun rise on the bad and the good, and causes rain to

fall on the just and the unjust. For if you love those who love you, what recompense will you have? Do not the tax collectors do the same? And if you greet your brothers only, what is unusual about that? Do not the pagans do the same? So be perfect, just as your heavenly Father is perfect (Mt 5:45–48).

God knows how difficult it is to be "nice" even to the people we "like" or "love" in our ordinary sense. To "love" them in the gospel sense is next to impossible. After hearing Jesus' teaching on divorce, the disciples are reported to have said, "If that is the case between man and wife, it is better not to marry" (Mt 19:10). Jesus' teachings on love are hard sayings, but he does not impose them on people as burdens from the outside. This would contradict his most profound understanding of the law as a yoke that is light. "Whoever can accept this teaching ought to accept it" (Mt 19:12). The love of enemies to which Jesus calls his disciples must be a grace (Mt 19:11), a gift from God, rooted in the relationship with the Father into which Jesus invites them. As the Gospel of John insists, disciples can find in his death the greatest example of the kind of inclusive and self-giving love Jesus taught (Jn 15:3). On the cross Jesus becomes the parable of God *par excellence*.

THE COMMUNITY OF DISCIPLES

From the time of John's baptism, Jesus is never without his disciples. Simon, whom Jesus renamed Peter (Cephas in Aramaic, Jn 1:43), and his brother Andrew, along with Zebedee's two sons, James and John, were among the first to be called (Mk 1:16–20). In addition to Andrew and Simon, John's gospel also includes Philip and Nathaniel among the first disciples (Jn 1:35–51).

From his disciples Jesus chose "the twelve" (Mt 10:2–4; Mk 3:16–19; Lk 6:13–16). They were his constant companions during the public ministry. They received special instructions from him, were *sent out* (the meaning of *apostle*) by Jesus to preach and heal as he had done, and they shared in the meals of fellowship that anticipated the kingdom and culminated at the last supper. In general the twelve shared in Jesus' life and ministry.

In the gospels, all of Jesus followers, including the twelve, are often called disciples. *Disciple* is a general term that literally means student or one who is taught. It would not be unusual for a traveling sage such as Jesus to attract a group of followers. The selection of a core group of twelve (probably for the twelve tribes of Israel) is to be interpreted in the eschatological context of Jesus' ministry. The twelve represent Israel and form the foundation of the new community that anticipates the restoration of Israel.

In addition to Peter and the others, Jesus also had women disciples whose names are mentioned in Luke 8:1–4 along with the twelve.

> Afterward he journeyed from one town and village to another, preaching and proclaiming the good news of the kingdom of God. Accompanying him were the Twelve and some women who had been cured of evil spirits and infirmities, Mary, called Magdalene, from whom seven demons had gone out, Joanna, the wife of Herod's steward Chuza, Susanna, and many others who provided for them out of their resources (Lk 8:1–3).

Mary Magdalene was one of the first witnesses to Jesus' resurrection. As a member of Herod Antipas' household, Joanna was perhaps the source for Luke's special material on Herod Antipas. On the strength of Luke 10:38–42, the story of Martha and Mary, we can conclude that Jesus instructed his women disciples as well as the men. Mary "sat beside the Lord at his feet listening to him speak" (Lk 10:39). When her sister Martha challenged Mary's behavior as an irresponsible neglect of "the serving," Jesus defended her choice to "sit at his feet," a common phrase referring to a disciple's receiving instruction from a master. "Mary has chosen the better part and it will not be taken from her" (Lk 10:41).

Jesus' disciples were the beginnings of the church. They were a community with common purse (Jn 12:6), to which the women disciples made substantial contribution (Lk 8:3). They had left their jobs and their families to follow him who had nowhere to lay his head. They traveled around Palestine, finding hospitality at places like Bethany and Capernaum at the houses of Martha and Mary and Peter's mother-in-law.

When the evangelists write about Jesus' disciples, they always have a twofold purpose. The first is to tell the story of what

Jesus' disciples were like. Given the context of the gospels in the life of the early church, it is hard to imagine that the evangelists were free to take too many liberties with the early careers of those like Peter who had become the church's "pillars." Second and more importantly, the evangelists want to instruct disciples who are their contemporaries. They write at a time when those who had known Jesus, the giants of the apostolic church, had begun to die. Peter, Paul, and James of Jerusalem all died before the destruction of Jerusalem in A.D. 69–70. The evangelists want to make Jesus present to a new generation of disciples. They want Jesus to instruct the new disciples just as he had instructed Peter and James and John. They want to provide a model for new disciples to identify with, an eye through which to see Jesus as the first disciples had seen him.

We can summarize the gospel portrayal of the disciples in three short sentences:

1. Disciples come when Jesus calls.
2. Disciples do what Jesus does.
3. Disciples remain everyday people.

Disciples Come When Jesus Calls

That a traveling sage like Jesus should have a gathering of disciples comes as no surprise. That this gathering included women disciples seems unusual. Ordinarily we might expect disciples to seek out the master the way students today choose a college. But the evangelists emphasize Jesus calling his disciples. They present these callings in stark fashion. The call of the fishermen, Simon and Andrew, is a good example. Jesus saw them casting their nets into the sea. He said, "Come after me; I will make you fishers of men." Mark concludes simply: "They immediately abandoned their nets and became his followers" (Mk 1:18). Luke presents the call of the tax collector, Levi (Matthew), in a similar way. "Afterward he went out and saw a tax collector named Levi sitting at his customs post. He said to him, 'Follow me.' Leaving everything behind, Levi stood up and became his follower" (Lk 5:27–28).

Even if we allow for some sense of urgency about the coming kingdom on the part of Jesus, or for some literary exaggeration on the part of the evangelists, the point seems clear enough. Being Jesus' disciple is a very serious commitment. Our usual commitments of family and work and concern for our livelihood are portrayed as subordinate to it (Mt 8:18–22). One of Jesus' starkest sayings, and one that seems to reflect his view that the law was not absolute (Sanders, 252–255), is given in answer to a would-be disciple who asks if he can postpone following Jesus until after he buries his dead father, a very serious obligation indeed. Jesus answers, "Follow me, and let the dead bury their dead" (Mt 8:22). Sanders' conclusion that this saying is authentic is a good example of the application of the criterion of discontinuity discussed at the beginning of Chapter XI.

Disciples Do What Jesus Does

Just as Jesus patterned his life after his understanding of the Father, so disciples are to conform their lives to his. They share in his mission and ministry. They leave their homes and tramp around Palestine with him. Each of the synoptics reports Jesus' sending them out on a mission to preach and heal as he did (Lk 9, Mt 10, Mk 6). Their sharing in his life and ministry would extend even to the death.

According to Mark, when James and John asked Jesus if they could sit one at his right and one at his left in the kingdom, he replied, "You do not know what your are asking. Can you drink of the cup I shall drink or be baptized in the same bath of pain as I?" (Mk 10:38). According to Christian tradition (Eusebius, *Ecclesiastical History*, Books 2 and 3), his closest followers did indeed eventually drink of Jesus' cup, dying as martyrs or "witnesses" for their faith in him.

Paul's Christ mysticism, the deep sense of being newly alive in Christ that pervades his letters, draws upon the gospel tradition of discipleship as the following or imitation of Christ. "Whoever wishes to come after me must deny himself, take up his cross, and follow me" (Mk 8:34).

Disciples Remain Everyday People

God confounds the wise and the strong with the foolish and the weak. This is a commonplace of biblical wisdom. Accordingly,

Jesus' disciples are neither heroic nor powerful human figures. Far from being the great success stories of first century Palestine, theirs are quite modest lives. Their characters have more than a fair share of human weakness and ineptitude.

As an editor of gospel traditions, Mark makes the haplessness of the disciples one of the themes of his work. Peter and the others are close to slapstick in their bumbling efforts to follow in Jesus' steps. Doubtless Mark exaggerates by his selection and arrangement of traditions. But after Peter had become one of the pillars of the church, Mark could hardly have portrayed him in such an embarrassing way unless the failings of Jesus' inner circle were an authentic part of the tradition. The most likely conclusion is that the gospels do not idealize the disciples because, like most of us, they were far from ideal.

After reading the above descriptions of gospel love and discipleship, one might be moved to exclaim with the bewildered disciples, "Then who can be saved?" (Mk 10:26). This theme of the disciples as everyday people is one of the most comforting aspects of the gospel tradition. Far from being an excuse for mediocrity, it testifies both to the need for and the present offer of God's grace. It both softens and humanizes the seeming impossibility of real love and discipleship. "For human beings it is impossible, but not for God. All things are possible with God" (Mk 10:27).

From the call stories cited above, we learn that Andrew and Peter were fishermen. Matthew was one of the hated publicans or tax collectors. Tax collectors were notorious for skimming and bilking the people. We can assume that Andrew and Peter and their partners probably hauled a good living out of the Sea of Galilee. As a member of Herod's household, Joanna was probably fairly well off. Though none of them was hurting financially, they did not come from the ranks of the rich and powerful. The gospels show no evidence that any of the disciples were well educated. Of most of them we know little. The other Simon is described as a member of the Zealot party and Judas Iscariot is remembered as the one who betrayed Jesus. They were an ill-assorted lot.

In addition to being quite ordinary in origin and stature, the disciples suffer, in Mark's portrayal, from chronic dullness and lack of faith (Senior, *Jesus*, 60–61). Not only do they fail to comprehend what they have seen and heard, but they can also be found doing exactly the opposite of what he has taught them. In Mark 8:17–21, Jesus becomes exasperated with this ragtag bunch, who will eventually become the foundations of the church. "Do you still not see or comprehend? Are your minds completely blinded? Have you eyes but no sight? Ears but no hearing? . . . Do you still not understand?"

The disciples do not *see*. They have an especially difficult time with the strange reversals of common sense that typify Jesus' wisdom teaching. Strength comes out of weakness. The last shall be first. Authority is service. Life comes out of death. If these are more than clever paradoxes and really reflect deep truths about the human condition and God's purpose, who can be surprised at the disciples' lack of understanding? "Whoever wishes to save his life will lose it" (Mk 8:35). What are we to make of such wisdom? What are we to make of the prodigal son's father, of the good Samaritan? Is this really how it is?

PETER AS "EVERY DISCIPLE"

If there is one character besides Jesus whose obvious presence shines through the gospel pages, it is Simon, the Galilean fisherman, Cephas, the most unlikely rock. He is impetuous, loyal but weak, filled with false bravado and a golden heart. A would-be disciple seeking instruction from Mark's gospel would not need much imagination to identify with Peter's struggle to be faithful to Jesus and follow in his steps. From Lloyd C. Douglas' *The Big Fisherman* (1948) to Walter Murphy's *Upon This Rock* (1987), Peter is the stuff of which historical novels are made. If Jesus is the ever-elusive and surprising child of wisdom, playing in the mists of history (Prov 8:30; Sir 24:3), Peter the rock is ever accessible.

Mark's gospel builds to a literary climax in the middle of chapter 8. The question of Jesus' identity has been raised and various possible answers have been given. Finally Jesus asks his disciples, "But who do you say that I am?" (Mk 8:29). Without hesitation Peter answers with a profession of faith, "You are the Messiah." In Matthew Peter's profession of faith is followed by the oft-quoted "primacy text," in which Jesus makes Peter the rock (Cephas) and entrusts to him the keys to the kingdom of heaven (Mt 16:17–19). At Jesus' mention of his impending suffering and death in both accounts, Peter objects, takes Jesus aside, and begins to "rebuke" him. At this Jesus calls him "Satan." "You are thinking not as God does, but as human beings do" (Mk 8:31–33). In spite of his beginning faith, his willingness to step forward and profess it, and even in spite of his new pre-eminence, the rock has much to learn about God's ways. Peter's dramatic misunderstanding gives Jesus another opportunity to instruct them.

He speaks again of his impending death (Mk 9:31). The disciples "did not understand the saying, and they were afraid to question him" (9:32). On the way back to Capernaum from Caesarea Philippi, the disciples argue about which one of them was the most important (9:34). For the third time Jesus instructs them on how to see with the eyes of God. At this point James and John come forward and ask for places of honor (10:37). When they hear this, the other ten "became indignant at James and John" (10:41). Again Jesus instructs them on authority as service. By this time, the systematic misunderstanding has reached near-comic proportions.

This series of episodes most likely reflects the tremendous difficulty Peter and the others must have had with Jesus' passion and death on the cross. It is at his death that the disciples, especially Peter, fail Jesus most miserably. At Mark's last supper scene, Peter makes a public profession of love and loyalty to the master: "Even though all should have their faith shaken, mine will not be" (14:29). When Jesus predicts Peter's threefold denial, he reasserts, "Even though I should have to die with you, I will not deny you." And Mark adds, "And they all spoke similarly" (14:31). There follows the sorry catalogue of denial and human failure in faith.

Jesus asks his three closest friends, Peter and James and John, to pray with him as he agonizes over his death. They fall asleep not once but three times. Jesus wakes Peter with these words, "Could you not keep watch for even an hour?" (14:37). Next, after Judas betrays Jesus and hands him over to the crowd, the disciples "all left him and fled" (14:50). Unable to desert the master completely, Peter followed at a distance and made his way to the courtyard outside the place where Jesus was being questioned.

Finally, when confronted with the accusation that he was a disciple of Jesus, the rock crumbles before the servant girl's questions. Amid the telltale cock crows, he denies Jesus three times. The third time he even denies knowing who Jesus is. At this point, like the prodigal son among the pigs, Peter hits bottom. "He broke down and wept" (14:72).

Of all Jesus' disciples, only Mary Magdalene and the other women remain faithful and stay with Jesus as he dies on Golgotha (15:40–41). The gospels credit Mary Magdalene with bringing, at Jesus' own request, the news of the resurrection to Peter and the others.

Who among would-be disciples can claim that they would have remained faithful where Peter failed? However deeply moving the story of his denial may be, its pathos is exceeded by John's account of Peter's reconciliation with the risen Lord. Peter and his partners had returned to their fishing boats on the Sea of Galilee. At the sight of Jesus on the shore, Peter, in his usual impetuous fashion, jumps from the fishing boat—he did take the time to put on some clothes—and swims ashore to meet Jesus. As he had done with Mary Magdalene in the previous chapter, Jesus calls Peter by name and then asks him three times, one for each denial, "Simon, son of John, do you love me?" (Jn 21:15–17). Three times Peter assures him that he does.

According to the gospels, the reconciling experience of the resurrected Lord, along with the outpouring of the Holy Spirit, changed the lives of the disciples. They were finally given the wisdom to understand and to recognize Jesus. They received the grace to die in faith. If Peter did not die upside down on a cross, as tradition has it, such a fate is nevertheless in keeping with the gospel portrait of him. The good news about Peter's failure and lack of faith is that Jesus, like the father of the prodigal son, surprised him with forgiveness and the other gifts that made him strong when he needed to be.

Questions for Review and Discussion

1. Give a Christian theological response to the question, "Was it possible for Jesus to pray?"

2. If we assume that Jesus behaved as a pious and observant Jew, what would this tell us about his life of prayer and religious observance?

3. What are the three different kinds of testimony in the gospels about Jesus' prayer? Give examples of each.

4. What is the basic theme of Jesus' prayers as the gospels record them? How is this theme related to Jesus' baptism by John?

5. What is the significance of Jesus addressing the Father in prayer as Abba?

6. Summarize what Jesus teaches his disciples about prayer.

7. What is a parable or story parable? What do the parables of "the laborers in the vineyard" and "the prodigal son" tell us about how Jesus imagined Abba? Which of the characters in these parables represent God and what is their attitude toward people?

8. What was Jesus' attitude toward *Torah*? Give specific examples.

9. What are the two "great commandments" and what is distinctive about Jesus' interpretation of them?

10. How does the Father enter into Jesus' understanding of and teaching about love?

11. Jesus told parables about the kingdom of God and taught his disciples to pray for its coming. Using Chapter XI as background, what is the kingdom of God? What do we learn about it from Jesus' parables?

12. Using Peter as an illustration, summarize the gospel portrait of Jesus' disciples. By means of this portrayal of the disciples of Jesus, what are the evangelists trying to teach readers of their gospels about Christian discipleship in general?

13. What is the significance of Jesus' inclusion of women among his disciples? Name some of them.

14. List and discuss some of the main problems the disciples had with Jesus.

For Writing and Reflection

1. Using the theme of Jesus' relationship with the Father, his "Abba experience," write an essay that ties together Jesus' prayers, parables, and teaching about the law. Emphasize the Father's role in each of these sets of traditions about Jesus' words.

2. Jesus often approached moral questions from a narrative perspective. When people asked him moral questions, he often replied with stories. Pick the most troubling and serious moral question you can think of, one that you really care about, but that you really don't think you know the answer to. From your sense of what Jesus was like, and of his understanding of the Father, write a parable that Jesus might tell in answer to your question. In other words, pose your question to Jesus in your imagination and then imagine how he would answer it.

   Keep two things in mind in writing your parable. First, the parable has to be based on your sense of who Jesus is. You have to try to get inside him and try to figure out what you think he would say. Second, the parable has to be a real story. It can't be a speech that gives moral advice from on high. Before writing your parable, you should familiarize yourself with the parables Jesus tells in the gospels. Try to speak with his voice.

3. Keeping in mind that we don't really know what Jesus looked like—the New Testament never describes him—write an essay describing your image of him. Since Jesus is part of western culture, one doesn't have to be a Christian believer to have an image of him. It is your image of him that is important for this essay and not what you say you believe or don't believe about him. How do you imagine him speaking and acting? Is your imagination dominated more by human or by divine images of Christ? Does this preference (divine over human or vice versa) have any effects on your religious life (if you have one)? One interesting way of getting at your image of Jesus is to think

about the kinds of religious art you are most attracted to. You might go to the library and look at some books on Christian art before you write your essay.

For Further Reading

E.P. Sanders, *Jesus and Judaism* (Philadelphia: Fortress Press, 1985). An excellent reconstruction of the historical Jesus that emphasizes his continuity with Judaism.

Edward Schillebeeckx, *Jesus, an Experiment in Christology*. Another similar and excellent portrait of the historical Jesus. Not as accessible to the general reader as Sanders.

Donald Senior, *Jesus, A Gospel Portrait* (Dayton: Pflaum Publishers, 1975). Written by a distinguished New Testament scholar, this book is informative, engaging and extremely clear; the best popularization of historical Jesus research that I know of. Students never failed to respond positively to it. A revised edition was published by Paulist Press in 1992.

Ivan Havener, *Q: The Sayings of Jesus*, with a Reconstruction of Q by Athanasius Polag (Wilmington, Del.: Michael Glazier, 1987). An analysis of the hypothetical Q or sayings source used by Matthew and Luke. The section on Jesus as Wisdom's agent (78–83) is helpful.

Joachim Jeremias, *The Prayers of Jesus*. Cited in the last chapter as an excellent entry into the work of Jeremias. Bears directly on the contents of this chapter.

Elizabeth A. Johnson, *She Who Is, the Mystery of God in Feminist Theological Discourse* (New York: Crossroad, 1992). Provides a look at Jesus and "Abba" from a feminist perspective, emphasizing the fluidity of Jesus' language about God and the intent of "Abba" as analogical language. Chapter 5 also contains a section on "Jesus-Sophia."

Brad H. Young, *Jesus and His Jewish Parables* (New York/ Mahwah: Paulist Press, 1989). A scholarly but readable study of the parables that emphasizes their role in teaching people how to live the law in daily life.

Pheme Perkins, *Love Commands in the New Testament* (New York/Mahwah: Paulist Press, 1982). Clearly written and accessible study of Jesus' teaching on the law.

Leonard Swidler, *Yeshua, a Model for Moderns* (Kansas City: Sheed & Ward, 1988). In a readable style, this book makes Jewish scholarship on Jesus available to the general reader. Emphasizes his similarity to the Pharisees as well as his openness to women.

Gerard S. Sloyan, *Is Christ the End of the Law?* (Philadelphia: Westminster Press, 1978). A theological treatment of the relationship between Christianity and Judaism, and, most importantly, a theological treatment of law.

John Pawlikowski, *Jesus and the Theology of Israel* (Wilmington, Del.: Michael Glazier, 1989). A theological essay on Jesus and Judaism.

Declaration on the Church's Relationship to Non-Christian Religions, in Tanner, ed., *Decrees of the Ecumenical Councils*, II, 970. Paragraph 4 of this document contains Vatican II's statement on Jewish-Christian relations.

Walter F. Murphy, *Upon This Rock, the Life of St. Peter* (New York: Macmillan, 1987). An engaging historical novel.

Terms To Identify

Abba	neighbor
parable/story parable	*Torah*
shema	Abba experience (Jesus')
disciple	kingdom of God
apostle	eschatological (see Ch. XI)
the twelve	halakhist

Chapter XIII

Miracles

In Chapters XI and XII, we examined, from an historical-theological point of view, Jesus' context in first century Judaism. We also examined some of the gospel traditions about his words. In Chapter X, we saw that one of the factors separating moderate from skeptical critics is how they approach the New Testament's supernatural claims about Jesus. The New Testament's claims for Jesus are based on his own at least implicit claims as God's special agent in bringing about the kingdom.

In the context of preaching about the Father's kingdom, Jesus worked what we have come to call *miracles*. In the section on skeptical historical criticism in Chapter X, we considered some of the questions raised by the New Testament's claim that Jesus worked miracles. Now it is time to examine these claims and questions in more depth. One thing we can note at the outset is the near unanimous agreement among scholars that at the earliest strata of the gospel traditions we find the memory of Jesus as a worker of wondrous or startling deeds.

We shall examine a statement of this consensus made by Bultmann in 1926. The terms he uses serve also to raise the philosophical questions about miracles that will occupy us in this chapter.

> The Christian community was convinced that *Jesus had performed miracles* [original emphasis], and told a good many miracle stories about him.

Bultmann regarded most of the miracle stories in the gospels as "legendary," or at least embellished with legend. But, he continued:

> There can be no doubt that Jesus did the kind of deeds which were miracles to his mind and to the minds of his contemporar-

305

ies, that is deeds which were attributed to a supernatural divine cause; undoubtedly he healed the sick and cast out demons (*Jesus and the Word*, 173).

Jesus' contemporaries generally did not question the fact of his wondrous deeds. Rather they questioned their meaning. Did Jesus' mighty works come from God or from some other source (Mk 3:22–27)? As Bultmann's careful language suggests, *our* problem is precisely with the fact of miracles as such, not their interpretations. One contemporary commentator describes modern people as "allergic" to miracles. We have trouble believing that the kinds of works attributed to Jesus are possible. This is a philosophical issue. It is a question of how we conceive the world in which we live.

Bultmann's comments make this clear. He speaks of "the kind of deeds which were miracles to his mind [Jesus'] and to the minds of his contemporaries." The wording indicates that Bultmann didn't share this mind. In his remarks, we see the question about whether Jesus actually performed miracles dissolve into the philosophical question about what the term *miracle* means.

By the phrase "deeds which were attributed to a supernatural divine cause," Bultmann indicates that for him miracles are supposed interferences by God, conceived as an external agent among agents, in the closed system of nature. We might imagine the long arm and hand of God from Michelangelo's Sistine Chapel as it reaches in from above to tinker with the world. This is what Bultmann says we cannot today continue to believe in.

As we saw in Chapter X, Bultmann accepts the enlightenment understanding of *miracle* as a "violation of the laws of nature" and accordingly rejects *miracle* as a religious category referring to events having some sort of objective claim on observers. Using David Hume's essay "Of Miracles," we will now examine this understanding of miracles.

DAVID HUME'S "OF MIRACLES"

In Chapter IX, in the context of discussing enlightenment views on religion, we mentioned briefly David Hume's approach to the miraculous. Since Hume's approach represents a relentlessly consistent application of the enlightenment worldview to religious questions, we will examine it more closely here.

Hume's eighteenth century contemporaries who defended "rational Christianity" emphasized the role of miracles and prophecies in establishing Christianity's pre-eminence among the religions. Modern apologists regarded miracles as proofs or demonstrations of Christianity's claims. In 1758 when Hume came to publish a new edition of his philosophical essays, he included among them for the first time his essay "Of Miracles." It became Section X of his popular philosophical work *An Inquiry Concerning Human Understanding*.

As a skeptic who understood himself as an empiricist, that is, one who based knowledge on sense experience, Hume was not prepared to make such statements as "There is no God" or "Miracles are impossible." Rather he was committed to the position that, on questions that could not be decided by an appeal to sense experience, he had to say simply that he did not know. Christian theologians in Hume's day tended to treat miracles as demonstrations coercing belief from the outside in the way that one must assent to mathematical conclusions or proofs for geometrical theorems. Hume found such claims immodest. In a brilliant display of ironic ridicule, his essay cuts the ground from under his contemporaries, all the while professing his deference to "our holy religion."

The main purpose of "Of Miracles," therefore, is not so much to argue directly that miracles are impossible (an immodest claim by Hume's standards) but to argue that an intelligent person could not reasonably believe that one had occurred. Against the apologists of his day, Hume concluded:

> . . . and therefore we may establish it as a maxim that no human testimony can have such force as to prove a miracle and make it a just foundation for any such system of religion (137).

Systems of religion cannot be based on human testimony to miracles. This is Hume's conclusion. Because the Bible comes to us from divine rather than human testimony, Hume excepts it from his conclusion. But this is merely a rhetorical evasion necessitated by the lack of full religious liberty in Britain. That Hume intends his conclusion to apply to Christianity is clear from his repeated use throughout the essay of the example of testimony that someone had risen from the dead.

Hume's primary argument is not explicitly metaphysical (having to do with claims about the nature of reality) but epistemological. It has to do with the order of knowledge. How, he asks, could an otherwise reasonable person come to recognize a miracle? How could we ever reasonably conclude that one had occurred? If one were to ask how Christians can reasonably believe that the Bible comes to us on divine rather than human testimony, it would become clear that, despite his pious statements to the contrary, Hume's conclusion applies to Christianity just as well as to other religions.

Hume divides "Of Miracles" into two parts. The first is more formal and establishes the basic structure of the argument. The second part is more historical and applies the argument to some historical examples.

Testimony to Miracles Versus Sense Experience of Nature's Regular Behavior

As a form of evidence, the testimony of others is inferior to the evidence of our own senses. Belief in miracles is based on the testimony of others, usually from the distant past. Hume does not consider the possible case of experiencing an apparent miracle oneself. This is probably because his primary concern is with the New Testament miracles his contemporaries regarded as "proofs" of Christianity.

Hume defines a miracle as "a violation of the laws of nature" (122). In asking how a reasonable person, one who proportions belief to evidence, might come to believe that such a violation had occurred, Hume pits the experience of the senses against the inferior form of evidence, human testimony. Imagine an analytical balance such as "Blind Justice" holds in our sculptures of her. On the one side of the balance, Hume places our experience of nature's regular behavior, our sense experience upon which the "laws of nature" are based. If we step out a three-story window and into the air, we expect to fall down.

On the other side of the balance he places some human testimony that our regular experience of nature's laws has been "violated." The very term *violation* strongly connotes something that's not supposed to happen. Violating laws is usually not desirable. The term *violation* appeals to the prevalent enlightenment sense of the unfittingness of the miraculous as unworthy of God.

Now we have our lifetime of sense experience on one side of the balance as witness to nature's regular or predictable behavior. On the other side we have someone else's testimony against this experience. The example Hume uses is "that a dead man should come to life" (122). Hume argues that for a reasonable person the former (sense experience) ought generally to outweigh the latter (testimony). He then proposes a possibility he considers highly remote, if not impossible, namely that the testimony would "be of such a kind that its falsehood would be more miraculous than the fact which it endeavors to establish" (123). This would result in a "mutual destruction of arguments" (123).

> When anyone tells me that he saw a dead man restored to life, I immediately consider with myself whether it be more probable that this person should either deceive or be deceived, or that the fact which he relates should really have happened (123).

Apparently the "mutual destruction of arguments" leaves reason to weigh one miracle against the other, and "always reject the greater." I say *apparently* because Part I's last sentence could be read as taking back Hume's conclusion. Part of the lack of clarity is due to the equivocal use of *miraculous*. It is hard to see how the falsehood of a testimony could be *miraculous* in the same sense as a dead man restored to life, i.e. how it could violate the laws of nature.

In any case, Hume concludes that no testimony—even if its falsehood could be figuratively described as miraculous—ought to be able to convince a reasonable person that a miracle as a violation of the laws of nature has occurred. For Hume, miracles are by definition not so much impossible (a metaphysical claim) as impossible to believe in (an epistemological claim). Thus by implication, the "miraculous nature" of an event is tantamount to its "absolute impossibility" (133).

How Would One Recognize a Miracle as God's Action?

In the second part of the essay, Hume examines some examples of past testimony to miracles and arrives at an historical conclusion: "Upon the whole, it appears that no testimony for any kind of miracle has ever amounted to a probability, much less to a proof" (137).

But what about the hypothetical future case? He examines two imaginary examples. For the first he proposes eight days of universally attested total darkness. This he finds plausible and would lead the reasonable person to look for natural causes.

The second example is telling. It involves widespread testimony to the death and return from the dead of Queen Elizabeth I. Hume concludes that the reasonable person would have to regard the queen's death as "pretended." Even if it were attributed to God in the name of some new religion or other, he would still have to reject the testimony. Here Hume raises the key difficulty. How would one recognize a miracle as God's action?

> Though the Being to whom the miracle is ascribed be in this case the Almighty, it does not upon that account, become a whit more probable, since it is impossible for us to know the attributes or actions of such a Being otherwise than from the experience which we have of his productions in the usual course of nature (139).

OPENING HUME'S CLOSED WORLD

If one were to push Hume's view of nature's predictability or regularity in an explicit metaphysical direction, i.e. a direction asking questions about what reality is like in the last analysis, one would most likely reach a "closed naturalism" or metaphysical determinism. Hume's view of miracles assumes that "any event must be natural—that it must be according to the laws of nature or contrary to those laws." This is how Germain Grisez begins his insightful critique of Hume on the miracle question (*Beyond the New Theism, A Philosophy of Religion*, 332–335). To put it in another way, Hume has closed the world prematurely. He lives in an overly mechanized world where it is difficult to account even for the uniquely human, not to mention possible manifestations of God.

To speak of an implied metaphysical horizon of closed naturalism is to raise the critical question of human freedom. As an example of a free human action, Grisez chooses Hume's writing "Of Miracles." Hume's physical and psychological performance in writing the essay was doubtless in accord with the "laws of nature." But his writing it "hardly seems to follow from any natural law or set of such laws" (332). Nature did not require Hume to write "Of Miracles" and then decide to publish it in 1758.

Grisez's move against Hume is an example of the kind of Socratic dialectic we saw in Chapter II. Its point is simply that, in order to account for Hume's own act of writing "Of Miracles," the world we live in cannot be as closed and mechanical as Hume's definition of miracles implies. Hume's writing the essay is in some meaningful sense a new and even unique act, free within the limits of our world. Hume conceived of the world according to Newton's physics, a form of mechanics. Contemporary physics, with its emphasis on indeterminacy, is more congenial to a view such as Grisez's than to that of Hume. The world and our experience of it must be more open and unpredictable than Hume would have us believe. If this is so, then human testimony must be of greater value than Hume allowed in this essay. Hume seems remotely aware that he has undervalued testimony and hedges at the end of Part I in the discussion of testimony whose falsehood would be "miraculous." Grisez uses the example of testimony to one's unconditional love for another.

Christianity claims that, with the arrival of Jesus, something new and unparalleled, something unpredictable and unique occurred. God visited his people. This claim is continuous with Jesus' own sense of deep personal union with the Father, and with his sense of himself as the Father's special agent in bringing about the kingdom. If we believe either of these claims, we should not be surprised that he did "incredible" deeds. "The blind regain their sight, the lame walk, lepers are cleansed, the deaf hear, the dead are raised to life, and the poor have the good news proclaimed to them" (Mt 11:5).

Having pried open Hume's universe, we are in a position to entertain Christian claims seriously. But we are still left with

Hume's conclusion that miracles understood as violations of the laws of nature cannot serve as the foundation for religious belief. They cannot coerce faith from outside. Further, we are left with the problem posed by Hume of how an otherwise reasonable person might come to believe that a "miracle" had occurred. We might call this the question of "recognition of miracles."

GOD AND WORLD REFLECT CHURCH AND STATE

Hume's understanding of miracles as violating the laws of nature is based on an implied understanding of the world as a closed system in which all events must have "natural" explanations. Of course we should expect the "natural" but, as Grisez's argument shows, we must remain open to the unpredictable, the unknown, the free. Hume's refusal to do this expresses the enlightenment's sense of the world's autonomy and independence, its secularity. The world or nature runs by itself. It has its own laws. Miracles as divine interventions into the affairs of the world are, therefore, highly offensive to the enlightened. For deists miracles so understood are unworthy of God. For skeptics they are virtually impossible.

Perhaps some brief attention to the political experience of Hume and other enlightened critics of Christianity would help us to appreciate better both the sense and the passion of their position. Hume lived in a modern state with an established church. So did Voltaire and Reimarus and D.F. Strauss. The ironic protestations of belief that pepper "Of Miracles" are for the benefit of those who would censor him as well as Hume's own amusement. Living in a similar situation in Germany, Reimarus feared to publish his lengthy life of Jesus manuscript during his own lifetime. When D.F. Strauss published his *Life of Jesus* nearly a century after Hume, it spelled the ruin of his academic career in state-sponsored theological faculties.

In the enlightenment critique of miracles, it is not difficult to catch an echo of the passionate concern of people like Hume and Voltaire for civil liberty. God's miraculous interferences in the affairs of secular nature were not unlike ecclesiastical interference in the affairs of secular states. Hume's critique of miracles is not simply an abstract philosophical argument. It is also a political statement. The enlightened criticized Christianity in the name of science. Perhaps their critique is more closely related to their aspirations for political freedom than our own experience of separation of church and state allows us to suspect. In a different kind of political situation, one in which we are no longer much concerned with banishing established churches from the affairs of autonomous states, perhaps we are free to think about miracles in a different way.

NATURE VERSUS CREATION

In order to do this, we must first try to think of the world more as creation than as nature. The term *nature*, inherited from the Greeks, connotes and emphasizes the world's autonomy and secularity. The more biblical term *creation* suggests a world distinct from but intimately related to the God whose constant presence holds it in being. Just as we have discovered that it is not as easy to banish religious faith from the realm of politics as the enlightened thought, so we might try to understand God as more intimately involved with creation than a deist would have it.

As Hume has made clear, interventions of a deist deity into a closed natural system are by definition virtually impossible, and in any case cannot force belief out of intelligent people. Only those who already believe in God on other grounds and who view the world as God's creation can be open to the unpredictable possibilities of the miraculous. But the wondrous or miraculous must be understood in a different way from Hume's. If we believe in God, we might ask whether the unfathomable Creator ever makes self-manifestations in our history. As Grisez would have it, does God ever send us signals? It is in the context of such a question that the term *miracle* can become meaningful as a "signal from the Creator." This is Grisez's definition of a miracle. Significantly, he introduces it only after a lengthy argument on other grounds for the reality of God as Creator. Speaking more biblically than philosophically, we might simply call miracles "signs" from God.

In order to appreciate this definition, it is necessary to unlearn practical deism as a way of thinking and a way of living in or being with the world. If we understand God as Creator as always present to creation (Acts 17:27–28), then such "signs" are better taken as *manifestations* than as *interventions* or *interpositions* (Hume, 123, note). The term *intervention* acquires its offensiveness in the context of a deist conception of the God who intervenes. The term *manifestation* presumes a different and more intimate relationship between Creator and creation. God is already here and doesn't need to reach in from without.

Recall the discussion of the analogical approach to religious experience in Chapter III. Without the radical separation of God and the world so typical of modern thought, "tiny whispering sounds" (1 Kgs 19:11–13) already mediate God's presence. In this context, more dramatic "signs" lose the offensiveness they might give to the deist mind. Though his approach to God and to religious experience seems more dialectical than the present one, it is not clear that Bultmann's discussion of Jesus' "Belief in Miracles" (*Jesus and the Word*, 172–179) is at odds with what has been said here. Here is Bultmann's conclusion:

> Whoever affirms Jesus' thought [his belief in miracles] accepts also the paradox that an event which from the observer's viewpoint must be regarded as a natural occurrence, as part of the world process determined by law, is in reality something different, that is, a direct act of God. When he says "miracle" he suspends the concept of nature, the category of cause and effect, which otherwise dominates his thinking. He knows however that he cannot do this at will, and of himself has no right to do it. For God is the distant God, whom the course of nature hides from his eyes; God is near only for faith, and faith originates only in miracle. The "natural" view of the world is for man the unbelieving view, from which he cannot free himself by his own desire (*Jesus and the Word*, 179).

MIRACLES AS SIGNS FROM GOD

In Chapter 9 of St. John's gospel, we find the story of Jesus' cure of the man born blind. Jesus' summary of his ministry, cited above from Matthew 11, speaks of the blind recovering their sight. For the sake of discussion, let us suppose that Jesus really did cure the man born blind. This Johannine example is particularly apt because the man is said to have been blind from birth. This condition would minimize the possible role of auto-suggestion in the cure and maximize the possible role of God's creative power. What would be the difference between understanding the cure of the blind man as "a violation of the laws of nature" and as "a sign from God"?

In the terms of Hume's definition, we would be struck most forcefully by the mere occurrence of such an event. Hume's definition focuses our attention on the inert physical aspect of the event. The term *violation* suggests both the offensiveness and virtual impossibility of such a cure. Our ordinary experience of the world, Hume might point out, perhaps with characteristic sarcasm, does not lead us to expect that blind people can be made to see simply by smearing mud made with saliva on their eyes (Jn 9:6). How can reasonable people be expected to believe this, even if John's gospel testifies to it? But what if we point out that John's testimony is not merely human testimony but inspired by the Holy Spirit, or that Jesus cured the man born blind by God's own creative power? Hume might rejoin, not without a note of triumph, "How do you know?" If miracles are violations of the laws of nature, the only possible reply would be something like, "Well, I just believe it and I have a right to my opinion." At this point, we would not be surprised if Hume snickered derisively, turned his back, and walked away.

Here we confront the issue of recognition. How could intelligent people—without completely abandoning their intelligence—come to believe that Jesus cured by God's own creative power the man born blind? Some Christians might glory in the position of completely abandoning their intelligence. Hume counts on this. But such a sacrifice of intellect would be at odds with the entire western theological tradition.

Grisez and other Christian thinkers who treat miracles as signs from God describe a process by which believers might come to acknowledge something like the blind man's recovery of sight as a sign from God. In order for religious people to believe intelligently that the mysterious Lord of creation has sent them a sign, at least two conditions must be met (Grisez, 335–342). The first is some extraordinary occurrence, the healing of a man born blind, or some striking and well-documented twentieth century cure. But even the occurrence of such an astounding event would not get us very far. Considered purely from the physical point of view as the cure of someone who was blind, such an event would remain ambiguous. How would we know what it meant? As it stands, it is simply an extraordinary event to be wondered at and filed under the unexplained.

This leads to the second condition. We must have some positive reason for interpreting the extraordinary occurrence as a sign from God. Signs require interpretation. Interpretation of an event occurs within a context or field. For the cure of the man born blind to appear as a sign from God, we must be able to locate it in an explicitly religious context or field of meaning.

JESUS' PERSON AND MISSION AS THE CONTEXT FOR HIS MIRACLES

The religious context for Jesus' miracles is clear. It is his mission as the Son-Servant-Wisdom of the Father. Jesus heals and exorcises in the context of his proclamation of the coming of the Father's reign. The religious context for Jesus' extraordinary works is well illustrated in the episode where John, having been imprisoned by Herod Antipas, sends some of his disciples to question Jesus (Mt 11:2–6; Lk 7:18–23; Havener, *Q*, 62–67). Jesus' behavior perplexed the Baptist. Jesus proclaimed the presence of the kingdom and called people to repent. But in addition to his talk of how sudden the kingdom's final inbreaking would be, he also told parables about its gradual growth and about the Father's patient mercy. Weeds and wheat, sinners and the righteous, would grow side by side. Jesus called sinners to his table. He refused to fix a date for the judgment John had prophesied (Mk 13:32).

John instructed his disciples to ask Jesus, "Are you 'He who is to come' or do we look for another?" (Mt 11:3). Jesus replies:

> Go and tell John what you hear and see: the blind regain their sight, the lame walk, lepers are cleansed, the deaf hear, the dead are raised, and the poor have the good news proclaimed to them (Mt 11:4–6).

Here in this saying from the hypothetical Q source, Jesus claims that his works of healing clarify his identity and mission. Although preaching the good news to the poor might not strike us as very extraordinary, John may have recognized in it echoes of the prophetic text of Isaiah 61 with which Jesus begins his public ministry in Luke 4:16–19. Thus not only do we find reference to Jesus' works of healing in the oldest traditions about him, but we also find strong indications of how these works are to be interpreted.

The field of meaning or interpretive context for Jesus' miracles is the entire event or spectacle of his ministry. The miracles have an inner relationship to what Jesus says. Jesus' healings defeat sin and restore creation to its original wholeness. They dramatize his words about God. They are microcosms of the kingdom, mini-episodes in the drama of its coming. They anticipate in miniature, at an individual level, the fullness of the kingdom that has begun, is now growing, and will burst into completion with the suddenness of a thief in the night.

Jesus does his extraordinary works in the context of his proclamation of the kingdom and his claim to a special role in bringing it about on behalf of the Father. Within this field of meaning, people of faith have interpreted Jesus' miracles as signs from the Father, testifying to his mission. Apart from this context, such works remain ambiguous displays.

CONTEMPORARY MIRACLES?

The New Testament makes clear the early Christian belief that, in the Holy Spirit, the kinds of extraordinary works Jesus did were still possible in the apostolic church. In his discussion of the variety of gifts in the one Spirit, St. Paul mentions "the gifts of healing" and "mighty deeds" (1 Cor 12:9–10). In the Acts of the Apostles, after the Holy Spirit's outpouring at Pentecost, Peter heals a man "crippled from birth" with the words, "In the name of Jesus Christ the Nazorean, walk!" (Acts 3:6).

Some Christian theologians have argued that such miraculous gifts or "charisms" ended with the apostolic age. But such theologians are often members of educated elites. In more popular forms of Christianity, the belief in miracles as "signs" from

God has tended to persist with varying degrees of theological sophistication.

Among Catholics, healing has been associated most commonly with belief in the "communion of saints." Living Christians remain united in Christ with dead Christians in a communion that death does not have the power to break. The interpretive context or field of meaning for healing in modern Catholicism, therefore, has been intercessory prayer, i.e. asking the prayers of Mary and the other saints who remain in Christ.

Among American Protestants, the belief in the gift of healing has been most dramatically preserved by "pentecostal" Christians. Pentecostal Christians believe that God regularly continues to send the gifts the apostles experienced at Pentecost (Acts 2), e.g. tongues, healing, etc., to contemporary Christians. In the pentecostal tradition, God's healing occurs through the prayers of a living human agent—sometimes called a "faith healer"—rather than through the prayers of the saints. Through the contemporary Catholic charismatic renewal and other means, beliefs and practices of the pentecostal tradition have found their way back into Catholicism. Readers may, therefore, be familiar with "healing services" in their churches or with various "healing ministries."

Doubtless some so-called "faith-healers" are misguided, dishonest, or both. Christians ought not to be overly gullible about claims associated with contemporary healings, but should examine them carefully to see if they can be explained "naturally." At the same time, when extraordinary and unexplained healings occur in a context of faith and prayer and in the name of Jesus, Christians ought not to dismiss out of hand the possibility that they have encountered a "sign" from God. Unless one chooses to adopt some form of closed naturalism, one need not assume that God stopped sending "signs" to Jesus' disciples with the end of the apostolic generation.

Among Catholics, perhaps the best-known contemporary setting for miraculous healing is in France, at the grotto of Lourdes, where in 1858 Jesus' mother is said to have appeared to a young French woman, Bernadette Soubirous. In his 1982 novel *Miracle*, Irving Wallace makes a popular and not entirely theologically inadequate fictional presentation of the phenomenon of Lourdes. In his book *The Miracles of Jesus and the Theology of Miracles*, the French-Canadian theologian René Latourelle reports that since 1858 twelve hundred healings "have been acknowledged by physicians to be scientifically inexplicable: the Church, however, has recognized only fifty-four as miracles" (313–314). These figures illustrate both the extraordinary character of the Lourdes phenomenon and the church's care in examining reported cures in the public, on-site medical facilities at Lourdes. Though miracles remain offensive to the enlightened or modern worldview, we have widespread and various contemporary Christian testimony that God has not left the world bereft of his healing touch.

MIRACLES AS CALLS TO FAITH

If one were to encounter in a religious context such an event as an unexplained healing, one would not be bound to interpret it as a sign from God. Signs are ambiguous and require interpretation. This is easily seen in the fact that all who witnessed Jesus' works did not necessarily become his disciples. Some interpreted him as being "out of his mind." Others thought Jesus did his marvelous works "with the help of 'the prince of demons' " (Mk 3:21–22). Understood as signs from God, miracles summon people to conversion and faith in God. Miracles cannot coerce faith from outside, nor can they be perceived outside the context of faith.

While a religious person might be reasonably justified in interpreting an extraordinary and otherwise unexplained healing as a sign from God, another might simply decide to leave it in the unexplained file. In either case, we need not assume that the laws of nature have been "violated." We might assume instead that unknown factors are at work in the processes of creation. If God is Creator and the world is creation, the signs God sends ought to be in keeping with the order of creation. Biblical miracles are for the most part not sensational spectacles. Jesus does not create three-headed dogs and other "unnatural" prodigies for his own aggrandizement and the amusement of his audience. The synoptic tradition contains its own critique of such "pseudo-miracles" (Latourelle, *Miracles of Jesus*, 257–258). Jesus' compassionate touch is not that of a wizard or sorcerer. He restores people to a

"natural" state of wholeness. What Jesus accomplishes is in keeping with nature's apparent purposes, but not something we could
have expected nature to accomplish on its own. As C.S. Lewis
argues in his book *Miracles*, God's signs seem to work in accordance with nature's laws and with due respect for them.

WHY DOESN'T GOD HEAL EVERYONE?

The gospels portray Jesus' miracles as genuine acts of compassion for those who suffer. When I hear accounts of miraculous
healings, I tend to think of all the sufferers who have not been
healed. What about them? I think of relatives and friends, good
people of faith, who have suffered cruelly from cancer. Why
didn't God heal them? I think of the haunting figure of the crucified on the cover of Gustavo Gutierrez' *A Theology of Liberation*.
It reminds me of all those who have suffered and died in the
struggle for justice in Central America, South Africa, and Eastern
Europe. Why didn't God heal them?

Some Christians might say that these people lacked strong
faith or that the inscrutable God simply did not happen to choose to
use them as his instruments. Or perhaps suffering and sickness are
tests or punishments from God. Some well-meaning Christians
presume to console those who mourn with assurances that what
they are mourning is part of "God's plan." How do they know?
How could Auschwitz, for example, be part of any plan of God?

In the spirit of Job's last reply to God (Job 42:1–6), such
pious attempts to "justify God" must be repudiated as dishonor-
ing God. A God who planned Auschwitz for some "good," or
who afflicts people with AIDS in order to test them, is at odds
with all that Jesus taught about God. Such a God would be mor-
ally inferior to most people. How could we worship such a mon-
ster? In the wisdom of Jesus, the Father numbers our very hairs
and knows us all by name. He delays the judgment and awaits
patiently the prodigal's return.

In the end I must confess that I simply do not know why God
doesn't heal everyone. I do not know why God's compassion,
revealed in Jesus, does not always come in recognizable form to
those who suffer. I am left to take consolation from Jesus' own

attitude in the face of suffering and death. Some Christians confess with the scriptures and the ancient councils that Jesus was truly human. But then they introduce some theological hypothesis about his human knowledge that makes it impossible to accept the clear gospel testimony that Jesus agonized over his death. In plausible Jewish fashion, he made lamentation to the Father. In the end, he simply had to trust that Abba would not abandon him. After having done what we could to prevent or alleviate suffering, lamenting, in the spirit of the psalmist, in the spirit of Jeremiah amid the ruins of the holy city, in the spirit of Jesus on the cross, is perhaps the only response to it.

In a moving meditation on "God and Suffering," Hans Küng describes Jesus' God-forsakenness as "unparalleled and boundless." He was "left utterly alone by him on whose presence he had staked everything" (*On Being a Christian*, 428–436, 433). Reflecting on Christ's descent into hell, Hans Urs von Balthasar writes in a similar vein. In his descent into the reality of death, Christ experienced "from within" that from which he redeemed us, namely, hell, or exclusion from the presence of God. He describes Jesus as the "last of the Old Testament saints that cry to God: 'Why hast thou forsaken me?' "

> No one could utter this cry more intensely than he whose life it is to be everlastingly generated by the Father and, in this generation, to see the Father. Now he, too, experiences what it means to lose God . . . (*The God Question and Modern Man*, 133).

In the descents into hell or dark nights of Christians, von Balthasar finds the possibility of an imitation by grace of Christ's experience of Holy Saturday, his loss of God.

Such speculations bear stark and even shocking testimony to the magnitude of Jesus' trust in the Father. In this his disciples can find a model and a support. The good news of the resurrection is that God did not abandon Jesus and will not abandon us. This hope and not hope in miracles must see Christians through their sufferings. If a miracle should come, it will be one of those surprising moments of grace, a sign to the church and an anticipation of God's final manifestation.

CONCLUSIONS

1. *Jesus healed people*. To our previous conclusions about Jesus, we can add that he healed people in what the New Testament variously calls "works of power," "wonders," or "signs." *Miracle* is a modern word derived from the Latin for *wonder*. In the careful words of Schillebeeckx, we have "a historically firm base for affirming, as the New Testament does, that Jesus acted as both healer and exorcist" (*Jesus*, 189). He points to "a growing conviction that Jesus carried out historical cures and exorcisms," shared by "the majority of critical exegetes." We find these healings and exorcisms attested to at the oldest levels of the tradition. Their impact on his contemporaries ought not to be minimized. Doubtless it contributed to his disciples' sense that he was more than an ordinary man, one in whom they experienced God's real offer of salvation.

2. *Jesus disciples interpreted his healings as signs from God.* While those who follow Hume would require "natural" explanations for Jesus' works, we have seen that otherwise reasonable people have interpreted them, in the non-deist religious context of Jesus and his mission, as signs from God. While historical and literary factors may lead scholars to conclude that individual miracle stories have been either embellished or created whole, we need not conclude that reason requires us to look for "purely natural" explanations for all of them.

3. *From an historical point of view, each miracle story must be examined individually.* In *The Miracles of Jesus*, Latourelle makes such a comprehensive examination of twenty-eight miracle stories from the gospels. His conclusions are quite conservative, tending strongly to favor historicity in almost every case. A less extensive examination by Schillebeeckx (*Jesus*, 183–200) yields more modest or skeptical conclusions. Neither opposes the miracle stories in principle. They differ only on their historical evaluations of individual stories.

Questions for Review and Discussion

1. In Chapter X, this quote appeared from Bultmann's essay "New Testament and Mythology": "It is impossible to use the

electric light and the wireless [radio] and to avail ourselves of modern medical and surgical techniques and, at the same time, to believe in the New Testament world of spirits and miracles." Why? As presumably one of the people he's talking about, do you agree with him? Explain.

2. What role did miracles play in the Christian theology of Hume's day? How does this help to explain the purpose of the essay "Of Miracles"?

3. How does Hume define *miracle*? Summarize his argument that an intelligent person cannot reasonably believe that a miracle (in his sense) has occurred.

4. How does Grisez try to show the "closed" and "mechanical" nature of the world implied by Hume's definition?

5. Make an analogy between Hume's philosophical opposition to God's intervention in the world and the general modern political opposition to interference by established churches in secular or worldly affairs.

6. Briefly, distinguish *metaphysical* from *epistemological* claims. Give examples of them from Hume's essay as discussed in the chapter.

7. What is the difference between regarding the world as *nature* and regarding it as *creation*? What is the corresponding difference between regarding God's action as *intervention* and regarding it as *manifestation*?

8. How does Grisez define *miracle*? Summarize his argument that an intelligent person could reasonably believe that a miracle (in his sense) has occurred.

9. What is the context or field of meaning in the gospels in terms of which Jesus' miracles are interpreted as "signs" from God? How is this context illustrated in the reply Jesus sent to the imprisoned John the Baptist?

10. Do you think that miracles in Grisez's sense still occur in the contemporary world?

11. In what sense are miracles "calls to faith" rather than proof?

12. How does this chapter deal with the question of why God doesn't heal everyone? Do you think this approach is successful?

For Writing and Reflection

This chapter treats two divergent understandings of the term *miracle*: 1) miracle as a "violation of the laws of nature" (Hume), and 2) miracle as "signal from the creator" or sign from God (Grisez). In John 9 you will find the story of Jesus' cure of a man said to have been "blind from birth." From the perspectives of the two different understandings of *miracle*, discuss the story of Jesus' cure of the man born blind. Apply the details of each definition to the details of the story. The gospel story, for example, is giving *testimony* about a miracle, exactly the subject of Hume's essay. Each discussion or application of the definition to the story will yield different results. Demonstrate that you have a sympathetic and accurate understanding of each definition and how it works. Finally, draw a conclusion about which understanding of the story of the man born blind you find more convincing and why.

For Further Reading

Rudolf Bultmann, *Jesus and the Word*. Bultmann's treatment of Jesus' "Belief in Miracles" appears on pp. 172–179.

David Hume, *An Inquiry Concerning Human Understanding* (1758 edition). The citations in the chapter are from the Library of Liberal Arts edition edited, with an introduction, by Charles W. Hendel.

Germain Grisez, *Beyond the New Theism, A Philosophy of Religion*. Grisez's treatment of miracles as signals from the Creator appears in Chapter 22, pp. 326–342. This is the best philosophical treatment of the issue that I have read.

C.S. Lewis, *Miracles, A Preliminary Study* (New York: Macmillan Co., 1947). A more popular study of miracles than Grisez's by one of the greatest Christian apologists of the twentieth century. Lewis defines miracle as "an interference with Nature by supernatural power," p. 15.

Edward Schillebeeckx, *Jesus, An Experiment in Christology.* Schillebeeckx' treatment of Jesus' miracles appears on pp. 183–200.

René Latourelle, *The Miracles of Jesus and the Theology of Miracles,* translated by Matthew J. O'Connell (New York/ Mahwah: Paulist Press, 1988). The heart of this book is Chapter 5, which makes individual studies of 28 miracle stories from the gospels. The theological perspectives in the closing chapters are valuable.

Hans Küng, *On Being a Christian,* trans. by Edward Quinn (Garden City, NY: Doubleday, 1976).

Hans Urs von Balthasar, *The God Question and Modern Man,* trans. by Hilda Graef, foreword by John Macquarrie (New York: Seabury Press, 1967). See the section on "The Journey through Hades," 129–142.

Terrence W. Tilley, *The Evils of Theodicy.* A powerful critique of the modern "theodicy project," i.e. the attempt to justify belief in God by solving in the abstract the "problem of evil."

Nicholas Wolterstorff, *Lament for a Son* (Grand Rapids, Mich.: Eerdmans, 1987). In this moving example of the genre of the lament, a Christian philosopher in the Reformed tradition mourns for his dead son.

Wilfrid Harrington, O.P., *The Tears of God, Our Benevolent Creator and Human Suffering* (Collegeville, Minn.: Liturgical Press, 1992). Biblical meditations on the question of suffering.

Terms To Identify

miracle (Hume, Grisez)

epistemological

metaphysical

laws of nature

nature

lament

analogical approach (to religious experience, Ch. III)

creation

indeterminacy

pentecostal

faith healer

Lourdes

Chapter XIV

Resurrection

OVERVIEW OF THE CHAPTER

Jesus' resurrection is the subject of the last and longest chapter. After three preliminary considerations on Jesus' death and the question of Christian origins, the chapter is divided into three parts. Parts I and II form the heart of the chapter and deal with the two key components of the Christian resurrection proclamation. Part I treats the proclamation that Jesus was raised. Part II treats his appearances. Part III asks about what the resurrection proclamation invites us to believe now, nearly 2,000 years after it was first announced.

THREE PRELIMINARIES

1. Jesus' Execution

The Roman execution of Jesus on the cross is the most certain historical fact we know about him. Christians often wonder why such a one as Jesus was disposed of so cruelly. Stress on Jesus' continuity with Judaism intensifies the question of why he was executed. Obviously he aroused opposition. But from whom?

Though the gospel accounts differ in their details, they agree that Jesus was executed by the Romans. This is also the testimony of our extra-biblical sources. The *Testimonium Flavianum* says that Pilate condemned Jesus to death "because of an accusation made by the leading men among us" (*Antiquities*, 18:3). The gospels speak variously of the instigation of Jesus' Jewish contemporaries.

Jesus, as we have seen, swam in the same eschatological stream as John the Baptist, the Essenes, and the Pharisees. Though they may have found some of his words and actions offensive and even blasphemous, it is not likely that the initiative in favor of Jesus' execution came from the Pharisees of his day. The Sadducees or "chief priests," as John calls them, emerge as the party most likely to have made this initiative.

Faced with the Roman occupation, the Sadducees had chosen to preserve Jewish identity by a strategy of adaptation and assimilation. This strategy was grounded in genuine devotion to the written law. The Sadducees did not share the variously expressed eschatological hopes that animated the others. Those who proclaimed these hopes and acted on them would prove dangerous to Judaism. Most influential among the Jewish priests were the aristocratic Jerusalem families associated with the temple. From among their number, the high priests were chosen. Of all Jesus' Jewish contemporaries, the temple priests are the ones he was most likely to antagonize.

In Jerusalem, at the feast of Passover, Jesus overturned the moneychangers' tables in the temple area. Sanders interprets this gesture as intended by Jesus to symbolize the temple's destruction, which he prophesies in Mark 13:1–2. Its context is Jesus' expectation of a new temple that would accompany the restoration of Israel (*Jesus and Judaism*, Chapter 1). In his discussion of the episode, Schillebeeckx calls it "a prophetic act, intended by Jesus to engender penitence and the conversion of Israel, in the latter days" (*Jesus*, 244).

However Jesus intended this prophetic symbolism, it most likely offended the temple priests. Such public displays of eschatological hope would have been disturbing to the Sadducees. Sanders thinks that the overturning of the tables in the temple area was the catalyst or "crucial act which led to his execution" (*Jesus and Judaism*, 334). He sees the "priestly aristocracy" as the "prime movers behind Jesus' execution" (289). It would not have been difficult for the priestly leaders associated with the temple to translate Jesus' behavior into the kind of "king of the Jews" language needed to convince a Roman governor, worried about his position in the capital ("If you release him, you are not a Friend of Caesar" [Jn 19:12]), to execute Jesus.

The story of Jesus' shameful suffering and execution impressed itself deeply into the memory of the early church. The gospel passion narratives, read during the liturgy of holy week, preserve this memory with more detail than is given to any other aspect of Jesus' life. From a redactional point of view, the gospels present Jesus' suffering and dying in faith as a model for their Christian readers, especially those in churches suffering persecution.

2. Jesus' Redemptive Death

From a theological point of view, the New Testament presents various interpretations of Jesus' death. Some liken it 1) to a "ransom" paid for sinners (1 Cor 6:20; Mt 20:28; Mk 10:45; 1 Tim 2:56); or 2) to the sacrifices of the Mosaic law (Ex 24:7–8; Mk 14:24; Jn 3:16; Heb 9:12–14). The most common categories for understanding the meaning of Jesus' death come from 3) deutero-Isaiah's description of the redemptive suffering of God's Servant (Is 52:13–15; 53:1–12; Wis 2:12–20; 4:20–5:5; 1 Pet 2:21–25; Acts 3:13, 26; 4:27, 30; Jn 15:12–13). These comparisons contain the seeds for the various theologies of redemption or atonement that have arisen in the course of Christian history. In view of Jesus' understanding of God and his relationship with God, the third interpretation deserves a certain primacy. Whether Jesus used it himself is a difficult question to answer from a purely historical point of view.

3. The Historical Riddle of Christian Origins

Why did anyone bother to think about Jesus' death and what it meant? How did a crucified prophet-teacher from Palestine eventually find himself the posthumous center of one of the most dynamic and long-lived religious movements in human history? Why didn't the disciples he had gathered simply return to their former lives and forget about him? Because of Christianity's tremendous impact on world history, these are very serious historical questions.

Many have attempted to answer them in purely natural terms. Space will not permit a survey of them, but they can be classified into three groups by way of summary:

> *First*, explanations based on fraud and deception. Some deliberate deception lies at the root of Christianity. Perhaps it was a

pretended death or a substitution of someone else for Jesus. Perhaps his disciples stole the body (cf. Mt 28:13). This original deception was followed by the lie that Jesus had risen from the dead.

Second, psychological explanations. Peter, Mary Magdalene, and the others didn't lie. They were sincere but deluded. Their minds played some sort of tricks on them and they only thought they had seen Jesus after his death. Perhaps they hallucinated or experienced visions caused by contagious hysteria. They were victims of their own mass-delusion.

Third, explanations from the history of religions. This approach is usually combined with one of the first two. It accounts for how the crucified prophet became the dying and rising Savior. This type was borrowed from other religions in a gradual process of mythologizing.

As for Jesus' disciples, they tell us that they continued to gather after his death because of what we call Easter. Their claim appears in one of its most primitive forms in Peter's preaching in the early chapters of Acts.

But God raised him up, releasing him from the throes of death, because it was impossible for him to be held by it (Acts 2:24).

The first Christians believed that something had happened to Jesus after he died. They attributed this to the Father and described it with language about Jesus having been "raised" up. Within the first decades after Jesus' death, Paul could write:

And if Christ has not been raised, then empty [too] is our preaching; empty, too, your faith (1 Cor 15:14).

Later generations of Christians have heard this and similar statements so many times that they tend to overlook how truly amazing it is, from an historical point of view, that such a thing as Christianity even exists. Jesus was clearly dead, after all. His disciples were in complete disarray. How did such a vigorous

religious movement as Christianity originate from the appearance
of such colossal failure? Hans Küng has put the question well:

> After the disastrous outcome of this life, what gave the initial
> impetus to that unique world historical development: a truly
> world transforming religion emerging from the gallows where
> a man was hanged in shame? (*On Being a Christian*, 345).

Are the kinds of natural explanations surveyed above really
enough to account for the development Küng describes? Is the
disciples' Easter proclamation really more fantastic than these
other explanations for Christianity's origin? The first Christians
remembered the passion story because they had an Easter story
that made them see Jesus' execution in a completely different
light. In the following sections of this chapter, we will explore this
Easter claim. As we do, readers should continue to ask themselves whether any of the alternative explanations offer answers
to Küng's question that are obviously better accounts for Christianity than the Easter claim.

PART I

JESUS WAS RAISED

Jewish Hope in Resurrection of the Dead

Talk of God raising the dead has its religious home in second
century B.C. apocalyptic expressions of Jewish eschatological
hopes. This was the time of the Seleucid persecution and the
Hasmonean revolt described at the beginning of Chapter XI. In
this situation, the "assembly of the pious" (1 Macc 2:42), forerunners of the Pharisees and Essenes, produced in the book of Daniel
a reinterpretation of Israel's prophetic tradition. They looked forward to the dramatic downfall of the Seleucid tyrant Antiochus
IV. The visions that conclude the book of Daniel (chapters 7–12)
anticipate Antiochus' defeat. Written in the second century B.C.,
the book of Daniel is one of the earliest examples of the literary
genre and mindset known as *apocalyptic*.

In the book of Daniel's last vision, we find one of the Bible's earliest uses of resurrection language. "Many of those who sleep in the dust of the earth shall awake; some shall live forever, others shall be an everlasting horror and disgrace" (Dan 12:2). Those sleeping in the dust of earth are the many "victims of the sword, of flames, of exile, of plunder," who have suffered under Antiochus' persecution (Dan 11:33).

Resurrection as God's vindication of the martyrs of Israel who have suffered unjustly appears in developed form in 2 Maccabees, probably written toward the end of the second century B.C. A good example is the story in chapter 7 of a nameless mother and her seven sons. They are tortured and executed by Antiochus for their refusal to eat pork and violate the law. According to the story, the mother was the last to die and her exhortations to her sons, "in the language of their forefathers" (2 Macc 7:21), give eloquent voice to the hope of the pious that God would raise the righteous dead.

> Therefore since it is the Creator of the universe who shapes each man's beginning, as he brings about the origin of everything, he in his mercy, will give you back both breath and life, because you now disregard yourselves for the sake of his law (2 Macc 7:23; cf. 2 Macc 7:14).

In what is called by some the "Apocalypse of Isaiah" (chapters 24–27), we see the eschatological context of the hope that God will raise the dead. Here the hope in the resurrection of the dead is clearly associated with hope in God's final vindication or restoration of Israel: "But your [God's] dead shall live, their corpses shall rise; awake and sing, you who lie in the dust" (Is 26:19).

The Earliest Christian Proclamation

Around A.D. 50, during the second of his missionary journeys, St. Paul founded a church at the Greek seaport city of Corinth. His first epistle to the Corinthians was written five or six years later. In the intervening years, divisions had grown up within the Corinthian community (1 Corinthians 1). One of them concerned the "resurrection of the dead."

Like most of us, the Corinthian Christians were troubled about what would happen to them when they died. Paul writes to address this concern. He tries to comfort them with the promise that what happened to Christ after his death will happen to them. They will be "raised." In the process, Paul recalls the gospel he proclaimed when he first came to Corinth. Here we find what is widely regarded as "our earliest example of resurrection proclamation" (Pheme Perkins, *Resurrection*, 88):

> I delivered to you as of first importance what I also received,
> *that* Christ died for our sins in accordance with the scriptures,
> *that* he was buried,
> *that* he was raised on the third day in accordance with the scriptures,
> and *that* he appeared to Cephas, then to the twelve.
>
> Then he appeared to more than five hundred brethren at one time [most of whom are still alive, though some have fallen asleep].
> Then he appeared to James, then to all the apostles.
> [Last of all, as to one untimely born, he appeared also to me] (1 Cor 15:3–8 RSV).

We should note both the early date and the creedal or proclamatory nature of this text.

1. *Early date*. In the introductory verse (3), Paul makes clear that he is handing on to the Corinthians a gospel or proclamation of which he was not the author. It had been handed on to him. Who gave Paul this tradition? The passage mentions both Cephas (Peter—from the Aramaic) and James. In his letter to the Galatians, one of his earlier writings, Paul mentions his previous contact with Peter and James at Jerusalem: "I went up to Jerusalem to get to know Cephas, with whom I stayed fifteen days. I did not meet any other apostles except James the brother of the Lord" (Gal 1:18–19). Paul dates this visit about three years after his conversion. Around A.D. 37 or 38 is a likely date. If Paul did receive the traditions in this passage from Peter and James at Jerusalem, late in the same decade during which Jesus died, then his testimony in 1 Corinthians 15 puts us in the presence of an extremely early witness to the primitive Christian faith that Jesus

was "raised." In any case, the passage is based on earlier traditions that clearly pre-date Paul's founding of the Corinthian church at mid-first century.

2. *Creedal or proclamatory nature of 1 Corinthians 15:4–5.* The four clauses introduced by the word *that* (vv. 4–5) have the look of a creedal formula. Say them aloud and they sound like the professions of faith still used in Christian churches. I have placed the second part of verse 6 and all of verse 8 in square brackets. This indicates that they are clearly from the hand of Paul. The first refers to the time when Paul was writing. The second refers to his own experience. They cannot, therefore, be part of what he is handing on to the Corinthians. This leaves the creedal formula (vv. 4–5), probably of liturgical origin, to which Paul has added a list of witnesses to the Lord's "appearances." The last witness is himself (Perkins, *Resurrection*, 88–89).

3. *Raised and appeared as key terms.* The key terms *raised* (Greek *egēgertai*) and *appeared* (Greek *ōphthē*) will help clarify for us Paul's understanding of this early resurrection proclamation. As we have seen above, Paul understands what it means for Jesus to have been "raised" in the context of what he calls the "resurrection of the dead."

WHAT DOES "RAISED" MEAN?

1. *To say that God "raised" Jesus from the dead is to make an eschatological proclamation.* Resurrection of the dead is clearly associated in Judaism with eschatological hope. The dead rise at the end of this age, when God acts to vindicate his faithful ones and restore Israel. Talk of resurrection of the dead occurs most consistently in the context of "a judgment to establish divine justice" (Perkins, *Resurrection*, 39). Resurrection of the dead is a subsidiary part of a broad and fluid constellation of images having to do with such themes as judgment, exaltation, vindication, and restoration (Perkins, *Resurrection*, 55), all used to express the eschatological hopes of pious Jews. When the first Christians proclaimed that Jesus had been "raised," they meant to imply that the "last things" had begun. In Jesus, God had begun the final fulfillment of Israel's eschatological hopes.

2. *To say that God "raised" Jesus is to proclaim that Jesus has been "transformed."* The second century texts as well as Paul compare resurrection of the dead to awaking from sleep. As we might say, "I woke up this morning," a speaker of *koinē* Greek would say, "I arose." Paul uses the passive of this verb to convey what happened between Jesus and the Father after Jesus' death. In the context of eschatology, this language indicates "a transition from one mode of existence (existence in this age) to another (existence in the age to come)" (Reginald Fuller, *The Formation of the Resurrection Narratives*, 17). The dead who arise do not simply return to their previous state; rather they are transformed (Pannenberg, *Jesus God and Man*, 78ff). The words of Jesus to the Sadducees at the end of an exchange about the resurrection of the dead use common imagery to convey this sense of transformation, and counter a more physicalist understanding of resurrection: "When they rise from the dead, they neither marry nor are given in marriage, but they are like the angels in heaven" (Mk 12:27).

3. *To say that God "raised" Jesus is to proclaim that God has acted to vindicate the righteous Son-Servant-Wisdom.* In the context of Israel's eschatological hopes, talk of God raising the dead is born of a deep hunger for justice for the victims of faithful suffering and death. Contrary to all appearances, God will not in the end abandon those who suffer and die faithfully. This is not so much a reward for a job well done, but God responding, "in his mercy" (2 Macc 7:23), to a faith and trust that in its ideal form, as expressed in the gospel passion narratives or in 2 Maccabees 7, has been unconditional. In this sense, God's raising of Jesus is the vindication of God's righteous one.

As Paul tried to assure the Corinthians, God's care for God's own does not cease with death. This hope in God beyond death is characteristic of the understanding of God among the pious and their religious descendants. The texts we have seen speak of God's awakening the dead as a communal hope. The Christian proclamation we have been examining applies this language to Jesus as an individual who anticipates the final fulfillment of the communal hope. This is why Paul designates Christ "now raised from the dead" as "the first fruits of those who have fallen asleep" (1 Cor 15:20). In terms of the previous chapter, Israel's eschatological hopes give us a context in which to interpret or understand the meaning of the raising of Jesus. It appears to the eyes of faith as a "sign" from God. It confirms Jesus' life and mission and points to a further future fulfillment.

Why the Proclamation of Jesus' Death and Resurrection Belong Together

In the eschatological context of the resurrection of the dead, it is not difficult to see why Jesus' death and resurrection are proclaimed together in the early formula preserved by Paul in 1 Corinthians 15. As we have seen, the resurrection of the dead is associated originally with the vindication by God of those suffering victims who have remained faithful even in death. This is precisely how the synoptic gospels present Jesus' death. Like the Maccabean martyrs and the Isaian servant, his trust in God remains even to the death. He joins the long history of victims who have suffered and died unjustly. God's raising him from the dead is, as we have seen, God's vindication of Jesus. Despite all appearances, Jesus' Abba did not forsake him on the cross. His deep and intimate personal union with the Father proved stronger than death. Thus the apostolic preaching (see Acts 2:26–27) applies to Jesus the words of Psalm 16:10–11:

> Therefore my heart is glad, my soul rejoices;
> my body also dwells secure,
> For you will not abandon me to Sheol,
> nor let your faithful servant see the pit.

In some of the apocalyptic scenarios of Jesus' day, a great tribulation would precede God's definitive revelation of his glory. The passion narratives (e.g. Mk 15:33, 38; Mt 27:51–53) indicate that some early Christians saw in Jesus' suffering and death this anticipated apocalyptic trial or great tribulation. It preceded the definitive revelation that came with his resurrection and began the end of the ages.

From the Kingdom of God to the Death and Resurrection of Christ

Jesus preached the kingdom of God. The first Christians proclaimed the death and resurrection of Christ. In the context of

Israel's eschatological hopes, these two proclamations need not be viewed as discontinuous. For Paul, Jesus' resurrection is the beginning of the resurrection of the dead. He is "the firstfruits of those who have fallen asleep" (1 Cor 15:20) and "the first-born of many brothers" (Rom 8:29; cf. Col 1:18; Rev 1:5). With Jesus' resurrection, the last days or the end of the ages had begun.

From this perspective, Jesus' resurrection begins and anticipates the fulfillment of what can be variously imagined in Jewish eschatology as: the coming of the kingdom, the restoration of Israel, the new creation, God's final judgment, and work of salvation. The resurrection can thus be interpreted as the fulfillment, or the beginning of the fulfillment, of Jesus' preaching about the kingdom.

Such an interpretation has consequences for our understanding of the church as well. In anticipation of the restoration of Israel or the coming kingdom, Jesus gathered a group of disciples around him with the twelve at its core. After the resurrection they continued to gather. Those among them who began the Gentile mission could, with Paul, view the early church as the beginning of a restored or spiritual Israel. Abraham is "father of all of us" (Rom 4:16). His descendants now include the Gentiles (Gal 3:24). "[A]nd the promise may be guaranteed to all his descendants, not to those who only adhere to the law but to those who follow the faith of Abraham, who is the father of all of us" (Rom 4:16). Paul and the other apostles of the Gentile mission saw the early church as a legitimate development of Israel's eschatological hopes.

"Christ Has Died, Christ Is Risen, Christ Will Come Again"

During the centuries before Constantine, the eschatological perspective remained alive in the church. But the view of Jesus' resurrection as the fulfillment of his preaching and the beginning of the last days implies a further fulfillment. "Christ the firstfruits; then, at his coming, those who belong to Christ" (1 Cor 15:23). Often Christians were able to view the sporadic persecutions and the gruesome fate of the martyrs in the same way the gospels viewed Jesus' suffering and death. Persecution and martyrdom were sometimes seen in the early church as the tribulations that would precede the second coming. In the third century, Tertullian could still write, "We are those upon whom the ends of the ages have come."

The eschatological interpretation of the proclamation of Jesus' death and resurrection, continuous with his own proclamation of the kingdom, requires for its fulfillment a third moment: the *parousia* or second coming. The eucharistic acclamation recalls this expectation, as well as its relationship to the death and resurrection of Christ: "Christ has died, Christ is risen, Christ will come again!"

How long will the last days last? It has been 2,000 years. Many have doubted. Many have abandoned hope. Some Christians have experienced periodic convulsions of renewed eschatological hope. Such hopes have been dashed or reinterpreted. Others have come to interpret the first eschatological hopes in a highly individualistic way. Eschatology becomes the study of death, judgment, heaven, and hell for individuals. Still, every liturgy reminds those present that we commemorate the Lord's death and resurrection "until he comes." What are we to make of his delay?

The apparent delay of the parousia is best interpreted in light of what we have learned about the Father from Jesus and from the long prophetic tradition of delay in judgment. Walter Kasper points out that "The tension between immediate expectation and the delay of the *parousia* is not just a New Testament problem, but pervades large sections of the Old Testament" (Kasper, *Jesus the Christ*, 78). Following the lead of the Jewish philosopher Martin Buber, Kasper approaches this problem by appealing to a biblical view of history as a dialogue or conversation of call and response between God and human beings. God's promises and prophecies about their fulfillment acquire a certain conditional character. If history is really such a dialogue, what happens there depends in part on human response to God (see Pannenberg, *Jesus God and Man*, 106–108).

PART II

HE APPEARED

What Does "Appeared" Mean?

The brief formula of faith that Paul hands on in 1 Corinthians 15 probably ends with the words, "that he appeared to Cephas, then to the twelve." Paul goes on to list other witnesses of appearances of the risen Lord. As we have concluded from the previous discussion of *raised*, resurrection is transformation rather than resuscitation. According to the gospels, resuscitation is what happened to Jairus' daughter (Mk 5:21–24 & parallels), the son of the widow of Nain (Lk 7:11–17), and Lazarus of Bethany (Jn 11:1–45). We can assume that, like our contemporaries who return from "clinical death," Lazarus, the widow's son, and Jairus' daughter would all have had to die again. For Jesus it is quite otherwise. Death could not hold him. "Now he lives, no more to die," as the Easter sequence has it. If resurrection is transformation rather than resuscitation, what did the disciples experience when Jesus "appeared" to them?

For each of the five appearances he lists, Paul uses the same Greek word for *appeared* (*ōphthē*). The root of the word refers to sight and is literally translated "was seen." In the Septuagint, or Greek translation of the Hebrew scriptures, this verb is used in the passive, as it is here, to refer to manifestations of God or his angelic messengers. We saw an example of this in Chapter III above when we looked at the story of Moses and the burning bush from Exodus. The emphasis in the Septuagint, as well as in our text, is on the initiative of God rather than on the experience of the person involved (Fuller, *Formation of the Resurrection Narratives*, 30).

We are left to speculate. Certainly Paul did not think that he or any of the others had hallucinated (Pannenberg, *Jesus God and Man*, 93–98). What did Cephas, James, and Paul see? What were the Easter experiences like? We have only one first-hand account. It is from Paul in Galatians 1. In the context of defending his legitimacy as an apostle, Paul speaks of his experience of the risen Lord on the Damascus road. He describes it as a *revelation* (Gal

1:12, 16). The Greek word for *revelation* that Paul uses is *apocalypsis*, and that is certainly consistent with the eschatological nature of resurrection. Paul insists that his experience was similar to that of Peter and James and the other disciples. Did God's revelation of his Son to Paul take the form of a vision or some sort of mystical or ecstatic experience? We shall pursue this question about the nature of the Easter experiences by examining the appearance stories in the gospels.

The Gospel Appearance Narratives

The gospel appearance narratives are much more detailed than Paul's sparse accounts. But for that reason, as we shall see, they are difficult to interpret. There are two sets of appearance narratives, one centered in Galilee, the other in Jerusalem.

Galilee Appearances. In Mark's final chapter, Mary Magdalene, Mary the mother of James, and Salome go to the tomb to anoint Jesus' body. They find the stone rolled away, the tomb empty, and a young man in a white robe. At this, "they were utterly amazed" (Mk 16:5). Though the young man's proclamation directs the women to Galilee, our best manuscripts have Mark's gospel ending at 16:8 with no appearance stories.

> "Do not be amazed! You seek Jesus of Nazareth, the crucified. He has been raised; he is not here. Behold, the place where they laid him. But go and tell his disciples and Peter, 'He is going before you to Galilee; there you will see him, as he told you.' " Then they went out and fled from the tomb, seized with trembling and bewilderment. They said nothing to anyone, for they were afraid (Mk 16:6–8).

The last chapters of Matthew (28) and John (21) both have Galilean appearances. In John 21 Jesus appears to Peter and six other disciples who are fishing in the Sea of Galilee. In Matthew 28 Jesus appears to the eleven on a mountain in Galilee. Both texts involve an apostolic commissioning.

Jerusalem Appearances. In the first part of Matthew 28, Jesus appears to Mary Magdalene and "the other Mary" at the empty tomb (Mt 28:9–10). Mark's Salome has slipped out of the story. In Luke, Mary Magdalene and Mary the mother of James are joined at the tomb by Joanna. Like Mark's, Luke's final chapter has no appearances to the women at the tomb. Instead Luke 24 has two Jerusalem appearances: 1) to two unidentified disciples walking from Jerusalem to Emmaus (cf. Mk 16:12); 2) to the eleven and others gathered with them (cf. Mk 16:14). In both of these episodes, the disciples recognize Jesus in the setting of a meal. At the conclusion of Luke's gospel (24:50), Jesus takes his final leave of the disciples not from a mountain in Galilee as in Matthew 28, but from Bethany. Finally, in John 20, Jesus appears to Mary Magdalene, who is weeping at the empty tomb, then to the disciples in the upper room with Thomas absent, and then to the disciples in the upper room with Thomas present.

Interestingly, the gospels contain no account of an appearance to James, the brother of the Lord. This is in spite of the fact that we know from both Josephus and Paul that James was a leader in the Jerusalem church. We also notice that Paul's formula in 1 Corinthians 15 makes no mention of the empty tomb or of an appearance to Mary Magdalene, one of the chief characters in the gospel Easter story.

We might expect the gospels to supplement the simplicity and sparseness of the early proclamation from 1 Corinthians 15 or Acts 2 and 3. Instead we find that, although the gospels present more detail, these details are difficult to harmonize or fit together into a single narrative. What are we to make of the discrepancies of detail in the gospel appearance narratives? In spite of these discrepancies, can we still learn something from the gospels about what *appeared* means, about what the Easter experiences of Mary and Peter, Paul, and James were like? We shall examine three approaches to the resurrection appearances: the mythical, the strictly historical, and the theological-literary.

A MYTHICAL APPROACH

Surprisingly, no New Testament book makes any mention of witnesses to the "raising" or resurrection of Jesus. They find the empty tomb and meet the risen Lord in his appearances, but no one sees the actual event. Some commentators have concluded from this that the resurrection is the kind of event that can only be proclaimed and not narrated. Perhaps this is too easy a way around the mysteriousness of the resurrection, but it does serve to focus our attention on the difficulties involved in imagining and thinking about such a claim as this.

Not until the mid-second century, in the apocryphal Gospel of Peter, do we find an attempt to describe the resurrection itself. The Gospel of Peter sets Jesus' resurrection in the sight of the soldiers at the tomb and the Jewish authorities.

> And whilst they were relating what they had seen, they saw again three men come out from the sepulchre, and two of them sustaining the other, and a cross following them, and the heads of the two reaching to heaven, but that of him who was led of them by the hand overpassing the heavens. Gospel of Peter, 10.39–40 (cited in Fuller, 190).

Its blatant contrast with the relative modesty and restraint of the canonical gospels makes this text from the Gospel of Peter a helpful beginning for our exploration of the appearances. In its emphasis on the spectacular, the Gospel of Peter presents a supermarket tabloid approach to the resurrection. The sheer physical size of the risen Lord is the central literary given. He is so big that his head surpasses heaven. The motion of the inanimate cross, following at a distance behind the three figures, adds a sensational special effect. One thinks of the possibilities involved if Steven Spielberg and George Lucas teamed up to do the resurrection.

The Gospel of Peter's emphasis on the sensational highlights the simplicity of the New Testament. The gospels communicate the wonder and mysteriousness of the first Easter without resorting to such heavy-handed special effects. In its attempt to capture the mystery, this text succeeds only in a painfully clumsy physicalism and objectivism.

HISTORICAL APPROACHES TO
THE GOSPEL APPEARANCE NARRATIVES

Until recently, commentators often thought it necessary to harmonize the gospel appearance narratives. The difficulty in doing this should not be exaggerated and some commentators still attempt it. But what we have learned about the process of tradition transmission by which the gospels came about leads to the conclusion that harmonization is probably not the best approach to the resurrection narratives. This is true not only because of the literary nature of the gospels but also because of the nature of the event these particular narratives are trying to talk about—the disciples' encounter with Jesus after he was dead.

The discrepancies of detail and setting make it difficult to make sense out of these texts at a purely historical level. There are at least three causes for these discrepancies. First, the evangelists are at some distance from the event they are trying to describe. Second, the event is quite extraordinary. Third, a comparison of the appearance narratives indicates that the literary conventions according to which the evangelists worked were different from our own. They appear to have more freedom to edit their sources by rearranging and amplifying them than the standards of contemporary historical scholarship would permit. The evangelists are not enlightened historians.

This is not to imply that the evangelists did not believe that Jesus appeared to his disciples after his death. Nor does it imply that the appearance narratives come to us in a form that, according to our literary conventions, is best described as fiction. 1 Corinthians 15 makes it clear that the appearance traditions are ancient and well-attested. The evangelists are neither novelists nor liars.

THEOLOGICAL-LITERARY APPROACHES TO THE GOSPEL
APPEARANCE NARRATIVES

The difficulties with interpreting the gospel appearance narratives from a purely historical point of view suggest that perhaps this modern method is not suited to their purpose and intent. Instead of focusing attention primarily on questions of chronology (Galilee or Jerusalem?) or questions of detail (which women were at the tomb?), perhaps a more theologically oriented or literary approach would be more fruitful. In Chapter VI above, we saw that determining literary form and intent were important aspects of biblical interpretation. What then did the evangelists want to communicate to their readers about Jesus' appearances to the disciples?

The New Testament gives evidence of multiple appearance traditions. Mary Magdalene, and Peter, James, and Paul seem to stand out in the early church's memory of the first Easter. The gospels emphasize Jesus' appearance to the twelve. In 1973 Raymond Brown published a very important essay on "The Problem of the Bodily Resurrection of Jesus." In it he drew upon previous form-critical work of C.H. Dodd and pointed to "a general similarity of pattern" in the gospel stories of Jesus' appearance to the twelve. This pattern emerges in spite of the differences of detail. It reflects an experience of real encounter with Jesus who was crucified. He is no longer dead but alive in a new and transformed way. Thus the proclamation, "He is risen!"

The following fivefold pattern is based on Brown's use of Dodd ("Bodily Resurrection," 107–108):

1. The disciples are disappointed and despondent, "bereft" of Jesus (Lk 24:21; Jn 20:19);
2. Jesus appears (Jn 20:19; Lk 24:15; Mt 28:9);
3. Jesus greets the confused disciples (Jn 20:19; Mt 28:9);
4. They recognize him (Jn 21:7; Jn 20:20; Mt 28:9, 17);
5. Jesus commissions the disciples (Jn 20:21; Jn 21:15; Lk 24:47; Mt 28:19).

This pattern is similar to what Paul tells us about his experience. He claimed that the gospel he preached had come "through a revelation of Jesus Christ." It was "not of human origin." "For I did not receive it from a human being, nor was I taught it, but it came through a revelation of Jesus Christ" (Gal 1:11–12). The implication is clearly that in his encounter with the risen Lord, God had communicated with Paul. Such communication, e.g. of Paul's gospel, requires some medium. This is where interpretation of the appearance narratives becomes most difficult. Did God speak in some literal or symbolic fashion? Was the communication in the form of some vision or other kind of mystical experience? We do not know.

But we can draw conclusions about what the evangelists wanted to teach. They wrote in the contexts of the doubts and questions, as well as the liturgical and communal lives of their churches. They hoped to communicate a sense of what Peter and Mary and the others had received from the risen Lord. We can summarize what the risen Lord communicated to the disciples under three headings:

1. a revelation of his true identity;
2. shalom—peace in the form of reconciliation and forgiveness;
3. vocation to the apostolic mission.

"MY LORD AND MY GOD"

The crucifixion left the disciples in disarray. Their behavior indicates that they didn't believe they would ever see Jesus again. Mary in the garden, Peter in the boat, the disciples on the road or in the upper room do not at first recognize Jesus. He has been transformed; he has entered into his glory. The evangelists want to stress that the "appearances" finally enabled the disciples to *see* Jesus. "Are your minds completely blinded? Have you eyes but no sight?" (Mk 8:17-18), Jesus had asked them in exasperation. In Luke's account of Paul's experience on the Damascus road, Paul is actually blinded by the light of his encounter with the risen Christ (Acts 9:8). Gradually his blindness is lifted and he comes to understand what has been revealed to him.

One of the literary keys to the appearance narratives is the theme of "recognition." Recognition of Jesus involves a certain conversion. Each of the various disciples reacts differently but in the end they all are finally given to see Jesus with the eyes of God. John captures this theme most dramatically in Thomas' profession of faith, "My Lord and my God" (Jn 20:28). In Jesus' words to Thomas, we have the fourth gospel's prayer for later generations of Christian disciples: "Blest are they who have not seen and have believed" (Jn 20:29).

"PEACE BE WITH YOU"

From its use in the liturgy, this greeting will sound familiar to Catholics and many other Christians. John links it to the reception of the Holy Spirit and the forgiveness of sins. In the Spirit, the disciples are to forgive sins as Jesus did. The liturgical ring of John 20:21–23 seems unmistakable. Here we need to recall that, with the exception of the women and the mysterious "beloved disciple" of the fourth gospel, all the disciples to whom Jesus appeared had failed him miserably and abandoned him. He does not come down on them or try to make them feel guilty. Rather he responds to them as he had taught them to respond to others by his parables and instructions on the law. He offers them "peace"—*shalom*—a one-word summary of Jewish hope. It means the justice for those who suffer, the forgiveness and reconciliation that are characteristic of the new creation.

Both Luke and John present the appearances in a way that is designed to suggest the liturgical and communal lives of their churches. The reference to the forgiveness of sins and the reception of the Spirit suggests baptism. In Luke 24, the disciples recognize Jesus "in the breaking of the bread," a term Luke uses for the eucharistic meal. Jesus shares the disciples' food again as he had before his death. He appears in the upper room, the scene of the last supper.

The evangelists give their readers an emphatic push in the direction of the liturgical and communal lives of their churches. It is here they should expect to encounter the risen Lord and his gifts. The risen Christ brings peace, reconciliation, forgiveness—*shalom*—the kinds of gifts Paul associates with life in the Spirit (Gal 5:22).

"GO THEREFORE AND MAKE DISCIPLES OF ALL NATIONS"

The Easter experiences are vocational. They confirm the disciples in their pre-Easter sharing in Jesus' life and mission. Peter and Paul and the others are called to preach the gospel of Jesus' death and resurrection. They are to take the good news to the ends of the earth, to "make disciples of all nations" (Mt 28:19).

Here it would make sense to include Mary Magdalene and other women disciples in this apostolic commission to witness to the resurrection. Always at the center of the gospel Easter stories, Mary Magdalene must be regarded as "a major witness to Jesus' resurrection" (Gerald O'Collins, *Interpreting the Resurrection*, 22–38). Except on prior theological grounds, it would be hard to deny that there must have been women present among the gathering of "the eleven and those with them" (Lk 24:33) when the risen Lord commissioned them as "witnesses" (Lk 24:46–49). Unless women disciples were understood to share in the missionary mandate of the risen Lord, it would be hard to explain Prisca, Junia

(Rom 16:3–5, 7), and other women missionaries who were Paul's contemporaries and co-workers (Perkins, *Resurrection*, 167; Schüssler-Fiorenza, *In Memory of Her*, Chapter 5).

The Empty Tomb

In discussing the gospel appearance narratives, we have mentioned the "empty tomb." All four gospels report the discovery by Mary Magdalene and other women that the tomb in which Jesus had been buried was empty. Though this in itself proves nothing, it is on the face of it a possible "sign" requiring interpretation. The women who find the tomb empty do not yet have the context to interpret it. The tomb could have become empty in a variety of ways. Matthew 28:13 indicates that already at the time Matthew was written Christians had been accused of stealing Jesus' body by night. The gospels do not claim that the empty tomb proves the resurrection.

The empty tomb tradition has been a controversial piece of evidence. Paul doesn't mention the empty tomb in 1 Corinthians 15. Some have argued that it is a late legend, fabricated to support the resurrection proclamation. But if the empty tomb were a legend, it should have been easy enough to refute it at Jerusalem. As the German Lutheran theologian Wolfhart Pannenberg has put it:

> How could Jesus' disciples in Jerusalem have proclaimed his resurrection if they could be constantly refuted merely by viewing the grave in which his body was interred? (*Jesus God and Man*, 100ff, and Perkins, *Resurrection*, 94).

Beyond a Humean aversion for its possible implications, there seems no good historical reason to doubt that, shortly after his execution and burial, some of Jesus' women disciples went to his grave and found it empty. Viewed in the context of the resurrection proclamation and appearances, the empty tomb becomes a subordinate or subsidiary "sign" of the resurrection.

The Shroud of Turin

In John 20, Mary Magdalene tells Peter and the beloved disciple that Jesus' tomb is empty. They run to see. The beloved disciple arrives first. As he peers into the empty tomb, he notices "the burial cloths" (Jn 20:5). In the fourteenth century, a French knight claimed to have discovered these same "burial cloths" of Jesus. The Shroud of Turin is a piece of linen cloth about fourteen feet long and three and a half feet wide. The shroud bears a haunting, life-sized image of a man. The image looks like a photographic negative of a picture of a man whose wounds show that he has been crucified.

At the time the French knight made his claim, the local bishop denounced the shroud as the work of a contemporary artist. People were fascinated by it nonetheless. The shroud eventually found its way to the cathedral at Turin, Italy, where up to the present it has been venerated as the "burial cloth" of Jesus. Some Christians have thought of the image as having been "burned on" as Jesus was raised from the dead. In the late 1970s a team of scientists began studying the shroud. They tried to determine its date and some explanation for how the mysterious image came about. Their results were inconclusive.

By 1988 advances in technology had made it possible to subject the shroud to carbon-dating tests without destroying a large piece of it. A small piece was cut from the shroud and subdivided into three postage stamp size pieces. They were sent to laboratories in three different countries where carbon-14 dating tests were performed on them. In October of 1988, the archbishop of Turin announced that all three series of tests had independently dated the lined fragments between A.D. 1260 and 1380. The tests claim a 95 percent degree of accuracy. While the shroud is still venerated as an "icon" of Christ, and the presence of the mysterious image has yet to be explained, the Shroud of Turin can no longer be regarded as any sort of "sign" of Jesus' resurrection.

Spiritual Bodies

In summing up the early Christian resurrection belief, we can say the following. The early Christians believed that Abba did not abandon Jesus to the grave. After Jesus was dead, something happened between him and the Father and he was no longer dead. From Jewish eschatology and its image of the "resurrection of the dead," they took the language for the first proclamation that God had "raised" Jesus. This raising was neither a simple resuscitation nor a purely spiritual event. It involved Jesus as an incarnate or embodied person. Christians speak of it as a "bodily" resurrection. It is best understood as a "transformation" by which the risen Jesus is related to the world of time and space in a different way. This was not just something that happened to Jesus. It was interpreted eschatologically as the beginning of the fulfill-ment of Israel's hopes.

Thus Paul sought to console the Corinthian Christians with the hope that they would eventually share in the resurrection of the dead which Jesus had begun. But just as we might expect twentieth century people to respond, these first century Chris-tians from Corinth asked a lot of questions about what this resur-rection of the dead would be like. Paul grew impatient. "But someone may say," he wrote, "'How are the dead raised? With what kind of body will they come back?' " (1 Cor 15:35). Despite his rhetorical move to dismiss this question as nonsensical, Paul must have realized that it was a fair question. In any case, he tried to answer it as best he could. He tells the Corinthians that when the dead rise, they will have "spiritual" bodies.

To explain this he uses a comparison from nature. He com-pares the difference between our present bodies and "spiritual" or transformed bodies to the difference between a seed that is planted and what eventually comes out of the ground after the seed has died.

> So also is the resurrection of the dead. It is sown corruptible; it is raised incorruptible. It is sown dishonorable; it is raised glorious. It is sown weak; it is raised powerful. It is sown a natural body; it is raised a spiritual body (1 Cor 15:42–44).

"For that which is corruptible," he goes on, "must clothe itself with incorruptibility, and that which is mortal must clothe itself with immortality" (1 Cor 15:53). This is what Paul thought had already happened to Jesus and what he hoped for himself and for his Corinthian disciples. In paraphrases of Isaiah 25:8 and Hosea 13:14, Paul exclaims in conclusion:

Death is swallowed up in victory.
Where, O death, is your victory?
Where, O death, is your sting?
(1 Cor 15:54–55)

When they portray the risen Jesus as not limited by the ordinary constraints of space and time, the evangelists exhibit a similar view of the resurrected body. Probably against over-spiritualized views of the resurrection, the gospels of Luke and John emphasize the bodily condition of the risen Jesus. Not only do the disciples see Jesus but they also touch him and watch him eat. This raises the interesting question of how someone with an incorruptible body can eat fish (O'Collins, *Interpreting the Resurrection*, 39–52).

We could speculate at length on the "spiritual" or transformed body of the resurrection of the dead. Perhaps Paul was too impatient with the Corinthians' questions. After all, if one is to hope, one must have some clue about what one is hoping for. So Paul relents and talks about "spiritual" bodies. His emphasis, however, is always on the hope we can have in Christ rather than on what we might call the "physics" of spiritual bodies. But this emphasis raises serious questions. Can twentieth century people really find hope in images of "spiritual bodies" (1 Cor 15) and living "like angels in heaven" (Mk 12:25)? Such images come to us from a distant world where apocalyptic expressions of Israel's eschatological hopes became the medium through which God consoled his people in their suffering. But what about our hope and our suffering?

PART III

RESURRECTION HOPE NOW

Resurrection of the Dead, Human Hope and Christian Hope

1. *Jewish eschatology gives voice to human hope*. Christian hope rather than physics is the emphasis of the resurrection proclamation. But even if this is so, the question remains: How can we

find God's own consolation in the exotic, far-away world of Jewish eschatology? Out of this complex of images and ideas Paul and other early Christians took the image of the resurrection of the dead. They used it to talk about what the Father had done for Jesus after his death. Though resurrection of the dead comes to us from a particular place and time in history, this should not blind us to the possibility that people from other times and places can hear in this proclamation an address to their own deepest hopes. If this were not true, we would be hard-pressed to understand how the early Christians converted anyone with their proclamation.

In Chapter I, we looked at some of the deep questions that arise out of human experience. We called them the great questions. They are not merely theoretical questions. They concern the meaning of human life, and we are all passionately involved with human life. We saw that upon reflection, human experience is ambiguous. Sometimes life leads us to hope that it makes sense and will turn out well. At other times, life leads us to fear that maybe there is no meaning at all, just death and empty cold.

Such hopes and fears become acute when we remember those who have died: the ones we have loved, our parents and families, the ones whose lives have been cut short, the ones who have suffered and died for the sake of justice, the innocent sufferers. Most of us want to hope that what is best about our lives, human trust and love and solidarity, the dignity of those who struggle for justice, the joy of song and play, will not be for nothing. We want to hope that somehow we are still in solidarity with those who have died. Most people want to hope but fear they will be disappointed or deceived by hope.

The proclamation of the resurrection invites us to trust that God will not allow these deepest hopes of ours to go unfulfilled. It invites us to go about our lives trusting the Father as Jesus did. This is not easy. Doubtless we will suffer, often cruelly and unjustly. The proclamation of Jesus' resurrection invites us to hope that no matter what the appearances, God will not in the end abandon us. This hope is not a counsel to resignation. Often it involves resisting the causes of needless human suffering.

2. *Jesus' resurrection confirms eschatological hope*. Even if Jewish eschatology does give voice to our deepest hopes, why should we pay any attention to this strange-sounding, distant

voice? From the point of view of Christian hope, this question can have only one answer. It is a stark, consoling, and deeply difficult saying. It is the simple resurrection proclamation: Jesus was crucified and God "raised" him up. This "raising" of Jesus is a sign. This sign means, among other things, that God really was and still is communicating with all God's people through the images and language of Jewish eschatology. Jesus' resurrection is God's sign that this eschatological hope is not in vain. Those who hear this proclamation and recognize the sign are summoned to respond in hope.

3. *Biblical eschatology challenges our own hopes*. Many twentieth century theologians have interpreted the tension between our worldview and that of ancient Jewish eschatology as a very serious problem for Christian faith. But we can interpret this tension in another way. If God really has used Jewish eschatology to console God's people, then we can interpret this tension as God's own challenge to our modern worldview and the kinds of hopes it inspires in us. Even if we can recognize in ancient Jewish eschatology an address to our own deepest hopes, we must also admit that its images challenge our own hopes at crucial points. In general we can say that the images of ancient Jewish eschatology challenge our own hopes to become more universal or inclusive. More specifically, the image of the "resurrection of the dead," presupposed by Paul in 1 Corinthians 15, challenges modern Christians to refashion their hopes in three ways. Biblical eschatology challenges Christians first to a less private and more communal hope, second to a hope that shares God's concern for justice, third to a hope that includes creation and the renewal of the face of the earth.

A COMMUNAL HOPE

Biblical eschatology challenges Christians to a more communal hope. Modern hopes tend to be private and individualistic. They focus on ourselves and often extend only to our families. The world of Jewish eschatology presents us with a much more extensive and inclusive vision. As we have already seen, resurrection of the body is not merely a private but also a communal hope. Jesus' resurrection is good news because it anticipates a general resurrection. Obviously any general resurrection will have to be a resurrection of individuals. The point is that the image of resurrection of the dead considers people in their human solidarity rather than as isolated individuals.

A HOPE FOR JUSTICE

Biblical eschatology challenges our hope to become larger and share God's love for the victims of unjust suffering. The image of resurrection of the dead expresses a deep hunger for justice and a solid trust in God's fidelity. Heirs of the modern west can hear in the proclamation of the resurrection of the dead a timely reminder that God's justice is not blind like our own. Rather it is actually "biased" in favor of those who suffer unjustly. Instead of making us feel guilty and helpless in the face of human suffering, God's justice calls Christians to expand their hopes to include those who suffer.

A HOPE FOR THE EARTH

Finally, biblical eschatology challenges Christians to expand their hope so far that it includes all of creation. The image of resurrection of the body is easily associated in biblical eschatology with the hope that God will "renew the face of the earth." Often Christians pray, "Come, Holy Spirit, renew the face of the earth," without realizing the eschatological context of such a request. In images associated with a physics much like Hume's, we have learned to imagine the "physical world" as a relatively inert aggregation of separated bodies. Each human individual is one of those separate bodies. We have become accustomed to moving around the other bodies in the aggregate when necessary. Though it has produced short-term wonders, such a disconnected view of the world has generally not served creation well in the long run. Biblical eschatology challenges Christians to imagine the world in a different way. The New Testament texts that speak of the risen Christ as the Lord of creation provide some clues for such imaginings (Rom 8:19–23; Col 1:15–20; Eph 1:9–10, 22–23). So do the strains of Christian thought that have developed out of reflection on this theme of the cosmic Christ. The final stage of Paul's hope in 1 Corinthians 15:28 is that "God may be all in all."

Experiences of Resurrection

The great German Catholic theologian Karl Rahner (1904–1984) once wrote:

> I have experienced God himself, not human words about him. This experience is not barred to anyone. I want to communicate it to others as well as I can (cited in Herbert Vorgrimler, *Understanding Karl Rahner*, [1986], 11).

Rahner claimed to experience God in the events of everyday life—in the silence of aloneness that punctuates the din of the routine, in various unconditional forms of joy, faithfulness to promises, fear, freedom, responsibility, and love. The sum of all these events communicated to Rahner a mystery at the heart of our lives. This mystery calls us to fuller forms of life, joy, love, and the like, for which our everyday experiences can only offer hints and clues. The American Catholic theologian John Shea has developed and popularized Rahner's approach in a series of books encouraging believers to read their lives as "stories of God" and "stories of faith."

For Christians, this experience of God in the everyday can take a specifically Christological form. Christians are people who experience God in their lives in terms of the story of Jesus' life and death and resurrection. The liturgical and communal lives of the church fill the heads and hearts of Christians with images that actually shape and color their experiences. I am thinking of the crib and the cross, the supper, the madonna and child. These lend a particular Christian hue to experience.

Of all these images, the cross is probably the most volatile and powerful. Generations of Catholics have been taught to unite their sufferings to Christ's. But what of the resurrection in our everyday experience? Following Rahner's lead, some contemporary theologians have suggested a way to understand better Jesus' resurrection, the disciples' experience of the appearances, and our own hopes for resurrection. It is to compare these Easter experiences to our own experiences of resurrection. In our everyday experiences, we find "foretastes of resurrection life" (William Thompson, *The Jesus Debate*, 232).

We all have "transforming experiences." Perhaps we associate them with "special moments of fellowship, reconciliation and solidarity" (Dermot Lane, *The Reality of Jesus*, 60–61). Because we cannot control or orchestrate them, we experience them as gratuitous, as moments of grace. In the words of the Irish Catholic theologian Dermot Lane, such experiences can "disarm and surprise, lift and renew, change and transform our lives." In terms of the story of Jesus, Christians can experience these moments as little resurrections, Thompson's "foretastes of resurrection life." In these experiences of ours, we also find analogies that help us understand what happened to the disciples when they encountered the risen Lord.

We emphasized above that Christians need to allow biblical eschatology to challenge and expand their hopes. We should keep this thought in mind when discussing experiences of transformation in our lives as hints or "foretastes" of resurrection. We ought to expect our experiences of transformation to extend, just as resurrection hope does, to the communal, to hunger and thirst for justice, and to our very relationship with creation. As Thompson points out, the resurrection experiences of the disciples did not simply manifest Jesus for the disciples to recognize. The disciples had to change and expand. They were challenged to see in a new way. This involved moments of "liberation" or freeing from the kinds of things that oppose Christ and his work, from selfishness to social injustice. Our protests against injustice, our hopes and struggles for a more free and inclusive future, the various short-of-complete human liberations we achieve—all of these too, along with interpersonal transformations, can be experienced in Christ as "foretastes of resurrection" (Thompson, *Jesus Debate*, 231–233).

Father, Son, and Spirit

The historical-theological portrait of Jesus in the previous chapters emphasized the theme of the union between Jesus and the Father. This union has an eschatological context. Jesus is the Son-Servant-Wisdom, the Father's anointed agent in proclaiming and bringing about the new age. In this eschatological context, the resurrection is the Father's vindication of Jesus' faithful life and work. It is in the final age, beginning with Jesus' resurrection, that biblical eschatology looks for the outpouring of the Spirit of God. We see this in the New Testament accounts of the Easter and Pentecost experiences.

Christian revelation is Christ-centered. Jesus' life, death, and resurrection reveal what God is like. The final word about God we learn from Jesus' life is that we come closest to expressing what God is really like when we speak of God as a Father, Son, and Spirit. As we have seen in Chapter VIII, the councils of the church have taught us how to use the trinitarian language about God, but we can see already in the context of Jesus' life the reality of the Crucified One, his Father, and their Spirit.

Questions for Review and Discussion

1. Among Jesus' Jewish contemporaries, which group would have been most likely to favor his execution? Why?

2. What are three images used in the New Testament to convey the significance of Jesus' death?

3. What is the "historical riddle of Christian origins"? What are three ways of answering it "in purely natural terms," i.e. without supposing that Jesus was really raised from the dead?

4. What is the significance of the resurrection of the dead in the Jewish tradition, especially in the book of Daniel?

5. Where can we find the earliest known Christian proclamation of Jesus' resurrection? How do we know that it's so early?

6. What is the meaning of *raised* (*egēgertai*) and *appeared* (*ōphthē*) in Paul's early resurrection proclamation?

7. What does it mean to say that God "raised" Jesus from the dead? What meanings and connotations come with this word *raised*?

8. In the proclamation of Jesus' death and resurrection, why do the two belong together?

9. How can the proclamation of Jesus' death and resurrection by Christians be interpreted as in continuity with Jesus' own proclamation of the kingdom of God?

10. Why is the second coming (*parousia*) implied in the proclamation of Jesus' resurrection? What are some possible explanations for why the second coming has been delayed for so long?

11. Why are the gospel narratives of the appearances of the risen Jesus so hard to harmonize? What is the fivefold similarity of pattern that they exhibit?

12. What did the risen Lord communicate to his disciples?

13. What does Paul say about our resurrection as "spiritual bodies"?

14. How does the resurrection of Jesus relate to the great questions of Chapter I?

15. How does biblical eschatology challenge our own hopes?

16. How can Christians experience a sort of resurrection in daily life? How is this related to the analogical approach to religious experience in Chapter III?

For Writing and Reflection

1. When St. Paul was summoned before King Agrippa (Acts 26), he posed this question to the king: "Why is it thought unbelievable among you that God raises the dead?" (Acts 26:8). The king found the idea of the resurrection of the dead unbelievable in part because he was unfamiliar with the context in which such a belief would be plausible. Help the king out. Beginning with the understanding of miracle as a sign from God (Chapter XIII), explain to the king what the resurrection of Jesus is supposed to be a sign of. Signs require interpretation. Interpretation requires context. In order to explain what the resurrection is a sign of, you have to use the context of biblical eschatology. Write an essay in which you use the Bible to show, a) what biblical eschatological hope is, and b) what the resurrection means as a sign. Having placed in its proper context the belief that God raises the dead, conclude with a brief explanation to the king of what the Christian proclamation of Jesus' resurrection asks him to believe about Jesus and to hope for himself. Suggest some reading for him.

2. Theologian William Thompson speaks of the possibility of Christians experiencing in daily life what he calls "foretastes of resurrection." The chapter provides some examples. Write an essay about experiences you've had that strike you as "foretastes of resurrection." Relate these experiences to the discussion of the "analogical" approach to religious experience in Chapter III.

For Further Reading

Pheme Perkins, *Resurrection: New Testament Witness and Contemporary Reflection* (Garden City, NY: Doubleday & Co., 1984). A comprehensive study of the resurrection by a distinguished New Testament scholar.

Reginald H. Fuller, *The Formation of the Resurrection Narratives* (New York: Macmillan Co., 1971). A pioneering study. Emphasizes the importance of beginning with 1 Corinthians 15.

Raymond E. Brown, "The Problem of the Bodily Resurrection of Jesus" in *The Virginal Conception and Bodily Resurrection of Jesus* (New York/Ramsey: Paulist Press, 1973). An important essay.

Wolfhart Pannenberg, *Jesus God and Man*, translated by Lewis L. Wilkins and Duane A. Priebe (London: SCM Press Ltd, 1973), Chapter 3. Important work by a great German Lutheran systematic theologian. Places the resurrection of Jesus squarely in the context of Jewish belief in resurrection of the dead. Discusses the delay of the parousia.

Gerald O'Collins, *Interpreting the Resurrection: Examining the Major Problems in the Stories of Jesus' Resurrection* (New York/Mahwah: Paulist Press, 1988). Four popular essays on the resurrection. The one on "Mary Magdalene as Major Witness to Jesus' Resurrection" is especially worthwhile.

Elisabeth Schüssler-Fiorenza, *In Memory of Her: A Feminist Theological Reconstruction of Christian Origins* (New York: Crossroad, 1983). Chapter 5 on the early Christian missionary movement emphasizes the role of women as Christian missionaries.

William M. Thompson, *The Jesus Debate: A Survey and Synthesis* (New York/Mahwah: Paulist Press, 1985). A comprehensive discussion of contemporary Christology. On the resurrection, see pp. 220–247.

Walter Kasper, *Jesus the Christ*. Chapters VI and VII deal with the resurrection.

Dermot A. Lane, *The Reality of Jesus* (New York/Ramsey: Paulist Press, 1975). A popular survey of Christology. Readable. Chapters 4 and 5 deal with the resurrection.

Terms To Identify

eschatology, eschatological	Shroud of Turin
resurrection of the dead	Cephas
Paul	James
book of Daniel	Mary Magdalene
resuscitation	*raised*
spiritual body	*appeared*
parousia	*koinē*
shalom	Corinth
ōphthē	empty tomb
egēgertai	firstfruits of those who have fallen asleep
Thomas	
Gospel of Peter	

Conclusion

BUT IS JESUS REALLY GOD?

In Chapter VIII, we reviewed classical Christology as expressed in the early conciliar interpretations of Jesus from Nicaea to Chalcedon. Jesus is "one in being with the Father" (Nicaea). There are not two Jesuses but only one (Ephesus). Jesus is one person in two natures. He is one in being with the Father in his divine nature. He is one in being with us in his human nature (Chalcedon). We emphasized the importance of interpreting these creedal professions of faith in a way that does not lose sight of their worship context.

In Chapter IX, we saw that, for reasons that are as much political as scientific, modern thinkers radically challenged the historical basis of classical Christology. This gave rise to the application of historical-critical method to the Bible. In Chapter X, we surveyed a spectrum of positions on the gospels as historical sources for information about the life of Jesus. Chapters XI through XIV form a kind of experiment. In it we adopted a posture of moderate historical criticism and tried to sketch from the gospels an historical-theological portrait of Jesus. This portrait, it was hoped, would be 1) sensitive to enlightened questions about Christianity's historical origins, 2) faithful to the church's traditional profession of faith, and 3) religiously compelling.

The portrait that emerged was based on the theme of Jesus and the Father. In terms drawn from various strains of Jewish eschatology, we spoke of Jesus as God's Son-Servant-Wisdom. As we might have expected, many of the most certain conclusions about Jesus from an historical point of view are those most consistent with Chalcedon's emphasis on Jesus' true humanity: his execution, his baptism by John, his life of prayer, his radical interpretation of the Jewish law, and his all-inclusive ministry that sought out sinners and the outcast.

Unless we insist on closing the world to the new and unique, we can also admit that a number of other historical conclusions about Jesus are open to Nicaea's profession of faith in his divinity: his sense of oneness with the Father, his sense of being on a decisive and all-important mission for the Father (variously understood in Son-Servant-Wisdom terms), his healings and exorcisms, and finally his being "raised." The gospel witness invites us to believe that in Jesus of Nazareth something very extraordinary and unusual happened. God came to us in human form and made a decisive offer of salvation.

This twofold aspect of our historical-theological portrait of Jesus need not mean that we have two Jesuses, one human and the other divine. Nor does it mean that the Jesus we do have can only be thought of as divine in some sort of metaphorical sense, but not in the real sense that the church has always held. Perhaps some have wondered, while reading Chapters XI through XIV, how we can really think of the Jesus of this historical-theological portrait as God. To readers with such questions these four concluding observations are addressed.

1. The Christian profession of faith in Jesus' divinity never simply identifies Jesus with God. Some Christians speak of Jesus during his earthly life simply as God, as in "God took bread, blessed it . . . ." However reverent the intent of such language, it is, technically speaking, monophysite and/or docetic. The man Jesus of Nazareth is not simply identical with God. Rather he is God incarnate (Jn 1), God enfleshed, the visible image of the invisible God (Col 1:15), God in human form, truly God and truly human, one person in two natures. The Christ of traditional Christianity has a real human face, not the mere human mask of docetism.

2. Our understandings of the Christian profession of faith in Jesus' divinity must be consistent with the scriptural witness to his true humanity. The figure of Jesus occupies a central place in the religious lives of Christians and in western culture. Painters, musicians, novelists, filmmakers, and other artists have shared the fascination with Jesus. However necessary and intriguing our imaginings about him may be, we cannot imagine or know with certainty what it felt like to be Jesus of Nazareth.

Christians as religious people cannot avoid thinking and imagining about Jesus. When they do, however, they should take care to be guided in their thinking and imagining by the scriptures and church tradition. The scriptures tell us that Jesus really prayed and really agonized over his death and really died. If this is not sufficient, Chalcedon explicitly affirms Jesus' true humanity. Subsequent councils upheld this affirmation.

In the face of the witness of scripture and tradition to the true humanity of Jesus, we ought not construct in our imaginings or in our thoughts a Jesus who cannot really pray, who cannot really be tempted, who cannot really accept his death freely, or who cannot really die because then he wouldn't *really* be God. Christians ought not to construct such a Jesus even if it be for the religiously admirable motive of saving Jesus' true divinity.

Still some will say that, because Jesus was truly divine, he could not possibly have really prayed, really told a funny parable, perhaps even really have been a disciple of John the Baptist, or really agonized over his death. These were only appearances for our benefit. We can only ask those who make such statements how they learned to know so clearly what God is like and what God can do. Perhaps such knowledge comes from philosophers. It does not appear to come from God's revelation in Jesus. How then ought we to think and imagine about Jesus' divinity?

3. In thinking and imagining about Jesus' divinity, we should take our lead from the New Testament. It is precisely in his being human—in his really suffering and dying and entering fully into the human condition—that Jesus surprises us with the manifestation of what God is really like. It is in Jesus' true humanity that we meet God's real offer of salvation. It is in his true humanity that Jesus is the icon (image) of God. It is in Jesus' true humanity that we encounter God's own mercy and compassion, God's own love for everyday people, the outcast and the sinner. Jesus is God's wisdom and compassion, God's very own reality, present in human or incarnate form. This is why the Council of Ephesus teaches that Jesus is one. If this means that Jesus isn't *really* divine, we can only ask for some clarification of what it could mean to be *really* divine in some other non-monophysite and non-docetic way.

4. The Jesus of our historical-theological portrait is not the only possible way to think and imagine about Jesus. But it is a

plausible way. It is a way that is consistent with the deep sense of Jesus' true humanity that lives in Christian art and devotion in the west. The Jesus of this portrait need not blink in the face of modern challenges to his historical reality. This portrait is faithful to the ancient Antiochene concern for a Jesus whom Christians can imitate in truth. For those who can pry open the modern Humean universe sufficiently to allow God to deal with humanity in surprising ways, this portrait is also faithful to the ancient Alexandrian concern for a Jesus upon whose name we can call without fear of idolatry, just as we would call upon God. This may not be divinity as some humans would have imagined it apart from Jesus, but it is divinity as God has made it known in Jesus. Christian belief in Jesus' divinity ought not to alienate us from our own human condition. Rather we can think and imagine about Jesus as the supreme instance of human openness to and receptivity for God.

In spite of these observations, some will still believe that, in the interest of historical truth, they must think and imagine Jesus as a mere man who, in the course of Christianity's development, took on the trappings of divinity. Others will believe that, in order to be true to the ancient faith, they must think and imagine Jesus as a quite unearthly incarnation of God, a luminous divine presence, aware in advance of all that would happen to him. From this book's perspective, the wonder of the incarnation has escaped both groups. God isn't as we thought God ought to be. In Jesus, God *really* (in the strongest sense we can give this term—and yes, I mean *ontologically*) visited and remains among God's people. This is good news. Perhaps those for whom this is still too "soft" an understanding of Jesus' divinity might ask themselves, first, how they came to such a clear understanding of God, and, second, how well they have understood the terms *docetism* and *monophysitism*.

CHRIST-CENTERED ECCLESIOLOGY
AND MORAL THEOLOGY

In Chapter VII, we defined theology as the critical reflection of Christians on the relationship between their faith and their culture. Theology occurs when particular Christians reflect on their attempts to follow Jesus in particular cultural contexts. Theology is not interested in a mere adaptation of the life of faith to a particular culture. If adaptation were the sole concern of theology, it would become an activity in which culture devoured the life of faith. In addition to a genuine concern for cultural adaptation, theological reflection must recognize the points at which a living faith would challenge and possibly transform the limits of culture.

The life of Christian faith centers on the person of Jesus. Like Christian revelation, it is Christ-centered. As reflection on the life of Christian faith, Christian theology is Christ-centered, too. In the preceding chapters, we have tried to present a portrait of Jesus that would be helpful to further theological reflection.

This book has dealt primarily with theological foundations. It has presented some of the basic concepts needed to get theological reflection off the ground: revelation, church, scripture, tradition, inspiration, and theology itself. In all of this the church has been presupposed as the religious and historical context for the scriptures, tradition, the memory and present life of Jesus, as well as theology itself. Except briefly, e.g. in the discussion of scripture, we have not ventured explicitly into the field of ecclesiology, the study of the church. Nor have we said much, apart from considering Jesus' teaching, about moral theology. In spending so much time on Jesus, however, we hope to have laid some foundations for Christ-centered ecclesiology and moral theology.

Jesus is the standard by which Christians must judge what Christian churches should be and not be, and by which Christians must judge what Christian life should be and not be. If theology is the critical reflection of Christians on the relationship between their lives of faith and their cultural contexts, our historical-theological portrait of Jesus can serve as a standard by which we try to judge what that relationship should be.

Subject Index

Biblical Index